THE RATNĀVALĪ
OF ŚRĪ HARṢA-DEVA

THE

RATNĀVALĪ

OF

ŚRĪ HARṢA-DEVA

With an exhaustive Introduction, a new Sanskrit Comm., Various Readings, a literal English Translation, copious Notes and useful Appendices

Edited by

M.R. KALE

MOTILAL BANARSIDASS PUBLISHERS
PRIVATE LIMITED • DELHI

Reprint : Delhi, 1984, 1995, 2002, 2011
First Published: Bombay, 1921

ISBN: 978-81-208-1042-6 (Cloth)
ISBN: 978-81-208-1043-3 (Paper)

MOTILAL BANARSIDASS
41 U.A. Bungalow Road, Jawahar Nagar, Delhi 110 007
8 Mahalaxmi Chamber, 22 Bhulabhai Desai Road, Mumbai 400 026
203 Royapettah High Road, Mylapore, Chennai 600 004
236, 9th Main III Block, Jayanagar, Bangalore 560 011
Sanas Plaza, 1302 Baji Rao Road, Pune 411 002
8 Camac Street, Kolkata 700 017
Ashok Rajpath, Patna 800 004
Chowk, Varanasi 221 001

Printed in India
By Jainendra Prakash Jain at Shri Jainendra Press,
A-45 Naraina, Phase-I, New Delhi 110 028
and Published by Narendra Prakash Jain for
Motilal Banarsidass Publishers Private Limited,
Bungalow Road, Delhi 110 007

CONTENTS

PREFACE TO THE FIRST EDITION

This edition of Śrī Harṣa-Deva's *Ratnāvalī* is prepared on the same lines as my edition of the *Nāgānanda* two years ago, with a view to supply the University student with a text-book that will meet all his requirements. Care has also been taken to make the book useful to the general reader as well. A brief but sufficiently exhaustive new commentary in Sanskrit has been written, as there was no suitable ancient comm. available on this play. Another feature of this edition is the Introduction wherein all that has been known of the author and the play has been put together for ready reference and systematic study. The figures of speech and the various technicalities of Sanskrit dramaturgy are not given (except in a few cases) in the Notes as they are not of much use to the junior University students. They are, however, pointed out in the commentary. I have used the editions of Messrs. V.S. Ghate, Joglekar, and the Nirn. and the available Calcutta editions, and I am beholden to the editors of all these. But my special thanks are due to Śāstrī Nigudkar whose edition was useful to me in writing out the comm., and Prof. Ray's excellent edition of the play from which I got many useful hints. Any suggestions for improvement & c., will be gratefully welcomed.

BOMBAY, M.R. KALE
June 1921

INTRODUCTION.

I THE SANSKRIT DRAMA.[1]

We shall begin with a brief outline of the general structure and arrangement of the Sanskrit Drama, without a knowledge of which the technical remarks on the construction of the present play here, as well as those made in the Notes, will not be intelligible to the general reader.[2] Poetry in Sanskrit, from its inherent nature, as apart from its intrinsic merit, is divided into two kinds–दृश्य 'what is capable of being seen or exhibited' and श्रव्य 'what can only be heard or chanted.' The drama falls under the first division. 'Rúpaka' is the general term in Sanskrit for all dramatic compositions, which also comprises a subordinate class called *Uparúpaka*. The Rúpaka,[3] which has Rasa or Sentiment for its substratum, is divided into ten classes, *viz.*, नाटकं सप्रकरणं भाणः प्रहसनं डिमः। व्यायोगसमवकारौ वीथ्यङ्केहामृगा इति ॥. Of the Uparúpakas or Minor Dramas there are eighteen species, the most important of which are *Nâṭikas* such as the Ratnâvalî, Viddhaśâlabhañjikâ .&c., *Trotakas* such as the Vikramorvaśiya, &c.

Having thus disposed of the divisions into which the whole of the scenic art is capable of falling, we turn to the Principle of division among the *Rûpakas* themselves, which is

---

1 The first two Sections are nearly the same as those prefixed to the Nâg.

2 The information given here has been mainly culled from the Das'arûpaka. The minor particulars not noticed here will be found in my Sâhityasârasaṃgraha (Nir, Ed.).

3 अवस्थानुकृतिर्नाट्यं रूपं दृश्यतयोच्यते । रूपकं तत्समारोपाद्दशधैव रसाश्रयम् ॥ D.-R. रूप्यतेऽभिनयैर्यत्र वस्तु तद्रूपकं विदुः । नाटकाद्यैर्दशविधम्. *Nâṭya* is another and perhaps a wider term for the drama or the dramatic art, and is so called because it represents the different situations in (the scenes presented by) life. The sage Bharata is the founder of the science of music. and dramaturgy and his work is styled the *Nâṭya Sâstra*. *Nâṭya* is also called *Rûpa* inasmuch as it has *dṛis'yatâ* or the capability of being seen, and *Rûpaka* inasmuch as its subject-matter is represented by actors assuming particular characters.

threefold[1]—(1) वस्तु or the Plot of the play; (2) नेता or the Hero; and (3) रस or the Sentiment. These three are the essential constituents, nay, the very life-blood, of every dramatic piece. Each of these we shall succintly deal with in its order.

---

1 VASTU OR THE PLOT.

Vastu is primarily of two kinds: आधिकारिक or 'principal' and प्रासंगिक or 'accessary.' The Principal is that which relates to the chief characters or the persons concerned with the essential interest of the piece, and pervades the whole arrangement. The Accessary is that which appears in furtherance of the main topic, and is concerned with characters other than the Hero or the Heroine. This latter is of two kinds, *viz.*, *Patâkâ* and *Prakarî*. *Patâkâ* or 'banner' is an episode by which the progress of the plot is illustrated, furthered or hindered (so as to give additional interest to it). It is of considerable length and sometimes extends to the very end of a play. The *Prakarî* is also an episodical incident—of limited duration and minor importance—one in which the principal characters take no part. Besides these two, there are three other elements requisite for the development of the plot. These are बीज or the seed, बिन्दु or the drop, and कार्य or the final issue. *Bija*[2] is the circumstance leading to the ultimate end briefly stated, which, as the plot develops, bears multifarious results and which is, as it were, the seed of the plot. *Bîndu*[3] is what cements a break in the plot caused by the introduction of some other incident. *Kârya* is the final object of the plot which being attained the whole is finished. These five are technically called Arthaprakṛitis (अर्थप्रकृतयः).

The *Vastu*, which is thus divided into five classes, may again be divided into three classes according to the source of its derivation. It may be borrowed from history or tradition, or it may be fictitious, or mixed, *i.e.*, partly drawn from history and partly the creation of the poet's fancy. A *Nâṭaka* belongs to the first class, a *Prakarana* to the second.

As regards its development a dramatic plot has five stages or conditions called *Avasthâs*. They are (1) आरम्भ beginning

---

1 वस्तु नेता रसस्तेषां भेदकः ।.

2 स्वल्पोद्दिष्टस्तु तद्धेतुर्बीजं विस्तार्यनेकेधा ।.

3 अवान्तरार्थविच्छेदे बिन्दुरच्छेदकारणम् ।.

or setting on foot of the enterprise, (2) यत्न effort, (3) प्राप्त्याशा prospect of success, (4) नियताप्ति certain attainment through the removal of obstacles, and (5) फलागम obtainment of the desired object. While these five stages are in progress there must be some links to connect them with the principal and subordinate parts of the main action (the episodes and incidents). These are called the *Saṃdhis* or junctures. They are five in number, answering to the five *Arthaprakritis*, each of which they join with its corresponding stage, *viz.*, मुख (Protasis or the opening juncture) प्रतिमुख (Epitasis). गर्भ (catastasis), अवमर्श (Peripateia), and निर्वहण (Catastrophe), also called उपसंहृति or उपसंहार). Thus *Mukhasamdhi* is the combination of the Bîja and Ârambha, *i. e.*, wherein the seed is sown, so to speak, with all its *Rasas*. In the *Pratimukha* there is the means (*yatna*) to the chief end, as originally implied by the Bîja in the Mukha which herein sprouts up. In the *Garbha* there is attainment and non-attainment of the desired end, implying a further sprouting up of the original Bîja. There are impediments, but the main plot gains ground under resistance. The *Avamarshasaṃdhi* is that in which the seed attains a more luxuriant growth than in the *Garbha*, being accompanied by *Niyatâpti* of the end, but whose final result is postponed further off by fresh impediments of various sorts, as in the Śákuntala the King's forgetting S'ak. after marriage owing to Durvásas' curse. The *Nirvahaṇa* or consummation is the harmonious combination of all the aforesaid parts in the final catastrophe.

The subject-matter, whether historical, fictitious, or mixed, is from its inherent nature capable of a twofold division. It is divided into (1) सूच्य-deserving to be suggested or implied only, as being of a dry and otherwise unfit character; and (2) दृश्यश्रव्य-fit to be represented and heard as being highly sentimental aud pleasing. The suggestions or implications are made in five ways—विष्कम्भचूलिकाङ्कास्याङ्कावतारप्रवेशकैः ।. (1) For *Vishkambha* see Notes, Act I. (2) *Chûlikâ* is the suggestion of some incident from behind the scenes (नेपथ्ये). (3) An अङ्कास्य[1] । is one wherein is suggested by the actors at the time of their departure the connexion between the Act finished and the one to be commenced, which otherwise would look disconnected, as the speech of Kámandakî and others at the

1 अङ्कान्तपात्रैरङ्कास्यं छिन्नाङ्कस्यार्थसूचनात् ।.

end of the 3rd Act of the Mâl.-Mâdh. (4) अङ्कावतार[1] consists in implanting the seed of the subject-matter of an Act in the previous Act before it has drawn to its close, so that the Act following is a continuation of the one preceding; *e. g.*, the sixth Act of the S'âk., the germ of which is cast at the end of the fifth Act; Mâlav. II. and Mâl.-Mâd. II, are other instances. (5) For प्रवेशक see notes Act II.

The subject-matter is further divided into three kinds—सर्वश्राव्यं or प्रकाशं, अश्राव्यं or स्वगतं and नियतश्राव्यम्. The last is of two kinds, जनान्तिक and अपवारितक (which is explained in the Notes). Independent of these divisions there is one called आकाशभाषित (आकाशे) or Speech from the Void.

The styles or modes of action (वृत्तयः) to be followed in a drama are four in number, *viz.* शृङ्गारे कैशिकी वीरे सात्वत्यारभटी पुनः। रसे रौद्रे च बीभत्से वृत्तिः सर्वत्र भारती ॥. Of these the Kaiśikî (used in the Nâṭikâ) consists of music, dancing and love-sports, assisting the development of Śriṅgâra, and is delightful by that and from the fascinating dresses worn by women. (*See* S.-D., VI. 124). It has four *aṅgas*, *viz.* (1) नर्म or polite pleasantry, (2) नर्मस्फूर्ज (०स्फञ्ज according to D.-R.) or development of Love, (3) नर्मस्फोट or the distant indication of Love, and (4) नर्मगर्भ or covert action for the furtherance of love (यथा मालतीमाधवे सखीरूपधारिणा माधवेन मालत्या मरणव्यवसायवारणम्).

2 NETA OR THE HERO.

The Hero is required to be modest, decorous, comely, munificent, civil, of sweet address, eloquent, sprung from a noble family, &c.[2] Heroes are mentioned to be of four kinds, *viz.*, धीरोदात्त, धीरललित, धीरशान्त and धीरोद्धत. '*Dhîrodâtta,*' or the Hero of sublimes qualities, is one who is magnanimous, patient, not given to boasting, self-possessed, of firm resolve, whose high spirit is concealed and who is true to his engagements. We are not concerned with the other three classes of Heroes

1 अङ्कावतारस्त्वङ्कान्ते पातोऽङ्कस्याविभागतः।. The distinction, however, between an Aṅkâsya and an Aṅkâvatâra, is considered by some as merely imaginary. Vis'vanâtha actually supplants the latter by Aṅkamukha which he defines as that where in one Act the substance of all the other Acts is suggested.

2 नेता विनीतो मधुरस्त्यागी दक्षः प्रियंवदः। रक्तलोकः शुचिर्वाग्मी रूढवंशः स्थिरो युवा ॥ बुद्ध्युत्साहस्मृतिप्रज्ञाकलामानसमन्वितः। शूरो दृढश्च तेजस्वी शास्त्रचक्षुश्च धार्मिकः ॥ भेदैश्चतुर्धा ललितशान्तोदात्तोद्धतैरयम् ॥.

here. Each of these Heroes may be of one or other of four sorts. He may be दक्षिण or 'gallant,' *i. e.*, equally devoted to many women, though principally attached to one; or शठ 'sly' *i. e.*, one who being attached to one lady, covertly acts in a way unpleasant to her; or he may be धृष्ट 'bold,' openly making his professions to another, and not ashamed even when reproached; or lastly he may be अनुकूल 'favourable,' devoted to one Heroine only. The धीरोदात्त Hero has eight manly qualities—शोभा, विलास, माधुर्य, गाम्भीर्य, धैर्य, तेजस्, लालित्य and औदार्य.

Among the assistants of the Hero the principal is पीठमर्द, the hero of the Patâkâ or episode, clever in discourse, devoted to his master, and a little inferior to him in qualities. Next comes the Vidûshaka, his constant companion, whose business consists in the repartees of wit, in helping his friend in his love-intrigues, and thus assisting in the general *dénouement* of the play. The third, and of equal rank with the Vidûshaka, is Viṭa, who knows one art only and is thereby useful to the Hero. The Hero thus equipped may still take into his service ministers of state and ministers of religion, ascetics, allies &c., as well as eunuchs, mutes, barbarians (Yavanas) &c. Sometimes there may be a Rival-Hero called प्रतिनायक who is avaricious, bold, impetuous, criminal and of evil conduct.

The Nâyikâor the Heroine who must be possessed of qualities similar to those of the Hero is of three kinds[1]. She may be the wife of the hero (स्वीया), as Sîtâ in the Uttar.; or one belonging to another (अन्या or परकीया), or a common woman (सामान्या or साधारणस्त्री) as Vasantasenâ in the Mṛich. The परकीया may be a maiden (so called because she is in the power of her guardian) or the wife of another. But the latter must not be introduced as the Heroine in a play[2]. The maiden's love, however, better helps the *rasa* and is, therefore, the most favourite theme with many Sanskrit poets. Further divisions and subdivisions of the *Nâyikâ* are not introduced here, as they have very little to do with the construction of the drama. For her

---

1 स्वान्या साधारणस्त्रीति तद्गुणा नायिका त्रिधा ।

2 अन्यस्त्री कन्यकोढा च नान्योढाङ्गिरसे क्वचित्. "We may observe however, to the honour of Hindu drama, that the *Parakîyâ* or she who is the wife of another person, is never to be made the object of dramatic intrigue; a prohibition that would have sadly cooled the imagination, and curbed the wit, of Dryden and Congreve" Wilson: Select Specimens. Vol. I. p. 45.

assistants the Heroine may have a सखी, दासी, धात्रेयी, प्रतिवेशिका and others, possessing qualities corresponding to those of the friends of the Hero.

---

3 RASA OR SENTIMENT.

Rasa is that lasting impression of feeling produced to his overwhelming delight in a man of poetic susceptibility by the proper action of the *Vibhâvas* and *Anubhâvas*, as well as the *Sâttvika* bhâvas and the *Vyabhichâribhâvas*[1]. Bhâva (भाव) or 'feeling' is the complete pervasion of the heart by any emotion, whether of pleasure or of pain, arising from the object under sight. Vibhâva (विभाव) or an Excitant is that which being perceived nourishes the main sentiment. It is divided into (1) *A'lambana*, that which is, as it were, the support or substratum of the Rasa—the person or thing with reference to whom or which a sentiment arises—such as the Hero or the Heroine, and (2) *Uddîpana* or what excites or enhances (adds to the development of) the sentiment, such as the moon, the beauties of the vernal season, &c.; beauty, decorations, &c. of the principal characters, in the case of शृङ्गार. *Anubhâva* or an Ensuant is the outward manifestation of the internal feeling through the eyes, face &c. The Sâttvika or natural *bhâvas* are a subdivision of *Ānubhâva*, and are mentioned as eight in number—स्तम्भप्रलयरोमाञ्चाः स्वेदो वैवर्ण्यवेपथू । अश्रुवैस्वर्यमित्यष्टौ ।. The *Vyabhichâris* or the Accessaries are those *bhâvas* which are not strictly confined to any *Rasa*, but appearing and disappearing, like waves in the ocean, they serve as feeders to the prevailing sentiment and strengthen it in different ways. *Sthâyibhâva* (स्थायिभाव) or the Permanent Sentiment[2] of a composition 'is one—the ocean melting all salt into water—which not being interrupted by any sentiment contrary or akin to its nature occurring at intervals, converts all of them into its own nature.' Now a *Rasa* would prove contrary to another if the आश्रय or substratum of both were the same. But as अङ्गी (principal) and अङ्ग (subordinate) a रस may be mixed with one or more of others.

---

1 विभावैरनुभावैश्च सात्त्विकैर्व्यभिचारिभिः । आनीयमानः स्वाद्यत्वं स्थायी भावो रसः स्मृतः ॥ सुखदुःखादिकैर्भावैर्भावस्तद्भावभावनम् । ज्ञायमानतया तत्र विभावो भावपोषकृत् ॥ आलम्बनोद्दीपनत्वप्रभेदेन स च द्विधा । अनुभावो विकारस्तु भावसंसूचनात्मकः ॥.

2 विरुद्धैरविरुद्धैर्वा भावैर्विच्छिद्यते न यः । आत्मभावं नयत्यन्यान्स स्थायी लवणाकरः ॥.

There are eight Sthâyibhâvas, रति, हास, शोक, क्रोध, उत्साह, भय, जुगुप्सा, and विस्मय on which are based respectively the sentiments—शृङ्गार the Erotic, हास्य the Comic, करुण the Pathetic, रौद्र the Furious, वीर the Heroic, भयानक the Terrible, बीभत्स the Loathsome, and अद्भुत the Marvellous. There is a ninth sentiment, that of शान्त the Quietistic, having शम or tranquillity for its Sthâyibhâva. But it is not suited to dramatic purposes and rarely occurs as a main sentiment in a drama. Of these eight sentiments शृङ्गार and हास्य, वीर and अद्भुत, बीभत्स and भयानक, and रौद्र and करुण are akin to each other as they proceed from the same condition of the mind. As we are here mainly concerned with the Erotic, that being the prevailing sentiment in most Sans. plays, we will say something about it here. शृङ्गार is mainly divided into विप्रलम्भ or Love-in-separation and संभोग or Love-in-union. The former, the Daśarûpaka sub-divides into two kinds, अयोग the Non-consummation of marriage, and विप्रयोग the Separation of the lovers deep in love after marriage. The former, which arises from the dependent position of one or the other of the parties or through distance or through the intervention of adverse fate, has ten stages, अभिलाष, चिन्ता &c. mentioned in the com.; चिन्ता occurs through मान, प्रवास or some such cause; मान 'jealous anger,' arises from a breach in the duties of love (प्रणयभङ्ग) and may be on both sides (rarely, however, the Nâyaka is *Mânî*). This मान has several varieties, such as ईर्ष्यामान, आनुमानिकमान &c. It is capable of being dispelled in six ways: साम्ना भेदेन दानेन नत्युपेक्षारसान्तरैः—and is called गुरु, लघु or मध्यम according to the greatness or the smallness of the effort required to make the Nâyikâ give it up. संभोग is when the two lovers are in the enjoyment of each other's company, engaged in looking at each other, kissing each other &c.

---

4 THE GENERAL CONDUCT OF THE NÂTAKA.

Every dramatic piece opens with a Prelude or Prologue (प्रस्तावना) which is itself introduced by what is called the *Nândî*. This *Nândî* according to some must suggest the gist of the whole plot. The Sûtradhâra may sometimes retire after the recital of the Nândî, in which case another actor, called स्थापक (for he *establishes* as it were the topic of the play), takes his place. In the Prelude, which may begin with a brief allusion to the poet's literary attainments, his genealogy, &c., the Sûtradhâra or the Sthâpaka suggests the subject in the form of the Bîja, or by a simple beginning, or by naming the character about to enter, as in the Śâkuntala. He must please the audience with sweet songs descriptive of some season and couched in the Bhâratî vṛitti. The प्रस्तावना is of two kinds—(1) प्ररोचना as in the Rat., and (2) आमुख, in which the Sûtradhâra holds conversation with the actress or his assistants, bearing on the subject to be introduced. This latter is of three kinds, of which one is प्रयोगातिशय. When the entry of a character is directly indicated by the Sûtradhâra, saying 'Here he enters,' that is Proyogâtis'aya.

The Prelude being over, the piece is commenced, being hereafter arranged and exhibited in the manner indicated in the three foregoing Sections. The whole matter should be well determined and divided into Acts and Scenes. A Nâṭaka may consist of from five to ten acts. The Hero should be of the Dhîrodâtta class. The Sentiment should be शृङ्गार or वीर (or sometimes करुण), others being introduced as conducive to its development. Nothing should be introduced in to the play which either misbeseems the Hero or is discordant with the main sentiment. An Act must not be tiresomely long, should be full of *Rasa*, and introduced by *Vishkhambaka* &c., according to necessity. Its close is marked by the exit of all characters. Such incidents as journeys, massacres, wars &c., should not be represented in a play: they may only be indicated. The death of the Hero must never be exhibited. This accounts for the somewhat monotonous character of Sanskrit plays, and the absence of tragedies in Sanskrit[1]. The play should end, as it began, with a Benediction or

---

1 Wilson observes—They (the Hindu plays) never offer a calamitous conclusion, which, as Johnson remarks, was enough to constitute Tragedy in Shakespeare's days; and although they propose to excite all the emotions of the human breast, terror and pity included, they never effect this object by leaving a painful impression upon the mind of the spectator. The Hindus in fact have no Tradegy.........The absence of tragic catastrophe in the Hindu dramas is not merely an unconscious omission; such a catastrophe is prohibited by a positive rule. The conduct of what may be termed the classical drama of the Hindus is exemplary and dignified. Nor is its moral purport neglected; and one of their writers declares, in an illustration familiar to ancient and modern poetry, that the chief end of the Theatre is to disguise, by the insidious sweet, the unpalatable, but salutary bitter, of the cup.

prayer, called the Bharatavâkya, which is repeated by the principal personages and contains an expression of their wishes for general prosperity and happiness. The Unity of interest or action must be maintained throughout.

As regards the language to be used in a piece, the Hero and the higher characters speak in classical Sanskrit, while females and the minor characters speak in the different Prakrit dialects.

The student will see from the foregoing sketch, that the characteristic peculiarities of the Indian Drama are mainly three—(1) its peculiar structure; (2) the absence of the distinction between Comedy and Tragedy; and (3) the diversity of Laguage to be spoken by the characters. The above-mentioned general characteristics of a Nâṭaka belong with certain modifications to the other divisions of the Rûpaka as well.

Of the Uparûpakas we are concerned here with the Nāṭikâ alone. We therefore give below its special features.

The *Nâṭikâ* :—This is defined by the Sâhitya-Darpaṇa as :—नाटिका क्लृप्तवृत्ता स्यात्स्त्रीप्राया चतुरङ्किका । प्रख्यातो धीरललितस्तत्र स्यान्नायको नृपः ॥ स्यादन्तःपुरसंबद्धा संगीतव्यापृताथ वा । नवानुरागा कन्यात्र नायिका नृपवंशजा ॥ संप्रवर्तेत नेतास्यां देव्यास्त्रासेन शङ्कितः । देवी भवेत्पुनर्ज्येष्ठा प्रगल्भा नृपवंशजा ॥ पदे पदे मानवती तद्वशः संगमो द्वयोः । वृत्तिः स्यात्कैशिकी स्वल्पविमर्शाः संधयः पुनः ॥ The Nâṭikâ should be based on an invented story, should consist of four Acts, and abound in female characters. Its Hero should be an illustrious King and of the *Dhîralalita* class. The Heroine should be a maiden of royal family (or a celestial one)[1] newly touched with Love, and should be either connected with the inner apartment (as an attendant of the Queen), or engaged in musical performance. The Hero should proceed in his love-affair cautiously from fear of the Queen. The Queen should be a grown up lady, bold, and also of royal family. She should display her indignation at every step, and the union of the lovers should depend on her consent. The Kaiśikî, with all its four parts, must be the *Vritti* employed, and the *Samdhis* should be without the Vimarsha (as explained by the comm.). The principal *Rasa* should be S'riṅgára.[2]

---

1 दिव्या चाथ मनोहरा । *Das'a-Rûpka.*

2 शृङ्गारोऽङ्गी सलक्षणः D.—R.

The points of difference between a Nâṭaka and a Nâṭikâ are:—(1) The plot of a nâṭaka should be well-known, *i. e.*, derived in its main features from history, while that of a Nâṭikâ should be mainly invented. (2) In the former the Hero is Dhîrodâtta, while in the latter he is Dhîralalita. (3) While a Nâṭaka should have many males engaged in important affairs, the Nâṭikâ should have many females. (4) The former should have one principal sentiment, which may be either शृङ्गार, or वीर, or करुण, while the latter should have शृङ्गार only. (5) A Nâṭaka may consist of five, seven, or even ten Acts; a Nâtikâ of *four* only.

II THE POET

The chronology of Sanskrit literature has been a perplexing problem to scholars and antiquarians, and it is no unusual experience for the serious student to have to face confusing statements and many-sided arguments before he can reach a safe conclusion about even the most famous of Sanskrit authors or their works. The authorship of the three plays, the Priyadars'ikâ, the Ratnâvalî and the Nâgânanda, has not escaped the common fate, and has provided the speculative critic with a most convenient dumping ground for all kinds of fanciful theories. There are some who doubt, in the first place, whether all the three dramas were written by the same person, and are inclined to differentiate between the author of the Nâgânanda, and that of the Priyadars'ikâ and the Ratnâvalî. Some have believed that Bâṇabhaṭṭa, the author of the Kâdambarî and the Harshacharita, wrote the Ratnâvalî also; while others have put forth with insistence the claims of Dhâvaka or Bhâsa. Tradition, however, has been consistent in ascribing the authorship of all the three plays to King S'rî-Harsha, or Harsha-Deva, of Kanouj. Scholars have generally accepted this view, and it is one with which, it might be stated at the outset, we are in entire agreement. But questions have been raised about the identity of this Harsha, since it is another common feature of all similar inquiries that they are hampered by a plurality of Sanskrit writers[1] bearing the same, or similar, names and titles. And

1 Compare in this connexion the existence of a number of poets bearing the names Kâlidâsa, Daṇḍin, Râjas'ekhara, and many others.

opinion has even been rife that the royal personage was merely a pa tron, the real author of the plays being some poet at his court, who wrote them and presented them to the public as those of his distinguished benefactor.

It is not easy to unravel this entanglement without clearing the ground before us by examining if there is any internal evidence leading up to any definite statement. Happily we are here on a firmer basis than in the case of other poets and writers, who have not deigned to vouchsafe any information about themselves. The Prastâvanâ of the Rátnavalî (p. 5) reads—

सूत्रधारः ॥ अलमतिविस्तरेण । अद्याहं वसन्तोत्सवे सबहुमानमाहूय नानादिग्देशागतेन राज्ञः श्रीहर्षदेवस्य पादपद्मोपजीविना राजसमूहेन उक्तः । यथा अस्मत्स्वामिना श्रीहर्षदेवेन अपूर्ववस्तुरचनालंकृता रत्नावली नाम नाटिका कृता सा चास्माभिः श्रोत्रपरंपरया श्रुता न तु प्रयोगतो दृष्टा । तत् तस्यैव राज्ञः सकलजनहृदयाह्लादिनः बहुमानात् अस्मासु चानुग्रहबुद्ध्या यथावत्प्रयोगेण त्वया नाटयितव्या इति ।............श्रीहर्षो निपुणः कविः etc.

From this it is clear that, since the time when the play was originally composed, it has been received as the work of King श्रीहर्षदेव (or merely श्रीहर्ष, if we omit the regal title *Deva.*) And this is corroborated by similar Prologues in the two sister-dramas—

(1) सूत्रधारः ॥ (परिक्रम्य।) अद्याहं वसन्तोत्सवे सबहुमानमाहूय नानादिग्देशागतेन राज्ञः श्रीहर्षदेवस्य पादपद्मोपजीविना राजसमूहेन उक्तः । यथा अस्मत्स्वामिना श्रीहर्षदेवेन अपूर्ववस्तुरचनालंकृता प्रियदर्शिका नाम नाटिका कृता इत्यस्माभिः श्रोत्रपरंपरया श्रुता न तु प्रयोगतो दृष्टा । तत् तस्यैव राज्ञः सर्वजनहृदयाह्लादिनः बहुमानात् अस्मासु चानुग्रहबुद्ध्या यथावत्प्रयोगेण त्वया नाटयितव्या इति । ....श्रीहर्षो निपुणः कविः etc.

—From the *Priyadars'iká*, Act I.

(2) सूत्रधारः ॥ अलमतिविस्तरेण । अद्याहं इन्द्रोत्सवे सबहुमानं आकार्य नानादिग्देशागतेन राज्ञः श्रीहर्षदेवस्य पादपद्मोपजीविना राजसमूहेन उक्तः । यथा अस्मत्स्वामिना श्रीहर्षदेवेन अपूर्ववस्तुरचनालंकृतं विद्याधरजातकप्रतिनिबद्धं नागानन्दं नाम नाटकं कृतं अस्माभिः श्रोत्रपरंपरया श्रुतं न तु प्रयोगतो दृष्टम् । तत् तस्यैव राज्ञः सकलजनहृदयाह्लादिनः बहुमानात् अस्मासु चानुग्रहबुद्ध्या यथावत्प्रयोगेण त्वया नाटयितव्यमिति।.........श्रीहर्षो निपुणः कविः etc.

—From the *Nágânanda,* Act I.

Indeed, as would be apparent on comparison, the three Prologues are almost indentical in their wording, and none of the theorists has yet directly challenged their genuineness, or the truth of the information therein conveyed, *viz.*, that the

King-Poet S'rî-Harsha composed the three dramas. In the face of this evidence one is surprised to find Dr. A. B. Keith stating categorically:—"The authorship of the Ratnâvalî is disputed, but it is absolutely impossible to decide the question, and the author must remain anonymous." (*Catalogue of Sk. MSS. in the Bodlein Library*, Oxford, 1909, p. 39). Our first task, therefore, is directed towards discovering and fixing the identity of this S'rî-Harsha.

There are three[1] well-known S'rî-Harshas known to ancient Indian history. One is the author of the famous नैषधीयचरित महाकाव्य in 22 cantos, who also wrote अर्णववर्णन, खण्डनखण्डखाद्य, गौडोर्वीशकुलप्रशस्ति, छन्दःप्रशस्ति, नवसाहसाङ्कचरित, विजयप्रशस्ति, शिवशक्तिसिद्धि, and स्थैर्यविचारण. All these works he mentions in the concluding stanzas of the several cantos of the Naishadhîya-charita, where he describes himself as the son of हीर and मामल्लदेवी. In one place[2] he describes himself, again, as receiving certain favours at the hands of his patron, the King of Kânyakubja. This then is assuredly not the author of the Ratnâvalî who is a King with a "पादपद्मोपजीवी राजसमूह." This fact alone is sufficient to disprove the supposed identity of the two. Moreover, the author of the Naishadhîyacharita, if he had written any or all of these three plays, would certainly have glorified himself by including their names, too, in the list which he so persistently presses on our notice. It should be noted, again, that the Naishadhîyacharita is a work of the 12th century,[3] and is never quoted in the earlier works on Indian rhetorics; while Dhanika, the commentator of the Das'arûpa, writing at the end of the 10th century, quotes[4] frequently from all the three plays. The author of the N.-Ch. could not then, evidently, have written them.

Another Harsha was the ruler of Kashmir between 1113 and 1125 A. D., and to him Prof. Wilson attributed the Ratnâ-

1 There are some minor authors who bore this name (*e. g.*, a S'rî-Harsha who wrote a commentary on the *Gîtagovinda*). But they are evidently modern, and none of them was a *King*.

2 ताम्बूलद्वयमासनं च लभते यः कान्यकुब्जेश्वरात् N.-Ch. XXII. 155.

3 See Pandit S'ivadatta's Ed. of the poem (Nirṇayasâgara Press, 1894), Introduction p. 9. This Harsha, the author of the खण्डनखण्डखाद्य, flourished under King Jayachandra of Kanauj (*circa* 1175).

4 See the English translation of the Daśarûpa in the Columbia Univ. Indo-Iranian Series (New York, 1912), Introduction p. xxxvi

valī in the early days of Sanskrit scholarship. Here certainly we have a *King* Harsha, but the discovery of the existence of the quotations in Dhanika's commentary has laid this theory finally at rest, and it is now forgotten.

There then remains the King S'rî-Harsha, better known as Harshavardhana, of Kanouj, originally of Thânesar, who must have been the author of these plays, and to whom scholars, both Indian and western, agree in ascribing them.

The reign of S'rî Harsha or Harshavardhana, from 606 to 647 A. D., was one of the brightest epochs in the history of ancient India. It is an epoch of which we possess detailed and more or less trustworthy records, and the researches of antiquarian Scholars have recently made further valuable additions to our knowledge of Harsha's political career, a brief account[1] of which may be given here.

In the latter part of the sixth century the city of Thanesar (in the holy land familiar to the Âryans as *Kuru-Kshetra*) was ruled over by a King named Prabhâkaravardhana, whose younger son was Harsha. His elder brother was Rájyavardhana, the crown prince, who ascended the throne in 605 A. D., on the death of his father; but he did not live long to enjoy his accession, having been treacherously murdered by the King of Bengal whom he had sought as an ally in an expedition against the Râjâ of Malwa. Rájyavardhana having died without leaving an heir, his ministers finally chose Harsha as his successor (October, 606). The wisdom and fitness of this choice were proved soon after by the energy and ability with which Harsha conducted himself in his new position. He first planned a methodical system of conquest (*dig-vijaya*), with the purpose of bringing the whole land under one political power, *viz.* his own. Within six years he had conquered large portions of the north-western regions and of Bengal, and his military strength at this time can be gauged from the fact that he could put in the field "60,000 war-elephants and

---

1 The standard account in Sanskrit is the *Harsha-Charita* of Bâṇa. The account given by Párkhî Shástrî in his Marathi Essay on श्रीहर्ष (1911) and the scholarly Introduction in Gujrâthî prefixed by Mr. K. H. Dhruva to his Guj. transl. of the Priyadarśikâ (2nd ed. 1917) are also very helpful. Consult especially V. A. Smith's *Early history of India* (3rd ed. 1914) pp. 335-359, from which mainly the above facts have been compiled.

100,000 cavalry." He then reigned for thirty-five years longer, most of which period was passed in peaceful development and the perfecting of the various schemes of administration and in making occasional additions to his already extensive empire. Towards the close of his reign his empire extended over the whole of the basin of the Ganges (including Nepal), from the Himálaya to the Narmadâ, besides Malwa, Gujarat and Sauráshtra (the modern Kathiawar). His long career of conquest was unbroken save for one defeat, which he sustained in 620 at the hands of Pulakes'in II. of the Chálukya family. The Chinese traveller-Houen Tsang gives an eye-witness's description of his civil administration, with which he was highly impressed. The principal source of revenue was of course land revenue, other taxes being light and negligible. Crimes were rare, and on the whole the people were prosperous and contented. Harsha in after life was strongly inclined towards the quietistic teachings of Buddhism, and he himself lived like a Buddhist devotee. Rest-houses (*dharma-S'âlâs*), religious establishments and benevolent and charitable institutions on the model of those of As'oka were founded throught his kingdom. He held religious assemblies, one at Kanouj and again at Prayága, where he freely gave away his wealth in charity. Having conquered Assam (Kámarûpa), he even sent a mission to China, between which country and India there was constant communication in those days. Harsha died in 646 (or 647) without leaving an heir. On his death the throne was usurped by one of his ministers. The removal of his mighty personality soon plunged the country in disorder which rapidly made his compact and solid state soon crumble to pieces.

Harsha was known as चक्रवर्ति श्रीहर्ष, or Harsha the Paramount Sovereign. He earned the title for himself by his extensive conquests, and we have seen how, during the forty years of his rule, he devoted his energy to the efficient administration of his wide dominions. Education was developed, and literature and learning flourished under government patronage. Two of the most famous poets at his court were Bâṇabhaṭṭa, the author of the Kâdambarî, and Mayûra, who composed the Sûryas'ataka. The King himself was a writer of considerable merit. As Mr. Smith says, "Besides a grammatical work, three extant Sanskrit plays and sundry compositions in verse are ascribed to his pen; and there is no reason for hesitating to believe that he had at least a large share in their composition; *for royal authors were not uncommon in ancient India.*"[1]

Taken by itself the reign of Harsha can be compared to that of the great Mogul Emperor Akbar, as regards the universal prosperity of the people, the efficiency of the administration, and the encouragement given to learning and the fine arts. Harsha's autograph has been preserved on an inscription, and those interested might find it at p. 342 of Mr. Smith's *History*. For nearly thirteen centuries, his plays have continued to enjoy an extensive popularity, and have furnished rhetoricians and literary critics with models and illustrations for their canons, their position in Sanskrit literature being very high.

Coming now to the various conflicting theories, we do not think there is any ground for urging that the same hand that worte the Priy. and the Ratn. could not have witten the Nâgânanda, so that it is necessary to provide the Nâgânanda with a different authorship. This argument seems to have been based on the general similarity of the subject-matter of the first two plays, and the totally distinct themo of the Nâgânanda. That is a very slender reed to relie upon; for nothing can prevent an author from choosing widely different subjets for his works, if he is so pleased. And in the plays themselves there are abundant traces and points of resemblance that leave no doubt as to their all having emanated from the same hand. There are, in the beginning, the प्रस्तावनाs, which agree almost literally with one another; and the भरतवाक्यs at the end have also the same ring of similarity. Many words, sentences and idioms, are common to all the plays, and these we have quoted in the Notes wherever they occur. Many verses are similar in sentiment or in phraseology (*cf.* the verse द्वीपादन्यस्मादपि &c. which occurs in the Priy. and in the Nâg. also). The प्रवेशक in Ratn. II. resembles the corresponding one in Nâg. II. Apart from the resemblance in words, incidents and ideas, the general simplicity of style, and characterization are almost uniform in the three plays, and the reader can hardly remain unconvinced that these plays

1 *E. g.*, S'ûdraka, Vis'âkhadatta, Bhoja, Yas'ovarman, and others. (The Italics in the quotation above are ours).

were composed by the same author, however dissimilar the subject of the Nāgânanda[1] may be from that of the two other plays.

It has been contended with great force and display of ingenuity, that King Harshavardhana did not himself write these plays, but some poet at his court did it for him, and this contention rests on a sentence in the Kâvyaprakās'a of Mammaṭa (Uch. I.)—"श्रीहर्षादेर्धावकादीनामिव धनम्।". Earning money is stated there to be one of the objects in composing a literary work; and as an instance the case of धावक getting money from श्रीहर्ष is pointed out. The commentator Uddyotakāra explains—"धावकः कविः। स हि श्रीहर्षनाम्ना रत्नावलीं कृत्वा बहु धनं लब्धवानिति प्रसिद्धम्।"; and he is followed in this by some other commentators. In some MSS. of the Kâvyaprakâs'a is found a variant, बाणादीनामिव धनम् for धावकादीनामिव धनम्, and this caught the imagination of the late Dr Hall, who was the first to attribute the Ratnâvalî to Báṇa. As it is, the whole of this argument turns upon the explanations of the *commentators* of the Kâvyaprakás'a, whom we need not implicitly follow; for there is another and a more natural interpretation of the passage in question, *viz.*, that Dhávaka and other poets got wealth from their (royal) patrons as a reward and as a mark of appreciation—and it is not necessary to suppose that authorships were *transferred* to the patrons in consideration of such gifts. Sensitive and honourable patrons themselves would fight shy of such wholesale transfers.

But, apart from that, there is no evidence whatever, internal or external, to believe Baṇa to have written the Ratnâvalî, since his style, as seen in his prose works, is completely removed from that of the dramas. The former is highly ornate and elaborate, the latter is simple and plain. Moreover, why Bâṇa should have sold the dramas only, and retained the Kâdambarî, which would have brought him a princely sum of money, would be a puzzle; again, Bâṇa was in sufficiently opulent circumstances, quite beyond the necessity which would drive an impecunious author to bargain for the

1 As it is well known that Harsha showed a leaning towards Buddhism towards the end of his reign, we can easily suppose that the Priy. and the Ratn. were his earlier works, while the Nâg. marks the beginning of the Buddhistic tenour of his thought-development.

sale of his works including their authorship. Dr. Hall also argued that the presence of the verse द्वीपादन्यस्मादपि etc. both in the Ratnâvalî and the Harshacharita proved Bâṇa's authorship of the former. But *no such verse exists in the Harshacharita*, and the learned doctor led scholars to follow a wild-goose chase for a time, till the theory was abandoned as both hasty and unsound. It was reserved for an enterprising scholar of South India, Mr. Nârâyan Shâstrī, to pursue the seemingly obscure reference to धावक in the Kâvyaprakâs a passage, and to deduce some very ingenious theories about the authorship of these plays. The learned scholar's conclusions and arguments, if they are proved to be correct, would disturb the chronology of many authors and make it necessary to revise and rewrite the early history of Kâvya literature; but for reasons shortly to be stated, we must say we are unable to concur in Mr. Shástrî's conclusions. Mr. Shástrî identifies धावक with the famous poet भास, who is eulogized by Kálidâsa, and thirteen of whose dramas have been recently discovered; he also identifies the हर्ष of the Preludes of these plays with a certain king Vikramâditya whom he places between 552 and 457 *B. C.*; and he ascribes the authorship of our plays to Bhâsa, a court-poet of this S'rî Harsha-Vikramâditya, thus carrying back the age of the plays by some ten centuries or so!

This edifice of conjecture and theory is based on a quotatio given by Mr. Shástrî from the कविविमर्श of राजशेखर, which runs as follows :—

भासो रामिलसोमिलौ वररुचिः श्रीसाहसाङ्कः कवि—
मेंण्ठो भारविकालिदासतरलाः स्कन्धः सुबन्धुश्च यः ।
दण्डी बाणदिवाकरौ गणपतिः कान्तश्च रत्नाकरः
सिद्धा यस्य सरस्वती भगवती के तस्य सर्वेऽपि ते ॥
कारणं तु कवित्वस्य न संपन्नकुलीनता ।
धावकोऽपि हि यद्भासः कवीनामग्रिमोऽभवत् ॥
आदौ भासेन रचिता नाटिका प्रियदर्शिका ।
निरीर्ष्यस्य रसज्ञस्य कस्य न प्रियदर्शना ॥
तस्य रत्नावली नूनं रत्नमालेव राजते ।
दशरूपककामिन्या वक्षस्यत्यन्तशोभना ॥
नागानन्दं समालोक्य यस्य श्रीहर्षविक्रमः ।
अमन्दानन्दभरितः स्वसभ्यमकरोत्कविम् ॥
उदात्तराघवं नूनमुदात्तरसगुम्फितम् ।
गद्दीक्ष्य भनभुस्याया: पणिन्युर्नाटकानि वै ॥

शोकपर्यवसानाऽस्य नवाङ्का किरणावली ।
माकन्दस्येव कस्यात्र प्रददाति न निर्वृतिम् ॥
भासनाटकचक्रेऽपि च्छेकैः क्षिप्ते परीक्षितुम् ।
स्वप्नवासवदत्तस्य दाहकोऽभून्न पावकः ॥

Dhâvaka, *lit.* 'a washerman', was a title by which, no doubt, Bhása was known, as it is said he was a washerman by profession. But since Bhâsa preceded Kálidâsa[1], the श्रीहर्षविक्रम in the quotation above cannot be identified with the king Harshavardhana of the seventh century, and hence Mr. Shástrî discovered an earlier Harsha, from a verse of the Rájataraṃgiṇî.[2] Mr. Shástrî further argued from the similarity in idiom and ideas between the Priyadars'ikâ and the Málavikágnimitra, that the former play of Bhâsa must have served as a model for Kâlidâsa's work. The latest supporter of the theory of Bhâsa's authorship of the plays is Prof. S. M. Paranjpe[3] of Poona.

It is not possible so easily to brush aside the quotation given by Mr. Shástrî. But the manner in which it was originally offered is highly suspicious, and creates in our mind grave doubts whether such a work as कविविमर्श, from which those verses are cited, actually exists. And till that work comes to light, no inquiry can be profitably conducted to enable us to form a conclusion directly on the strength of this statement ascribed to Râjas'ekhara. Because, when Pandit R. V. Krishnamachariar, the learned editor of the Priyadars'ikâ in the Vani Vilas Sanskrit Series (Srirangam, 1906) challenged Mr. Shástrî to produce the source of his information, the latter wrote back in reply that he borrowed the quotation from *a friend of his*,[4] and thus the whole thing, apparently based on hearsay, came to almost nothing. And therefore it becomes necessary to suspend judgment on other questions arising out of these quoted verses. Prof. Paranjpe, fully conscious of the weakness of Mr. Shástrî's position

---

1 Kâlidâsa mentions Bhâsa in the Prologue to his Mâlavikâgnimitra.

2 तत्रानेहस्युज्जयिन्यां श्रीमान्हर्षापराभिधः । एकच्छत्रश्चक्रवर्ती विक्रमादित्य इत्यभूत् ॥ Râjat. III. 125.

3 In an article in Marathi in the monthly *Chitramaya Jagat* for December 1915.

4 See p. xxvii. of the Sanskrit Bhúmikâ of the Priyadars'ikâ, Vani Vilas Edition

which was thus rendered quite untenable, passes over that point and tries to argue independently that Bhâsa was the real author of the Nâgânanda. He has picked up similar ideas[1] and grammatical and literary peculiarities,[2] from the published writings of Bhâsa and the two plays Nâgânanda and Priyadars'ikâ; and relying on them he endeavours to show that the same hand must have produced all the plays. We must say with reference to this attempt that the learned critic has relied too much on a generous imagination, and he is prejudiced as he starts with a declared purpose to be on the look-out for similar ideas. If we are to apply the same argument, almost any classical work in Sanskrit can be shown to be written by almost any famous poet, as there is bound to be some similarity, more or less, everywhere. Similarity of ideas is to a certain extent common in all works having similar themes; very frequently it arises out of the fact that the works owe their composition to a common source, as in the case of the Panchatantra and the Hitopades'a; still more frequently it arises when an author, who is acquainted with the works of his predecessors, deliberately imitates them or unconsciously repeats the ideas and words with which he is familiar. Thus the works of Kálidâsa are abundantly bestrewed with phrases, constructions, similes and ideas from Válmîki's Rámâyaṇa. But who will venture to assert that Kâlidâsa had a hand in the composition of the Rámáyaṇa or *vice versa*? In fact, Prof. Paranjpe has stepped beyond the limits which a cautious critic must always set to such an argument. There is not a shred of evidence to deny King Harshavardhana's authorship of the Nâgánanda. Granting that all these resemblances set forth by Mr. Paranjpe, and many more, do occur, we can at the best argue that Harshavardhana must have read and admired the plays of Bhâsa. To jump at any other conclusion would be unsafe and is most certainly unwarranted. For in

---

1 *E. g.*, the worship of Agastya; the extreme heat of the *s'arad* season; the idea of कन्यका हि निर्दोषदर्शना भवन्ति (Nâg. p. 17) similar to that of कन्यकादर्शनं निर्दोषमिति कृत्वा (Bhâsa's Pratijñâ-Yaugandharâyaṇa); the affection of the Heroines for trees and plants; the attempt at suicide by hanging; and some others.

2 The most common of these is the recurrence of the phrase आपस्तावत्, which Prof. Paranjpe compares to समागय जलं at Nág. p. 118 (variant given in the foot-notes to our ed. of the play).

the first place there is the question of style. Bhasa's style is comparatively crude and his language more easily flowing; it must have evidently belonged to an earlier date than the polished refinement of Harsha's works, whose style resembles much more that of Kâlidâsa. Next it might be urged, though it lacks confirmation, that Harsha might have written these plays on the model of, and as revised or modified versions of, those of his predecessor, Bhása, in the same way in which Śūdraka wrote his *Mṛichchhakatika* on the basis of Bhása's *Chârudatta*. But for this we must wait till more plays of Bhása come to light, including *his originals of* Nâg., Priy. and Ratn., if at all he wrote these. But the most convincing testimony, to our mind, to prove that King Harsha of Kanouj wrote the Nágânanda in the seventh century, is afforded by the Chinese traveller-pilgrim I Tsing,[1] with which for the present we can safely conclude this brief inquiry into the genesis of our play. He writes:—" King Śilâditya[2] versified the story of the Bodhisattva Jîmútavâhana who surrendered himself in place of a Nâga. This version was set to music; he had it performed by a band, accompanied by dancing and acting, and thus popularized it in his time."

III THE PLAY.

(1) The Story of the Ratnávali.

The *Ratnávalî* or the *'Jewel Necklace'* is a drama in four Acts; it is so named after the Heroine, the Siṃhala princess Ratnâvalî, whose union with King Udayana of Kauśâmbî forms the theme of the play. In order that the student may fully understand the various points subsequently to be discussed, it is desirable that he should be acquainted with the outline of the plot, which is therefore given below :—

Act. I. After the Benediction (Nándî), the Sûtradhâra in the Prelude (Prastâvanâ) introduces to the audience the play to be enacted *viz. Ratnávali* by King Srî-Harshadeva. After this begins the Act proper. King Vikramabâhu of Siṃhala had a daughter, named Ratnâvalî. A sage (*siddha*) had prophesied that whoever would marry her would be a paramount sovereign (Sârvabhauma). Yaugandharâyaṇa, the chief minister of King

1 English Tr. by Takakusu, p. 163.

2 This was one of the titles of King Harshavardhana.

Udayana, heard this rumour, and acting upon it, sought Ratnâvalî in marriage for his master. King Udayana had already a wife, the Queen Vâsavadattâ, and for fear of offending her, the request was disallowed by king Vikramabâhu. Thereupon Yaugan. got a rumour circulated that Queen Vâsavadattâ perished in a fire at Lâvâṇaka. The only objection to the proposed marriage being thus removed, Vikramabâhu gave his consent, and sent Ratnâvalî to Kauśâmbî on board a ship. The ship was wrecked in mid-ocean; the princess, however, was luckily rescued by a trader of Kauśâmbî while she was clinging to a plank. He recognized her by the Jewel-Necklace (Ratna-mâlâ-whence her name Ratnâvalî), which she always wore. The minister Yaugandharâyaṇa, to whom the rescued princess was brought by the trader, did not announce her identity, for obvious reasons, but introduced her into the Queen's apartments, where she worked as an attendant maid appropriately named *Sâgarikâ* (rescued from the sea). In a soliloquy on the stage Yaugandharâyaṇa explains all these previous incidents. The ship which carried Ratn. also carried Bâbhravya (Udayana's chamberlain) and Vasubhúti (Vikramabâhu's minister) as the escorts of the princess. They, too, were rescued, but they were unaware of the similar rescue of Ratnâvalî. Hence, believing her to have perished, they kept the affair to themselves, and straightway joined the army of General Rumaṇvat, whom Udayana had ordered to lead an expedition against the Kosala country. Thus the only two persons who could have disclosed Sâgarikâ's identity were away, and Yaugandharâyaṇa thought that she (Sâgarikâ) would be able by means of her uncommon beauty to win Udayana's heart under her assumed name and position as a common maiden; it would then be happier and better to make known her identity as a princess of the royal blood. These plans also are briefly touched upon in Yaugaddharáyaṇa's soliloquy. Then enters on the stage Udayana, accompained by the court-jester (Vidúshaka). They discuss and describe the annual Cupid's carnival which was then in full swing. Then enter two maid-servants, Madanikâ and Chútalatikâ, who dance and sing on the stage. The Vidúshaka, too, feels inclined to join them in a spirit of general gaiety. After a little diversion, the maids deliver a message from the Queen to the King, requesting his presence that day in the Makaranda garden. The King and the Vidúshaka accept the invitation and forthwith repair there, where shortly arrives the Queen accompanied by her attendants, Kâñchanamâlâ, Sâgarikâ (*i. e.* Ratnâvalî) and others. The Queen perceives the necessity of keeping the extremely young and beautiful Sâgarikâ out of the sight of her husband, and sends her away on some pretext. But Sâgarikâ, who was full of curiosity as to how the Cupid's festival was celebrated in this strange land, hides herself behind a tree and looks on. In the meanwhile the Queen offers worship to Cupid, and then to her husband.

Sâgarikâ, who had never seen the King before, feels for him love-at-first-sight, and later, learning that he was the same King Udayana to whom she had been betrothed and sent by her father on board the ship, her love waxes strong. It being evening, the festival closes with the departure of the royal party off the stage.

Act II.

In an Interlude (Praves'aka) two maid-servants announce that the King was to go that day to visit the *Navamâlikâ* creeper with a view to try upon it an experiment which would make it blossom out of season, and that Sâgarikâ had gone to a bower of *kadalî* plants with painting materials. We are then introduced to Sâgarikâ herself who is love-sick and diverting her longing by drawing the picture of her lord and looking at it. In this state she is observed by Susaṅgatâ, her friend, to whom she had entrusted the cage of the Queen's pet bird (a sârikâ). A conversation ensues between them in which Sâgarikâ confesses her love for the King. A diversion is created at this stage by the news that a monkey had got loose and was frightening women and children. Sâgarikâ and the maid Susaṃgatâ who was with her, both leave the stage in a hurry; the *sârikâ* flies away from her cage which was broken open by the monkey. Then enters the Vidúshaka with the news of the success of the experiment on the creeper *Navamâlikâ*, which he relates to the King. They then come upon the bird (*Sârikâ*) who, parrot-like, repeats in their hearing the impassioned utterances of Sâgarikâ which she had listened to, as well as the replies of Susaṃgatâ to them. There are no names mentioned, and the King and the Vidúshaka discuss as to whom those words could refer to. They wander about, and come upon the painting hastily left behind by Sâgarikâ. The Vidúshaka therein recognized the King, but neither of them could recognize Sâgarikâ whom Susaṃgatâ had painted at his side and whom they had not seen before. In the meanwhile Sâgarikâ and Susaṃgatâ come back for their bird and painting-board; and finding there the King with the Vidúshaka, they listen to their conversation. It soon becomes clear to them that the King too has fallen in love with the unknown maiden (*i. e.* Sâgarikâ) of the picture; Susaṃgatâ thereupon introduces her friend to the King. Apprehending a visit from the Queen, Sâgarikâ goes away. Then enters Queen Vâsavadattâ who catches sight of the painting-board, recognizes her maid therein by the side of her husband, gets angry with the latter who gives evasive answers, and leaves in a huff. The crest-fallen King, thereupon, departs with the Vidúshaka.

Act III.

In an Interlude (Praves'aka) two maid-servants relate how Susaṃgatâ has planned to bring about a meeting between the King and Sâgarikâ who is to be disguised as the Queen, Susaṃgatâ taking the diguise of the Queen's maid Kâñchanamâlâ. Then enters the King whom the Vidúshaka acquaints with this scheme. Then they both repair to the place of rendezvous. In the meanwhile the Queen, too, learns of the plot and she also arrives there. The King and the Vidúshaka take her for Sâgarikâ (disguised), and address her as such; the King perceives his mistake and tries to reconcile her, but the Queen departs in high dudgeon. Then there comes the real Sâgarikâ (dressed like Vâsavadattâ) but she proceeds to commit suicide by hanging herself in despair as she suspects the plot being discovered by her royal mistress. The King now mistakes her for Queen Vásavadattâ, and when he goes forth to rescue her, he sees his mistake and is very much rejoiced at having been unexpectedly united with his beloved. But just then the Queen, repenting of her ill-temper towards the King, comes back prepared to be reconciled to him, and finds him engaged in paying his attentions to Sâgarikâ. The King feels now thoroughly abashed, and the curtain drops on the scene as the Vidúshaka is marched off, bound, along with Sâgarikâ, by the Queen who follows both herself.

Act IV.

The Queen circulates a report that Sâgarikâ was sent away to her father at Ujjayinî, while she keeps her secretly a prisoner in her palace so as to prevent her being seen by anybody. In an Interlude the maid Susaṃgatâ gives to the Vidûshaka the jewelled-necklace which was worn by Sâgarikâ and which the latter had handed over to her to be given to some Brâhmaṇa as a gift, when she herself despaired of her own life. The Vidúshaka visits his royal master, informs him that Sâgarikâ was said to have been sent to Ujjayinî and shows him the jewel-necklace. In the interval news is brought about the success of the expedition against the Kosala country in which Rumaṇvat had been engaged. Then enters a magician whose performance the King witnesses; but this is interrupted by the arrival of Bâbhravya and Vasubhúti, who were with the army of Rumaṇvat, and who had now returned to the capital. Vasubhúti sees the jewel-necklace with the Vidûshaka and recognizes it as the same that once belonged to the Princess Ratnâvalî. He next proceeds to give a full account of the proposed marriage between Ratnâvalî and Udayana, but the narration is interrupted by the commotion caused by the news of a fire having broken out in the royal household. Vâsavadattâ is afraid that Sâgarikâ (who was a prisoner) might lose her life in the fire, and in her terror she asks the King to save her. The King promptly rushes to the rescue, and brings Sâgarikâ safe out of the fire. It is then discovered that the fire was unreal, having been the work of that magician. Vasubhúti at once recognizes his princess in Sâgarikâ, and then everything is satisfactorily cleared up. Vâsava-

dattâ regrets the treatment she gave to her rival, who turns out to be her cousin; Yaugandharâyaṇa enters next to explain his part in the affair; the magician had been sent in by him in order to bring about the release of Sâgarikâ. Everyone is happy, and the Queen consents to the long-deferred marriage of Udayana and Ratnâvalî. The play then closes with the customary *Bharatavâkya*, praying for peace, prosperity and contentment all round.

---

(2) THE SOURCE OF THE PLOT.

It is a noticeable feature of dramatic literature in Sanskrit that few, if any, play-writers have troubled themselves with inventing *entirely* original plots for their plays. Most of them, among whom is our author, have been content to borrow their plots from ancient sources, either from the inexhaustible fund of the great Indian Epics, or from the semi-legendary stories current among the people. The largest collection of these legends, ever made, was probably the *Bṛihatkathâ*, attributed to Guṇâḍhya. This work, which is supposed to date from the first century A. D., was written in the Pais'âchî[1] language. It is, however, unfortunately no longer extant in the original; but we have two excellent and fairly extensive abstracts of it in Sanskrit both compiled in the 11th century, the Bṛihatkathámañjarî of Kshemendra and the Kathásaritságara of Somadeva. The latter (which is larger and less condensed than the version of Kshemendra) is a veritable mine of ancient Hindu legendary lore and makes as entertaining reading as the *Arabian Nights' Entertainments*. The originals of the plots of Harsha's three plays would be found in the Kathásaritságara. But it is difficult to pass any definite criticism on these originals and the changes worked in them by the poet. For, the Kathásaritságara is a later paraphrase, which was not before Harsha, who probably had direct access to the Bṛihatkathá itself: and we do not know how far Somadeva has improved upon the Bṛihatkathá in minor details.

In our edition of the Nágánanda we have given a long extract to show how closely the plot of that play was taken from the Bṛihatkathá. The plots of the two plays Priya-

---

1 "A term applied to a number of low Prakrit dialects spoken by the most ignorant and degraded classes"—Macdonell.

darśiká and Ratnávalí have also been borrowed from the same source; but it should be stated that the borrowings here have not been wholesale as in the case of the Nágánanda. The story of the loves of king Udayana of Kauśâmbî and his Queen Vásavadattá, seems to have been exceedingly popular in ancient India, as it is referred to by many poets of note, including Kálidása—(who says in his Megh. प्राप्यावन्तीनुदयनकथाकोविदग्रामवृद्धान्, प्रद्योतस्य प्रियदुहितरं वत्सराजोऽत्र जह्रे &c.) and Śûdraka (in his Mṛichchh. यौगन्धरायण इवोदयनस्य राज्ञः). It is given at length in the Kathásaritságara. As Harsha does not borrow that story we have not given any extracts from it here; the curious student may consult the beginning of the third Lambaka for the same. In the Kathás. is given an account of how Yaugandharáyaṇa, the minister of Udayana, brought about a marriage of his king with Padmávatî. Harsha has taken this broad fact for his basis, and some names (such as यौगन्धरायण, the General रुमण्वत्, वसन्तक, वासवदत्ता, कौशाम्बी, लावाणक &c.) are common to his play and the original story. But the actual development of the plot, as it runs through the four Acts to the *dénouement*, is practically his own invention. In the Kathás. the princess is the daughter of king Pradyota of Magadha, Padmâvatî[1] by name, and it was prophesied by a seer that she was destined to be the wife of Udayana; but Harsha names her Ratnávalî and makes her a daughter of King Vikramabáhu of Ceylon. The rumour of Vásavadattá being killed in the Lávāṇaka fire is common to both the accounts, but the use made of it by Harsha is not in the original and constitutes a novel feature, as also does the prophecy of the sage concerning Ratnávalî.

In short, while originality of plot has to be denied to our poet, it must be admitted that in the Ratnávalî his inventive genius and constructive skill shine out so pre-eminently as to make his indebtedness to the original quite insignificant. This has endeared the Ratnávalî to the later critics and students of the play, and Dámodaragupta, a poet of the eighth century,

---

1 The poet Bhâsa, thirteen of whose dramas have been recently recovered, has written two plays on the Udayana and Vâsavadattâ story, the *Svapnavâsavadatta* and the *Pratijñāyaugandharāyaṇa*. These follow the original as represented by the Kathâs. much more closely than the *Ratnâvalî*. Harsha, therefore, does not appear to be indebted to Bhâsa in this respect.

has in his Kuṭṭanîmata[1] given a detailed summary of the first Act of Ratnávalî, with the encomium—

आश्लिष्टसंधिबन्धं सत्पात्रसुवर्णयोजितं सुतराम् ।
निपुणपरीक्षकदृष्टं राजति रत्नावलीरत्नम् ॥ (924)

—which undoubtedly it deserves.

---

(3) TIME-ANALYSIS OF THE PLAY.

The action of the Ratnávalî is spread over a period of four consecutive days (probably more), roughly according with the four Acts. The time when the action begins is the season of Spring (*cf.* अद्याहं वसन्तोत्सवे p. 5, प्रद्योतस्य सुता वसन्तसमय: p. 10).

Act I.—begins late in the afternoon of one of the days of the Madana-festival; and this must be the full-moon-day[2] of the month of Chaitra (इह प्रथमं मधुमास: I. 15). For this is clearly shown by the fact that the moon is described as rising just after the sun has set (*cf.* उदयतटान्तरितमियं प्राची सूचयति दिङ् निशानाथम् p. 27). The actual events narrated probably take up two hours, when the Sun sets and the Act ends (नभस: पारं प्रयाते रवौ p. 26, संप्रति परिणतमह: p. 27).

Act II. The time of this Act cannot be conclusively ascertained; but that it comes the next day immediately after the events of Act I. is sufficiently clear. For in Act I. Ságariká hands over the bird Sârikâ to Susaṃgatâ (p. 22); as she has forgotten to take it back, Susaṃgatá is shown at the beginning of Act II. as seeking her friend in order to restore the bird to her keeping (p. 29). This must be evidently the next day. The time, though not definitely mentioned anywhere, is probably early afternoon; for it was on that same day (अद्य p. 29) that the King learnt the कुसुमसंजननदोहद from श्रीखण्डदास, and that must have happened in the morning. Again, Sâgarikâ is mentioned as going to the

---

1 See the ed. of the Kuṭṭanîmata in Kávyamâlâ, Guchchhaka III. (1889) pp. 105—110. Dâmodaragupta not only mentions सागरिका, काञ्चनमाला, the Sârikâ मेधाविनी &c., but actually quotes the verse उदयनगान्तरितमियं &c. from the first Act of the play.

2. And not the 13th, as supposed by Prof. Jackson; see P. 91 of his article in the *Journal of the American Oriental Society*, Vol. 21 (1900). For the मदनमहोत्सव see p. 9 of our text.

plantain-bower, with a picture-board and painting materials; this must have been in the afternoon as then alone she could have got leisure to do it. The subsequent events follow consequently without a break, and the Act ends some time *before* sunset, for otherwise a description of sunset would most likely have come at the end.

Act III.—begins late in the evening of the next day. Some[1] have imagined that the events of Acts II. and III. take place on the same day, with only an interval of two or three hours between. But this appears hardly likely. For the King is described as being love-sick and in ill-health (न खलु सागरिकां वर्जयित्वा p. 61, and the Queen as sending Kāñchanamâlâ to learn about the condition of his health; अस्वस्थशरीरस्य भर्तुः p. 62). Surely, at least a day's interval is necessary for the King to manifest signs of his indisposition and the Queen to get anxious on his account. The action begins at about dusk. (प्रदोषे p. 61, पर्यवसितमहः p. 66), and is continued for a few hours, the darkness (प्रसरति पूर्वदिशं प्रच्छादयंस्तिमिरसंघः p. 69) affording a ready ground for the series of mistaken identities upon which so much of the interest of this Act depends. Later on there is moon-rise (स्थितः पुरस्तान्निशानाथः p. 74), the Act thus closing late in the night of probably the 2nd day of the dark half of the month.

Act IV. The events of this Act follow the very next day; the reference to Ságariká being said to have been sent away at "mid-night" (उपस्थितेऽर्धरात्रे p. 86) obviously indicates the mid-night intervening between the two days on which respectively the events of Acts III. and IV. take place. As to the actual time of this Act, there is no conclusive proof, but it may be taken to be early afternoon, in the absence of any mention to the contrary.

---

(4) TECHNICAL REMARKS.

The *Ratnávalî* is pre-eminently a Sanskrit play which conforms strictly to the various canons of Sanskrit dramaturgy, and is for this reason more often quoted in the later treatises on dramaturgy than many other plays.[2] It belongs to the class

1 *E. g.* Prof. M. Windisch as quoted by Prof. Jackson *op. cit.*

2. In this respect it is to be compared with the Veṇîsaṃhâra which also is very largely drawn upon in Sanskrit treatises on dramaturgy.

of Uparūpakas known as the *nāṭikā* and is divided into four Acts. As regards the three chief requisites, the वस्तु or Plot is प्रख्यात or historical, as the story of Udayana and Vásavadattá was popularly received as history in the poet's own days. The नेता here is धीरललित, "Firm, sportive and tender-hearted" (निश्चिन्तो धीरललितः कलासक्तः सुखी मृदुः D.-R. II. 3). The Heroine belongs to the variety known as मुग्धा, who is defined as मुग्धा नववयःकामा रतौ वामा मृदुः क्रुधि (D. R., II. 16). There is no प्रतिनायक or प्रति-नायिका as in other plays. The prevailing रस or sentiment is शृङ्गार (Love). There is an occasional infusion of करुण as in the lament of Ságariká (p. 79) and of हास्य as in the jokes of the Vidûshaka; but these are all subordinate to शृङ्गार which permeates the whole. The अर्थप्रकृतिs, कार्यावस्थाs, the five संधिs and their various अङ्गs, have been pointed out in the commentary in the various places.

As regards the *dénouement* and the external setting, the play opens with the customary नान्दी. Then in the प्रस्तावना or Prelude the Sûtradhâra informs the audience of the name of the poet, the title of the play and the occasion of its performance. Then there is a विष्कम्भक in which the minister Yaugandharāyaṇa briefly relates that portion of the story which is anterior to the period where the play actually begins. Then each of the three succeeding Acts has a प्रवेशक or interlude, and finally there is the भरतवाक्य as usual. This is the broad structural outline of the arrangement of the play; for details and minor divisions and sub-divisions of topics (*e. g.* फलयोग, करण, नर्म, पुष्प, तोटक and others too numerous to mention) the student may consult the Das'arūpaka which deals with these fully.

---

(5) THE GEOGRAPHY OF THE PLAY.

The scene of the play is laid at Kaus'âmbî, the capital of king Udayana, who ruled over the Vatsa country. Vatsa is thus described in the Kathâs.—अस्ति वत्स इति ख्यातो देशो दर्पोपशान्तये । स्वर्गस्य निर्मितो धात्रा प्रतिमल्ल इव क्षितौ ॥. The city of Kaus'âmbî was very famous in ancient times, being mentioned in the Râmâyaṇa of Vâlmîki. The Kathâs. describes its grandeur as लक्ष्मीविलासवसतिर्भूतलस्येव कर्णिका (II. 1. 5). In many Ceylonese books it is named as one of the nineteen capital cities of ancient India. It was founded by Kus'âmba (son of

Kus'a). tenth in descent from Purúravas. Time has deprived it of its glory and now it is represented by the comparatively insignificant village of Kosam, on the river Jamná, about 30 miles above Allahabad.

कोसल—The country of Kosala against which Rumanvat led an expedition, is the southern Kosala, as it is mentioned in the fourth Act that the Kosala king had taken refuge in the Vindhya fortress (विन्ध्यदुर्गावस्थितस्य p. 93). This is distinct from the Uttara Kosala, where reigned the celebrated kings of the solar dynasty (see Rag. IX. 1). It lay to the south of the Ganges and stretched as far as the modern Berar. According to the Vâyupurâṇa, Kus'a, the son of Râma ruled over this country at his capital कुशस्थली or कुशावती, built in the defiles of the Vindhya mountain.

सिंहल—is identified by some with the modern Ceylon. Others hold that it was an island different from Ceylon as the two are separately mentioned in the Bhâg.-P. Sk. V., जम्बुद्वीपस्य च राजन्नुपद्वीपानष्टौ येक उपदिशन्ति । तद्यथा—स्वर्णप्रस्थश्चन्द्रशुक्र आवर्तनो रमणको मुदाहरणः पाञ्चजन्यः सिंहलो लंकेति । Varahâmihira also mentions these differently; see Bṛh.-Saṃ. Ch. XIV. 11, 15 (कांची मरुचीपत्तनचेर्यार्यकसिंहला ऋषभाः ।).

लावाणक—was the name of a village adjacent to Magadha and was probably situated on the south bank of the Jamnâ, near its confluence with the Ganges.

---

(6) CRITICAL AND GENERAL REMARKS.

Of the three plays of Śrî Harshadeva, the Nâgánanda which is a Nâṭaka, is of a unique type and stands quite by itself, being intended to teach a lofty moral; while the two remaining ones (Ratnâvalî and Priyadarśikâ) may be called sister plays, their subject being common, *viz.* the love-intrigue of King Vatsa. They are, like the Mâlavikágnimitra and Vikramorvaśîya of Kâlidâsa, essentially love-plays, and

---

1 The plot of the Mâl. resembles that of our play in some details. There also we find Mâlavikâ, the Heroine, like Ratnâ, thwarted in her assignations with the King Agnimitra by his second queen Iravali. There also Mâlavikâ is put in fetters and confined in a room by the chief queen Dhârinî and is released by means of a scheme, and the queen herself, as here, gives her in marriage to the King.

the poet herein neither desires to teach any moral nor aims at illustrating any of the great concerns of worldly life. Thus these plays lie on a lower plane than the Nágánanda; none the less they are sufficiently interesting on the stage. The Râtnâvalî, in particular, by reason of its well-conceived and well-developed plot, has attracted admirers ever since the days when it was first exhibited at Harsha's royal theatre. We have already quoted the enthusiastic praise accorded to it by Damodaragupta; and we might here quote Dr. Macdonell, who writes:[1] "Altogether, *Ratnâvalî* is an agreeable play, with well-drawn characters, and many poetical beauties." His play which has thus elicited admiration from both eastern and western scholars, holds no insignificant position in Sanskrit literature, and, as has been stated elsewhere, is very frequently quoted (by way of illustration or authority) by writers on poetics. Evidence of style shows that the *Ratnávalî*, which is mere polished and distinctly more graceful than the *Priyadarśikâ*, must be a later production, while the Nâgânanda must be put last as it was obviously written[2] during the closing years of Harsha's life.

The Ratnâvalî is deservedly the best of the works of Harsha; it observes the unities of time and place, and maintains the spectators' interest in the story right up to the end, where finally the ingenious little plot of the minister, Yaugandharâyaṇa, is revealed to the King. How cleverly the poet has manipulated the incidents for keeping up the interest may be observed in each Act. Thus he ingeniously makes use of the talking-bird, Sáriká, both for the purpose of frightening the Vidúshaka and allowing the audience to enjoy a joke at his expense (कोऽपि भूतः पतिवसति p. 40) and of informing the King of the beginnings of his own love-affair. Next in Act III. the poet has, by dressing Ságariká as Vásavadattá,

1 *A History of Sanskrit Literature*, p. 362. *Cf.* also "The story is romantic, the incidents are well contrived, the situations are eminently dramatic, and although the spectator is let into the secret of the plot from the beginning, the interest is very successfully maintained. The intrigue corresponds perfectly with the definition given by Schlegel; it is the union of un-expected combinations, resulting from the contending operation of accidental occurrences and premeditated designs."—(Wilson).

2 See p. XLVI. of our ed. of the play.

and Susamgatâ as Kâñchanamâlâ, finely used the opportunity thus provided for creating a number of mistaken identities which not only help the plot but must also have been very amusing to the spectators. The fire-scene in the last Act is again an excellent display of ingenuity, without which the entrance of Sâgarikâ on the stage at the required time would not have been possible, except in some bare, humdrum, manner. That Yaugandharâyaṇa should have planned and worked out the whole marriage scheme on his own responsibility, without letting the King know anything about it, seems strange. The minister himself feels it when he says स्वेच्छाचारि भीत एवास्मि भर्तुः (p. 9). But by the above device the poet has given such a finish to the whole thing as to make it impossible for the King to blame his minister, or the Queen to withold her consent to the intended match. The only draw-back in the play is that the poet has represented the Heroine as somewhat simple-minded. For, in his anxiety to describe the supreme handsomeness of his Hero, he makes Sâgarikâ conceive him as Cupid in bodily form (p. 25) and then suddenly recognize him as a human personage. Another weak point is the hanging-scene in the third Act; the poet seems to be rather fond of painting his Heroines as unable to hold out against distress even for a short time and seeking relief therefrom in this extreme and exaggerated fashion; for he has used a similar device in the second Act of the Nâgânanda also. At any rate, it does not speak much for the Heroine's strength of mind.

The Ratnâvalî is a court-comedy and not a social comedy like the Mrichchhakaṭika; hence it is natural if it does not give us much detailed information about the social customs or the domestic habits of the people in those days. It appears that music (p. 15), dancing (p. 14) and painting (p. 30) were the fine arts cultivated by cultured ladies then—a contrast with the present day Hindu society. Shipping is referred to as a commercial enterprise (p. 8). Magic seems to have had a firm hold on the popular mind (*cf.* अचिन्त्यो हि मणिमन्त्रौषधीनां प्रभावः p. 39, and also the ऐन्द्रजालिक-scene in the fourth Act). Belief in ghosts was then as common as it is now (*cf.* how the Vidûshaka is frightened at p. 40). Beyond these stray facts we get few glimpses into the daily life of the people of Harsha's timec.

The style of Harsha is simple and easy-flowing, though consciously elaborate in a few places. It has not the grace or rhythm of Kâlidâsa, but it is also remarkably free from the artificial ponderousness of later-day Sanrkrit. S'rî Harsha evidently took Kâlidâsa for his model and many of his stanzas and sentences are reminiscent of Kâlidâsa. Thus प्रारम्भेऽस्मिन्स्वामिनो वृद्धिहेतौ &c. (p. 9) reminds us of इष्टाधिगमनिमित्तं प्रयोगमेकान्तसाधुमपि मत्वा &c. (Mâlavik. IV. 5). Compare also न कमलाकरं वर्जयित्वा राजहंस्यन्यत्राभिरमते (p. 32) with सागरमुज्झित्वा कुत्र वा महानद्यवतरति &c. (S'âk. III.), दुल्लहजणाणुराओ (p. 35) with दुल्लहो पिओ मे (Málavik. II. 4) and many other passages pointed out in our Notes. Verses like उद्यत्तटान्तरितमियं &c. (p. 27) and दृशः पृथुतरीकृता जितनिजाब्जपत्रत्विषः &c. (p. 53) are not unworthy of the distinguished author of the Śákuntala. It has to be admitted, however, that coming after Kâlidâsa, Harsha has not quite escaped from the deterioration in style that is observable in post-Kálidásian authors. Puns like those in लीलावधूतपद्मा कथयन्ती पक्षपातमधिकं नः &c. (p. 45) or दृशामुदयनस्येन्दोरिव &c. (p. 27), long compounds like संध्यामृष्टावशिष्टस्वकरपरिकरस्पष्टहेमारपङ्क्ति (p. 66) or सान्द्रोद्यानद्रुमाग्रग्लपनपिशुनितात्यन्ततीव्राभितापः, and jingling collocations of words like those in अस्त्रव्यस्तशिरस्त्रशस्त्रकषणोत्कृत्तोत्तमाङ्गे (p. 94) are of very rare occurrence in Kálidása's verse.

In simplicity and easy intelligibility of style, Harsha would rank next to Kâlidâsa, and above Bhavabhûti. But the same cannot be said of him as a dramatic artist, or a master of language either. As the author of the three plays taken together, Harsha's position among Sanskrit writers is in the second class. He calls himself, in modesty, only a निपुणः कविः (p. 5); but Jayadeva (the author of the Prasannarâghava) calls him the Delight of the Muse of Poetry (हर्षो हर्षः—कविताकामिन्याः). It is possible that in his enthusiasm and love of alliteration Jayadeva was led into conferring upon our author a position to which sober critics would demur. We on our part are content to endorse the poet's own estimate of his work, that he was a "skilful" (निपुण) writer, a star of lesser brilliancy than Kâlidâsa or Bhavabhûti, but certainly not inferior to Bhaṭṭa Nârâyaṇa or Viśâkhadatta in constructive art.

(7) THE PRINCIPAL CHARACTERS IN THE PLAY.

Vatsarája (*Hero*).

It may be remarked at the outset that the interest in the story of this play depends on the incidents and not so much on the development of any particular character; this is also due to the fact that the action of the play is spread over the very short period of a few days, and not over a number of months or years in which latter case there is sufficient scope for developing a character more fully. As it is, we shall content ourselves with pointing out the salient characteristics of the dramatis personae as delineated by the poet. They are all cast in the conventional mould. The Hero is King Udayana of the Vatsa country, chosen for the purpose of showing him in the enjoyment of courtly life, the charming incidents of his public life (लोके हारि च वत्सराजचरितं p. 5) having already won for him great popularity. He was a good ruler who understood and discharged his duties and responsibilities (*cf.* राज्यं निर्जितशत्रु योग्यसचिवे न्यस्तः समस्तो भरः सम्यक्पालनलालिताः प्रशमिताशेषोपसर्गाः प्रजाः I. 9). We get few glimpses into his political career, as this is not a political play; still one stray remark that falls from him in appreciation of a vanquished foe (साधु कोसलपते साधु। मृत्युरपि ते श्लाघ्यो यस्य शत्रवोऽप्येवं पुरुषकारं वर्णयन्ति। p. 94) shows his generous and noble nature; while his surprise at Yaugandharáyaṇa's action (कथमसौ मामनिवेद्य किंचित्करिष्यति p. 108.) shows that the minister had to consult him in all state matters before they were finally disposed of. We need not look askance at his love-intrigue; polygamy was common in India among sovereigns in those days and it is excusable if the King felt attracted by a new face. He himself was very handsome, as is shown by his being mistaken by Sâgarikâ for Cupid (p. 25). That this was not his first love-affair is clearly shown when he narrates his covert experiences in verses like उद्दामोत्कलिकां &c. (p. 38) and प्रणयविशदां दृष्टिं वक्त्रे &c. (p. 70). Although forced to tell a lie when the occasion demanded it, as when he denied having ever seen Sâgariká (न तु दृष्टपूर्वा p. 57), he does it equivocally and does not tell a downright lie. Being a past master in dealing with jealousies and counter-jealousies in his harem, he is careful not to wound the feelings of his old love, as is shown by his uniform respect for his Queen

Vâsavadattá and his constant endeavours to conciliate her. Gallant speeches like मदनिके नन्वाज्ञापयतीत्येव रमणीयम् and ननु वक्ष्यसुस्तवान्तरमापतितमिति (p. 17) are a further testimony to his courtesy towards the Queen. He is a kind master, as is clear from the familiar manner in which Susaṃgatâ speaks to him at p. 51.

THE VIDU'SHAKA.

The Vidúshaka is a necessary conventional character in most of the Sanskrit plays. He is a Bráhmaṇa, the privileged court-wit and a constant companion of the Hero. His appearia stupidit yand generel air of self-conceit serve to excite laughter on the stage; he is generally described as ugly in appearance (*cf.* how he is mistaken for a monkey; p. 37). His business is also to assist in forwarding the progress of love-affairs of his friend the hero; this he accomplishes in this play to a great extent, and the rendezvous in Act III. is brought about by his agency. He is made to dance and sing with the two maid-servants (p. 16) to show him up as a simpleton. His character as a glutton is shown by his constant references to मोदक (pp. 16, 86). As a Bráhmaṇa he is fond of boasting of his knowledge of the Vedas; what that consists of is known when he mistakes a गाथा for a ऋक् (p. 42). His taste for study is seen in his remark यदि पठ्यते तदलमेतेन (p. 16). He is somewhat greedy and is ever ready to receive gifts and presents (pp. 17, 45). His wits are not really dull, however; they can become quite sharp if the occasion requires it (*e. g.* वयस्य नैते मधुकरा नूपुरशब्दमनुहरन्ति। नूपुरशब्द एवैष देव्याः परिजनस्य: p. 20). His emotions are easily excited; he is easily frightened (*e. g.* एतस्मिन्बकुलपादपे कोऽपि भूतः प्रतिवसति p. 40; भो लब्धावकाश। वेपत इव मे हृदयम् p. 93) and as easily and readily delighted (*e. g.* at p. 56 when he dances in wild joy and lets fall the picture-board). generally considered, he constitutes the chief source of the comic element on the stage. Nevertheless now and then we get a glimpse of the nobility of his mind. For although the *Ratnamálâ* was given to him as a present (p. 86) he hands it over to the King for his diversion, without saying a word about it (p. 91) and finally restores it to Ratnâvalî (according to one reading; see p. 109). Again his love for his master is unboundeds–to him none is as great—as is clear from his words अथवा कोऽन्यः कुसुमचापव्यपदेशेन निन्ह्यते (p. 43), and भो वयस्य यस्य पुनः...... आत्मन उपरि कः पराभवः &c. (p. 48.).

SÂGARIKÂ.

Although the play is named Ratnâvalî after the Heroine, yet for reasons already stated in the case of the Hero, there is nothing especially noteworthy about her character. She is described as a young and an uncommonly beautiful princess charming and accomplished—one who captivates the Hero's mind at the mere sight of her picture. Her character is not drawn with a view to represent her in the glory of a maiden of high birth like Mâlatî or to paint her in the grandeur of married life either. The chief noticeable thing about her is her great love for the King, with whom she falls in love-at-first-sight, thinking him as handsome as Cupid (p. 25). Her another trait is her extreme sensitiveness of feeling, and the slightest untoward incident plunges her into a depth of despondency so that she immediately thinks of death and suicide. Compare सर्वथा मरणमेव मम मन्दभागिन्या उपस्थितम् p. 31, जीवितमरणयोरन्तरे वर्ते p. 47, and वरमिदानीं स्वयमेवात्मानमुद्बध्योपरता न पुनर्ज्ञातसंकेतवृत्तान्तया देव्या परिभूता p. 79, इयं रत्नमाला जीवितनिराशया तया &c. p. 85. This representation of weakness detracts not a little from her character as a Heroine. The only relieving feature of her character indirectly indicated is her high sense of family honour which prevents her from disclosing her identity to even her friend Susaṃgatá.

VA'SAVADATTA.

She is the chief Queen, elderly and staid; her love for her lord is deep-rooted and is recognized as such by the latter when he remarks प्रिया मुञ्चत्यद्य स्फुटमसहना जीवितमसौ प्रकृष्टस्य प्रेम्णः स्खलितमविषह्यं हि भवति (p. 77). She is well aware of the King's fondness for a pretty face, and hence tries (p. 21) her best to keep Sâgarikâ out of his sight. Failing there, she is naturally jealous and as such interrupts the King in his love passages; but she is really affectionate at heart and her anger is of short duration. This is amply illustrated by her almost instantaneous repentance at having spurned the King's reconciliation (p. 81). Her tenderness of heart is shown when she readily confesses her secret, *viz.* the imprisonment of Sâgarikâ in fetters, the moment she perceived her to be in danger of life. Her magnanimity is shown finally when she willingly accepts Sâgarikâ as her rival and sharer in her lord's affection, her character thus appearing in a generous and lovable light.

IMPORTANT ABBREVIATIONS.

Ak., *Amara.*—Amarakośa.
Amaru.—Amaruśataka.
Bg.—Bhagavadgîtâ.
Bhar.—Bhartṛihari's Śatakas (N. and V.).*
Bhaṭṭi.—Bhaṭṭikāvya (I.-V.)*
Bṛih.-S.—Bṛihatsaṃhitá.
Bṛih.-Up.—Brihadáraṇyakopanishad.
Cf.—Compare.
Ch.—Chapter.
Com.—Commentary, Commentator.
Dic.—Dictionary.
D.-K.—Daśakumáracharita.*
D.-R.—Daśa-Rúpaka.
Gît.—Gîtagovinda.
H.-Ch.—Harshacharita.
H. S. Gr.—Higher Sanskrit Grammar (by the Editor).
Hitop.—Hitopadeśa.*
Kâd.—Kádambarî.*
Kathás.—Kathásaritságara.
Káv., *K.-D.*—Kávyádarśa.
Kir.—Kirátārjunîya (I-.III.).*
K.-P.—Kávyaprakáśa.
Kum.—Kumárasaṃbhava (I.-VII.).*
Madhyam.—Madhyamavyáyoga of Bhása.*
Mah.-Bh.—Mahábhárata.
Málav.—Málavikágnimitra.*
Malli.—Mallinátha.
Mál.-Mádh.—Málatî-Mádhava.*
M.-S.—Manusmṛiti.
Megh.—Meghadûta.*
Mṛich.—Mṛichchhakaṭika.
Mudrá.—Mudrárákshasa.*
M.-W.—Monier-Williams.
Nág.—Nágánanda.*
N.-Ch.—Naishadhîyacharita.
Páṇ.—Páṇini's Ashṭádhyáyî
Pañchar.—Pañcharátra of Bhása.*
Priy.—Priyadarsśiká. (N. Ed.)
Pt.—Pañchatantra.*
Ragh.—Raghuvaṃśa (I.-X.)*
Râm.—Râmáyaṇa.
Ratn.—Ratnávalî.*
Ṛig.-V.—Ṛig-Veda.
Ṛitus.—Ṛitusaṃhára.*
S.—Sûtra.
Śâk.—Śákuntala of Kálidása.*
S.-D.—Sáhityadarpaṇa.
Sid.-Kau.—Siddhánta-Kaumudî.
Ś.Ś.—Śiśupálavadha.
Subhá.—Subháshita.
Śv.-Up.—Śvetāśvataropanishad.
Svap.-Vâs.—Svapnavâsavadatta of Bhása.
Uttar.—Uttararâmacharita.*
Várt.—Vârtika.
Veṇî.—Veṇîsaṃhâra.*
Vikr.—Vikramorvaśîya.*
Vikr.-Ch.—Vikramâṅkadevacharita of Bilhaṇa.

* Annotated by the Editor.

DRAMATIS PERSONAE.

——:o:——

MALES.

सूत्रधारः—The stage-manager.

राजा (उदयनः)—The Hero, king of Kauśâmbî.

विदूषकः (वसन्तकः)—A Brâhmaṇa. the Hero's companion and court-wit.

यौगन्धरायणः—The chief minister.

विजयवर्मा—The nephew of Rumaṇvat who is the commander-in-chief of the King.

बाभ्रव्यः—The chamberlain of the King.

वसुभूतिः—The minister of Vikramabâhu, the king of Siṃhala.

ऐन्द्रजालिकः—A magician.

FEMALES.

नटी—The stage-manager's wife.

रत्नावली (known as सागरिका)—The Heroine, daughter of king Vikramabâhu of Siṃhala.

वासवदत्ता—The Queen, wife of Udayana.

काञ्चनमाला—An attendant-maid of the Queen.

सुसंगता—A maid-servant, friend of the Heroine.

चूतलतिका—A maid-servant.

मदनिका—A maid-servant.

निपुणिका—A maid-servant.

प्रतीहारी (वसुंधरा)—The door-keeper.

PERSONS &c. MENTIONED.

विक्रमबाहुः—The king of Siṃhala, and father of the Heroine.

रुमण्वान्—The commander-in-chief of the King.

मेधाविनी (सारिका)—A talking-bird.

SCENE.

Kaus'âmbî, the capital city of king Udayana.

———

भूमिका ।

यस्याश्चोरश्चिकुरनिकुरः कर्णपूरो मयूरो
भासो हासः कविकुलगुरुः कालिदासो विलासः ।
हर्षो हर्षो हृदयवसतिः पञ्चबाणस्तु बाणः
केषां नैषा कथय कविताकामिनी कौतुकाय ॥

—जयदेवस्य ।

इह खलु सकलविद्याकलाकलापादिपीठेऽस्मिन्भारते वर्षे निजयशःसुरभीकृतदिगन्तरालाः प्रतिभाशालिनः परःशताः कवीश्वरा भासकालिदासादयः स्वकृत्याभरणैर्वाग्वधूं मण्डयन्ति स्म । तेषां च केचन प्रबन्धप्रमोदितरसिकमण्डलाः शब्दसर्गार्जितोर्जितयशस्का विदग्धधुरीणाः प्रतापसंतापितारिचक्रा वक्रेष्वप्यार्जवमुत्पादयन्तश्चक्रवर्तिनो राजानोऽभूवन्नित्यहो नवनवाश्चर्यनिर्माणचातुरी विधेः । श्रीसरस्वत्योः ख्यातनिसर्गभिन्नास्पदयोरप्येकसंस्थानं कस्य हि सहृदयस्य चेतः कुतूहलितं प्रमोदनिर्भरं च न कुर्यात्। एतेषु श्रीमच्छूद्रकयशोवर्मभीमटभोजादिषु कविनृपेष्वग्रेसरीभूतः **श्रीहर्षा**भिधः स्थानेश्वरेश्वरः **चक्रवर्तिश्रीहर्षवर्धना**ख्यया पुरावृत्तकोविदैरुद्घुष्यमाणकीर्तिर्नृपतिरितस्त्रयोदशशताद्वर्षेभ्यः प्राग्भारतभूमण्डलं प्रशशास । यस्य च **प्रियदर्शिका—रत्नावली—नागानन्द**समाख्यं रूपकत्रयमद्य यावद्रसिकान्तःकरणग्रहणेनात्मनो निर्मातुर्यथार्थनामत्वं प्रख्यापयद्रसिकानां हर्षं संवर्धयन्नाटकनिबन्धेषु गुणानुकूल्याद्धुरीवर्ति । यस्य चेभ्यस्य सभ्यो गद्यकविमूर्धन्यपदवीमारूढः कादम्बर्याः प्रणेता श्रीभट्टबाणः स्वस्वामिनः शूरस्य वदान्यस्य विक्रान्तस्योदारचरितस्य चरितमाख्यायिकारूपेण सुललितपदबन्धं निबबन्ध । सोऽयं चित्तचमत्कारी **हर्षचरिता**ख्यो गद्यप्रबन्ध एव श्रीहर्षनृपतेरितिवृत्तादिविज्ञाने प्रधानतया सहायतां समुपगच्छति प्राचीनवार्ताविविदिषूणामिति सुविदितमेव सुधियाम् । केचित्तु नव्यशिक्षिता नागानन्दादिरूपकप्रणेतृत्वं न श्रीहर्षवर्धननृपतेः किं तु कस्याप्यपरस्य तदनुजीविनः कवेरिति साग्रहं प्रत्यवतिष्ठन्ते । तेष्वपि भिन्नभिन्नमतप्रणाल्या महती विप्रतिपत्तिः । केचित्त्रयोविंशतिसंख्यकरूपककृतः श्रीमतो भासस्य, अन्ये हर्षवर्धनाश्रितपण्डितपारिषदानामेकतमस्य धावकस्य, अपरे चोपरिनिर्दिष्टगद्यगीर्वधूप्राणस्य श्रीबाणस्य न कथंचिदपि तावच्छ्रीहर्षस्य त्रितयमिदं रूपकाणामिति नानापरंपरानुसरणशीला बम्भ्रम्यमाणाः कष्टयन्ति चेतः शिष्टानाम् । सोऽयं सर्वोऽप्यूहसमूहो न विश्वसनीयत्वकक्षामवगाहत इति सविस्तरं विमर्शितमन्यत्रास्माभिरिति नात्र परतरं प्रस्तूयते ।

श्रीमान्हर्षः सर्वत्र भासकालिदासादिमहाकव्युपदिष्टपथानुसरणपरः स्वकृतिषु वैदर्भीमेव रीतिमवलम्बितवानिति स्फुटमेवावलोकयताम् । यां च रीतिं श्रीबिल्हण

इत्थमुपवर्णयामास—" अनभ्रवृष्टिः श्रवणामृतस्य सरस्वतीविभ्रमजन्मभूमिः । वैदर्भ-रीतिः कृतिनामुदेति सौभाग्यलाभप्रतिभूः पदानाम् ॥" इति । प्रसादश्लेषमाधुर्यादिकाव्यगुणैर्द्विगुणीकृतसरसत्वमस्य प्रबन्धत्रये सर्वतः समुल्लसतितराम् । पद्ये ह्यसमस्तपदप्रचुरप्रचारान्नये च सरलायाः सुस्पष्टाया वाचो निबन्धनात्कविरयं भवभूत्यादिपश्चात्तनकव्यपेक्षया सुतरां संमानार्ह इति संमतमेव विपश्चिताम् ।

एतदीयप्रबन्धत्रये परस्परानुगुणगुणगणनक्रमेण **रत्नावली**समाख्या नाटिकैव शेखरीभूता यामुद्दिश्याह कुट्टनीमते श्रीदामोदरगुप्तः— "आश्लिष्टसंधिबन्धं सत्पात्रसुवर्णयोजितं सुतराम् । निपुणपरीक्षकदृष्टं राजति **रत्नावलीरत्नम्** ॥" इति । तदपेक्षया **प्रियदर्शिका** न्यूनगुणाऽथ चैतदपेक्षातो **नागानन्दं** न्यूनगुणतरम् । एवमधराधरक्रमानुस्यूतमपि नागानन्दमस्य कवेः चरमैव कृतिर्भवेदिति तस्य शान्तरसप्रधानाद्वस्तुस्वरूपात्सुव्यक्तमेव । कालानुक्रमेण **रत्नावलि**रियं मध्यस्थतामारूढा । अस्या नाटिकात्वेन चत्वार एवाङ्काः । अत्र नायकः सुविख्यातचरितसौरभो बृहत्कथादिषु वर्णितहारिवृत्तान्तो वत्सराज उदयनो नाम धीरललितः । नायिका च सिंहलेश्वरविक्रमबाहोरात्मजा रत्नावली यस्या अत्र सागरिकेतिनाम्ना व्यवहारः । सा च मुग्धा । रसोऽत्र प्रधानः शृङ्गार एवाङ्गी । इतिवृत्तं चास्या आधारभूतं बृहत्कथावर्तिवत्सराजचरितं यदुपजीव्य प्रादुरासन्बहूनां कविप्रकाण्डानां प्रबन्धाः । अस्यां च नाटिकायामुपवर्णितं कथावस्त्वङ्कानुक्रमतो विभक्तं सारांशरूपेण सुखावबोधायात्रोपनिबध्यते—

प्रथमाङ्के तावदादौ नान्दीपठनम् । ततः प्रस्तावनायां सूत्रधारनटीसंवादेन नाटिकाया अस्याः कर्तृत्वाभिधानादीनामुपन्यासः । ततो विष्कम्भके वत्सराजप्रधानामात्यस्य यौगन्धरायणस्य प्रवेशस्तन्मुखेन च पूर्ववृत्तस्य वस्तुनः किमपि निवेदनम् । तद्यथा । वत्सराजे महीं शासति केनापि सिद्धेनादिष्टं सिंहलेश्वरस्य विक्रमबाहोर्नृपतेर्दुहितू रत्नावल्या यः पाणिं ग्रहीष्यति स सार्वभौमो राजा भविष्यतीति । ततस्तत्प्रत्ययात्तेन मन्त्रिणोदयनस्य स्वामिनोऽर्थे बहुवारं प्रार्थितोऽपि विक्रमबाहुः प्रथमपरिणीताया देव्या वासवदत्तायाश्चित्तखेदं परिजिहीर्षन्नास्य प्रणयं स्वीचकार । तदा लावाणिकेन वह्निना वासवदत्ता दग्धेति प्रसिद्धिमुत्पाद्य यौगन्धरायणः सिंहलेश्वरान्तिकं बाभ्रव्यं कञ्चुकिनं पुना रत्नावलीं प्रार्थयितुं प्रेषयामास । प्रदत्ता च रत्नावली सिंहलेश्वरेण पश्चात्तदमात्येन वसुभूतिना बाभ्रव्येण च सहागच्छन्ती समुद्रे यानभङ्गान्निमग्ना । किं तु दैववशात्फलकमासाद्य जीवितं धारयन्ती सा केनापि कौशाम्बीयेन वणिजा सिंहलेभ्यः प्रत्यागच्छता संभाविता रत्नमालां च तत्कण्ठगतां विलोक्य प्रत्यभिज्ञाय कौशाम्बीं प्रापय्य यौगन्धरायणहस्ते समर्पिता । सोऽथ सागरतः प्राप्तेयं दारिकेति भणित्वा तां सागरिकेतिनाम्ना परिज्ञायमानां देव्या वासवदत्तायाः परिजनत्वेन स्थापितवान् । इमं कथांशं लघु निवेद्य निष्क्रान्ते यौगन्धरायणे वत्सराजविदूषकयोर्मदनमहोत्सवं सादरं च सानन्दं चावलोकयतोः प्रवेशः । तत्र

नृत्यन्त्योश्चेट्योः साकं विदूषकोऽपि नृत्यति गायति क्रीडति च। चेटीमुखेन वासवदत्तायाः संदेशः—'प्रवृत्ते मदनोत्सवेऽद्य खलु मया मकरन्दोद्यानं गत्वा रक्ताशोकपादपतले संस्थापितस्य भगवतः कुसुमायुधस्य पूजा निर्वर्तयितव्या। तत्रार्यपुत्रेण संनिहितेन भवितव्यम्' इत्येवंविधं समुपलभ्य यावच्च राजा तत्र गच्छति तावद्वासवदत्ताऽपि सपरिजना तत्रोपस्थिता। परिजनमध्यगतां चाद्भुतमनोरमलावण्यां सागरिकां दृष्ट्वा यस्य दर्शनात्प्रयत्नेन रक्ष्यते तस्यैव दृष्टिगोचरे पतिता भवेदिति कृत्वा राज्ञी कुत्रचिदन्यत्र प्रेषितवती। सागरिका तु मदनपूजाकुतूहलाक्रान्तचित्ता तत्रैव प्रच्छन्नाऽतिष्ठत्। वत्सराजं दृष्ट्वा च तस्मिन्बद्धभावा बभूव।

द्वितीयाङ्के प्रथमं तावत्प्रवेशके सुसंगतानिपुणिकासंवादाज्ज्ञायते यन्मदनोत्क्षिप्तहृदया सागरिका गृहीतचित्रफलकवर्तिकाद्युपकरणा कदलीगृहं प्रविश्यावस्थितेति। ततस्तथाविधां नायिकां सुसंगतोपातिष्ठत्। सागरिकयाऽऽलिखिते वत्सराजे तद्भावं ज्ञात्वा सुसंगताऽपि तत्पार्श्वे सागरिकामालिखितवती। ततो युक्त्या ज्ञातसखीहृदया सा तस्या अभिलाषमभिननन्द। मिथो मन्त्रयमाणयोस्तयोरालापस्य गृहीताक्षरा पञ्जरस्था मेधाविनी नाम सारिका बभूव। अत्रान्तरे कोऽपि वानरो मन्दुरायाः प्रभ्रष्टस्तयैव दिशागमिष्यतीति शङ्कयोभे निष्क्रान्ते। सारिका च वानरेणोद्घाटितपञ्जरोड्डीयापससार। ततो वत्सराजविदूषकौ प्रविशतः। तयोश्च समीपे वृक्षस्था सारिका यानि मदनपरवशतया सागरिकया वचांस्युक्तानि तान्येव भणितुमुपक्रम्य सर्वं तद्रहस्यं तयोः श्रवणपथं प्रापयामास। उड्डीय गतां तामनुसरन्तौ द्वावपि सागरिकया त्वराक्रान्तया विस्मृतं चित्रफलकं दृष्टवन्तौ। ततः सुसंगतापि फलकापनयनव्याजेन तत्रागत्य राजानं नर्मवचोभिः प्रसाद्य तस्य सागरिकया संगमं कारितवती। ततश्च वासवदत्तागमनभयेन निष्क्रान्ते सुसंगतासागरिके। आगतया च वासवदत्तया चित्रफलकं विलोक्य कृतः कोपानुबन्धः निष्क्रान्ता च साऽकृत्वैव प्रसादम्।

तृतीयाङ्के प्रवेशक आदौ मदनिकाकाञ्चनमालयोः संवादेनेदं ज्ञाप्यते यद्राजानमस्वस्थशरीरं दृष्ट्वा वसन्तकः सुसंगतया सह संकेतं कृतवान्। यथा—सुसंगते न हि सागरिकां वर्जयित्वान्यत्किमपि राज्ञोऽस्वस्थतायाः कारणं तच्चिन्तयात्र प्रतीकारमिति। तया च प्रत्युक्तं यथा—विरचितवासवदत्तावेषां सागरिकां गृहीत्वाहमपि देव्याश्चेट्याः काञ्चनमालाया वेषधारिणी भूत्वा प्रदोषे माधवीलतामण्डपं समागत्य तत्रैव तया सह भर्तुः समागमं संपादयिष्यामीति। एतं संकेतमनु वसन्तकेनानुगम्यमानो वत्सराजः प्रसृते तिमिरसंघाते रजनीमुखवेलायां माधवीलतामण्डपमुपागमत्। तत्रैव चोपस्थिता कथमप्युपलब्धोदन्ता देवी वासवदत्ता। ततो वासवदत्तामेव संकेतिनीं सागरिकां मन्यमानो राजा यावत्प्रणयवचनैस्तामाराधयितुमुपचक्रमे तावत्सा सरोषमवगुण्ठनमपनीयात्मानं दर्शितवती। निष्क्रान्ता चाकृत्वैव भर्तुः प्रसादम्। गतायां च तस्यां वासवदत्तावेषधारिणी सागरिकैकाकिनी तमेवो-

देशं प्राप। किं तु देव्या आत्मसंकेतो ज्ञात इति समुपलभ्य निराशाक्रान्तहृदयः सात्मानमुद्बध्य लतापाशेन व्यापादयितुमुपचक्रमे यावत्तावद्राजा विदूषकोऽपि तां दृष्ट्वा सहसोपसृत्य तस्या आरम्भं निष्फलं व्यदधाताम्। एतस्मिन्नेवान्तरे जातानुतापा देवी वासवदत्ता राजानमनुनेतुं तत्रैव प्रत्यागतवती। उभयोश्चमे लग्नं दृष्ट्वा भृशं संक्रुद्धा तेनैव लतापाशेन विदूषकं भर्तुः साहाय्यकरं बद्धा सागरिकामग्रे कृत्वा निर्जगाम

चतुर्थाङ्के प्रवेशके सुसंगता "सागरिका वासवदत्तयोज्जयिनीं नीयत इति प्रवादं कृत्वोपस्थितेऽर्धरात्रे कुत्रापनीता तन्न ज्ञायते। इयं च रत्नमाला सागरिका-कण्ठस्था तया जीवितनिराशया आर्यवसन्तकस्य हस्ते प्रतिपादयेति भणित्वा मम हस्ते समर्पिता। तदङ्गीकरोत्वेतां भवान्" इति विदूषकेण सह संलापं कृतवती विदूषकोऽपि तां गृहीत्वा राज्ञः समीपमुपससर्प। सागरिकायाश्च यथोपलब्धं वृत्तान्तं वयस्याय कथयित्वा रत्नमालां चादर्शयत्। ततो विरहपर्याकुलो राजा यावत्तिष्ठति तावत्कोसलोच्छित्तये गतवता सेनापतिना रुमण्वता जिताः कोसलाः इति प्रवृत्तिं तद्भागिनेयाद्विजयवर्मण उपलभ्य किंचित्समाहितान्तःकरणो बभूव। अत्रान्तरे कोऽप्यैन्द्रजालिको यौगन्धरायणप्रयुक्त आगम्यात्मनो खेलनस्य दर्शनाय राजानं व्यज्ञापयत्। उपक्रान्ते खेलनेऽसमापित एव सिंहलेश्वरामात्यो वसुभूतिः कञ्चुकिना बाभ्रव्येण सह नृपं द्रष्टुमागतः। ततो विश्रम्यतामिति प्राप्ताज्ञ ऐन्द्रजालिकः "एको मम खेल उर्वरितो देवेनावश्यं प्रेक्षितव्यः" इति संप्रार्थ्य निश्चक्राम। प्रवृत्तायां च बाभ्रव्य-वसुभूतिवत्सराजसंकथायामन्तःपुरेऽग्निरुत्थित इति महान्कोलाहलः संबभूव ततो वासवदत्ता "मया निर्घृणयाऽन्तःपुरे निगडसंयमिता संस्थापिता सागरिका विपत्स्यते। तत्परित्रायतामेनामार्यपुत्रः" इति राजानमुक्तवती। सोऽपि वह्निं प्रविश्य सागरिकां बहिरानयत्। तस्मिन्नेव क्षणे प्रशान्तो वह्निः। ततः किं न्विद-मिन्द्रजालमिति सर्वे शशङ्किरे। बहिरानीता च सागरिका वसुभूतिना बाभ्रव्येण चापि प्रत्यभिज्ञाता। यौगन्धरायणश्चागत्य सर्वमात्मनो निपुणमुपक्रमं स्वप्रयुक्तं चैन्द्र-जालिकवृत्तान्तं समाचख्यौ। ततो या सागरिका सैव स्वभगिनी रत्नावलीति समभि-ज्ञाय वासवदत्ता स्वीयाभरणैस्तामलंकृत्य हस्ते गृहीत्वा देवीशब्दभागिनीं च कृत्वा "गृहाणेमां रत्नावलीमार्यपुत्रः" इति भर्त्रे समर्पयामास। एवं च सर्वेषां प्रिय-संजननमुपदर्श्य कविरन्ते भरतवाक्येनेमं वत्सराजचरितैकदेशमुपसंजहार॥

The Metres used in the Play, their Definitions and Schemes.

———:o:———

1. Sanskrit verse is regulated by quantity, and not, as in English, by accent. A पद्य (stanza) consists usually of four पाद्s (quarters). A पाद् is regulated either by the number of syllables (अक्षरs), or of syllabic instants (मात्राs). When the पाद्s are all similar, it is called a सम वृत्त, to which type most of the metres conform; there are अर्ध-सम वृत्तs, wherein the first quarter corresponds with the third, and the second with the fourth, called respectively the *odd* (विषम) and *even* (सम) quarters. A third class comprises विषम वृत्तs, but these are very seldom used.

2. The vowels अ, इ, उ, ऋ and ऌ are short, and the rest long. The quantity of a syllable is determined by its vowel. A syllable with a short vowel is called लघु ('light'), and a syllable with a long vowel is called गुरु ('heavy'). But a लघु syllable is considered as गुरु if it is followed by an *anusvára*, or a *visarga,* or a conjunct consonant, or when it comes at the end of a पाद्.[1]

3. A set of three successive syllables is called a गण (foot). Marking a short syllable as ◡ and a long one as —, the different गणs,[2] which are 8 in number, may be exhibited as follows :—य ◡ – –; र – ◡ –; त – – ◡; भ – ◡ ◡; ज ◡ – ◡; स ◡ ◡ –; म – – –; and न ◡ ◡ ◡. In the definitions which are given below, a short syllable is indicated by the letter ल and a long one by ग.

4. Excepting nine stanzas (I. 13, 14, 15; II. 1, 7; IV. 7, 8, 9, 10) of Prakrit verse, the Ratnâvalî has 78 stanzas, distributed over 13 different metres, which we give below arranged in the alphabetical order of their names. The metre is also named in the com. in this edition, except in the case of अनुष्टुभ्.

---

1 सानुस्वारश्च दीर्घश्च विसर्गी च गुरुर्भवेत् ।
वर्णः संयोगपूर्वश्च तथा पादान्तगोऽपि वा ॥

2 आदिमध्यावसानेषु यरता यान्ति लाघवम् ।
भजसा गौरवं यान्ति मनौ तु गुरुलाघवम् ॥

अनुष्टुभ्—(also called श्लोक). Def. श्लोके षष्ठं गुरु ज्ञेयं सर्वत्र लघु पञ्चमम् । द्विचतुःपादयोर्ह्रस्वं सप्तमं दीर्घमन्ययोः ॥. This is the shortest metre in ordinary use. There are many varieties of this metre, but the one defined is the most common. Each *Pâda* of it consists of 8 syllables of which the 6th is long and the 5th short, and the 7th is *short* in the second and fourth *pâdas* and *long* in the first and third. The rest of the syllables may be either short or long. *Exmples*:—I. 22; II. 6, 10, 18; III. 2. 16; IV. 4, 15, 18.

आर्या—Def. यस्याः प्रथमे पादे द्वादश मात्रास्तथा तृतीयेऽपि । अष्टादश द्वितीये चतुर्थके पञ्चदश साऽऽर्या ॥. This belongs to the class of metres which are regulated by the number of मात्राs or syllabic instants. The four *pádas* contain respectively 12, 18, 12 and 15 मात्राs. *Examples*:—I. 6, 19, 21, 24; II. 9, 12, 19; III. 10, 12.

[इन्द्रवज्रा—See उपजाति below].

उपजाति—Def. [स्यादिन्द्रवज्रा यदि तौ जगौ गः उपेन्द्रवज्रा जतजास्ततो गौ।] अनन्तरोदीरितलक्ष्मभाजौ पादौ यदीयावुपजातयस्ताः ॥ इत्थं किलान्यास्वपि मिश्रितासु वदन्ति जातिष्विदमेव नाम ।. An उपजाति is a mixture of one or more pádas of इन्द्रवज्रा [11 syllables, Scheme—त, त, ज, ग, ग], with one or more of उपेन्द्रवज्रा [11 syllables, Scheme—ज, त, ज, ग, ग], so as to form one stanza; a mixture of other metres also, in this manner, is called an उपजाति. The student should scan and find out in each case whether a páda is in इन्द्रवज्रा or उपेन्द्रवज्रा. Examples:—II. 15 (उ०, इ०, उ० and इ०).

[उपेन्द्रवज्रा—See उपजाति above].

पुष्पिताग्रा—अयुजि नयुगरेफतो यकारो युजि च नजौ जरगाश्च पुष्पिताग्रा। This is an अर्धसम metre; the first and third pâdas consist each of 12 syllables (Scheme—न, न, र, य) and the second and fourth pâdas consist each of 13 syllables (Scheme—न, ज, ज, र, ग). *Examples*:—I. 4.

पृथ्वी—Def. जसौ जसयला वसुग्रहयतिश्च पृथ्वी गुरुः ।. 17 Syllables. Scheme—ज, स, ज, स, य, ल, ग. The pause occurs after the 8th syllable. *Examples*:—II. 16; IV. 17.

प्रहर्षिणी—Def. म्नौ ज्रौ गस्त्रिदशयतिः प्रहर्षिणीयम् ।. 13 Syllables. Scheme—म, न, ज, र, ग. The pause occurs after the 3rd syllable. *Examples*:—II. 8.

मालिनी—Def. ननमयययुतेयं मालिनी भोगिलोकैः ।. 15 Syllables. Scheme—न, न, म, य, य. The pause occurs after the 8th syllable. *Examples*.—II. 14; III. 17; IV. I6.

वसन्ततिलका—Def. उक्ता वसन्ततिलका तभजा जगौ गः । 14 Syllables. Scheme—त, भ, ज, ज, ग, ग. *Examples*:—I. 8, 12, 20; II. 17; III. 6, 14; IV. 2, 3, 19.

शार्दूलविक्रीडित—Def. सूर्याश्वैर्यदि मः सजौ सततगाः शार्दूलविक्रीडितम् ।. 19 Syllables. Scheme—म, स, ज, स, त, त, ग. The pause occurs after the 12th syllable. This metre is very frequently used in this play. *Examplas*:—I. 1, 2, 5, 9, 11, 17, 23, 25: II. 3, 4, 5, 11, 21; III. 1, 3, 11, 13, 18, 19; VI. 1, 6, 12, 20, 21. And the additional stanza after I. 2.

शालिनी—Def. मात्तौ गौ चेच्छालिनी वेदलोकैः ।. 11 syllables. Scheme—म, त, त, ग, ग. The pause occurs after the fourth syllable. *Ex*.—I. 7.

शिखरिणी—Def. रसै रुद्रैश्छिन्ना यमनसभलागः शिखरिणी ।. 17 syllables. Scheme—य, म, न, स, भ, ल, ग. The pause occurs after the 6th syllable. *Ex*.—II. 13, 20; III. 4, 7, 15; IV. 13.

स्रग्धरा—Def. म्रभ्नैर्यानां त्रयेण त्रिमुनियतियुता स्रग्धरा कीर्तितेयम् । 21 syllables. Scheme—म, र, भ, न, य, य, य. The pauses occur after the 7th and the 14th syllables. This is the longest metre in ordinary use. *Ex*.—I. 3, 10, 16, II. 2; III. 5, 8; IV. 5, 11, 14. 22.

हरिणी—Def. नसमरसला गः षड्वेदैर्हयैर्हरिणी मता 17 syllables. Scheme—न, स, म, र, स, ल, ग. The pauses occur after the 6th and the 10th syllables. *Ex*.—III. 9.

महाकविश्रीहर्षदेवविरचिता

रत्नावली ।

प्रथमोऽङ्कः ।

पादाग्रस्थितया मुहुः स्तनभरेणानीतया नम्रतां
शम्भोः सस्पृहलोचनत्रयपथं यान्त्या तदाराधने ।
ह्रीमत्या शिरसीहितः सपुलकस्वेदोद्गमोत्कम्पया
विश्लिष्यन्कुसुमाञ्जलिर्गिरिजया क्षिप्तोऽन्तरे पातु वः ॥ १ ॥

ब्रह्मानन्दनिमग्नाय चित्स्वरूपाय केवलम् ।
भक्तकामप्रदात्रे च कस्मैचिद्योगिने नमः ॥

अथ तत्रभवान् कविप्रवरः श्रीहर्षदेवः काव्यस्य यशआदिसंपादनद्वारा श्रेयः-साधनतां पश्यन् 'नाट्यं भिन्नरुचेर्जनस्य बहुधाप्येकं समाराधनम्' इत्याद्युक्त्या श्रव्यकाव्याद् दृश्यकाव्यस्य औत्कृष्ट्यं निश्चित्य दृश्यकाव्यप्रभेदं शृङ्गाररसस्य सर्वाह्लादकत्वाच्छृङ्गाररसप्रधानां रत्नावलीं नाम नाटिकां निर्ममे । नाटिकादिलक्षणानि उपोद्घाते लिखितानि तत्र द्रष्टव्यानि । तत्राप्रत्यूहसिद्धिकाम आदौ मङ्गलभूतां–' आशीर्नमस्क्रिया-वस्तुनिर्देशो वापि तन्मुखम्'–इति वचनानुरोधेनाशीरूपां नान्दीमवतारयति–**पादाग्रेति।** गिरिजया पार्वत्या शम्भोः शिवस्य शिरसि ईहितः । पातयितुमिष्ट इति यावत् । किं तु क्षिप्तः सन् अन्तरे उभयोः मध्ये विश्लिष्यन् विशीर्णः पतन् कुसुमाञ्जलिः वः सामाजिकान् । अस्मांश्च । पातु इत्यन्वयः । कीदृश्या गिरिजयेत्याह– तदाराधने शम्भोः सेवावसरे इत्यर्थः । पादयोः अग्रे पादाग्रे ताभ्यां स्थितया । तथापि मुहुः स्तनयोः भरः भारः स्तनभरः । भृ भरणे इत्यस्मात्–ऋदोरप् इत्यप् । तेन मुहुः पुनः पुनः नम्रतामवनतिं आनीतया प्रापितया । पुनश्च शम्भोः । स्पृहया इच्छया सहितं सस्पृहं तच्च तल्लोचनत्रयं तस्य पन्थाः ०त्रयपथः । ऋक्पूरब्धूःपथामानक्षे इति अप्रत्ययः समासान्तः । तं यान्त्या गच्छन्त्या । सस्पृहलोचनैस्तेन दृष्टयेति यावत् । पुनश्च कीदृश्या । पुलका रोमाञ्चाः स्वेदोद्गमः घर्माविर्भावः उत्कम्पः वेपथुः तैः सहिता तया सपुलकस्वेदोद्गमोत्कम्पया । अनेन सात्त्विकभावोदयेन मदनाविर्भावः सूचितः । अत एव ह्रीमत्या जातलज्जयेत्यर्थः । अत्र स्तनभरेत्यादिह्रीमत्यान्तानां पदानामञ्जलिविश्लेषे हेतुत्वात्काव्यलिङ्गमलंकारः ।'हेतोर्वाक्यपदार्थत्वे काव्यलिङ्गमुदाहृतम्' इति तल्लक्षणात् । शार्दूलविक्रीडितं वृत्तम् । तल्लक्षणं तु 'सूर्याश्वैर्यदि मः सजौ सततगाः शार्दूलविक्रीडितम् ।' इति । नान्दीश्लोकत्वादेवास्यादौ मगणः प्रयुक्तः । तदुक्तं भामहेन–' क्षेमं सर्वगुरुर्दत्ते

---

१ पुरः. २ यास्या. ३ सदाराधने.

अपि च ।

> औत्सुक्येन कृतत्वरा सहभुवा व्यावर्तमाना ह्रिया
> तैस्तैर्बन्धुवधूजनस्य वचनैर्नीताभिमुख्यं पुनः ।
> दृष्ट्वाग्रे वरमात्तसाध्वसरसा गौरी नवे संगमे
> संरोहत्पुलका हरेण हसता श्लिष्टा शिवायास्तु वः ॥ २ ॥

अपि च ।

> संप्राप्तं मकरध्वजेन मथनं त्वत्तो मदर्थे पुरा
> तद्युक्तं [किं युक्तं] बहुमार्गगां मम पुरो निर्लज्ज वोढुं [वोढुर] तव ।
> तामेवानुनयस्वभावकुटिलां हे कृष्णकण्ठग्रहं
> मुञ्चेत्याह रुषा यमद्रितनया लक्ष्मीश्च पायात्स वः ॥

मगणो भूमिदैवतः । ' इति ॥ १ ॥ बहुविघ्नशङ्कया तन्निरासाय पुनर्मङ्गलमेव तनोति- अपि चेति । **औत्सुक्येनेति** । नवे सङ्गमे विवाहानन्तरं प्रथमसमागमे औत्सुक्येन उत्सुकस्य भाव औत्सुक्यं तेन हेतुना कृता त्वरा संरम्भो यया सा कृतत्वरा । सह भवतीति सहभूः तया सहजया ह्रिया लज्जया व्यावर्तमाना परावर्तमाना । बन्धुवधूनां जनस्य समूहस्य तैस्तैः समग्रैः वचनैः प्रोत्साहनभाषणैः । वीप्सायां द्विर्वचनम् । पुनः आभिमुख्यं नीता पत्युः संमुखं प्रापिता । ततः अग्रे पुरतः वरं परिणेतारं दृष्ट्वा आत्तः साध्वसस्य भयस्य रसो यया सा आत्तसाध्वसरसा । यद्वा आत्तौ साध्वसं च रसः रागश्च साध्वसरसौ यया तादृशी । तथा च संरोहत्पुलका संरोहन्तः पुलका रोमाञ्चा यस्याः सा तथोक्ता । तथाविधां दृष्ट्वा हसता हरेण श्लिष्टा कृतालिङ्गना गौरी वः शिवायास्तु कल्याणं विदधातु इत्यर्थः । अत्र नवोढाया यथावत्क्रियावर्णनात्स्वभावोक्ति- रलंकारः । तदुक्तं-स्वभावोक्तिस्तु डिम्भादेः स्वक्रियारूपवर्णनम् । इति । शार्दूल- विक्रीडितं वृत्तम् । लक्षणमुक्तम् ॥ २ ॥ अतः परं प्रक्षिप्तमपि पद्यं व्याख्यायते—

अद्रितनयासमुद्रतनययोः स्वस्वभर्तारमुद्दिश्य श्लिष्टोक्त्या सरोषवचनान्याह । तत्र शिरःस्थितां गङ्गां दृष्ट्वा सपत्नीद्वेषादद्रितनयोक्तमाह—हे कृष्णकण्ठ नीलकण्ठ पुरा तपश्चरतस्तव विवाहार्थं मनआकर्षणकाले मकरो ध्वजो यस्य स मकरध्वजः कामस्तेन मदर्थे । मां पुरस्कृत्योद्यतत्वात् । त्वत्तः मथनं संप्राप्तं मृत्युर्लब्धः । तत्तस्मात् हे निर्लज्ज हर । यस्या मम कृते कामेनापि प्राणास्त्यक्तास्तस्या ममोपेक्षणादिति भावः । मम पुरः समक्षं बहुभिः मार्गैर्गच्छतीति बहुमार्गगा त्रिपथगा गङ्गा तां वोढुं युक्तं खलु इत्युपहासः । यद्वा युक्तमिति काकुः । न युक्तमेव इत्यर्थः । स्वभावेन प्रकृत्या कुटिलां वक्रां नदीत्वात् । तामेव गङ्गामेव अनुनय चाटूक्तिभिरावर्जय । ग्रहं मदनुनयाग्रहं मद्देहग्रहणं । आलिङ्गनमिति यावत् । वा मुञ्च । इति यं हरमद्रितनया पार्वती रुषा कोपेनाह स हरः वः पायाद्रक्षतु । आशिषि लिङ् । पक्षे—स्वीकृतायां कुब्जायां परिणी- तायां सरस्वत्यां वा हे कृष्ण पुरा दुग्धोदधिमन्थनकाले मकरध्वजेन मकरलाञ्छनेन सागरेण मदर्थे । लक्ष्म्या मध्यमानसागरोत्पन्नत्वात् । त्वत्तः भगवता मन्दरधारणा- दिति भावः । मथनं मन्थनं संप्राप्तम् । तत्तस्माद् हे निर्लज्ज । बहूनां मार्गं गच्छ-

१ व्यावर्त्य०. २ परं; दृष्ट्वा गोचरमा०. ३ संरोहोत्पु०. ४ नः.

अपि च ।

क्रोधेद्धैर्दृष्टिपातैस्त्रिभिरुपशमिता वह्नयोऽमी त्रयोऽपि
त्रासार्ता ऋत्विजोऽधश्चपलगणहृतोष्णीषपट्टाः पतन्ति ।
दक्षः स्तौत्यस्य पत्नी विलपति करुणं विद्रुतं चापि देवैः
शंसन्नित्यात्तहासो मखमथनविधौ पातु देव्यै शिवो वः ॥ ३ ॥

अपि च ।

जितमुडुपतिना नमः सुरेभ्यो द्विजवृषभा निरुपद्रवा भवन्तु ।
भवतु च पृथिवी समृद्धसस्या प्रतपतु चन्द्रवपुर्नरेन्द्रचन्द्रः ॥ ४ ॥

तीति । कुब्जत्वात् । तां कुब्जाम् । अथ वा बहुमार्गैः श्रुतिस्मृत्यादिभिः वैदर्भीगौडीयादिभिर्वा गच्छतीति तां सरस्वतीम् । वोढुं युक्तमिति पूर्ववत् । भावेनाभिप्रायेण कुटिलां वक्रां श्लेषवक्रोक्त्यादियुतां पक्षे भावेन हृद्गतेनाभिप्रायेण अङ्गविक्षेपादिचेष्टया वा कुटिलाम् । तामेवानुनयस्व प्रीणय । कण्ठस्य ग्रहं ग्रहणं मुञ्च । इति लक्ष्मीः यं रुषा आह स कृष्णः वः पायात् । श्लेषालंकारः । शार्दूलविक्रीडितं छन्दः ॥

क्रोधेद्धैरिति । मखमथनविधौ मखस्य दक्षसंभृतयज्ञस्य मथनं विध्वंसः तस्य विधिः विधानं । तस्मिन् विषये तमधिकृत्येत्यर्थः । देव्यै पार्वत्यै । क्रियया यमभिप्रैति इति सम्प्रदानम् । इति वक्ष्यमाणप्रकारेण शंसन् कथयन् । आत्तः गृहीतः हासो येन स आत्तहासः । वस्य स्वाभाविकलीलाकृतसंरम्भदर्शनादिति भावः । अट्टहास इति पाठे अट्ट उच्चो हासो यस्येत्यर्थः । शिवः वः पातु इति योजना । उक्तमेवाह—क्रोधेन रोषेण इद्धैः प्रदीप्तैः । ञि इन्धीत्यस्मात् क्तप्रत्ययो नलोपश्च । त्रिभिः दृष्टिपातैः तिसृणां दृष्टीनां पातैः पतनैः अमी प्रसिद्धाः त्रयोऽपि दक्षिणगार्हपत्याहवनीयाख्याः वह्नयः उपशमिताः निर्वापिताः । त्रासेन भयेन वीरभद्रोग्ररूपदर्शनजेन आर्ताः विह्वलाः । चपलैः चञ्चलैः गणैः प्रमथादिभिः हृताः उष्णीषार्थे शिरोवेष्टनार्थे पट्टाः उष्णीषपट्टा येषां ते तथोक्ताः । ऋत्विजो याजकाः पतन्ति । इतस्ततो धावन्त इति शेषः । दक्षः स्तौति । मम कोपप्रशमनार्थमित्यर्थात् । अस्य पत्नी करुणं दीनं यथा तथा विलपति क्रोशति । देवैरपि विद्रुतं पलायितं च । क्षोणिदेवैः इति पाठे ब्राह्मणैः इत्यर्थः । 'भूदेववाडवाः । विप्रश्च ब्राह्मणः' इत्यमरः । इति शंसन्निति सम्बन्धः । अत्र पुरा किल विततयज्ञेन दक्षेणोपस्थितः शिवोऽपमानितो जटास्फोटनोत्पन्नेन वीरभद्रेण तद्यज्ञं विध्वंसयामासेत्यादि कथानुसन्धेया । विशेषस्तु भागवते चतुर्थस्कन्धे द्रष्टव्यः । अत्रानुप्रासः स्फुट एव । स्रग्धरा वृत्तम् । म्रभ्नैर्यानां त्रयेण त्रिमुनियतियुता स्रग्धरा कीर्तितेयम् । इति तल्लक्षणम् ॥ ३ ॥ पुनरपि मङ्गलमेव विस्तारयति-

जितमिति । उडूनां नक्षत्राणां । तारकाप्युडु वा स्त्रियाम् इत्यमरः । पतिश्चन्द्रस्तेन जितं सर्वोत्कर्षेण स्थितं । तेन तं प्रति प्रणतोऽस्मीत्यर्थो लभ्यते । चन्द्रवंशीयेन

---

१ क्रोधोद्धैः, क्रोधान्धैः, क्रोधोत्थैः. २ मुहुरु०. ३ त्येव. ४ प्रल०. ५ कृपणा-णं. ६ क्षोणिदेवैः, देवि दे०, चाधिदेवैः. ७ हासैः, अट्टहासः, आत्तहर्षो. ८ धूर्जटिः पातु युष्मान्. ९ देवः, देव्याः. १० भवति, जयति. ११ वीर.

(नान्द्यन्ते ।)

राज्ञा श्रीहर्षेण इत्यपि ध्वनितम् । सुरेभ्यः नमः । द्विजवृषभा ब्राह्मणश्रेष्ठाः । स्युरुत्तरपदे व्याघ्रपुंगवर्षभकुञ्जराः । सिंहशार्दूलनागाद्याः पुंसि श्रेष्ठार्थगोचराः ॥ इत्यमरः । उपमितं व्याघ्रादिभिः सामान्याप्रयोगे इति समासः । निर्गत उपद्रवो येषां ते निरुपद्रवाः पीडारहिता भवन्तु । पृथिवी च समृद्धं विपुलं सस्यं व्रीह्यादि । एतत्प्रसत्रान्तरस्याप्युपलक्षणम् । यस्यां सा समृद्धसस्या भवतु । नरेन्द्रः चन्द्र इव । द्विजवृषभवत्समासः । नरेन्द्रचन्द्रः राजश्रेष्ठः चन्द्रवपुः चन्द्रस्य इव वपुर्यस्य तथा सन् प्रतपतु । सर्वान् सुखयन्प्रतापं दर्शयतु इत्यर्थः । समासगा उपमालंकारः । पुष्पिताग्रा वृत्तम् । अयुजि नयुगरेफतो यकारो युजि च नजौ जरगाश्च पुष्पिताग्रा इति लक्षणात् ॥ ४ ॥ एवं श्लोकचतुष्टय (मतान्तरे श्लोकत्रितय) घटितेयं नान्दी । नान्द्यां मनाक् काव्यार्थसूचनं कर्तव्यमित्युक्तत्वात्तदपि प्रदर्श्यते—तत्र प्रथमश्लोकेन प्रथमाङ्कार्थः सूचितः । तदित्थं—गिरिजाशब्देन सागरिका पुष्पाञ्जलिक्षेपेण तत्कृतं कामदेवपूजनं च सूचिते । शम्भोः लोचनत्रयपथं यान्त्या इत्यनेन नायकस्य दृष्टिपथाद्रक्षितायाः सागरिकायाः वासवदत्तया दर्शनं तेन च अहो प्रमादः परिजनस्य इत्यादिः—काञ्चनमालाया हस्ते समर्पय इत्यन्तः संदर्भः सूचितः । औत्सुक्येन कृतत्वरेत्यादिना हृदय प्रसीद प्रसीद इत्यारभ्य सुसंगता—भर्तः अतिकोपना खल्वेषा तद् हस्ते गृहीत्वा प्रसादयैनामित्यन्तः काव्यार्थः सूचितः । दृष्ट्वाग्रे वरमात्तसाध्वसरसेत्यनेन सागरिका—राजानं दृष्ट्वा सहर्षं ससाध्वसं... एनं प्रेक्ष्य अतिसाध्वसेन न शक्नोमि पदात्पदमपि गन्तुं तत्किंवात्र करिष्ये इति काव्यार्थः सूचितः । हरेणेत्यनेन राजा गौरीत्यनेन गौरवर्णा सागरिका । श्लिष्टेत्यनेन—राजा—(सानन्दं ।)—यथाह भवती । (सागरिकां हस्ते गृहीत्वा ।) इत्यादि ग्रन्थः सूचितः । एवं द्वितीयश्लोकेन द्वितीयाङ्कार्थः सूचितः । तृतीयश्लोके—क्रोधेद्धैरित्यनेन वासवदत्ताक्रोधः । दक्षः स्तौतीत्यनेन राज्ञा कृतं वासवदत्तासान्त्वनं, अस्य पत्नी करुणं विलपतीत्यनेन—सागरिका—हा तात एषाहमनाथाऽशरणा विपद्ये इति सागरिकाविलपनं—इत्यादिस्तृतीयाङ्कार्थः । तथा च उपशमिता वह्नय इत्यनेन त्रासार्ता इत्यादिना च चतुर्थाङ्कप्रतिपादितः ऐन्द्रजालिकप्रदर्शिताग्निकृतसंरम्भः तत्प्रशमनं चेत्यर्थजातं सूचितम् । जितमुडुपतिनेति पद्यं नान्द्यन्तर्गतमेवेति मन्यमानानां मते जितमित्यनेन चतुर्थाङ्कनिर्दिष्टो रुमण्वतो विजयः राज्ञा च रत्नावलीलाभः सूचितः । **नान्द्यन्ते** इति—नान्दीपदव्युत्पत्तिर्नाट्यप्रदीपे—नन्दन्ति काव्यानि कवीन्द्रवर्गाः कुशीलवाः पारिषदाश्च सन्तः । यस्मादलं सज्जनसिन्धुहंसी तस्मादियं सा कथितेह नान्दी ॥ इति । नान्दीलक्षणमादिभरते—आशीर्नमस्क्रियारूपः श्लोकः काव्यार्थसूचकः । नान्दीति कथ्यते तस्यां पदादिनियमोऽपि वा । नान्दीपदैर्द्वादशभिरष्टाभिर्वाप्यलंकृता ॥ इति । पदस्वरूपं नाट्यप्रदीपे—श्लोकपादः पदं केचित्सुप्तिङन्तमथापरे । परेऽवान्तरवाक्यैकस्वरूपं पदमूचिरे ॥ इति । तत्र श्लोकपादः पदमिति मते द्वादशपदा षोडशपदा वेयं नान्दी । इयं च पत्रावलीसंज्ञा । तदुक्तं नाट्यदर्पणे—

सूत्रधारः—अलमतिविस्तरेण । अद्याहं वसन्तोत्सवे सबहुमानमाहूय नानादिग्देशागतेन राज्ञः श्रीहर्षदेवस्य पादपद्मोपजीविना राजसमूहेनोक्तो यथा—अस्मत्स्वामिना श्रीहर्षदेवेनापूर्ववस्तुरचनालंकृता रत्नावली नाम नाटिका कृता । सा चास्माभिः श्रोत्रपरंपरया श्रुता न तु प्रयोगतो दृष्टा । तत्तस्यैव राज्ञः सकलजनहृदयाह्लादिनो बहुमानादस्मासु चानुग्रहबुद्ध्या यथावत्प्रयोगेण त्वया नाटयितव्या इति । तद्यावदिदानीं नेपथ्यरचनां कृत्वा यथाभिलषितं संपादयामि । (परिक्रम्य अवलोक्य च ।) अये आवर्जितानि सकलसामाजिकानां मनांसीति मे निश्चयः । कुतः ।

श्रीहर्षो निपुणः कविः परिषदप्येषा गुणग्राहिणी
लोके हारि च वत्सराजचरितं नाट्ये च दक्षा वयम् ।
वस्त्वेकैकमपीह वाञ्छितफलप्राप्तेः पदं किं पुन-
र्मद्भाग्योपचयादयं समुदितः सर्वो गुणानां गणः ॥ ५ ॥

यस्यां बीजस्य विन्यासो ह्यभिधेयस्य वस्तुनः । श्लेषेण वा समासोक्त्या नान्दी पत्रावलीति सा ॥ इति । उडुपतिनेति चन्द्रनिर्देशाच्चन्द्रनामाङ्किता च । **सूत्रधार** इति । सूत्रं प्रयोगानुष्ठानं धारयतीति सूत्रधारः । तदुक्तं—वर्तनीयतया सूत्रं प्रथमं येन सूच्यते । रङ्गभूमिं समाक्रम्य सूत्रधारः स उच्यते ॥ इति । **अलमिति** । अतिविस्तरोऽधिकमङ्गलश्लोकपठनं तेन किंचिद्विधेयं नास्ति । स मास्तु इत्यर्थः । अलं भूषणपर्याप्तिशक्तिवारणवाचकम् । इत्यमरः । वसन्तोत्सवः प्रायः फाल्गुनपौर्णमासीमारभ्य पञ्चमीपर्यन्तं वर्तते । नाना दिशः येषां ते नानादिशः । ते च ते देशाश्च तेभ्य आगतेन । पादौ पद्मे इव पादपद्मे ते उपजीवतीति तच्छीलेन । सुप्यजातौ इत्यादिना णिनिः । अविद्यमानं पूर्वं यस्याः सा अपूर्वा । अपूर्वा या वस्तु इतिवृत्तं तस्य रचना तया । श्रोत्राणां परम्परा तया । यथा अर्हतीति यथावत् । यथावत्प्रयोगः यथावत्प्रयोगः तेन । नाटयितव्या अभिनेतव्या । नेपथ्यरचनां नेपथ्यं प्रसाधनं रङ्गभूमिः वा । तस्य रचनां व्यवस्थापनम् । नेपथ्यं स्याज्जवनिका रङ्गभूमिः प्रसाधनम् । इत्यजयः । इति संभ्रमे अव्ययम् । अये क्रोधविषादयोः । संभ्रमे । इति हैमः । आवर्जितानि अभिमुखीकृतानि । समजन्त्यस्मिञ्जना इति समाजः । घञ् अधिकरणे । समाजं समवयन्ति सामाजिकाः । समवायान्समवैति इति ठक् । **श्रीहर्ष इति** । निपुणः प्रवीणः । परितः सीदन्त्यस्यां जना इति परिषत् । लक्षणया तत्स्था जनाः । गुणान्गृह्णाति तच्छीला । ताच्छील्ये णिनिः । अवश्यं हरतीति हारि मनोहरम् । वत्सराज उदयनः । नाट्ये अभिनयेनावस्थानुकृतौ । दक्षा निष्णाताः । इह नाटिका

---

१ अतिप्रसङ्गेन. २ देशादागतेन, देशान्तराग०. ३ यासावस्म० कृतेत्यस्मा० श्रुता-श्रुतं न च. ४ राज्ञः श्रीहर्षदेवस्य सर्वजन०. ५ वा, ०बुद्ध्या वा. ६ वस्तुप्र०. ७ तदिदानीं ने०; तद्यावन्ने०. ८ ०यामि । आत्म० च मया सामाजिकम०; ०राज-जन-म०. ९ परिषदमव०, परितो विलोक्य. १० दसौ.

तद्यावद् गृहं गत्वा गृहिणीमाहूय संगीतकमनुतिष्ठामि । (परिक्रम्य नेपथ्याभिमुखमवलोक्य च ।) इदमस्मदीयं गृहम् । यावत्प्रविशामि । (प्रविश्य ।) आर्ये इतस्तावत् ।

(प्रविश्य ।)

नटी—आर्यपुत्र इयमस्मि । आज्ञापयत्वार्यः को नियोगोऽनुष्ठीयतामिति । (क)

सूत्रधारः—आर्ये रत्नावलीदर्शनोत्सुकोऽयं राजलोकः । तद् गृह्यतां नेपथ्यम् ।

नटी—(निःश्वस्य । सोद्वेगम् ।) आर्यपुत्र निश्चिन्त इदानीमसि त्वं तत्कस्मान्न नृत्यसि । मम पुनर्मन्दभाग्याया एकैव दुहिता । सापि त्वया कस्मिन्नपि देशान्तरे दत्ता । कथमेवं दूरदेशस्थितेन भर्त्रा सहास्याः पाणिग्रहणं भविष्यतीत्यनया चिन्तयात्मापि मे न प्रतिभाति । किं पुनर्नर्तितव्यम् । (ख)

(क) अज्जउत्त इअम्हि । आणवेदु अज्जो को णिओओ अणुचिट्ठीअदित्ति ।

(ख) अज्जउत्त णिच्चिन्तो दाणिं सि तुमं ता कीस ण णच्चसि । मह उण मन्दभाँआए एक्का ज्जेव दुहिदा । सावि तुए कहिंपि देसंन्तरे दिण्णा । कहं एव्वं दूरदेसट्ठिदेण भत्तुणों सह से पाणिग्गहणं भविस्सदित्ति इमाए चिन्ताए अप्पावि मे ण पडिहादि । किं पुण णच्चिदव्वम् ।

प्रयोगे । एकैकमपि वस्तु वाञ्छितं अभीष्टं यत्फलं सामाजिकहृदयावर्जनरूपं तस्य प्राप्तेर्लाभस्य पदं स्थानम् । किं पुनः मम भाग्यं मद्भाग्यं तस्य उपचयः समृद्धिः तस्मात् । समुदितः सम्भूय मिलितः अयं गुणानामनुकूलवस्तूनां गणः वाञ्छितफलप्राप्तेः पदं भवेदिति वक्तव्यम् । शार्दूलविक्रीडितं वृत्तम् ॥ ५ ॥ एवं कविप्रभृतीनां प्रशंसनेन सभ्यानां प्रस्तुताभिनयोन्मुखीकरणाद् भारतीवृत्तेः अङ्गभूता प्ररोचना इयम् । तदुक्तं दशरूपके—उन्मुखीकरणं तत्र प्रशंसातः प्ररोचना । इति । संगीतमेव संगीतकम् । स्वार्थे कः । नृत्तं गीतं तथा वाद्यं त्रयं संगीतमुच्यते । इति संगीतरत्नाकरे । अस्माकमिदमस्मदीयं । वृद्धाच्छः । आर्यपुत्रेति—सर्वस्त्रीभिः पतिर्वाच्य आर्यपुत्रेति यौवने । इति भरतः । नाटकादिषु स्त्र्यादीनां शौरसेनी भाषैवोचिता । तदुक्तं मातृगुप्ताचार्यैः- आर्यावर्तप्रसूतासु सर्वास्वेव हि जातिषु । शौरसेनीं समाश्रित्य भाषां काव्ये प्रयोजयेत् ॥ इति । रत्नावली लक्षणया रत्नावलीनाटिकाप्रयोगस्तस्या दर्शने उत्सुकः । नेपथ्यं वेषः । रामादिव्यञ्जको वेषो नटे नेपथ्यमिष्यते । इति भरतः । सोद्वेगं उद्वेगेन सहितं

---

१ विलोक्य. २ उच्चैः, म० उच्चैः. ३ नसमु०. ४ तत्क्रियतां संगीतकम्. ५ सावेगम्. ६ अज्ज... ०अदि. ७ ०भाइणीए; नास्त्येतत्कचित्. ८ तुए णिक्करुणेन. ९ दूरदेस०. १० जामातुणा.

सूत्रधारः—आर्ये दूरस्थितेनेत्यलमुद्वेगेन । पश्य ।

द्वीपादन्यस्मादपि मध्यादपि जलनिधेर्दिशोऽप्यन्तात् ।
आनीय झटिति घटयति विधिरभिमतमभिमुखीभूतः ॥ ६ ॥

(नेपथ्ये ।)

साधु भरतपुत्र साधु । एवमेतत् । कः संदेहः । (द्वीपादन्यस्मादिति पठति ।)

सूत्रधारः—(आकर्ण्य । नेपथ्याभिमुखमवलोक्य । सहर्षम् ।) आर्ये एषं मम कनीयान्भ्राता गृहीतयौगन्धरायणभूमिकः प्राप्त एव । तदेहि । आवामपि नेपथ्यग्रहणाय सज्जीभवावः ।

(इति निष्क्रान्तौ ।)

प्रस्तावना ।

यथा तथा । ब्रवीतीति शेषः । एवमग्रेऽपि । दत्ता वाग्दत्तेत्यर्थः । उद्वेगेन विमनस्कतया । **द्वीपादिति** । विधिः दैवम् । अभिगतं मुखमस्य असौ अभिमुखः न अभिमुखः अनभिमुखः । अनभिमुखः अभिमुखः सम्पन्नः अभिमुखीभूतः अनुकूलः । च्विप्रत्ययः । सन् । कुगतिरिति समासः । अन्यस्मादपि द्वीपात् । द्विर्गता आपः अत्र इति द्वीपः । ऋक्पूर—इति अः समासान्तः । द्व्यन्तरुपसर्गेभ्योप ईत् इति ईदादेशः । जलानि निधीयन्ते अस्मिन्निति जलनिधिः सागरः । कर्मण्यधिकरणे च इति किप्रत्ययः । तस्य मध्यादपि । दिशः अन्तादपि । अभिमतं इष्टं वस्तु झटिति द्रुतमानीय घटयति मेलयति संपादयति वा । अतो दूरे वर इति चिन्ता न कार्या । आर्या वृत्तम् । यस्याः पादे प्रथमे द्वादश मात्रास्तथा तृतीयेपि । अष्टादश द्वितीये चतुर्थके पञ्चदश सार्या ॥ इति तल्लक्षणम् ॥ ६ ॥ प्रवेशं विनैव यज्जवनिकान्तरे उच्यते तत् नेपथ्ये इत्युच्यते । यौग०—एवमेतत् इत आरभ्य मुखसन्धिः । अस्यान्येषां चाङ्गानां लक्षणानि इह विस्तरभिया नोच्यन्ते । द्वीपादिति पठति । अत्र यौगन्धरायणो वत्सराजस्य रत्नावलीप्राप्तिहेतुभूतमनुकूलदैवं स्वव्यापारं बीजत्वेनोपक्षिप्तवानिति उपक्षेपो नाम मुखसन्धेरङ्गमिदम् । गृहीता यौगन्धरायणस्य वत्सराजप्रधानामात्यस्य भूमिका वेषान्तरं येन । नेपथ्यग्रहणाय वेषान्तरग्रहणाय । **इति निष्क्रान्तौ** इति । तदुक्तं—एषामन्यतरेणार्थं पात्रं वाक्षिप्य सूत्रभृत् । प्रस्तावनान्ते निर्गच्छेत्ततो वस्तु प्रपञ्चयेत् ॥ इति । **प्रस्तावना**—अस्या लक्षणं दशरूपके—सूत्रधारो नटीं ब्रूते मार्षं वाथ विदूषकम् । स्वकार्यं प्रस्तुताक्षेपि चित्रोक्त्या यत्तदामुखम् ॥ प्रस्तावना वा तत्र स्युः कथोद्धातः प्रवृत्तकम् । प्रयोगातिशयश्चाथ वीथ्यङ्गानि त्रयोदश ॥ इति । अत्र द्वीपादित्यादिवाक्यं गृहीत्वा प्रवेशात्कथोद्धातरूपा प्रस्तावनेयम् । तदुक्तं-स्वेतिवृत्तसमं वाक्यमर्थं वा यत्र सत्रिणः ।

---

१ ०स्थेन. २ यतः. ३ नास्त्येतस्तुस्त्कान्तरे. ४ आर्ये किमतः परं विलम्बसे-स्थने-विलम्बनेन । नन्वयं मम. ५ तदहमपि परसेश्वरभूमिकां संपादयामि; तद्वयमप्यनन्तरकरणीयवेशग्रहणेनापरभूमिकया सज्जीभवामः ।. ६ अस्मात्परं—नटी—जं—एवं—जं—अज्जो आणवेदि, इ०.

(ततः प्रविशति यौगन्धरायणः ।)

यौगन्धरायणः—एवमेतत् । कः संदेहः । (द्वीपादन्यस्मादिति पुनः पठित्वा ।) अन्यथा क्व सिद्धादेशप्रत्ययप्रार्थितायाः सिंहलेश्वरदुहितुः समुद्रे यानभङ्गमग्नोत्थितायाः फलकासादनं क्व च कौशाम्बीयेन वणिजा सिंहलेभ्यः प्रत्यागच्छता तदवस्थायाः संभावनं रत्नमालाचिह्नायाः प्रत्यभिज्ञानादिहानयनं च । (सहर्षम् ।) सर्वथा स्पृशन्ति नः स्वामिनमभ्युदयाः । (विचिन्त्य ।) मयापि चैनां देवीहस्ते सगौरवं निक्षिपता युक्तमेवानुष्ठितम् । श्रुतं च मया—बाभ्रव्योऽपि कञ्चुकी सिंहलेश्वरामात्येन वसुभूतिना सह कथं कथमपि समुद्रादुत्तीर्य कोशलोच्छित्तये गतवता रुमण्वता मिलित इति । तदेवं निष्पन्नप्रायमपि प्रभुप्रयोजनं न मे धृतिमावहतीति कष्टोऽयं खलु भृत्यभावः । कुतः—

गृहीत्वा प्रविशेत्पात्रं कथोद्घातो द्विधैव सः ॥ इति । **यौग० एवमेतदित्यादि** । अत्र वत्सराजस्य रत्नावलीप्राप्तिहेतुरनुकूलदैवो यौगन्धरायणव्यापारः कः सन्देह इत्यादिना प्रारम्भेस्मिन्स्वामिनो वृद्धिहेतौ इत्यन्तेन विष्कम्भके न्यस्तो बीजम् । तदुक्तं—स्वल्पोद्दिष्टस्तु तद्धेतुर्बीजं विस्तार्यनेकधा । इति । सिद्धस्य प्राप्तयोगसिद्धेः आदेशः कथनं तेन जनितो यः प्रत्ययः विश्वासः तेन प्रार्थिताया याचितायाः । सिंहलो नाम लङ्कानिकटवर्ती द्वीपविशेषः तस्येश्वरः स्वामी । स्थेशभासपिसकसो वरच् इति ईशः वरच् । समीचीनाः उद्रा जलचरविशेषा यस्मिन्स समुद्रः । मुद्रया मर्यादया सहित इति वा । यानभङ्गेनेति । यानमत्र पोतः । तस्य भङ्गेन आदौ निमग्ना । समुद्रजले इत्यर्थात् । पश्चादुत्थिता तस्याः । पाठान्तरे प्रवहणस्य पोतस्य भङ्गः । प्रकृष्टमुह्यते अनेनेति प्रवहणम् । करणे ल्युट् कृत्यच इति णत्वम् । तेन निमग्नायाः जले मग्नायाः । क्व च—द्वौ क्वशब्दौ उभयोरत्यन्तासम्भवित्वं द्योतयतः । कुशाम्बेन निर्वृत्ता कौशाम्बी नगरी । तेन निर्वृत्तमिति अण् । अणन्तात् ङीप् । तत्र भवः कौशाम्बीयः । वृद्धाच्छः । सा अवस्था यस्याः सा तदवस्था तस्याः । रत्नमाला चिह्नं ज्ञापकं यस्याः तस्याः प्रत्यभिज्ञानं सा एव राजपुत्री इयमिति ज्ञानं तस्मात् । देवी वासवदत्ता । देवीति महिषी वाच्या राज्ञः परिजनेन तु । सगौरवं—सादरम् । **युक्तमेवेति**—योग्यत्वमत्र प्रकृतकार्यानुकूलत्वम् । **कञ्चुकी**—कञ्चुकः अस्त्यस्य इति । कञ्चुकिलक्षणं भरते—ये विद्यासत्यसम्पन्नाः कामदोषविवर्जिताः । ज्ञानविज्ञानकुशलाः कञ्चुकीयास्तु ते स्मृताः ॥ इति । अन्यत्र च—अन्तःपुरचरो राज्ञां वृद्धो विप्रो गुणान्वितः । उक्तिप्रत्युक्तिकुशलः कञ्चु-

---

१ यथानिर्दिष्टः—हृष्टः यौग०. २ पुनः श्लोकं पठति. ३ देशजनित. ४ सुतायाः. ५ अन्तःसमुद्रे. ६ निमग्नायाः; प्रवहणभङ्गनिमग्नायाः. ७ फलहका. ८ समासादनं. ९ सरत्नमालायाश्च परिज्ञाना०; स्वरत्नमालाचिह्नां च परिज्ञायेहानयनम्. १० न्यस्मत्स्वा०. ११ समर्पयता. १२ कथितं च मम...गतस्य रुमण्वतः; कोसलेश्वरस्यो०; रुमण्वता सह घटेते इति. १३ मनसो मे प्रीतिं नावहति. १४ अमात्य०. १५ यतः.

प्रारम्भेऽस्मिन्स्वामिनो वृद्धिहेतौ
दैवेनेत्थं दत्तहस्तावलम्बे ।
सिद्धेर्भ्रान्तिर्नास्ति सत्यं तथापि
स्वेच्छाचारी भीत एवास्मि भर्तुः ॥ ७ ॥

(नेपथ्ये कलकलः ।)

यौग०—(आकर्ण्य ।) अये यथायमभिहन्यमानमृदुमृदङ्गानुगतगीतमधुरः पुरः पौराणां समुच्चरति चर्चरीध्वनिस्तथा तर्कयामि मदनमहमहीयांसं पुरजनप्रमोदमवलोकयितुं प्रासादाभिमुखं प्रस्थितो देव इति । (ऊर्ध्वमवलोक्य ।) अये कथमधिरूढ एव देवः प्रासादम् । य एषः—

विश्रान्तविग्रहकथो रतिमाञ्जनस्य
चित्ते वसन्प्रियवसन्तक एव साक्षात् ।
पर्युत्सुको निजमहोत्सवदर्शनाय
वत्सेश्वरः कुसुमचाप इवाभ्युपैति ॥ ८ ॥

कीत्यभिधीयते ॥ इति । अमात्येन—अमा सह भवः अमात्यः । अव्ययात्त्यप् । तेन । अमाऽन्तिकसहार्थयोः इति मेदिनी । कथं कथमपि महता प्रयासेनेत्यर्थः । रुमण्वता तन्नामकसेनापतिना । निष्पन्नः सिद्धः प्रायः बाहुल्यं यस्य । धृतिं धैर्यं परितोषं वा । **प्रारम्भ इति** । स्वामिनः वत्सराजस्य वृद्धिः अभ्युदयः चक्रवर्तित्वलाभरूपः तस्य हेतौ कारणे अस्मिन्नारम्भे कर्मणि दैवेन इत्थं दत्तहस्तावलम्बे दत्तः हस्तेन हस्तस्य वा अवलम्ब आश्रयो यस्य तस्मिन् सति सिद्धेः साफल्यस्य । इष्टकार्यनिष्पत्तेः इत्यर्थः । भ्रान्तिः संशयो नास्ति । सत्यमिदम् । तथापि स्वस्येच्छा स्वेच्छा तया चरतीति तच्छीलः । सुप्यजातौ इति णिनिः ताच्छील्ये । यद्वा स्वेच्छया आचारः अस्यास्तीति स्वेच्छाचारी । राज्ञोऽनुमतिमन्तरेणास्मिन्कर्मणि प्रवृत्त इति यावत् । अहं भर्तुः वत्सराजात् भीत एवास्मि । शालिनी वृत्तम् । लक्षणं—मात्तौ गौ चेच्छालिनी वेदलोकैः । इति ॥ ७ ॥ **अये** इति संभ्रमद्योतकमव्ययम् । अये क्रोधविषादे च संभ्रमे स्मरणेपि च । इति मेदिनी । [पाठान्तरे । मधुरं यथा तथा] अभिहन्यमानाः ताड्यमाना ये मृदवः मृदुस्वनाः मृदङ्गास्तैरनुगतं यद्गीतं गानं तेन मधुरः मनोहरः । पुरे भवाः पौराः । तत्र भवः इत्यण् । तेषां चर्चरीध्वनिः करताडनशब्दः । चर्चरी वाद्यविशेष इति केचित् । अनेकशब्दानां मिश्रीभवनमित्यपरे । मदनस्य मह उत्सवः तेन महीयांसं महत्तरम् । महच्छब्दादीयसुन् टेरिति टिलोपश्च । प्रासादस्याभिमुखम् । **देवः** इति तदुक्तं—देवेति नृपतिर्वाच्यो भृत्यैः प्रकृतिभिस्तथा । इति । **विश्रान्तेत्यादि** । य एष साक्षात् कुसुमचापः कामदेव इवाभ्युपैति । उभयोः साम्यं प्रदर्शयन्नाह—विश्रान्त-

---

१ आर०. २ सिद्धे. ३ कर्णं दत्वा सहर्षम्. ४ मधुरम० सङ्गी० तर्कयामि यद्देवं... ५ सकलपुर०. ६ एष. ७ जन. ८ राज; ०चापधरोऽभ्यु०.

तद्यावर्द् गृहं गत्वा कार्यशेषं चिन्तयामि । (इति निष्कान्तः ।)

विष्कम्भकः ।

(ततः प्रविशत्यासनस्थो गृहीतवसन्तोत्सववेषो राजा विदूषकश्च ।)

राजा—(सहर्षमवलोक्य ।) सखे वसन्तक ।

विदूषकः—आज्ञापयतु भवान् । (क)

राजा—

राज्यं निर्जितशत्रु योग्यसचिवे न्यस्तः समस्तो भरः
सम्यक्पालनलालिताः प्रशमिताशेषोपसर्गाः प्रजाः ।
प्रद्योतस्य सुता वसन्तसमयस्त्वं चेति नाम्ना धृतिं
कामः काममुपैत्वयं मम पुनर्मन्ये महानुत्सवः ॥ ९ ॥

(क) आणवेदु भवं ।

विग्रहकथः विश्रान्ता उपरता शत्रोरभावात् विग्रहस्य युद्धस्य पक्षे अनङ्गत्वात् हरकोपाग्निना दग्धदेहत्वाद्वा शरीरस्य कथा यस्य स तथोक्तः । रतिमान् प्रजाप्रेमवान् अनुरागवान् वा । पक्षे रतिः स्वप्रिया तद्वान् । जनस्य चित्ते वसन् तद्वात्सल्यात्पक्षे मनसिजत्वादिति भावः । प्रियः वसन्तकः तन्नामा विदूषकः । पक्षे वसन्त एव वसन्तकः । स्वार्थे कन् । तत्संज्ञः ऋतुर्यस्य । पर्युत्सुकः सोत्कण्ठः सन् । निजः स्वयं प्रवर्तितत्वात् पक्षे आत्मानं उद्दिश्य कृतत्वात् यः महांश्चासौ उत्सवश्च महोत्सवः तस्य दर्शनाय एवाभ्युपैतीति सम्बन्धः । श्लेषालङ्कार उत्प्रेक्षालंकारश्च तयोरङ्गाङ्गिभावेन संकरः । छेकानुप्रासोऽनुप्रासश्च । वसन्ततिलकं वृत्तम् । तल्लक्षणं–ज्ञेयं वसन्ततिलकं तभजा जगौ गः । इति ॥ ८ ॥ तद्यावदित्यवधारणे । कार्यशेषं रत्नावलीप्राप्तिरूपं यत्कार्यं तत्र यदवशिष्टं तत् । **विष्कम्भकः**––एतल्लक्षणं दशरूपके–वृत्तवर्तिष्यमाणानां कथांशानां निदर्शकः । संक्षेपार्थस्तु विष्कम्भो मध्यपात्रप्रयोजितः ॥ एकानेककृतः शुद्धः संकीर्णो नीचमध्यमैः । इति । अयं च एकेन मध्यमपात्रेण कृतत्वाच्छुद्धः । **तत इति**––गृहीतः परिहितः वसन्तोत्सवस्य वेषो येन स तथा । **विदूषकः**––अस्य लक्षणं–कुसुमवसन्ताद्यभिधः कर्मवपुर्वेषभाषाद्यैः । हास्यकरः कलहरतिर्विदूषकः स्यात्स्वकर्मज्ञः ॥ इति दर्पणे । अन्यत्र च––नर्मभेदप्रयोगज्ञो हास्यकृन्नायकस्य च । नर्मवादी स वै नर्मसचिवश्च विदूषकः ॥ इति । अस्य प्राकृतं पाठ्यम् । तदुक्तं–विदूषकविटादीनां पाठ्यं तु प्राकृतं भवेत् । इति । **वसन्तक**––वयस्येत्यथ वा नाम्ना वाच्यो राज्ञा विदूषकः । इत्युक्तत्वान्नाम्ना निर्देशः । **राज्यमिति** । निःशेषेण जिताः । स्ववशमानीता इत्यर्थः । निर्जिताः शत्रवः यस्मिन् तथाभूतं मे राज्यम् । योग्यः राज्यकार्यक्षमः स चासौ सचिवः मन्त्री तस्मिन् समस्तः भरः राज्यतन्त्रचिन्ता न्यस्तः आहितः । प्रजाः प्रशमिताः विनाशिताः अशेषाः सकलाः उपसर्गाः यासां तादृश्यः । सम्यक् सुविहितं यत्पालनं रक्षणं तेन लालिताः संवर्धिताः वर्तन्ते । प्रद्योतस्य तदभिधस्य

---

१ दहमपि गृ०. २ अनुचि०, संपादयामि. ३ समन्तादु०; सानन्दम्; सादरम्. ४ अस्मात्परं–प्रियवयस्य पज्य. ५ ०वन्यस्तः. ६ लालनपा०.

विदूषकः—(सहर्षम् ।) भो वयस्य एवं न्विदम् । अहं पुनर्जानामि न भवतो न कामदेवस्य ममैवैकस्य ब्राह्मणस्यायं मदनमहोत्सवः यस्य प्रियवयस्येनैवं मन्त्यते । (विलोक्य ।) तत्किमनेन । प्रेक्षस्व तावदस्य मधुमत्तकामिनीजनस्वयंग्राहगृहीतशृङ्गकजलप्रहारनृत्यन्नागरजनजनितकौतूहलस्य समन्ततः शब्दायमानमर्दलोद्दामचर्चरीशब्दमुखररथ्यामुखशोभिनो प्रकीर्णपटवासपुञ्जपिञ्जरितदशादिशामुखस्य सश्रीकतां मदनमहोत्सवस्य। (क)

(क) भो वअस्स एव्वं ण्णेदम् । अहं पुण जाणामि ण भवदो ण कामदेअस्स मम ज्जेव एक्कस्स बम्हणस्स अअं मअणमहूसवो जेस्स पिअवअस्सेण एवं मन्तीअदि । ता किं इमिणा । पेक्ख दाव इमस्स महुमत्तकामिणीजणसअंगाहगहिदसिङ्गकजलप्पहारणच्चन्तणाअरजणजणिदकोदूहलस्स समन्तदो घुम्मन्तमद्दलुद्दामचच्चरीसद्दमुहररच्छामुहसोहिणो पइण्णपडवासपुञ्जपिञ्जरिज्जन्तदसदिसामुहस्स सस्सिरीअदं मअणमहूसवस्स ।

उज्जयिनीनृपस्य सुता वासवदत्ता रमणीयगुणा रतिसदृशी मम पत्नी । भोगानुकूलो वसन्तस्य समयः कालः । मम प्रियकरणदक्षः त्वं च । यद्वा वसन्तस्य इव समयः आचारः मम नर्मसहायत्वाद्यस्य तादृशः त्वम् । इति पूर्वोक्तेभ्यः षड्भ्यो हेतुभ्यः । कामः नाम्ना मदनमहोत्सव इति नाममात्रात् कामं पर्याप्तं यथा तथा धृतिं सन्तोषमुपैतु प्राप्नोतु । पुनः इति भेदे । अहं तु अयं महानुत्सवः । ममेति मन्ये । अत्र ममैवायमुत्सव इत्यस्य राज्यं निर्जितशत्रु इत्यादिभिर्हेतुभिः समर्थनात्काव्यलिङ्गमलंकारः । शार्दूलविक्रीडितं वृत्तम् ॥ अत्र धृतिर्नाम व्यभिचारी भावः । स च शङ्कितः (द. रू. ४.१२) । अत्र चिन्ताराहित्यादिध्वननात् धीरललितो नायक उक्तः । तदुक्तं—निश्चिन्तो धीरललितः कलासक्तः सुखी मृदुः । इति । विशेषस्तु दशरूपके द्रष्टव्यः ॥ ९ ॥ब्राह्मणबटुकस्येति पाठे ब्राह्मणश्चासौ बटुश्च ब्राह्मणबटुः क्षुद्रब्राह्मणः । कडारादित्वाद्ब्राह्मणशब्दस्य पूर्वनिपातः । अनुकम्पितः ब्राह्मणबटुः ब्राह्मणबटुकः । अनुकम्पायामिति कन् । अस्य मदनमहोत्सवस्य सश्रीकतां शोभां प्रेक्षस्वेति अन्वयः । कथंभूतस्येत्याह—मधुना मद्येन मत्तः मधुमत्तः । काम आसां विद्यते इति कामिन्यः अत इनिठनौ इति इनिः । ऋन्नेभ्यो ङीप् इति ङीप् । तासां जनः कामिनीजनः । मधुमत्तश्चासौ कामिनीजनश्च तस्य यः स्वयंग्रहः स्वेच्छाग्रहणं तेन गृहीतः । शृङ्गाण्येव शृङ्गकाणि तेषां ये जलप्रहारास्तैः हेतुभिः नृत्यन् यः नागरजनः तेन जनितं प्रेक्षकाणां कौतूहलं यस्मिन् । पुनः किंभूतस्य । शब्दायमाना ये मर्दला मृदङ्गास्तैः उद्दामा उद्दामो वा यः चर्चर्या गीतविशेषस्य शब्दस्तेन च मुखराणि सशब्दानि यानि रथ्यामुखानि तैः साधु शोभते तस्य । पुनश्च किंभूतस्य । प्रकीर्णाः विक्षिप्ता ये पटं

---

१ बम्हणबडुअस्स (बटुकस्य). २ जस्स किदे (कृते); जेण पिअव...मन्तीअदि (मन्यते). ३ ०वअस्सो एवं मन्तेदि. ४ सुच्छन्द (स्वच्छन्द), सुवत्त (सुवृत्त). ५ रज्जपइण्ण. ६ पिञरिद, ०ज्जन्तदिसामुहस्स, ०दसदिसस्स. ७ सिरिअं (श्रियं).

राजा—(समन्तादवलोक्य ।) अहो परां कोटिमधिरोहति प्रमोदः[2] पौराणाम् । तथा हि ।

कीर्णैः पिष्टातकौघैः कृतदिवसमुखैः कुङ्कुमक्षोदगौरै-
र्हैमालंकारभाभिर्भरनमितशिखैः[4] शेखरैः कैङ्किरातैः ।
एषा वेषाभिलक्ष्यस्वविभवविजिताशेषवित्तेशकोशा
कौशाम्बी शातकुम्भद्रवखचितजनेवैकपीता विभाति॥१०॥

अपि च ।

धारायन्त्रविमुक्तसंततपयःपूरप्लुते सर्वतः
सद्यः सान्द्रविमर्दकर्दमकृतक्रीडे क्षणं प्राङ्गणे ।
उद्दामप्रमदाकपोलनिपतत्सिन्दूररागारुणैः
सैन्दूरीक्रियते जनेन चरणन्यासैः पुरः कुट्टिमम् ॥ ११ ॥

वासयतीति पटवासः पिष्टातकस्तस्य पुञ्जास्तैः पिञ्जरितानि पीतीकृतानि दशदिशानां मुखानि यस्मिन् तथाविधस्य । **कीर्णैरिति** । एषा कौशाम्बी नगरी शातकुम्भे पर्वतविशेषे भवं शातकुम्भं सुवर्णं तस्य द्रवो रसः तेन खचिता व्याप्ता जना यस्यां सा शातकुम्भद्रवखचितजना इव । एकः मुख्यः पीतः पीतवर्णो यस्यां सा । एका केवला पीता चेति वा । एकपीता विभाति । तत्र हेतूनाह—कुङ्कुमं घुसृणं तस्य क्षोदः चूर्णं तेन गौरैः अरुणैः । अतः कृतं दिवसस्य मुखमारम्भः । प्रत्यूष इत्यर्थः । यैः तथाविधैः कीर्णैरितस्ततः क्षिप्तैः पिष्टातकस्य पटवासस्य ओघैः पुञ्जैः । तथा च हेम्नोलंकाराणां जनधृतानां भाभिः दीप्तिभिः । अपि च भरेण भारेण नमिताः नम्रीकृताः । णम् धातोर्णिजन्तात्कर्मणि क्तः । मितां ह्रस्वः इति ह्रस्वत्वम् । शिखाः शिरांसि इत्यर्थः यैः तादृशैः । किङ्किरातानामशोकानां लक्षणया तत्पुष्पाणां विकाराः कैङ्किराताः तैः । तस्य विकारः इति विकारार्थे अण् । पीताशोकपुष्पघटितैः शेखरैः आपीडैः च हेतुभिः । तथा च वेषेण वस्त्रालंकारादिधारणेन अभिलक्ष्यः उन्नेयः यः स्वविभवः निजैश्वर्यं तेन विजितः अशेषः सकलः वित्तेशस्य कुबेरस्य कोशो वित्तसंचयो यया तादृशी । अत्र कौशाम्ब्या उत्कर्षवर्णनादुदात्तालंकारः । शातकुम्भद्रवखाचितत्वोत्प्रेक्षणाद् हेतूत्प्रेक्षा च । सा चेवशब्दवाच्या । स्रग्धरा छन्दः ॥ १० ॥

धारायन्त्रेत्यादि । सर्वतः धारायन्त्रैः जलोद्गारयन्त्रैर्नलिकाभिर्वा विमुक्त उद्गीर्णः यः संततः अविरतः पयःपूरः जलसंघातस्तेन प्लुते प्लाविते । तथा च सद्यः तत्क्षणमेव सान्द्रः निबिडः यः विमर्दः पादैः निष्पेषस्तेन यः कर्दमः पङ्कस्तत्र कृता क्रीडा यस्मिन् । एतादृशे प्राङ्गणे उद्दामा उद्दामानो वा अप्रतिबन्धं नृत्यन्त्य इत्यर्थः । याः प्रकृष्टो मदो यासां ताः प्रमदाः तासां कपोलेभ्यो निपतन् यः सिन्दूररागः तेन अरुणैः रक्तैः चरणन्यासैः पादविक्षेपैः पुरः समीपवर्ति कुट्टिमं बद्धभूमिः क्षणं सैन्दूरीक्रियते सिन्दूरमयमिव सिन्दूररक्तं वा क्रियते । सिन्दूरस्य इदं सिन्दूरेण रक्तमिति वा

---

१ सहर्षं सम०. २ प्रमोदः पुरः. ३ क्षोदवासैः. ४ शिरःशे०. ५ लक्ष्या. ६ स्नुते. ७ रस-कृत-क्रीडाक्षमे. ८ विलसत्सिन्दूरसान्द्रारुणं; ०सिन्दूरचूर्णाकणे; चूर्णारुणैः; चूर्णा-रागा-रुणम्. ९ सैन्दूरं. १० जनस्य. ११ पुनः.

विदू०—(विलोक्य ।) इदमपि तावत्सुविदग्धजनभरितशृङ्गकजलप्रहारमुक्तसीत्कारमनोहरं वारविलासिनीजनविलसितमवलोकयतु प्रियवयस्यः।(क

राजा – (विलोक्ये ।) वयस्य सम्यग्दृष्टं त्वयाे । कुतः ।

अस्मिन्प्रकीर्णपटवासकृतान्धकारे
दृष्टो मनाङ्मणिविभूषणरश्मिजालैः ।
पातालमुद्यतफणाकृतिशृङ्गकोऽयं
मामद्य संस्मरयतीह भुजङ्गलोकः ॥ १२ ॥

विदूषकः—(विलोक्य ।) भोः एषा खलु मदनिका मदनवशविसंष्ठुलं वसन्ताभिनयं नृत्यन्ती चूतलतिकया सहेत एवागच्छति । तदवलोकयत्वेतां प्रियवयस्यः । (ख)

(क) ईमं पि दाव सुविअद्धजणभरिदसिङ्गकजलप्पहारमुक्कसिक्कारमणहरं वारविलासिणीजणविलसिदं ओलोएदु पिअवअस्सो । (ख) भो एसा क्खु मअणिआ मअणवसविसंठुलं वसन्ताभिणअं णच्चन्ती चूअलदिआए सह इदो ज्जेव आअच्छदि । ता अवलोएदु एदं पिअवअस्सो ।

सैन्दूरं । उभयत्र अण् । न सैन्दूरमसैन्दूरम् असैन्दूरं सैन्दूरं सम्पद्यमानं क्रियते सैन्दूरीक्रियते। अभूततद्भावे च्विः ।अनुप्रासालंकारः । शार्दूलविक्रीडितं वृत्तम्॥ ११॥ **सुविदग्धेति** । सुविदग्धाः तादृक्क्रीडापटवः ये जनाः तैः भरिताः पूरिताः । भर एषां सञ्जात इति भरिताः । तदस्य संजातं तारकादिभ्य इतच् इति इतच् । यद्वा भृत इति च्छाया । ये शृङ्गकास्तेषां जलेन ये प्रहारास्तैः हेतुभिः मुक्ताः सीत्कारास्तैर्मनोहरम् । वारस्य जनसमूहस्य विलासिन्यः वारविलासिन्यः गणिकाः । **अस्मिन्निति** । अस्मिन् प्रकीर्णश्चासौ पटवासश्च तेन कृतश्चासौ अन्धकारश्च तस्मिन् । अनेन प्रकीर्णपटवासपुञ्जानां सान्द्रत्वमतिप्रभूतत्वं च सूचितम् । मणिमयानि मणियुक्तानि वा पक्षे मणय एव विभूषणानि मणिविभूषणानि । तेषां रश्मिजालैः किरणसमूहैः । इह मनाक् किंचिदस्पष्टमिति यावत् । दृष्टः । उद्यताः फणा इव आकृतिर्येषां ते फणाकृतयः शृङ्गका येन । पक्षे फणाकृतयः शृङ्गका इव येन । उपमितं व्याघ्रादिभिरिति समासः । व्याघ्रादेराकृतिगणत्वात् । यद्वा उद्यतं फणाकृति फणारूपं शृङ्गकं चिह्नं येन । एवंविधः अयं भुजङ्गा विटास्तेषां लोकः समूहः । पक्षे सर्पलोकः । अद्य मां पातालं संस्मरयति । स्मृ आध्याने इति घटादौ पाठात् मित्त्वेन ह्रस्वः । स्मरणालंकारः श्लेषश्च । वसन्ततिलकं वृत्तम् ॥ १२ ॥ मदनस्य वशेन आयत्तत्वेन विसंष्ठुलं विषमं यथा

---

१ ०क्य सविस्मयम्; समन्तादवलोक्य. २ दृष्टं भवता; साधु दर्शितम्. ३ महा०. ४ विभूषितरत्न. ५ मणि. ६ तीव. ७ पुरोवलोक्य. ८ भो वअस्स इमं; वि०-(पुरोवलोक्य ।) इमिणा किं एदं पेक्ख; इमं-एदं. ९ ०अद्धविडजणो-णा-वहारिद (विटजनो-ना-पहृत शृ०); जणापुरिदसि०. १० प्पवाह. ११ वणिदालोअ. १२ अवलो०. १३ भो वअस्स पेक्ख एसा...च्छदित्ति अव०. १४ मअ(मद)वस०; मअणपरवसं णच्चन्ती; मअवसविब्भमदत्ताभिणअं, मअणरसविसअदत्ताभिणआ; मअणवसा वसन्ता०; मअपरवसा विसंवदन्ताहिणअं णच्चन्तीए चूदल०; मअणवसावेसं वहन्ती अभिणअं णच्चन्ती.

(ततः प्रविशतो मदनलीलां नाटयन्त्यौ द्विपदीखण्डं गायन्त्यौ चेट्यौ ।)

चेट्यौ—

कुसुमायुधप्रियदूतको मुकुलायितबहुचूतकः ।
शिथिलितमानग्रहणको वाति दक्षिणपवनकः ॥ १३ ॥
विकसितबकुलाशोककः काङ्क्षितप्रियजनमेलकः ।
प्रतिपालनासमर्थकस्ताम्यति युवतिसार्थकः ॥ १४ ॥
इह प्रथमं मधुमासो जनस्य हृदयानि करोति मृदुलानि ।
पश्चाद्विध्यति कामो लब्धप्रसरैः कुसुमबाणैः ॥ १५ ॥ (क)

(क) कुसुमाउहपिअदूअओ मउलीकिदबहुचूअओ ।
सिढिलिअमाणग्गहणओ वाअदि दाहिणपवणओ ॥
विअसिअबउलासोअओ कङ्क्षिअपिअजणमेलओ ।
पडिबालणासमत्थओ तम्मइ जुवईसत्थओ ॥

तथा । वसन्ताभिनयं वसन्तव्यञ्जकं यथा स्यात्तथा । मदनलीलां कामविलासम् । द्विपदी गीतिविशेषः । तदुक्तं—भवेद्द्विपदिका गीतिर्भरतेन प्रकीर्तिता । युक्ता चतुर्भिश्चरणैस्त्रयोदशकलात्मकैः ॥ तस्याः खण्डस्तम् । अत्र भरतः—शुद्धा खण्डा च मात्रा च संपूर्णेति चतुर्विधा । द्विपदी करणाख्येन तालेन परिगीयते ॥ खण्डा स्याच्छुद्धयार्धया । विशेषस्तु भरते द्रष्टव्यः । **कुसुमायुधेत्यादि** । दक्षिणः दक्षिणदिगुत्पन्नः । पवन एव पवनकः । अल्पार्थे कः । मन्द इत्यर्थः । दक्षिणश्चासौ पवनश्च दक्षिणपवनः वाति । कीदृश इत्याह । कुसुमान्यायुधान्यस्य कुसुमायुधः कामः तस्य प्रियश्चासौ दूतकश्च प्रियदूतकः । मुकुलायिताः मुकुलैरयिताः गमिताः । सञ्जातमुकुलाः कृता इत्यर्थः । बहवः चूतका आम्रवृक्षका येन स तथोक्तः । मुकुलीकृतेति पाठे मुकुला एषां विद्यन्ते इति मुकुलिनः । न मुकुलिनः अमुकुलिनः मुकुलिनः कृताः मुकुलीकृताः । अभूततद्भावे च्विः । शिथिलितं शिथिलं कृतं । त्याजितमिति यावत् । मानिनीनामिति शेषः । मानस्य रमणविषये प्रणयकृतस्याभिमानस्य ग्रहणं येन तादृशः ॥ १३ ॥ **विकसितेत्यादि** । विकसिताः । पुष्पिता इत्यर्थः । बकुलाश्च अशोकाश्च येन तथोक्तः । मधुगण्डूषदानेन पादताडनेन चेति भावः । एतच्च कविसमयात् । तदुक्तं—पादाहतः प्रमदया विकसत्यशोकः शोकं जहाति बकुलो मुखसीधुसिक्तः ॥ इति । विशेषोऽग्रेऽष्टादशश्लोकस्य व्याख्याने द्रष्टव्यः । कांक्षितः प्रियजनानां मेलकः समूहः येन । प्रतिपालने प्रियागमनकालप्रतीक्षणे असमर्थः । सुप्सुपेति समासः । स्वार्थे कः । सार्थ एव सार्थकः । युवतीनां सार्थकः समूहः ताम्यति ॥ १४ ॥ **इहेति** । इह अस्मिन्वसन्तावतारे मधुश्चासौ मासश्च मधुमासः । प्रथमं जनस्य हृदयानि मृदुलानि कोमलानि

---

१ गृहीतमदनोत्सववेषेण मदनावस्थां नाट०; ०शतः गृहीतवसन्तवेषे-वेषोत्सवे. २ मदनिका गायति. ३ मउलाइदघणचू०, कुसुमा...दूअअं मउलावन्तो चूअअं (कुसु०...दूतं मुकुलयंश्चूतं). ४ मोअओ (लामोदकः). ५ पिअअम(तम)ः टक्कण्ठिअ (उत्कण्ठित) पिअमेलओ. ६ अस्मात्परं-अइवा-अपरा इत्य० क्वचित्.

राजा—(निर्वर्ण्य सविस्मयम् ।) अहो निर्भरः क्रीडारसः परिजनस्य । तथा हि ।

स्रस्तः स्रग्दामशोभां त्यजति विरचितामाकुलः केशपाशः
क्षीबाया नूपुरौ च द्विगुणतरमिमौ क्रन्दतः पादलग्नौ ।
व्यस्तः कम्पानुबन्धादनवरतमुरो हन्ति हारोऽयमस्याः
क्रीडन्त्याः पीडयेव स्तनभरविनमन्मध्यभङ्गानपेक्षम् ॥ १६ ॥

विदूषकः—भो वयस्य अहमप्येतयोर्मध्ये गत्वा नृत्यन् गायन् मदनमहोत्सवं मानयिष्यामि । (क)

राजा—(सस्मितम् ।) वयस्य एवं क्रियताम् ।

विदूषकः—(उत्थाय चेट्योर्मध्ये नृत्यन् ।) भवति मदनिके भवति चूतलतिके मामप्येतां चर्चरीं शिक्षयतम् । (ख)

इह पढमं महुमासो जणस्स हिअआइं कुणइ मिउलाइं ।
पच्छा विद्धइ कामो लद्धप्पसरेहिं कुसुमबाणेहिं ॥

(क) भो वअस्स अहंपि एताणं मज्झे गदुअ णच्चन्तो गाअन्तो मअणमहूसवं माणइस्सम् । (ख) भोदि मअणिए भोदि चूअलदिए मंपि एदं चच्चरिं सिक्खावेहि ।

कुसुमशरभेदार्हाणीत्यर्थः । करोति । पश्चात् कामः लब्धः प्रसरः अवकाशः यैः तैः कुसुमबाणैः कुसुमरूपैर्बाणैः तानि हृदयानि विध्यति भिनत्ति । अरविन्दमशोकं च चूतं च नवमल्लिका । नीलोत्पलं च पञ्चैते पञ्चबाणस्य सायकाः ॥ इति कामस्य बाणाः ॥१५॥

अहो इत्याश्चर्ये । क्रीडारसः विहारासक्तिः । निर्भरोऽतिमात्रः । क्रीडारसस्य निर्भरत्वमिति यावत् । निर्भरत्वमेव प्रतिपादयति-**स्रस्त** इति । क्षीबाया मधुपानान्मत्तायाः । 'अनुपसर्गात्फुल्लक्षीबकृशोल्लाघाः' इति निपातनात्साधुः । अत एव स्तनयोर्भरः स्तनभरस्तेन विनमन् नम्रीभवन् यो मध्यः कटिभागस्तस्य भङ्गस्तत्र अनपेक्षा अनवधानं यस्मिन्कर्मणि तद्यथा तथा क्रीडन्त्याः अस्याः पुरो दृश्यमानायाः स्रस्तः बन्धनाद्विगलितः आकुलः व्यस्तः केशपाशः केशकलापः पीडयेव विरचितां स्रग्दाम्नः । तत्कृतामित्यर्थः । शोभां त्यजति । इमौ पादलग्नौ नूपुरौ मञ्जीरौ पीडयेव द्वौ गुणौ आवृत्ती यस्य तद्द्विगुणम् । अतिशयेन द्विगुणं द्विगुणतरं अत्यन्तमित्यर्थः । क्रन्दतः रुदित इव । उद्दामनर्तनाद्यः कम्पः अङ्गानां दोलनं तस्य अनुबन्धात्संततत्वाद् व्यस्तः इतस्ततः क्षिप्तोऽयं पुरो दृश्यमानः हारः मुक्ताहारः पीडयेव अनवरतं सततमुरो हन्ति । अत्र शोभात्यागादिक्रियाणां पीडाहेतुत्वेनोत्प्रेक्षणात् हेतूत्प्रेक्षालंकारः । स्रग्धरावृत्तम् ॥१६॥ एतासां बद्धपरिकराणामिति पाठे बद्धः परिकरः याभिः । वधूपरिजनानामिति पाठे वध्व

---

१ विलोक्य. २ अहो मधुरोयमासां नि०...रसः; (सहर्ष) अहो; (निर्वर्ण्य) अहो मधुरं प्रवृत्तः मदनमहोत्सवः. ३ पश्य. ४ तरमिवा. ५ मुच्चैः. ६ येव. ७ ०पेक्षम्. ८ एतन्नास्ति क्वचित्. ९ अस्मात्प्राक्—जं भवं आणवेदि इत्य०. १० नृत्यति. ११ अस्मात्परं-इति गायन्त्यौ नृत्यतश्चेट्यौ । इत्य०. १२ एदाणं वहू (वधू)परिजणाणं, बद्धपरिअराणं (बद्धपरिकराणां); णच्चन्तो मअण०. १३ चच्चरिअं.

उभे—(विहस्य।) हताश न खल्वेषा चर्चरी। (क)

विदूषकः—तत् किं खल्वेतत्। (ख)

मदनिका—द्विपदीखण्डं खल्वेतत् (ग)

विदूषकः—(सहर्षम्।) किमेतेन खण्डेन मोदकाः क्रियन्ते। (घ)

चेट्यौ—(विहस्य।) न हि न हि। पठ्यते खल्विदम्। (ङ)

विदूषकः—(सविषादम्।) यदि पठ्यते तदलं ममैतेन। वयस्यस्य सकाशमेव गमिष्यामि। (गन्तुमिच्छति।) (च)

उभे—(हस्ते गृहीत्वा।) एहि क्रीडामः। वसन्तक कुत्र गच्छसि। (इति बहुविधं वसन्तकमाकर्षतः।) (छ)

विदू०—(आकृष्य हस्तं प्रपलाय्य राजानमुपसृत्य।) वयस्य नर्तितोऽस्मि। न हि न हि। क्रीडित्वा पलायितोऽस्मि। (ज)

राजा—साधु कृतम्।

(क) हर्दास ण क्खु एसा चच्चरी। (ख) ताँ किं क्खु एदं। (ग) दुअई-खण्डं खु एदं। (घ) किं एदिणा खण्डेण मोदआ करीअन्दि। (ङ) णँहि णहि। पढीअदि क्खु एदं। (च) जँइ पढीअदि ता अलं मम एदिणा। वअँस्सस्स सआसं जेव्व गमिस्सम्। (छ) एँहि कीलम्ह। वसन्तअ कहिं गच्छसि। (ज) वअस्स णाच्चिदम्हि। णहि णहि। कीलिअ पलाइदोम्हि।

एव परिजनाः परिचारिका इत्यर्थः। मानयिष्यामि सत्करिष्यामि। हताश इति कुत्सायाम्। हताः आशा यस्य असौ हताशः। **किमेतेनेति**। खण्ड इति शब्दश्रवणेन खण्डशर्करेति मन्वानस्य मोदककरणसम्बद्धः प्रश्नः। विहस्येति। भोजनप्रियस्यास्य सर्वं भोजनसम्बद्धमेव इति विस्मयो हासकारणम्। बहुविधमनेकप्रकारं यथा तथा

---

१ सादरम्. २ अस्मात्प्राक्—(सविस्मयं) पढीअदि क्खु एदं (सवि०). ३ गन्तुमुद्यतः; तथा करोति. ४ भो वअस्स हदास...०री। दुवदीखण्डं क्खु एदं. ५ भोदि (भवति) किं. ६ भोदि; मोदआ लड्डुआ वा. ७ भो वअस्स, हदास-हदास पढिदव्वं क्खु एदं. ८ भो पढीअदि जइ क्खु एदं ता मम अलं इमिणा; जदि पढीअदि न भुञीअदि ता एदिणा न मम कज्जं. ९ वरं पिअ० ज्जेव सआ०. १० मदनिका-(हस्ते गृ०) हदास कहिं गच्छसि; हतास चच्चरिअं सिक्स; (इति बहुविधं ताडयति।); हदास चिठ्ठ। विना कीलिअं कहिं गमिस्ससि। (इति आकर्षतः—बहुविधं ताडयतः). विदू०—(बलाद्गच्छति। राजानमुपसृत्य) जअदु जअदु भट्टा। भो वअस्स णच्चिदम्हि गाइदम्हि।; उभे—आकर्षतः। विदू०—आकर्षति। मद०—हदास कहिं गच्छसि। इह ज्जेव कीलम्ह.

चूत०—हञ्जे मदनिके चिरं खल्वावाभ्यां क्रीडितम् । तदेहि। निवेदयावस्तावद्भर्त्र्याः संदेशं महाराजाय। (क)

मदनिका—सखि एवं कुर्वः। (ख)

उभे—(परिक्रम्य उपसृत्य च।) जयतु जयतु भर्ता। भर्तः देव्याज्ञापयति (इत्यर्धोक्ते लज्जां नाटयन्त्यौ।) नहि न हि। विज्ञापयति। (ग)

राजा—(विहस्य सादरम्।) मदनिके नन्वाज्ञापयतीत्येव रमणीयम्। विशेषतोऽद्य मदनमहोत्सवे। तत्कथय किमाज्ञापयति देवी।

विदू०—आः दास्याः पुत्रि। किं देवी आज्ञापयति। (घ)

उभे—एवं देवी विज्ञापयति–अद्य खलु मया मकरन्दोद्यानं गत्वा रक्ताशोकपादपतले संस्थापितस्य भगवतः कुसुमायुधस्य पूजा निर्वर्तयितव्या। तत्रार्यपुत्रेण संनिहितेन भवितव्यम्। (ङ)

राजा—(सानन्दम्।) वयस्य ननु वक्तव्यमुत्सवादुत्सवान्तरमापतितमिति।

विदूषकः—भो वयस्य तदुत्तिष्ठ। तत्रैव गच्छामो येन तत्र गतस्य ममापि ब्राह्मणस्य स्वस्तिवाचनं किमपि भविष्यति। (च)

(क) हञ्जे मअणिए चिरं क्खु अम्हेहिं कीलिदम् । ता एहि। णिवेदम्ह दाव भट्टिणीए संदेसं महाराअस्स। (ख) सहि एवं करिम्ह। (ग) जअदु जअदु भट्टा। भट्टा देवी आणवेदि–णहि णहि। विण्णवेदि। (घ) आः दासीए धीए। किं देवी आणवेदि। (ङ) एवं देवी विण्णवेदि-अज्ज क्खु मए मअरन्दोद्दाणे गदुअ रत्तासोअपाअवतले संठाविदस्स भअवदो कुसुमाउहस्स पूआ णिव्वत्तइदव्वा। तहिं अज्जउत्तेण संणिहिदेण होदव्वम्। (च) भो वअस्स ता उट्ठेहि। तहिं ज्जेव गच्छम्ह जेण तहिं गदस्स ममावि बम्हणस्स सोत्थिवाअणं किंवि भविस्सदि।

लज्जां नाटयन्त्यौ इति। आज्ञापनं हि स्वापेक्षया निकृष्टं प्रति भवति। राज्ञ्या राजानं प्रति तदनुचितम्। अतो वाण्यास्तथा निर्गतत्वाल्लज्जानाटनम्। कुसुमायुधस्यार्थात्तत्प्रतिकृतेः। अन्य उत्सव उत्सवान्तरम्। मयूरव्यंसकादित्वादन्यार्थकान्तरशब्देन समासः। स चास्वपदविग्रहः। स्वस्ति वाच्यते अनेन इति स्वस्तिवाचनम्। यद्वा स्वस्तिवायनमिति संस्कृतम्।

---

१ सानन्दम्; सहर्षं विहस्य सान०. २ षतश्चाद्य...तदुच्यतां. ३ किं. ४ चूदलदिए सुट्ठु तुए सुमरिदं (स्मृतं) एदं। एहि त्वरम्ह. ५ किं त्ति देवी आणवेदित्ति. ६ भो उट्ठेहि। लहुं गच्छम्ह। ममा वि क्खु तहिं ज्जेव्व सोत्थिवाअणणिमित्तओ बहुमाणो भविस्सदि.

राजा—मदनिके गम्यतां देव्यै निवेदयितुमयमहमागत एव मकरन्दोद्यानमिति ।

उभे—यद्भर्ताज्ञापयति । (इति निष्क्रान्ते ।) (**क**)

राजा—वयस्य एहि अवतरावः । (उभौ प्रासादावतरणं नाटयतः ।) वयस्य आदेशय मकरन्दोद्यानस्य मार्गम् ।

विदूषकः—यद्भवानाज्ञापयति । एत्वेतु भवान् । (**ख**)

(उभौ परिक्रामतः ।)

विदूषकः—(अग्रतोऽवलोक्य ।) भो एतत्तन्मकरन्दोद्यानम् । तदेहि । प्रविशावः । (**ग**) (इति प्रविशतः ।)

विदूषकः—(अवलोक्य सविस्मयम् ।) भो वयस्य प्रेक्षस्व प्रेक्षस्व । एतत्खलु तन्मलयमारुतान्दोलनप्रफुल्लत्सहकारमञ्जरीरेणुपटलप्रतिबद्धपटवितानं मत्तमधुकरमुक्तझङ्कारमिलितमधुरकोकिलारावसंगीतश्रुतिसुखं तवागमनदर्शितादरमिव मकरन्दोद्यानं लक्ष्यते । तत्प्रेक्षतां भवान् । (**घ**)

राजा—(समन्तादवलोक्य ।) अहो रम्यता मकरन्दोद्यानस्य । इह हि

(**क**) जं भट्टा आणवेदि । (**ख**) जं भवं आणवेदि । एदु एदु भवं । (**ग**) भो एदं तं मअरन्दुज्जाणम् । ता एहि । पविसम्ह । (**घ**) भो वअस्स पेक्ख पेक्ख । एदं क्खु तं मलअमारुदान्दोलणपहुल्लन्तसहआरमञ्जरीरेणुपटलपडिबद्धपडवितानं मत्तमहुअरमुत्तझङ्कारमिलिदमहुरकोइलारावसंगीदसुदिसुहं तुहागमणदंसितादरं विअ मअरन्दुद्दाणं लक्खीअदि । ता पेक्खदु भवं ।

मलयेति । मलयस्य मारुतो मलयमारुतस्तेन आन्दोलनं तेन प्रफुल्लन्त्यो याः सहकाराणामतिसौरभवतामाम्रवृक्षाणां मञ्जर्यस्तासां रेणवः परागास्तेषां पटलं तेन प्रतिबद्धं पटवितानं यस्मिन् । मत्ताश्च ते मधुकराश्च तैर्मुक्तः यः झङ्कारस्तेन मिलितो यः कोकिलारावः स एव संगीतं तेन श्रवणसुखम् । तवागमने दर्शित आदरो येन । तत्र इत्यस्य सापेक्षत्वेऽपि गमकत्वात्समासः । यद्वा त्वदागमनेति पठनीयम् ।

---

१ ०तुमहमा. २ वयस्य तदादेशय मार्गं मक ०स्य. ३ विलोक्य. ४ प्रवेशं नाटयतः. ५ दृष्ट्वा. ६ मक० परा श्रीः. ७ (अग्रतो भूत्वा) एदु एदु भवं. ८ भट्टा. ९ भो भोः एदं मअ० । ता पविसदु भवं. १० महाराअ. ११ मारुदान्दोलिदमउलन्त (मुकुलायमान) सह०; मारुदंदोलिअपरिसरन्त–मण्डलन्त–पल्लविद. १२ मिलिद; समन्तदोपसुण्वन्तमत्तमहुअरणिवह०. १३ लालाव (लालाप) संगीदमुहरअं (मुखरं). १४ बहुमाणदंसि०.

उद्यद्विद्रुमकान्तिभिः किसलयैस्ताम्रां त्विषं बिभ्रतो
भृङ्गालीविरुतैः कलैरविशदव्याहारलीलाभृतः ।
घूर्णन्तो मलयानिलाहतिचलैः शाखासमूहैर्मुहु-
र्भ्रान्तिं प्राप्य मधुप्रसङ्गमधुना मत्ता इवामी द्रुमाः ॥ १७ ॥

अपि च ।

मूले गण्डूषसेकासव इव बकुलैर्वास्यते पुष्पवृष्ट्या
मध्वाताम्रे तरुण्या मुखशशिनि चिराच्चम्पकान्यद्य भान्ति ।
आकर्ण्याशोकपादाहतिषु च रणतां निर्भरं नूपुराणां
झङ्कारस्यानुगीतैरनुरणनभिवारभ्यते भृङ्गसार्थैः ॥ १८ ॥

उद्यदिति । अधुना संप्रति अमी द्रुमाः मधोः वसन्तस्य मधुनः मद्यस्य च प्रसङ्गं प्रकृष्टसम्पर्कं प्राप्य मत्ताः पानक्षीबा इव भान्ति । भ्रान्तिमिति पाठे मधुप्रसङ्गः वसन्तसम्पर्कस्तत्सम्बन्धी यन्मधु तेन भ्रान्तिमुन्मादं प्राप्य मत्ताः पानशौण्डा इव दृश्यन्ते इति शेषः । तदेव प्रतिपादयति । उद्यतां प्ररोहतां विद्रुमाणां प्रवालानां कान्तय इव कान्तयो येषां तैः किसलयैः । हेत्वर्थे तृतीया । ताम्रां त्विषं कान्तिं बिभ्रतो धारयन्तः । मधुमत्तोऽपि रक्तवर्णां त्विषं धारयति । कलैः अव्यक्तमधुरैः भृङ्गालीनां भ्रमरपंक्तीनां विरुतैः गुञ्जितैः हेतुभिः । अविशदः अस्पष्टः यो व्याहारः भाषितं तस्य लीलां बिभ्रतीति व्याहारलीलाभृतः । मधुमत्ता जना इव अस्पष्टं व्याहरन्त इत्यर्थः । तथा च मलयानिलस्य दक्षिणपवनस्य आहतिभिस्ताडनैः चलैः शाखासमूहैः मुहुः पुनः पुनः घूर्णन्तः भ्रमन्तः । उत्प्रेक्षालंकारः श्लेषश्च । शार्दूलविक्रीडितं वृत्तम् ॥१७॥

मूल इति । बकुलैः केसरवृक्षैः कर्तृभिः चिरात् मूले यः तरुण्याः गण्डूषसेकासवः स पुष्पवृष्ट्या वास्यते सुरभीक्रियते । यद्वा मूले गण्डूषसेकासवे सति बकुलैः पुष्पवृष्ट्या वास्यते आच्छाद्यते । अधःप्रदेश इति शेषः । तरुण्या मुखं एव शशी मुखशशी तस्मिन् मधुना आताम्रे ईषद्रक्ते सति । पटुमृदुहसनरूपदोहदप्रापणादित्यर्थः । चिरादद्य चम्पकानि चम्पकपुष्पाणि भान्ति आविर्भवन्ति इत्यर्थः । चम्पकशब्दात् पुष्परूपविकारे विहितस्याणः 'पुष्पमूलेषु बहुलम्' इति लुप् । भृङ्गसार्थैः भ्रमरसमूहैश्च अशोकेषु याः पादाभ्यामाहतयः दोहदपूरणार्थे ताडनानि तासु निर्भरं रणतां क्वणतां नूपुराणां झंकारस्य शिञ्जितस्य आकर्ण्य अनुगीतैः अनुकरणमारभ्यत इव । अत्र कविसमयः— स्त्रीणां स्पर्शात्प्रियंगुर्विकसति बकुलः सीधुगण्डूषसेकात्पादाघातादशोकस्तिलककुरबकौ वीक्षणालिङ्गनाभ्याम् । मन्दारो नर्मवाक्यात्पटुमृदुहसनाच्चम्पको वक्त्रवाताच्चूतो गीतान्नमेरुर्विकसति च पुरो नर्तनात्कर्णिकारः ॥ उत्प्रेक्षालंकारः । स्रग्धरा छन्दः । लक्षणमुक्तं

---

१ ताम्रास्त्विषः, ताम्रत्विषः. २ भृशं. ३ भ्रान्तिं. ४ जनितां. ५ रसतां, रसितं-रणितं. ६ स्यात्तगी०, गीतैरनुसरण-गणन. ७ वाभ्यस्यते.

विदूषकः—(आकर्ण्य ।) भो वयस्य नैते मधुकरा नूपुरशब्दमनुहरन्ति । नूपुरशब्द एवैष देव्याः परिजनस्य । (क)

राजा—वयस्य सम्यगुपलक्षितम् ।

(ततः प्रविशति वासवदत्ता काञ्चनमाला पूजोपकरणहस्ता सागरिका विभवतश्च परिवारः ।)

वासवदत्ता—हञ्जे काञ्चनमाले आदेशय मे मकरन्दोद्यानस्य मार्गम् । (ख)

काञ्चनमाला—एतु एतु भर्त्री । (ग)

वासव०—(परिक्रम्य ।) हञ्जे काञ्चनमाले अथ कियद्दूरे स रक्ताशोकपादपो यत्र मया भगवतः कुसुमायुधस्य पूजा निर्वर्तयितव्या । (घ)

काञ्चन०—भर्त्रि आसन्न एव । किं न प्रेक्षते भर्त्री । इयं खलु सा निरन्तरोद्भिन्नकुसुमशोभिनी भर्त्र्या परिगृहीता माधवीलता । एषाप्यपरा नवमालिका लता यस्या अकालकुसुमसमुद्गमश्रद्धालुना भर्त्रा अनुदि-

---

(क) भो वअस्स ण एदे महुअरा णेउँरसद्दं अणुहरन्ति । णेउरसद्दो ज्जेव्व एसो देवीए परिअणस्स । (ख) हञ्जे कञ्चणमाले आदेसेहि मे मअरन्दुज्जाणस्स मग्गं । (ग) एदु एदु भट्टिणी[६] । (घ) हञ्जे कञ्चणमाले अध केत्तिअ दूरे सो रत्तासोअपादवो जहिं मए भअवदो कुसुमाउहस्स पूआ णिव्वत्तइदव्वा ।

प्राक् ॥१८॥ उपलक्षितमवगतम् । पूजायाः उपकरणानि हस्ते यस्याः सा । हञ्जे—हञ्जे हण्डे हलाह्वाने नीचां चेटीं सखीं प्रति । इत्यमरः । **निरन्तरेति**—निर्गतमन्तरं यस्मात्तथा तथा निरन्तरं उद्भिन्नानि कुसुमानि तैः शोभते इति निरन्तरोद्भिन्नकुसुमशोभिनी । परिगृहीता आत्मीयत्वेन स्वीकृता । नवमालिका सप्तला (बटमोगरी इति महाराष्ट्रीयभाषायां ख्याता) । **अकालेति** । स्वकुसुमोत्पत्तिकालादन्यः कालः अकालः । तदन्यत्वं नञर्थः । तत्सादृश्यमभावश्च तदन्यत्वं तदल्पता । इति वचनात् । अकाले कुसुमानां

---

१ श्रुत्वा. २ गवधारितं, गवधार्यताम्. ३ उज्ज्वलनेशा वा०. ४ गृहीतपूजोपकरणा. ५ णिग्घोसमणुकरन्ति; सरन्ति; अणुहरन्दो (हरन्तः). ६ अस्मात्परं–(इति परिक्रामति ।). **काञ्चन०**—पेक्खदु भट्टिणी महुसमअकुसुमिआविविहतरुलदापरिगहदिमहुअरमुहुरामिदमअरन्दुज्जाणसस्सरीअदं । **वास०**—सुट्ठु दंसिदं । **काञ्च०**—एदं वि दाव आलोअदु भट्टिणी । कोमलकिसलअरत्तवसणमणहरा सहआरमञ्जरीगुच्छणिरन्तरणिलिनालिभरकेसपासा कलपरहुदाविरुदालाविणी चूदकाणणे भमन्ती विअ वसन्तलच्छी । **वास०**—जं सच्चं अदिसअरमणीअदावक्खित्ताहिअआए मे दिट्ठी कहिं वि पदेसे पविभट्टा ण णिवत्तदि । हञ्जे काञ्च० इ०. ७ दाणिं सो. ८ मअणस्स.

नमायास्यत आत्मा । तदेतामतिक्रम्य दृश्यत एव स रक्ताशोकपादपो यत्र देवी पूजां निर्वर्तयिष्यति । (क)

वासव०—तदेहि तत्रैव लघु गच्छामः । (ख)

काञ्चन०—एतु एतु भर्त्री । (ग)

(सर्वाः परिक्रामन्ति ।)

काञ्चन०—भर्त्रि अयं खलु स रक्ताशोकपादपो यत्र देवी पूजां निर्वर्तयिष्यति । (घ)

वासव०—तेन हि मे पूजानिमित्तान्युपकरणान्युपनय । (ङ)

साग०—(उपसृत्य ।) भर्त्रि एतत्सर्वं सज्जम् । (च)

वासव०—(निरूप्य आत्मगतम् ।) अहो प्रमादः परिजनस्य । यस्यैव दर्शनपथात्प्रयत्नेन रक्ष्यते तस्यैव दृष्टिगोचरे पतिता भवेत् । भवतु एवं तावद्भणिष्यामि । (प्रकाशम् ।) हञ्जे सागरिके कस्मात्त्वमद्य मदनमहोत्सवपराधीने

(क) भट्टिणि आसण्णो ज्जेव । किं न पेक्खदि भट्टिणी । इअं क्खु सा निरन्तरुब्भिण्णकुसुमसोहिणी भट्टिणीए परिगहिदा माहवीलदा । एसा वि अवरा णोमालिआ लदा जीए अआलकुसुमसमुग्गमसद्धालुणा भट्टिणा अणुदिणं आआसीअदि अप्पा । ता एदं अतिक्कमिअ दीसदि ज्जेव सो रत्तासोअपाअवो जहिं देवी पूआं णिव्वत्तइस्सदि । (ख) ता एहि तहिं ज्जेव्व लहु गच्छम्ह । (ग) एदु एदु भट्टिणी । (घ) भट्टिणि अअं खु सो रत्तासोअपाअवो जहिं देवी पूआं णिव्वत्तइस्सदि । (ङ) तेण हि मे पूआणिमित्ताइं उवअरणाइं उवणेहि । (च) भट्टिणि एदं सव्वं सज्जम् ।

समुद्गमः अकालकुसुमसमुद्गमः तस्मिन् श्रद्धालुना विश्वासवता । स्पृहिगृहि-इत्यादिना श्रच्छब्दोपपदे डुधाञ्धातोस्ताच्छील्ये आलुच् । आयास्यते कदा पुष्पोद्गमः स्यादिति चिन्तया खेदं नीयते । पूजा निमित्तानि पूजा निमित्तमेषामिति । उपक्रियते एभिरिति उपकरणानि । ल्युट् करणे । सज्जं संभृतम् । प्रमादः अनवधानता । दर्शनस्य पन्थाः दर्शनपथः तस्मात् । गावः इन्द्रियाणि चरन्त्यस्मिन्निति गोचरः विषयः । गोचरसंचरेत्यादिना अधिकरणे घः । दृष्टेः गोचरे दृष्टिगोचरे । ०गोचरमिति पाठे दृष्टेः गोचरं यथा तथा । परस्मिन्नधि इति पराधीनः । मदनमहोत्सवेन पराधीनः तस्मिन्मदन-

---

१ इति परि०. २ सहस्रो०. ३ सागरिकां दृष्ट्वा. ४ जीए किदे—०कुसुमसद्धा०. ५ ०दिअहं (दिवसं). ६ ता एदु एदु देवी (इति परिक्रामन्ति). ७ वास०—अअं सो...जहिं भई पूआं णिवत्तइस्सं । तेण हि-ता-मे पूआ० उवणेहि.

परिजने सारिकामुज्झित्वेहागता। तत्तत्रैव लघु गच्छ। एतदपि सर्वं पूजोपकरणं काञ्चनमालाया हस्ते समर्पय। (क)

साग०—यद्भर्त्र्याज्ञापयति। (इति तथा कृत्वा कतिचित्पदानि गत्वा। आत्मगतम्।) सारिका मया पुनः सुसंगताया हस्ते समर्पिता। एतदप्यस्ति मे प्रेक्षितुं कौतूहलं किं यथा तातस्यान्तःपुरे भगवाननङ्गोऽर्च्यते इहापि तथैव किमन्यथेति। तदलक्षिता भूत्वा प्रेक्षिष्ये। यावदिह पूजासमयो भवति तावदहमपि भगवन्तमनङ्गमेव पूजयितुं कुसुमान्यवचेष्यामि। (इति कुसुमावचयं नाटयति।) (ख)

वासव०—काञ्चनमाले प्रतिष्ठापयाशोकमूले भगवन्तं प्रद्युम्नम्। (ग)

काञ्चन०—यद्भर्त्र्याज्ञापयति। (तथा करोति।) (घ)

(क) अहो पमाओ परिअणस्स। जस्स ज्जेव दंसणपर्होदो पअत्तेण रक्खीअदि तस्स ज्जेव दिट्ठिगोअरे पडिदा भवे। भोदु एवं ताव भणिस्सम्। हञ्जे साअरिए कीस तुमं अज्ज मअणमहूस्सवपराहीणे परिअणे सारिअं उज्झिअ इहागदा। ता तहिं ज्जेव लहुं गच्छ। एदं वि सव्वं पूओबअरणं कञ्चणमालाए हत्थे समप्पेहि। (ख) जं भट्टिणी आणवेदि। सारिआ मए उण सुसंगदाए हत्थे समप्पिदा। एदं वि अत्थि मे पेक्खिदुं कोदूहलं किं जहा तादस्स अन्तेउरे भअवं अणङ्गो अच्चीअदि इह वि तह ज्जेव किं अण्णहेत्ति। ता अलक्खिदा भविअ पेक्खिस्सम्। जाव इह पूआसमओ होइ ताव अहं पि भअवन्तं अणंगं ज्जेव पूअइदुं कुसुमाइं अवचिणिस्सम्। (ग) कञ्चणमाले पडिट्ठावेहि असोअमूले भअवन्तं पज्जुण्णम्। (घ) जं भट्टिणी आणवेदि।

महोत्सवपराधीने। ०परिहीने इति पाठे ०त्सवेन परिहीने विरले। सारिका पक्षिविशेषः लघु द्रुतम्। कुसुमानामवचयः कुसुमावचयस्तम्। हस्तादाने चेरस्तेये इति घञि कृते अवचाय इति स्यात्। अत्र तु आदेयस्य प्रत्यासत्त्यभावाद्धञभाव इति समाधेयम्। अत्र–" वासवदत्ता–उपनय मे पूजोपकरणानि " इत्यारभ्य–" तदलक्षिता प्रेक्षिष्ये " इत्यन्तेन वासवदत्ताया रत्नावलीवत्सराजयोर्दर्शनप्रतीकारात्सारिकायाः सुसंगतार्पणेन अलक्षितप्रेक्षणेन च वत्सराजसमागमहेतोर्बीजस्योपादानात्समाधानं नाम मुखसन्धेरङ्गम्।

---

१ काञ्चनमालाया अर्पयित्वा...पदानि दत्त्वा; काञ्चनमालां समर्प्य. २ नास्त्येतत्कांचित्. ३ मे परि. ४ पधादेव इअं...ज्जेव कहं वि ०गोअरं गदा। ता भोदु...; गोअरं गदा भविस्सादि—भद्दे (विचिन्त्य). ५ मअ(मद)पराहीणपरिअणे इमास्सिं मअणमहूस्सवे. ६ मोत्तूण (मुक्त्वा). ७ एदं अ सव्वं कञ्च०ए सम०. ८ ०आदाव. ९ ज्जेव आदु (अथवा) अण्ण०. १० ०क्खिदा एव्व पे०; सिन्धुवारविडवान्तरिदा भविअ. ११ मअणं ज्जेव्व समच्चिदुं. १२ आणइस्सं.

विदू०—भो वयस्य यथा विश्रान्तो नूपुरशब्दस्तथा तर्कयामि आगता देव्यशोकमूलमिति । (क)

राजा—(अवलोक्य ।) वयस्य सम्यगवधारितम् । पश्येयं देवी या किलैषा

कुसुमसुकुमारमूर्तिर्दधती नियमेन तनुतरं मध्यम् ।
आभाति मकरकेतोः पार्श्वस्था चापयष्टिरिव ॥ १९ ॥

तदेहि उपसर्पावः । (उपसृत्य ।) प्रिये वासवदत्ते ।

वासव०—(विलोक्य ।) कथमार्यपुत्रः । जयतु जयत्वार्यपुत्रः । एतदासनम् । अत्रोपविशत्वार्यपुत्रः । (ख)

(राजा नाट्येनोपविशति ।)

काञ्चन०—भर्त्रि स्वहस्तदत्तकुङ्कुमचर्चिकाशोभितं कृत्वा रक्ताशोकपादपमर्च्यतां भगवान्प्रद्युम्नः । (ग)

वासव०—उपनय मे पूजोपकरणानि । (घ)

(काञ्चनमालोपनयति । वासवदत्ता तथा करोति ।)

(क) भो वअस्स जधा वीसन्तो णेउरसद्दो तहा तक्केमि आअदा देवी असोअमूलंत्ति । (ख) कधं अज्जउत्तो । जअदु जअदु अज्जउत्तो । एदं आसणं एत्थ उवविसदु अज्जउत्तो । (ग) भट्टिणि सहत्थदिण्णकुङ्कुमचच्चिआसोहिदं कदुअ रत्तासोअपाअवं अच्चीअदु भअवं पज्जुण्णो । (घ) उवणेहि मे पूजोवअरणाइं ।

बीजार्थस्योपगमनं तत्समाधानमुच्यते । इति तल्लक्षणम् । विश्रान्तः विरतः । अवधारितं निश्चितम् । **कुसुमेत्यादि** । कुसुममिव सुकुमारा मूर्तिः यस्याः सा । यष्टिपक्षे कुसुमान्येव सुकुमारा मूर्तिर्यस्याः सा । मदनधनुषः पुष्पमयत्वात् । नियमेन उपवासादिव्रतेन तनुतरमतिशयेन कृशं मध्यं कटिं पक्षे नियमेन तनुतरं पूर्वापरभागापेक्षया लघुतरं मध्यं दधती । मकरः केतुर्यस्य तस्य मकरकेतोः मदनस्य पार्श्वस्था तस्य चापयष्टिः धनुःकाण्डमिव आभाति । श्लेषानुप्राणितोत्प्रेक्षालंकारः । आर्या छन्दः ॥ १९ ॥ कथमिति संभ्रमे । कथं प्रश्ने प्रकारार्थे संभ्रमे संभवेऽपि च । इति हेमचन्द्रः । स्वहस्तेन त्वयात्महस्तेन दत्ता या कुङ्कुमस्य घुसृणस्य चर्चिका चर्चा तया शोभितं विभूषितम् ।

---

१ समन्तादव०; विलोक्य; वासवदत्तां दृष्ट्वा; (दृष्ट्वा) वयस्य इयं देवी येषा. २ सुपलक्षितं. ३ कुसुम०. ४ इत्युपसर्पतः. विदू०—(उपसृत्य) सोत्थि भोदीए । काञ्च०—भट्टिणि सहत्थ०. विदू०—भो वयस्स एहि उपसप्पम्ह । राजा—क्षणं तिष्ठ । मा भूत्समाधिभङ्गो देव्याः । निर्वर्तयतु पूजां मन्मथस्य । ५ पूजयति. अस्मात्परं-विदू० पेक्ख वअस्स अणंगं अच्चन्ती अहिअं सोहइ भट्टिणी । राजा०--सम्यगभिहितम् । ६ परिसन्तो ०रवो...संपत्ता (संप्राप्ता) देवी ०पाअवसमीपे—समीपं ७ अम्मो, कधं आअदो ज्जेव. ८ ०उत्तो । अलंकरेदु इमं देसं आसणपरिग्गहेण । एदं आसणं—इ० ९ ०णाहिं विलेवणं वि.

राजा—प्रिये[1]

प्रत्यग्रमज्जनविशेषविविक्तकान्तिः
कौसुम्भरागरुचिरस्फुरदंशुकान्ता।
विभ्राजसे मकरकेतनमर्चयन्ती
बालप्रवालविटपिप्रभवा लतेव ॥ २० ॥

अपि च।

स्पृष्टस्त्वयैष दयिते स्मरपूजाव्यापृतेन हस्तेन।
उद्भिन्नापरमृदुतरकिसलय इव लक्ष्यतेऽशोकः ॥ २१ ॥

अपि च।

अनङ्गोऽयमनङ्गत्वमद्य निन्दिष्यति ध्रुवम्।
यदनेन न संप्राप्तः पाणिस्पर्शोत्सवस्तव ॥ २२ ॥

काञ्चन०—भर्त्रि अर्चितो भगवान्प्रद्युम्नः। तत्कुरु भर्तुरुचितं पूजासत्कारम्। (क)

(क) भट्टिनि अच्चिदो भअवं पज्जुण्णो। ता करेहि भत्तुणो उइदं पूआसक्कारम्।

प्रत्यग्रेत्यादि। मकरकेतनं कामदेवमर्चयन्ती त्वं बाला नूतनाः प्रवालाः पल्लवा यस्य तादृशो विटपी वृक्षः स प्रभव उत्पत्तिस्थानं यस्याः तादृशी लता इव विभ्राजसे शोभसे। तत्र साम्यं दर्शयति विशेषणद्वयेन। प्रत्यग्रमचिरवृत्तं यद् मज्जनं स्नानं तेन विशेषेण अधिकं विविक्ता उज्ज्वला कान्तिर्यस्याः सा तथोक्ता। पक्षे प्रत्यग्रं यन्मज्जनं जलेन सिञ्चनं तेन विशेषेण विविक्ता पूता। स्वच्छेत्यर्थः। कान्तिर्यस्यास्तादृशी। पुनश्च कौसुम्भेन कुसुम्भपुष्पजन्येन रागेण रञ्जनद्रव्येण रुचिरं सुन्दरं यथा तथा स्फुरन् लसन् अंशुकान्तो यस्यास्तादृशी। पक्षे कौसुम्भं कुसुम्भपुष्पं तस्येव रागो लौहित्यं तेन रुचिरा चासौ स्फुरद्भिरंशुभिः किरणैः कान्ता रमणीया च सा तथोक्ता। उपमालंकारः। वसन्ततिलका वृत्तम्। उदाहृतमेतत्पद्यं काव्यप्रकाशे उपमादोषप्रकरणे। अत्र लता विभ्राजते न तु विभ्राजसे इति सम्बोध्यमाननिष्ठस्य परभागस्य असंबोध्यमानविषयतया व्यत्यासात्पुरुषभेदः इति भग्नप्रक्रमतादोषश्च दर्शितः। एतद्दोषवारणाय प्रिये इत्यनन्तरं भवती इति पदमध्याहृत्य विभ्राजते इति पठनीयम् ॥ २० ॥ स्पृष्ट इति। हे दयिते त्वया स्मरपूजायां व्यापृतेन व्यग्रेण हस्तेन स्पृष्टः अयमशोकः उत्पन्न उद्गतः अपरः विद्यमानेभ्यः अन्यः मृदुतरः किसलयः पल्लवः यस्य तथाविध इव लक्ष्यते। उत्प्रेक्षालंकारः। आर्यावृत्तम् ॥ २१ ॥ अनङ्ग इति। अयं नास्ति अङ्गं यस्य सः अनङ्गः कामः। अद्य आत्मनः अनङ्गत्वं गात्ररहितत्वं ध्रुवं निश्चितं निन्दिष्यति। यत् यस्मात्कारणादनेन तव पाणिस्पर्शः तस्माद्य उत्सवः। स एव उत्सव इति वा। न सम्प्राप्तः। शिवेन भालस्थनेत्राग्निना दग्धाङ्गत्वादिति भावः। उत्प्रेक्षालंकारः ॥ २२ ॥

१ (निरूप्य) प्रिये। प्रिये वासवदत्ते. २ द्युतिः. ३ विटप. ४ त्वयैव–यैक. ५ व्यापृतेन. ६ प्रिये. ७ त्वत्पाणिग्रहणोत्सवः. ८ भट्टिनि करेहि...समुइदं पू०.

वासव०—तेन हि उपनय मे कुसुमानि विलेपनं च । (क)

काञ्चन०—भर्त्रि एतत्सर्वं सज्जम् । (ख)

(वासवदत्ता नाट्येन राजानं पूजयेति ।)

सागरिका—(गृहीतकुसुमा ।) हा धिक् हा धिक् । कथं कुसुमलोभोत्क्षिप्तहृदययातिचिरमेव मया कृतम् । तद्यावदनेन सिन्धुवारविटपेनापवारितशरीरा भूत्वा प्रेक्षे । (तथा कृत्वा विलोक्य सविस्मयम् ।) कथं प्रत्यक्ष एव भगवान्कुसुमायुध इह पूजां प्रतीच्छति । अस्माकं तातस्यान्तःपुरे पुनश्चित्रगतोऽर्च्यते । तदहमपीह स्थितैवैभिः कुसुमैर्भगवन्तं कुसुमायुधं पूजयिष्ये । (कुसुमानि प्रक्षिप्य ।) नमस्ते भगवन्कुसुमायुध अमोघदर्शनो म इदानीं त्वं भविष्यासि । (इति प्रणम्य ।) दृष्टं यद्द्रष्टव्यम् । तद्यावन्न कोऽपि मां प्रेक्षते तावदेव गमिष्यामि । (इति कतिचित्पदानि गच्छति ।) (ग)

(क) तेण हि उवणेहि मे कुसुमाइं विलेबणं च । (ख) भट्टिणि एदं सव्वं सज्जं । (ग) हद्धी हद्धी । कहं कुसुमलोहोक्खित्तहिअआए अदिचिरं जेव्व मए किदम् । ता जाव इमिणा सिन्दुवारविडवेण ओवारिअसरीरा भविअ पेक्खामि । कहं पच्चक्खो एव्व भअवं कुसुमाउहो इह पूअं पडिच्छदि । अम्हाणं तादस्स अन्तेउरे उण चित्तगदो अच्चीअदि । ता अहं वि इह त्थिदा जेव्व इमेहिं कुसुमेहिं भअवन्दं कुसुमाउहं पूअइस्सं । णमो दे भअवं कुसुमाउह अमोहदंसणो मे दाणिं तुमं भविस्ससि । दिट्ठं जं दिट्ठव्वम् । ता जाव ण कोवि मं पेक्खदि तावज्जेव गमिस्सम् ।

पूजा एव पूजारूपो वा सत्कारस्तम् । कुसुमानां लोभः तेन उत्क्षिप्तं हृदयं यस्याः सिन्धुवारो निर्गुंडीवृक्षः तस्य विटपेन शाखाविस्तारेण अपवारितमन्तर्हितं शरीरं यस्याः सा तथा । कथं प्रत्यक्ष एव इत्यारभ्य पूजयिष्यामि इत्यन्तेन परिभावनाख्यं मुखसन्धेरङ्गमुक्तम् । अनेन वत्सराजस्यानङ्गरूपतयापह्नवादनङ्गस्य च प्रत्यक्षस्य पूजाग्रहणस्य लोकोत्तरत्वादद्भुतरसावेशः परिभावना । इति दशरूपकम् । अमोघं सफलं दर्शनं यस्य तथाविधः । ममाभीष्टस्य सम्पादयितेत्यर्थः । नमस्ते...प्रेक्षते तावद्गमिष्यामि इत्यने-

---

१ ०यति । सर्वे उपविशन्ति । २ दृष्ट्वा सवि०. ३ परिवृत्य कुसु०; इति पुष्पांजलिं गृहीत्वा; एतन्नास्ति क्वचित्. ४ ०मति. ५ परावृत्य पदद्वयं ददाति; निष्क्रामति. ६ दाव मे. ७ जं भट्टिणि आणवेदि । (तथा करोति ।) वास०—उपविसदु अज्जो । (राजा उपविशति ।). ८ अम्मो कुसुम०. ९ ०वारन्तरेण; विडवन्तरेण–विडवान्तरणवारिदसरीरा–पेक्खिस्सम्. १० कहं पेक्खिदो जेव्व अपूव्वो कुसुमाउहो । ११ पडिच्छदि । ता अहं वि...पूअइस्सं । (पुष्पाणि क्षिपति ।). १२ ०अदि इह पच्चक्खीकिदो । ता अहं; चित्तगदो वा पडिमग्गओ भअवन्तो अणंगो पूअं पडिच्छइ; ०अदि । सव्वथा, एत्थ अअं विसेसोत्ति । १३ ०उह सुभदंसणो मे भविस्ससि । दिट्ठं... । अमोघदंसणो मे भविस्ससि । १४ अस्मात्परं क्वचित्—अच्चरिअं अच्चरिअं । दिट्ठोवि पुणो पेक्खिदव्वो ता जाव इ०. १५ ताव तुरिदं.

काञ्चन०—आर्य वसन्तक एहि सांप्रतं त्वमपि स्वस्तिवाचनं प्रतीच्छ। (विदूषक उपसर्पति।) (क)

वासव०—(विलेपनकुसुमाभरणदानपूर्वकम्।) आर्य स्वस्तिवाचनं प्रतीच्छ। (इत्यर्पयति।) (ख)

विदू०—(सहर्षं गृहीत्वा।) स्वस्ति भवत्यै। (ग)

(नेपथ्ये वैतालिकैः पठति।)

अस्तापास्तसमस्तभासि नभसः पारं प्रयाते रवा-
वास्थानीं समये समं नृपजनः सायंतने संपतन्।
संप्रत्येष सरोरुहद्युतिमुषः पादांस्तवासेवितुं
प्रीत्युत्कर्षकृतो दृशामुदयनस्येन्दोरिवोद्वीक्षते॥ २३॥

(क) अज्ज वसन्तअ एहि संपदं तुमं वि सोत्थिवाअणं पडिच्छ। (ख) अज्ज सोत्थिवाअणं पडिच्छ। (ग) सोत्थि भोदीए।

नानन्तराङ्कप्रकृतनिर्विघ्नदर्शनारंभणात्करणं नाम मुखसन्धेरङ्गं दर्शितम्। आर्य–विदूषकस्य ब्राह्मणत्वादार्येति सम्बुद्धिः। आर्येति ब्राह्मणं ब्रूयादिति भरतः। प्रतीच्छ गृहाण। वैतालिकः विविधश्चासौ तालश्च वितालस्तेन चरतीति वैतालिकः। चरति इति ठक्। वितालः प्रयोजनमस्य। प्रयोजनम् इति ठञ् वा। **अस्तेत्यादि**। अस्ते अस्ताचले अपास्ताः निक्षिप्ताः समस्ताः भासः किरणा येन तादृशे रवौ नभसः पारं प्रयाते। सायंतने सायंभवे। सायंचिरमित्यादिना ट्युप्रत्ययस्तुडागमश्च। समये आस्थानीं राजसभाम्। आतिष्ठन्त्यस्यामिति आस्थानी। अधिकरणे ल्युट् टित्वान्ङीप्। सम्पतन् युगपत्प्राप्नुवन् एष पुरोदृश्यमानः नृपजनः सम्प्रति अधुना दृशां नयनानां प्रीत्युत्कर्षकृतः प्रीतेः आनन्दस्य उत्कर्षोऽतिशयस्तं करोतीति तस्य। उद् ऊर्ध्वमयनं गमनं यस्य तस्य उदयनस्य उदयमानस्येत्यर्थः। इन्दोश्चन्द्रस्य सरोरुहद्युतिमुषः सरोरुहाणां पद्मानां द्युतिं कान्तिं मुष्णन्ति हरन्तीति तथोक्तान्। चन्द्रोदये तेषां निमीलनात्। पादान् मयूखान् इव दृशां प्रीत्युत्कर्षकृतः। सम्यक्पालनेन प्रजानामानन्दजननादिति भावः। उदयनस्य एतन्नामकनृपतेस्तव। उदेष्यमाणस्येत्यपि ध्वनिः। सरोरुहद्युतिमुषः कमलतुल्यकान्तीन् पादानासेवितुमुद्वीक्षते उन्मुखः प्रतीक्षते इत्यर्थः। श्लेषाश्रय उपमालंकारः अनुप्रासश्च। शार्दूलविक्रीडितं वृत्तम्। अत्र वैतालिकमुखेन चन्द्रतुल्यवत्सराजगुणवर्णनया सागरिकायाः समागमहेत्वनुरागबीजानुगुण्येनैव विलोभनाद्विलोभनमिति। तथा च कुसुमायुधव्यपदेशगूढस्य वत्सराजस्यात्र उदयनस्येत्यनेन उद्भेदनाद् उद्भेद इति च मुखसन्धेरङ्गद्वयमुक्तम्॥ २३॥ कथमिति विस्मये। परस्य

---

१ ०मामि गृहीत्वा. २ ०लिकैः पठ्यते. ३ स्येव. ४ ०मुखः. ५ प्रत्यु०, कृतां दृशां, कृतो दृशां. ६ अज्ज एदं सो०; अज्ज वसन्तअ गहाण इदं सोत्थि०.

सागरिका—(श्रुत्वा[1] सहर्षं परिवृत्य राजानं सस्पृहं पश्यन्ती ।) कथमयं स राजा उदयनो यस्याहं तातेन दत्ता । (दीर्घं निःश्वस्य ।) तत्परप्रेषणदूषितमपि मे जीवितमेतस्य दर्शनेनेदानीं बहुमतं संवृत्तम् । (क)

राजा—अये[2] कथमुत्सवापहृतचेतोभिः[3] संध्यातिक्रमोऽप्यस्माभिर्नोपलक्षितैः[4] । संप्रति परिणतमहः[5] । देवि[6] पश्य ।

उदयतटान्तरितमियं[7] प्राची सूचयति दिङ्निशानाथम् ।
परिपाण्डुना मुखेन प्रियमिव हृदयस्थितं रमणी[8] ॥ २४ ॥

देवि तदुत्तिष्ठ[9] । आवासाभ्यन्तरमेव प्रविशावः । (सर्वे उत्थाय[10] परिक्रामन्ति ।)

सागरिका—कथं प्रस्थिता देवी । भवतु तदहमपि त्वरितं गमिष्यामि । (राजानं[11] सस्पृहं दृष्ट्वा । निःश्वस्य ।) हा धिक् हा धिक् । मन्दभागिन्या मया प्रेक्षितुमपि चिरं न पारितोऽयं जनः । (इति[12] राजानं पश्यन्ती निष्क्रान्ता ।) (ख)

(क) कहं अअं सो राआ उदअणो[13] जस्स अहं तादेण दिण्णा । ता परप्पेसण[14]दूसिदं पि मे जीविदं एदस्स दंसणेण दाणिं बहुमतं संवुत्तम् । (ख) कधं पत्थिदो[15] देवी । भोदु । ता अहंवि तुरिदं गमिस्सम् । हद्धी[16] हद्धी । मन्दभाइणीए मए पेक्खिदुमपि चिरं न पारिदो अअं जणो ।

प्रेषणं प्रेरणं पराज्ञानुष्ठानमिति यावत् । तेन दूषितम् । अत्र सागरिकायाः सुखागमाप्राप्तिरूपं मुखसन्धेरङ्गम् । उत्सवेनापहृतमाकृष्टं चेतो येषां तैः । अन्यत्किंचिदचेतयद्भिरित्यर्थः । **उदयेत्यादि** । रमणी विरहिणीति शेषः । परिपाण्डुना मुखेन हृदयस्थितं प्रियमिव प्रियं यथा सूचयति तथा इयं प्राची दिग् उदयस्य उदयाचलस्य तटेन अन्तरितं छन्नं निशानाथं चन्द्रं सूचयति । उपमालंकारः । आर्या ॥ २४ ॥

---

१ आकर्ण्य सोद्वेगम्; दृष्ट्वा सलज्जम्. २ (ऊर्ध्वमवलोक्य, सर्वतोऽवलोक्य ।) अये. ३ चेतसा...क्रमो मया. ४ परिकल्पितः. ५ नास्त्येतत्क्वाचित्. ६ तथा हि. ७ उदयगिरितटान्तरितं–तटस्थगितं–प्राची. ८ तरुणी. ९ तदेहि; तदुत्तिष्ठावः. १० उत्तिष्ठन्ति. ११ इति राजानं विलोक्य सकरुणं निःश्वस्य; राजानं सस्पृहमालोकयन्ती नि०. १२ इति निष्क्रान्ता; साभिलाषमालोकयन्ती नि०. १३ ०अनो वत्सराअ. १४ पोसण. १५ गदा देवी ता तुरिदं एव्व; उट्ठिदा देवी । अहं वि तुरिदं. १६ कथं मन्द०; णं मए मन्दभाअधेआए चिरं पेक्खिदुं ण पारिदं; कथं मन्दभाआए अदिचिरं पेक्खिदुं ण पारिअदि.

राजा—(परिक्रामन् ।)

देवि त्वन्मुखपङ्कजेन शशिनः शोभातिरस्कारिणा
पश्याब्जानि विनिर्जितानि सहसा गच्छन्ति विच्छायताम् ।
श्रुत्वा त्वत्परिवारवारवनितागीतानि भृङ्गाङ्गना
लीयन्ते मुकुलान्तरेषु शनकैः संजातलज्जा इव ॥ २५ ॥

(इति निष्क्रान्ताः सर्वे ।)

इति मदनमहोत्सवो नाम प्रथमोऽङ्कः ।

आवासाभ्यन्तरं गृहान्तर्भागम् । देवीति । हे देवि पश्य । अब्जानि शशिनः शोभातिरस्कारिणा शोभां श्रियं तिरस्करोति प्रत्यादिशतीति तेन । सुप्यजातौ णिनिः इति णिनिः । तव मुखमेव पङ्कजं तेन त्वन्मुखपङ्कजेन विनिर्जितानि अभिभूतानि सन्ति । सहसा अकस्मात् । विगता छाया कान्तिर्येषां तानि विच्छायानि तेषां भावो विच्छायता तां गच्छन्ति । परतिरस्कृतिजन्यविमनस्कतयेति भावः । तथा च तव परिवाराश्च ताः वारवनिताः गणिकाश्च तासां गीतानि श्रुत्वा भृङ्गाङ्गना भ्रमर्यः संजातलज्जा इव शनकैः मुकुलानां कमलकुड्मलानामन्तरेषु गर्भेषु लीयन्ते गूढास्तिष्ठन्ति । अत्र प्रतीपहेत्वलंकारयोरुत्प्रेक्षया संकरः । शार्दूलविक्रीडितं छन्दः ॥ २५ ॥ निष्क्रान्ताः सर्वे- तदुक्तं दशरूपके । एकाहाचरितैकार्थमित्थमासन्ननायकम् । पात्रैस्त्रिचतुरैरङ्कं तेषामन्तेऽस्य निर्गमः ॥ इति ॥ इति रत्नावलीटीकायां प्रथमोऽङ्कः ॥ १ ॥

---

१ छाया०. २ ते. ३ कुसुमा०. ४ प्रथमोऽङ्कः समाप्तः; रत्नावलीनामप्रधाननाटिकायां प्र०.

द्वितीयोऽङ्कः ।

(ततः प्रविशति सारिकापञ्जरव्यग्रहस्ता सुसंगता ।)

सुसंगता—हा धिक् हा धिक् । कुत्रेदानीं मम हस्ते सारिकापञ्जरं निक्षिप्य गता मे प्रियसखी सागरिका । तत्क पुनरेनां प्रेक्षिष्ये । (अग्रतोऽवलोक्य ।) कथमेषा खलु निपुणिकेत एवागच्छति । तद्यावदेनां प्रक्ष्यामि । (क)

(ततः प्रविशति निपुणिका ।)

निपुणिका—(सविस्मयम् ।) आश्चर्यमाश्चर्यम् । अनन्यसदृशः प्रभावो मन्ये देवतायाः । उपलब्धः खलु मया भर्तुर्वृत्तान्तः । तद्गत्वा भट्टिन्यै निवेदयिष्यामि । (इति परिक्रामति ।) (ख)

सुसं०—(उपसृत्य ।) सखि निपुणिके क्वेदानीं त्वं विस्मयोत्क्षिप्तहृदयेव इह स्थितां मामवधीर्येतोऽतिक्रामसि । (ग)

निपु०—कथं सुसंगता । हला सुसंगते सुष्ठु त्वया ज्ञातम् । एतत्खलु मम विस्मयस्य कारणम् । अद्य किल भर्ता श्रीपर्वतादागतस्य श्रीखण्डदासनामधेयस्य धार्मिकस्य सकाशादकालकुसुमसंजननदोहदं शिक्षि-

---

(क) हद्धी हद्धी । कहिं दाणिं मम हत्थे सारिआपञ्जरं णिक्खिविअ गदा मे पिअसही साअरिआ । तां कहिं पुण एणं पेक्खिस्सम् । कहं एसा खु णिउणिआ इदो ज्जेव आअच्छदि । ता जाव एदं पुच्छिस्सम् । (ख) अच्चरिअं अच्चरिअं । अणण्णसदिसो पभावो मण्णे देवदाए । उवलद्धो खु मए भट्टिणो वुत्तन्तो । ता गदुअ भट्टिणीए णिवेदइस्सम् । (ग) सहि णिउणिए कहिं दाणिं तुमं विम्हओक्खित्तहिअआ विअ इह ठिदं मं अवधीरिअ इदो अदिक्कामसि ।

अथ प्रथमाङ्कोपक्षिप्तस्य सागरिकाया वत्सराजदर्शनोत्पन्नस्य रत्याविर्भावस्योचितविभावानुभावादिभिः परिपोषार्थं परस्ताद्ग्रन्थमारभमाणः कविर्द्वितीयाङ्के नायिकायाः सागरिकायाः प्रवेशसूचनार्थमादौ प्रवेशकमारभते—**तत** इत्यादिना । सारिकायाः पञ्जरे व्यग्र आसक्तः हस्तो यस्याः सा सारिकापञ्जरव्यग्रहस्ता । अवधीर्य विगणय्य । अनालोक्य अतिक्रम्य पुरस्ताद्गमनादिति भावः । कथमिति सम्भ्रमे अकस्माद्दर्शनात् । श्रीपर्वतः श्रीशैलः । धर्मं चरतीति धार्मिकः साधुः । ठक् प्रत्ययः । योग्यादन्यः कालः अकालः । तदन्यत्वं नञर्थः । अकाले यत्कुसुमानां

---

१ गृहीतपञ्जरा. २ निरूप्य. ३ सहर्षम्; अस्मादारभ्य 'मन्ये देवतायाः' इत्यन्तः ग्रन्थः नास्ति क्वचित्. ४ अथ कहिं, कहिं उण. ५ ०आ भविस्सदि. ६ भोदु अण्णेस्सम्मि. ७ एदं पडिवालिअ (प्रतिपाल्य) पु०. ८ गदुअ जाव. ९ हला. १० गुरुअविम्हअक्खित्त. ११ पिअसही वि मं. १२ कुदो; अण्णदो गच्छसि.

त्वात्मनः परिगृहीतां नवमालिकां कुसुमसमृद्धिशोभितां करिष्यतीति। तत्रैतं वृत्तान्तं ज्ञातुं देव्या प्रेषितास्मि। त्वं पुनः कुत्र प्रस्थिता। (क)

सुसंगता—प्रियसखीं सागरिकामन्वेष्टुम्। (ख)

निपुणिका—सखि दृष्टा मया ते प्रियसखी सागरिका गृहीतचित्रफलकवर्तिकासमुद्गका समुद्विग्नेव कदलीगृहं प्रविशन्ती। तद्गच्छ त्वम्। अहमपि देव्याः सकाशं गमिष्यामि। (ग)

(निष्क्रान्ते।)

प्रवेशकः।

(ततः प्रविशति गृहीतचित्रफलकवर्तिका मदनावस्थां नाटयन्ती सागरिका।)

सागरिका—(निःश्वस्य।) हृदय प्रसीद प्रसीद। किमनेनायासमात्रफलेन दुर्लभजनप्रार्थनानुबन्धेन। अन्यच्च। येनैव दृष्टेन त ईदृशः

(क) कधं सुसंगदा। हला सुसंगदे सुठ्ठ तुए जाणिदं। एदं क्खु मम विम्हअस्स काअणम्। अज्ज किल भट्टा सिरिपव्वतादो आअदस्स सिरिखण्डदासणामधेअस्स धम्मिअस्स सआसादो अकालकुसुमसंजणणदोहलअं सिक्खिअ अत्तणो पडिगिहीदं णोमालिअं कुसुमसमिद्धिसोहिदं करिस्सदित्ति। तहिं एदं वुत्तान्तं जाणिदुं देवीए पेसिदम्हि। तुमं उण कहिं पत्थिदा। (ख) पिअसहिं साअरिअं अण्णेसिदुम्। (ग) सहि दिट्ठा मए दे पिअसही साअरिआ गहिदचित्तफलकवत्तिआसमुग्गआ समुव्विग्गा विअ कदलीघरअं पविसन्ती। ता गच्छ तुमं। अहं पि देवीए सआसं गमिस्सम्।

संजननमुत्पत्तिः तस्य। दोहं ददातीति दोहदः। आतोऽनुपसर्गे कः इति कः। पुष्पोत्पत्तिसाधनं किंचित्। तम्। तरुगुल्मलतादीनामकाले कुशलैः कृतम्। पुष्पाद्युत्पादकं द्रव्यं दोहदं स्यात्तु तत्क्रिया॥ इति शब्दार्णवः। कुसुमानां समृद्धिः विपुलता तया शोभिताम्। गृहीतः चित्रफलकः वर्तिका तूलिका तस्याः समुद्गकः संपुटकः च यया सा तथोक्ता। समुद्विग्ना विमनस्का। **प्रवेशक** इति। एतल्लक्षणं—प्रवेशकोऽनुदात्तोक्त्या नीचपात्रप्रयोजितः। अङ्कद्वयान्तर्विज्ञेयः शेषं विष्कम्भके यथा॥ इति। **हृदय प्रसीदेति**। इतः प्रतिमुखसन्धिः। अत्र वत्सराजसागरिकासमागमहेतोरनुरागबीजस्य प्रथमाङ्कोपक्षिप्तस्य सुसङ्गताविदूषकाभ्यां ज्ञायमानतया किंचिल्लक्ष्यस्य वासवदत्तया च चित्रफलकवृत्तान्तेन किंचिदुन्नीयमानस्य दृश्यादृश्यरूपतयोद्भेदः प्रतिमुखसन्धिः। इति दशरूपकम्। आयासः खेद एव आयासमात्रम्। मयूरव्यंसकादिः। तत्फलं

---

१ इति, उभे, नि०. २ शत्युपविष्टा मद०. ३ सकरुणं नि०. ४ (विलोक्य।) कहं. ५ कण्ट, खण्डदास०. ६ ०अ तेण. ७ ०स्सदि। ता तुमं दाणिं कहिं प०. ८ सहि; हला णिउणिए पिअ०. ९ दिट्ठा मए साअ०. १० ०रिआ. सुसं०—कहिं. निपु०—दिट्ठा गहीद. ११ गच्छ पिअसहीं, ०सआसं एव्व; ता गच्छदु पिअसही। अहं वि एदं वुत्तन्तं गदुअ देवीए णिवेदेम्हि. १२ गच्छामि.

संतापो ननु वर्धते तमेव पुनरपि प्रेक्षितुमभिलषसीत्यहो ते मूढता । कथं चातिनृशंस जन्मतः प्रभृति सहसंवर्धितमिमं जनं परित्यज्य क्षणमात्रदर्शनपरिचितं जनमनुगच्छन्न लज्जसे । अथ वा कस्तव दोषः । अनङ्गशरपतनभीतेन त्वयैवमद्य न्यवसितम् । (सास्रम्[1]।) भवतु । अनङ्गं तावदुपालप्स्ये । (अञ्जलिं बद्ध्वा[2]।) भगवन्कुसुमायुध निर्जितसकलसुरासुरो भूत्वा स्त्रीजनं प्रहरन्कथं न लज्जसे । (विचिन्त्य ।) अथ वा अनङ्गोऽसि । (दीर्घं निःश्वस्य ।) सर्वथा मम मन्दभागिन्या मरणमेवानेन दुर्निमित्तेनोपस्थितम् । (फलकमवलोक्य ।) तद्यावन्न कोऽपीहागच्छति तावदालेख्यसमर्पितं तमभिमतं जनं प्रेक्ष्य यथासमीहितं करिष्यामि । (सावष्टम्भमेकमना भूत्वा नाट्येन फलकं गृहीत्वा[3] निःश्वस्य ।) यद्यपि मेऽतिसाध्वसेन वेपते अयमतिमात्रमग्रहस्तस्तथापि नास्ति तस्य जनस्यान्यो दर्शनोपाय इति यथातथालिख्यैनं प्रेक्षिष्ये । (इति नाट्येन लिखति ।) (क)

(क) हिअअ पसीद[4] पसीद । किं इमिणा आआसमेत्तफलेण दुल्लहजणप्पत्थणाणुबन्धेण । अण्णं च । जेण एव्व दिट्ठेण[5] दे ईदिसो संतावो णु वड्ढदि[6] तं एव्व पुणो वि पेक्खिदुं अहिलससित्ति अहो दे मूढदा[7] । कहं अ अदिनिसंस[8] जम्मदो पहुदि सहसंवड्ढिदं ईमं जणं परिच्चइअ[9] खणमेत्तदंसणपरिचिदं जणं अणुगच्छन्तो ण लज्जसि । अह वा को तुह दोसो । अणङ्गसरपडणभीदेण[10] तुए एव्वं अज्ज ववसिदम्[11] । भोदु । अणङ्गं दाव उबालहिस्सं[12] । भअवं कुसुमाउह निज्जिअसअलसुरासुरो भविअ इत्थि[13]आजणं पहरन्तो कधं ण लज्जसि । अह वा अणङ्गोसि । सव्वहा[14] मम मन्दभाइणीए मरणं एव्व इमिणा दुण्णिमित्तेण उवत्थिदम् । ता जाव ण को वि इह आअच्छदि ताव आलेक्खसमप्पिदं[15] तं अहिमदं जणं पेक्खिअ जहासमीहिदं करिस्सम्[16] । जइ वि

यस्य स आयासमात्रफलस्तेन । दुर्लभश्चासौ जनश्च दुर्लभजनः वत्सराजरूपः तस्य प्रार्थना अभिलाष इति यावत् । तस्या अनुबन्धः तेन । क्षणमेव क्षणमात्रं क्षणमात्रं यद्दर्शनं तेन परिचितस्तम् । व्यवसितमाचरितम् । उपालप्स्ये दोषं दास्यामि इत्यर्थः । निर्जिताः सकलाः सुरा असुराश्च येन स तथोक्तः । **अनङ्गोऽसीति** । अतः शरीरराहित्यादन्तःकरणाभावादुचित एव ते लज्जाभाव इत्याशयः । मन्दः भागोऽस्या अस्तीति मन्दभागिनी दुर्भाग्या तस्याः । यथासमीहितं समीहितमनतिक्रम्य वर्तते इति ।

---

१ सास्रा, सास्रमञ्जलिं बद्ध्वा. २ बद्ध्वा जानुभ्यां स्थित्वा. ३ ०त्वाग्रहस्तकम्पं नाटयन्ती नि०. ४ समस्सस समस्सस. ५ ०ण अअं. ६ ०दि (सविस्मयं) पुणो वि तं एव्व. ७ ०दा णिल्लज्जदा अ. ८ अइ णिसंस हिअअ. ९ मं परि...अण्णं जणं. १० परिहरिअ. ११ खण्डण. १२ अज्झवसिदं (अध्यवसितं). १३ इत्थिजणे. १४ सव्वहा मरणं एव्व मे इमिणा णि०. १५ अवस्सं म०. १६ ०क्खगदं तं जणं कदुअ.

(ततः प्रविशति सुसंगता ।)

सुसं०—एतत्तत्कदलीगृहम् । तत्प्रविशामि । (प्रविश्याग्रतो विलोक्य सविस्मयम् ।) एषा मे प्रियसखी सागरिका । किं पुनरेषा गुरुकानुरागोत्क्षिप्तहृदयेव किमप्यालिखन्ती न मां प्रेक्षते । भवतु । तद्यावदस्या दृष्टिपथं परिहृत्य निरूपयिष्यामि किमेषालिखतीति । (स्वैरं पृष्ठतोऽस्याः स्थित्वा दृष्ट्वा सहर्षम् ।) कथं भर्तालिखितः । साधु सागरिके साधु । अथ वा न कमलाकरं वर्जयित्वा राजहंस्यन्यत्राभिरमते । (क)

साग०—आलिखितः खलु मयैषः । किं पुनरनवरतनिपतद्बाष्पसलिलेन न मे दृष्टिः प्रेक्षितुं प्रभवति । (मुखमुत्तानीकृत्याश्रूणि निवारयन्ती सुसंगतां दृष्ट्वोत्तरीयेण फलकं प्रच्छादयन्ती सविलक्षस्मितम् ।) कथं प्रियसखी सुसंगता । सखि इत उपविश । (ख)

सुसं०—(उपविश्य बलात्फलकमाकृष्य ।) सखि क एष त्वयात्रालिखितः । (ग)

मे अदिसद्धसेण वेवदि अअं अतिमेत्तं अग्गहत्थो तहा वि णत्थि तस्स जणस्स अण्णो दंसणोवाओ त्ति जहातहा आलिहिअ णं पेक्खिस्सम् ।

(क) एँदं तं कदलीहरअम् । ता पविसामि । एसा मे पिअसही साअरिआ । किं उँण एसा गुरुआणुराओक्खित्तहिअआ विअ किंवि आलिहन्ती ण मं पेक्खदि । भोदु । ता जाव से दिट्ठिपहं परिहरिअ णिरूवइस्सं किं एसा आलिहदित्ति । कहं भट्टा आलिहिदो । साधु साअरिए साधु । अह वा ण कमलाअरं वज्जिअ राअहंसी अण्णस्सिं अहिरमदि । (ख) आलिहिदो खु मए एसो । किं उण अणवरदणिवडन्तबाप्फसलिलेण ण मे दिट्ठी पेक्खिदुं पभवति । कहं पिअसही सुसंगदा । सहि इदो उवविश । (ग) सहि को एसो तुए एत्थ आलिहिदो ।

अग्रश्चासौ हस्तश्च अग्रहस्तः इति समानाधिकरणः समासः । अवयवावयविनोरभेदात्सामानाधिकरण्यम् । हस्ताग्राग्रहस्तयोर्गुणगुणिनोर्भेदाभेदात् इति वामनः । यथातथा यथाकथंचित् । भर्ता उदयन इत्यर्थः । न कमलाकरमित्यादि । वत्सराज एवोचितस्तवानुराग इति भावः । अनवरतं यथा तथा निपतद्बाष्पसलिलं तेन । हेतौ तृतीया । ०सलिलेति पाठे ०सलिलं यस्याः सा तथोक्ता । उत्तानीकृत्य ऊर्ध्वं कृत्वा ।

---

१ प्रवेशं नाटयति । अग्र०; प्रविश्यावलोक्य, प्रविश्य सागरिकां दृष्ट्वा. २ पश्यति. ३ विधारयन्ती, संहरन्ती; उत्तानीकृत्य सुसंगतां दृष्ट्वा मुखं परावृत्याश्रूणि सारयन्ती उत्तरीयेण फलकं पिधातुमिच्छन्ती सलज्जा. ४ स्मितं कृत्वा. ५ ०कं गृहीत्वा दृष्ट्वा च; (उपविश्यात्मगतं) कहं मं पेक्खिअ फलहको छादिदो; एसा मं पेक्खिअ विलक्खा होदि; एवं दाव । (प्रकाशं; फलकं गृहीत्वा दृष्ट्वा प्रकाशं) सहि दंसहि (दर्शय) को उण-आलिहिदो । कहं ण सुणादि । हला पिअसहि णं भणामि साअरिए को एसो तुए आलिहिदोत्ति । ६ तं जहा० आलिखिस्सम्. ७ एदं क्खु. ८ अध पुण एसा गुरुअरा(तरा)णुराअखिन्न०; समीवगदं वि मं. ९ भोदु भोदु । दिट्ठि० से. १० एसाए भट्टा. ११ एत्थ चित्तफलए.

साग०—(सलज्जम्।) सखि प्रवृत्तमदनमहोत्सवे भगवाननङ्गः। (क)

सुसं०—(सस्मितम्।) अहो ते निपुणत्वम्। किं पुनः शून्यमिवैतच्चित्रं प्रतिभाति। तदहमप्यालिख्य रतिसनाथं करिष्यामि। (वर्तिकां गृहीत्वा नाट्येन रतिव्यपदेशेन सागरिकां लिखति।) (ख)

साग०—(विलोक्य सासूयम्।) सुसंगते कस्मात्त्वयाहमत्रालिखिता। (ग)

सुसं०—(विहस्य।) सखि किमकारणं कुप्यसि। यादृशस्त्वया कामदेव आलिखितस्तादृशी मया रतिरालिखिता। तदन्यथासंभाविनि किं तवैतेनालपितेन। कथय तावत्सर्वं वृत्तान्तम्। (घ)

साग०—(सलज्जा स्वगतम्।) ननु ज्ञातास्मि प्रियसख्या। (सुसंगतां हस्ते गृहीत्वा प्रकाशम्।) प्रियसखि महती खलु मे लज्जा। तत्तथा कुरु यथा न कोऽप्यपर एतं वृत्तान्तं जानाति। (ङ)

सुसं०—सखि मा लज्जस्व। ईदृशस्य कन्यारत्नस्यावश्यमेवेदृशो वरे अभिलाषेण भवितव्यम्। तथापि यथा न कोऽप्यपर एतं वृत्तान्तं ज्ञास्यति

(**क**) सहि पउत्तमअणमहूसवे भअवं अणङ्गो। (**ख**) अहो दे णिउणत्तणम्। किं पुण सुण्णं विअ एदं चित्तं पॅडिभादि। ता अहं पि आलिहिअ रतिसणाहं करिस्सम्। (**ग**) सुसंगदे कीस तुए अहं एत्थ आलिहिदा। (**घ**) सैहि किं अआरणं कुप्पसि। जादिसो तुए कामदेवो आलिहिदो तादिसी मए रइ आलिहिदा। ता अँण्णधासम्भाविणि किं तुए एदिणा आलबिदेण। कहेहिं दाव सव्वं वुत्तन्तम्। (**ङ**) णं जाणिदम्हि पिअसहीए। पिअसहि महदी खु मे लज्जा। ता तहा करेसु जहा ण को वि अवरो एदं वुत्तन्तं जाणेदि।

अकारणे असति कारण इत्यर्थः। अविद्यमानं कारणं यस्मिन् तदकारणं तस्मिन् विषये। अकारणमिति पाठः साधीयान्। अन्यथा वास्तवादन्यप्रकारेण सम्भावयति कल्पयति इति उपपदसमासः। सुप्यजातौ इति णिनिः। ज्ञातास्मि मदनकृतैवेयं ममावस्था इति ज्ञातमिति तात्पर्यम्। ईदृशस्य त्यदादिषु इत्यादिना इदंशब्दे उपपदे दृशेः कञ्-

---

१ (विचिन्त्य फलकं दर्शयन्ती) सहि पउत्ते इ०. २ फलकं गृहीत्वा नाट्येन लिखति. ३ निर्वर्ण्य; सासूयं-सक्रोधं, सलज्जम्. ४ सुसंगताया हस्तं; प्रका०-सास्रम्. ५ पेक्खामि; एदं आलिहिदं. ६ सहि मा कुप्प।...तुए अअं काम०—रइत्ति. ७ अण्णसम्भा०; असम्भाविणि (असद्भाविनि) किं इमिणा। कहेहि दाव एतं; इमिणा सम्भमेण; सव्वं-सच्चं. ८ तं जाणिदं ज्जेव (तज्ज्ञातमेव).

तथा करोमि। एतया पुनर्मेधाविन्या सारिकयात्र कारणेन भवितव्यम्। कदाप्येषास्यालापस्य गृहीताक्षरा भूत्वा कस्यापि पुरतो मन्त्रयिष्यते। (क)

साग०—तत्किमिदानीमत्र करिष्यामि। अतोऽप्यधिकतरं मे संतापो वर्धते। (मदनावस्थां नाटयति।) (ख)

सुसं०—(सागरिकाया हृदये हस्तं दत्वा।) सखि समाश्वसिहि समाश्वसिहि। यावदस्या दीर्घिकाया नलिनीपत्राणि मृणालिकाश्च गृहीत्वा लघ्वागच्छामि। (निष्क्रम्य पुनः प्रविश्य च नाट्येन नलिनीपत्रैः शयनीयं मृणालैर्वलयानि च रचयित्वा परिशिष्टानि नलिनीपत्राणि सागरिकाया हृदये निक्षिपति।) (ग)

साग०—सखि अपनयेमानि नलिनीपत्राणि मृणालवलयानि च। अलमेतैः। किमित्यकारण आत्मानमायासयसि। ननु भणामि। (घ)

(क) सहि मा लज्ज। ईदिसस्स कण्णाँरैअणस्स अवस्सं एव्व ईदिसे वरे अहिलासेण होदव्वम्। तँहवि जहा ण कोवि अवरो एदं वुत्तन्तं जाणिस्सदि तह करेमि। एदाए उण मेधाविणीए सारिआए एत्थ काअणेण होदव्वम्। कदा वि एसा इमस्स आलावस्स गहिदक्खरा भविअ कस्स वि पुरओ मन्तइस्सदि। (ख) ताँ किं दाणिं एत्थ करइँस्सम्। अँदोवि अहिअदरं मे संतावो वड्ढैदि। (ग) सहि समस्सस समस्सस। जाव इमाओ दिग्घिआओ णलिणीवत्ताइं मुणालिआओ अ गिण्हिअ लहुं आअच्छामि। (घ) सहि अवणेहि इमाइं णलिणीवत्ताइं मुणालवलआइं अ। अलं एदेहिं। कीस अआरणे अत्ताणं आआसेसि। णं भणामि।

प्रत्ययः। इदंकिमोरीश्की इत्यनेनेशादेशः। प्रशस्ता मेधास्त्यस्या इति मेधाविनी धीर्धारणावती मेधा इत्यमरः। अत्र एतद्रहस्यप्रकाशने। अस्यास्मत्कृतस्य आलापस्य भाषणस्य गृहीतान्यक्षराणि। न त्वर्थः। यया। दीर्घिकाया वाप्याः। मृणाली बिसं एव मृणालिका। स्वार्थे कन् ततः टाप्। यद्यपि मृणालशब्दो बहुशो मृणालमिति नपुंसके उपलभ्यते तथापि क्वचित् स्त्रियामपि प्रयुज्यते। लघु शीघ्रम्। मृणालवलयानि—क्वचित् मृणालकानि इति पाठः। मृणालिकानीति पाठे क्वचित्स्वार्थिकाः प्रकृतितो लिङ्गवचनान्यतिवर्तन्ते इति न्यायेन समाधेयम्। तव श्रम आयासमात्रफलः स्यादिति

---

१ सन्तापं. २ (परिक्रम्य तथा कृत्वा नलिनीपत्रैरास्तरणं रचयित्वा सागरिकाया हृदये तानि दत्वा) समस्सदु समस्ससदु पिअसही। ३ कण्णआ. ४ ता ण...स्सदि। किं पुण एदाए मे० सा० सङ्किदव्वं; किंदु एसा मे० सा-सङ्किदव्वा. ५ नास्त्ये० पुस्तकान्तरे. ६ सहि सावसेसं संदावो बाहदि। (इति मूर्च्छां नाटयति). ७ बाधेदि. ८ (तानि क्षिपन्ती।) ता सहि अ० मे णलि० मुणालिआओ (मृणालिकाः) अ। एदेहिं अआ० अत्ताणअं सहि किं आआसेसि। भण्णं भ०.

दुर्लभजनानुरागो लज्जा गुर्वी परवश आत्मा ।
प्रियसखि विषमं प्रेम मरणं शरणं न वरमेकम् ॥ १ ॥ (क)

(इति मूर्च्छति ।)

सुसं०—(सकरुणम् ।) सखि सागरिके समाश्वसिहि समाश्वसिहि । (ख)

(नेपथ्ये ।)

कण्ठे कृत्तावशेषं कनकमयमधः शृङ्खलादाम कर्ष-
न्क्रान्त्वा द्वाराणि हेलाचलचरणरणत्किंकिणीचक्रवालः ।
दत्तातङ्कोऽङ्गनानामनुसृतसरणिः संभ्रमादश्वपालैः
प्रभ्रष्टोऽयं प्लवङ्गः प्रविशति नृपतेर्मन्दिरं मन्दुरायाः ॥ २ ॥

अपि च ।

नष्टं वर्षवरैर्मनुष्यगणनाभावादपास्य त्रपा-
मन्तः कञ्चुकिकञ्चुकस्य विशति त्रासादयं वामनः ।

(क) दुल्लहजणाणुराओ लज्जा गुरुई परव्वसो अप्पा ।
पिअसहि विसमं पेम्मं मरणं सरणं न वरमेक्कम् ॥

(ख) सहि साअरिए समस्सस समस्सस ।

यदुक्तं तदेव विशदयति–**दुर्लभ इति** । दुःखेन लभ्यत इति दुर्लभः दुष्प्रापः । दुर्लभश्चासौ जनश्च तस्मिन् अनुरागः । अतः ईदृशैरुपायैर्मम तापापनोदनमशक्यमिति भावः । एवं चेत्तमुपगम्य किमित्यात्मनः प्रेम नाविष्क्रियते इत्यत्राह–लज्जा गुर्वीति । तथापि लेखप्रेषणादिना तत्प्राप्त्युपायः कर्तव्य इति चेन्नेत्याह । यतः परस्य वासवदत्तायाः इत्यर्थः वशः परवशः आत्मा शरीरम् । एवं हे प्रियसखि ममैतत्प्रेमानुरागः विषमं विपरीतम् । अतः एकं केवलं मरणं वरं शरणमाश्रयः न किमिति शेषः । यद्वा नवरमित्येकं पदम् । नास्ति वरं यस्मात्तन्नवरं मरणमेकं शरणं रक्षितृ । नशब्देन समासः । नान्यदित्यर्थः ॥ १ ॥ **कण्ठ इति** । मन्दुराया अश्वशालायाः प्रभ्रष्टः निर्गतः । अश्वपालैः संभ्रमात्त्वरया अनुसृता अनुगता सरणिः मार्गः यस्य सः अनुसृतसरणिः । अयं प्लवंगः वानरः कण्ठे स्थितं कृत्तस्य शेषमवशिष्टं कनकस्य विकारः कनकमयं सुवर्णघटितं कनकप्रचुरं वा शृङ्खलाया दाम अधः कर्षन् । हेलया लीलया चलाः चञ्चला ये चरणाः तेषु रणत् शब्दायमानं किंकिणीनां क्षुद्रघंटिकानां चक्रवालं मण्डलं यस्य तथाभूतः । द्वाराणि क्रान्त्वा अतिक्रम्य अङ्गनानां स्त्रीणां दत्तः आतङ्कः भयं येन तथाविधः सन् नृपतेः मन्दिरं भवनं प्रविशति । स्वभावोक्तिरलंकारः । स्रग्धरा छन्दः ॥ २ ॥ **नष्टमिति** । वर्षवरैः षण्ढैः । मनुष्यगणनाभावात् मनुष्येषु गणना अन्तर्भावः तस्याभावो विरहः । पुंस्त्वस्त्रीत्वाभावादित्यर्थः । तस्मात् त्रपां लज्जामपास्य नष्टं विद्रुतम् । अयं पुरोवर्ती वामनः खर्वः त्रासात् वानरभयात्

---

१ भूमौ पतति. २ नेपथ्ये कलकलः. ३ कृत्वाव०. ४ लीला. ५ ०वालम्. ६ नष्टाः-ङ्ग०. ७ पुनस्तत्रैव. ८ धरैः. ९ ०दङ्कृत्वा.

पर्यन्ताश्रयिभिर्निजस्य सदृशं नाम्नः किरातैः कृतं
कुब्जा नीचतयैव यान्ति शनकैरात्मेक्षणाशङ्किनः ॥ ३ ॥

सुसं०—(आकर्ण्याग्रतोऽवलोक्य ससंभ्रममुत्थाय सागरिकां हस्ते गृहीत्वा ।) सखि उत्तिष्ठोत्तिष्ठ । एष खलु दुष्टवानर इत एवागच्छति । तदलक्षितं तमालविटपान्धकारे प्रविश्यैनमतिवाहयावः । (तथा कृत्वा उभे सभयं पश्यन्त्यौ स्थिते ।) (क)

साग०—सुसंगते कथं त्वया चित्रफलक उज्झितः । कदापि कोऽपि तं प्रेक्षते । (ख)

सुसं०—अयि सुस्थिते किमद्यापि चित्रफलकेन करिष्यसि । एष खलु दधिभक्तलम्पटो सारिकापञ्जरमुद्घाट्यापक्रान्तो दुष्टवानरः । मेधाविन्यप्युड्डीनैषा गच्छति । तदेहि । लघ्वनुसरावः । अस्यालापस्य गृहीताक्षरा कस्यापि पुरतो मन्त्रयिष्यते । (ग)

(क) सहि उट्ठेहि उट्ठेहि । एसो खु दुट्ठवाणरो इदो ज्जेव आअच्छदि । तं अलक्खिदं तमालविडवान्धआरे पविसिअ इमं अदिवाहेम । (ख) सुसंगदे कहं तुए चित्तफलहओ उज्झिदो । कदावि कोपि तं पेक्खदि । (ग) अइ सुत्थिदे किं अज्ज वि चित्तफलएण करिस्ससि । एसो क्खु दधिभत्तलम्पडो सारिआपञ्जरं उग्घाडिअ अवक्कन्दो दुट्ठवाणरो । मेहाविणी वि उड्डीणा एसा गच्छदि । ता एहि । लहुं अणुसरम्हं । इमस्स आलावस्स गहिदाक्खरा कस्स वि पुरदो मन्तइस्सदि ।

कञ्चुकिनः कञ्चुकस्य चोलकस्य अन्तः विशति । किरातैः किरं पर्यन्तभूमिमतन्ति गच्छन्तीति किराताः म्लेच्छभेदाः राजसेवायां वर्तमानास्तैः । पर्यन्तं प्रान्तभूमिं भयादाश्रयन्त इति तैः पर्यन्ताश्रयिभिः । निजस्य नाम्नः सदृशं कृतं चेष्टितम् । कुब्जा आत्मनः । कर्मणि षष्ठी । ईक्षणं वानरेणेति शेषः तत् शङ्कन्ते इति तथोक्ताः नीचतया अनुच्चतया एव यान्ति । अत्रापि स्वभावोक्तिः । उभयोः श्लोकयोर्भयानको रसः । शार्दूलविक्रीडितं वृत्तम् ॥ ३ ॥ तमालानां विटपाः शाखास्तेषामन्धकारः तस्मिन् । **सुस्थिते** इति । सुष्ठु स्थिता शोभनं स्थितमस्या इति वा सुस्थिता तत्सम्बोधनम् । सति त्वराकारणे किं निश्चिन्ता तिष्ठसीति भावः । तदेव व्यनक्ति किमित्यादिना । दध्ना भक्तः ओदनः दधिभक्तः । अन्नेन व्यञ्जनमिति समासः । तस्य लम्पटः लुब्धः । उड्डीना उत्प्लुता । उत्पूर्वात् डीङ् विहायसा गतौ इत्यस्मात्

---

१ ०र्ण्याग्रवलोक्य च ०मं समुत्थाय. २ तिष्ठतः; परिक्रम्योभे...एकान्ते पर्यवस्थित. ३ साग०—किं दाणिं करेम्ह । सुसं०—एहि इमस्सिं तमा०. ४ कदलीविडवन्तरे. ५ सहि किं; कहिं सो.... । मा कदावि...पेक्खिस्सदि । ६ ०एण ०फलहं गेण्हिअ । एसो क्खु...लम्पडदाए; एताए सारिआए; एसो क्खु नहिं उवगदो सारि०; एसा क्खु मेहा० उड्डीणा अण्णदो ग०. ७ ०रम्ह । (इति निष्क्रान्ते).

साग०—सखि एवं कुर्वः । (इति परिक्रामतः ।) (क)

(नेपथ्ये ।)

ही ही भोः आश्चर्यमाश्चर्यम् । (ख)

साग०—(विलोक्य सभयम् ।) सुसंगते ज्ञायते पुनरपि स दुष्टवानर आगच्छतीति । (ग)

सुसं०—(विदूषकं दृष्ट्वा विहस्य ।) अयि कातरे मा बिभीहि । भर्तुः पार्श्ववर्ती आर्यवसन्तकः खल्वेषः । (घ)

साग०—(सस्पृहमवलोक्य ।) सखि सुसंगते दर्शनीयः खल्वयं जनः । (ङ)

सुसंगता—अयि सुस्थिते किमनेन दृष्टेन । दूरे भवति खलु सारिका । तदेहि । अनुसरावः । (च)

(उभे निष्क्रान्ते ।)

(ततः प्रविशति प्रहृष्टो विदूषकः ।)

विदूषकः—ही ही भोः आश्चर्यमाश्चर्यम् । साधु रे श्रीखण्डदास धार्मिक साधु । येन दत्तमात्रेणैव तेन दोहदेनेदृशी नवमालिका संवृत्ता येन निरन्तरोद्भिन्नकुसुमगुच्छशोभितविटपा उपहसन्तीव लक्ष्यते देवीपरिगृहीतां माधवीलताम् । तद्यावद्गत्वा प्रियवयस्यं वर्धयिष्यामि ।

(क) सहि एव्वं करेम्ह । (ख) ही ही भो अच्चरिअं अच्चरिअम् । (ग) सुसंगदे जाणिअदि पुणो वि सो दुट्ठवाणरो आअच्छादित्ति । (घ) अई काअरे मा भेहि । भत्तुणो पासवत्ती अज्जवसन्तओ क्खु एसो । (ङ) सहि सुसंगदे दंसणीओ क्खु अअं जणो । (च) अइ सुत्थिदे किं इमिणा दिट्ठेण । दूरे भोदि खु सारिआ । ता एहि । अणुसरम्ह ।

क्तप्रत्ययः । ओदितत्वान्निष्ठानत्वम् । ही ही इति विदूषकस्य हर्षसूचको निपातः । ही ही वैदूषक इत्युक्तत्वात् । दत्तमेव दत्तमात्रं तेन । मयूरव्यंसकादित्वात्समासः । **निरन्तरेति** । निर्गतमन्तरं यस्मिन्कर्मणि तद्यथा तथा उद्भिन्ना ये कुसुमगुच्छाः तैः शोभिता विटपाः शाखा यस्याः सा । वर्धयिष्यामि दिष्ट्यावृद्धिं करिष्यामि ।

---

१ निष्क्रान्ते. २ दृष्ट्वा सबहुमानम्. ३ अवलोकयति. सुसं०—सहि किं पक्खिणा. ४ पटाक्षेपेण प्र०. ५ णं सुणीअदि. ६ अदिकादरे मा भाआहि मा भाआहि । भट्टिणो पस्सपरिवट्टि अज्ज० एसो आअच्छदि; ण भेहि...परिवत्ती क्खु एसो अज्ज०; अस्मात्परं–(ततः प्रविशति वसन्तकः–विदूषकः) वस०, विदू०—अच्चरिअं । साहु रे सिरिखण्डदास धम्मिअ साहु । ७ ण भोदि, दूरीभूदा.

(परिक्रम्यावलोक्य च ।) एष खलु प्रियवयस्यस्तस्य दोहदस्य लब्धप्रत्यय-तया परोक्षामपि तां नवमालिकां प्रत्यक्षामिव कुसुमितां प्रेक्षमाणः हर्षो-त्फुल्ललोचन इत एवागच्छति । तद्यावदेनमुपसर्पामि । (क)

(ततः प्रविशति यथानिर्दिष्टो राजा ।)

राजा—(सहर्षम् ।)

उद्दामोत्कलिकां विपाण्डुररुचं प्रारब्धजृम्भां क्षणा-
दायासं श्वसनोद्गमैरविरतैरातन्वतीमात्मनः ।
अद्योद्यानलतामिमां समदनां नारीमिवान्यां ध्रुवं
पश्यन्कोपविपाटलद्युति मुखं देव्याः करिष्याम्यहम् ॥ ४ ॥

तद्वृत्तान्तमुपलब्धुं गतो वसन्तकोऽद्यापि नायाति ।

(क) ही ही भो अच्चरिअं अच्चरिअम् । साहु रे सिरिखण्डदास धम्मिअ साहु । जेण दिण्णमेत्तेण ज्जेव तेण दोहएण ईदिसी णोमालिआ संवुत्ता जेण निरन्तरुब्भिण्णकुसुमगुच्छसोभिअविडवा उवहसन्ती विअ लक्खिअदि देवीपरिग्गहिदं माधवीलदं । ता जाव गदुअ पिअवअस्सं वड्ढावइस्सम् । एसो क्खु पिअवअस्सो तस्स दोहदस्स लद्धपच्चअदाए परोक्खंवि तं णोमालिअं पच्चक्खं विअ कुसुमिदं पेक्खन्तो हरिसुप्फुल्ललोअणो इदो ज्जेव आअच्छदि । ता जाव णं उवसप्पामि ।

लब्धः प्रत्ययो विश्वासः । जातानुभवादित्यर्थः । यस्य तस्य भावस्तत्ता तया लब्ध-प्रत्ययतया । कुसुमितां सञ्जातानि कुसुमानि यस्यास्तां तथोक्ताम् । तदस्य संजातं तारकादिभ्य इतच् इति इतच्प्रत्ययः । हर्षेण उत्फुल्ले विकसिते लोचने यस्य सः । **उद्दामेत्यादि** । अद्य इमां हृदयसन्निहितां उद्यानलतां मदेन सहिता समदना तां समदनामन्यां नारीमिव पश्यन् अहं ध्रुवं देव्या वासवदत्ताया मुखं कोपेन विपाटला विशेषेण श्वेतरक्ता द्युतिर्यस्य तत्कोपविपाटलद्युति करिष्यामि । उभयोः साम्यमाह— क्षणाद् दोहददानक्षणे नायकावलोकनक्षणे च इत्यर्थः । उद्दामोत्कलिकां उद्दामा अतिप्रभूता इत्यर्थः । उद्गताः कलिका यस्याः तादृशीम् । पक्षे उद्दामा अत्युत्कटा उत्कलिका उत्कण्ठा यस्यास्तथाविधाम् । विपाण्डुररुचं विशेषेण पाण्डुरा शुभ्रा विपाण्डुरा । सर्वत्र पुष्पोद्गमात् । पक्षे विमनस्कतया । रुक् कान्तिर्यस्याः तां तथोक्ताम् । तथा च प्रारब्धा जृम्भा कलिकाविकासः जृम्भणं च यया तादृशीम् । पुनश्च अविरतैः संततैः श्वसनानां वातानां पक्षे निःश्वासानां उद्गमैः आविर्भावैः आत्मनः आयासं खेदमातन्वतीम् । श्लेषालंकार उपमा च । शार्दूलविक्रीडितं वृत्तम् ॥ ४ ॥ यदुक्तमचिन्त्यो ही-

---

१ म्याग्रतो दृष्ट्वा. २ ०शति राजा. ३ जृम्भेक्षणात्. ४ तस्याः. ५ नास्त्येतद्वाक्यं क्वचित्. ६ ०दास णाम. ७ सा णोमा० लदा. ८ ०मच्छदा इअं निडवादो ञ्जव०...तं देवीए परि०; गुच्छाच्छादिअवि०. ९ णिवेदेमि. १० तस्स ज्जेव. ११ पेक्खिअ दोहल-(दोहद) रसोप्फुल्ल०. १२ अस्मात्परं—इति राजानं प्रति गतः । इत्य०.

विदूषकः—(सहसोपसृत्य)। जयतु जयतु प्रियवयस्यः । भो वयस्य दिष्ट्या वर्धसे । (जेण दिण्णमेत्तेण ज्जेव्व तेण दोहएण ईदिसी णोमोलिआ संवुत्तेत्यादि पठति ।) (क)

राजा—वयस्य कः संदेहः । अचिन्त्यो हि मणिमन्त्रौषधीनां प्रभावः । पश्य ।

कण्ठे श्रीपुरुषोत्तमस्य समरे दृष्ट्वा मणिं शत्रुभि—
र्नष्टं मन्त्रबलाद्वसन्ति वसुधामूले भुजङ्गा हताः ।
पूर्वं लक्ष्मणवीरवानरभटा ये मेघनादाहताः
पीत्वा तेऽपि महौषधेर्गुणनिधेर्गन्धं पुनर्जीविताः ॥ ५ ॥

तदादेशय मार्गं येन वयमपि तदवलोकनेन चक्षुषः फलमनुभवामः ।

विदूषकः—(साटोपम् ।) एत्वेतु भवान् । (ख)

राजा—गच्छाग्रतः ।

(उभौ सगर्वं परिक्रामतः ।)

विदूषकः—(आकर्ण्य सभयं परावृत्य राजानं गृहीत्वा ससंभ्रमम् ।) भो वयस्य एहि पलायावहे । (ग)

राजा—किमर्थम् ।

(क) जअदु जअदु पिअवअस्सो । भो वअस्स दिट्ठिआ वड्ढसि । (ख) एदु एदु भवं । (ग) भो वअस्स एहि पलाअम्ह ।

त्यादि तदेवोदाहरणेन समर्थयति—कण्ठेत्यादिना । पुरुषेषु उत्तमः पुरुषोत्तमः विष्णुः । सुप्सुपेति समासः । तस्य कण्ठे मणिं कौस्तुभाख्यं दृष्ट्वा शत्रुभिः नष्टं विद्रुतम् । मन्त्रबलात् हता हतवीर्या इत्यर्थः । भुजैः भोगैः गच्छन्तीति भुजङ्गाः । खचो डित्वाट्टिलोपः । वसुधामूले पाताले वसन्ति । पूर्वं रामरावणयुद्धे ये लक्ष्मणश्च वीराश्च ते वानरभटाश्च लक्ष्मणवीरवानरभटाः मेघनादेन इन्द्रजिता आहताः तेऽपि गुणानां विशल्यकरणादीनां निधिः गुणनिधिस्तस्याः महती चासौ ओषधिश्च तस्याः गन्धं पीत्वा आघ्राय पुनः जीविताः । तदुक्तं रामायणे युद्धकाण्डे चतुःसप्ततितमे सर्गे—तावप्युभौ मानुषराजपुत्रौ तं गन्धमाघ्राय महौषधीनाम् । बभूवतुस्तत्र तदा विशल्यावुत्तस्थुरन्ये च हरिप्रवीराः ॥ सर्वे विशल्या विरुजाः क्षणेन हरिप्रवीराश्च हताश्च ये स्युः । गन्धेन तासां प्रवरौषधीनां सुप्ता निशान्तेष्विव सम्प्रबुद्धाः ॥ इति । शार्दूलविक्रीडितं छन्दः ॥ ५ ॥ आटोपेन गर्वेण सहितं यथा तथा साटोपम् ।

---

१ उपसृत्य. २ सा णोमा०. ३ नितरां. ४ ०वरैः, ०बलैः. ५ अद्य. ६ किमिति. ७ एतन्नास्ति क्वचित्.

विदूषकः—एतस्मिन्बकुलपादपे कोऽपि भूतः प्रतिवसति । (क)

राजा—धिङ् मूर्ख विश्रब्धं गम्यताम् । कुत ईदृग्विधानामत्र संभवः ।

विदूषकः—भोः एष खलु स्फुटाक्षरमेव मन्त्रयते । तद्यदि मम वचनं न प्रत्येषि तदग्रतो भूत्वा स्वयमेव तावदाकर्णय । (ख)

राजा—(तथा कृत्वा श्रुत्वा च ।)

स्पष्टाक्षरमिदं यस्मान्मधुरं स्त्रीस्वभावतः ।
अल्पाङ्गत्वादनिर्ह्रादि मन्ये वदति सारिका ॥ ६ ॥

(**ऊर्ध्वं** निरूप्य ।) कथं सारिकैवेयम् ।

विदूषकः—(ऊर्ध्वमवलोक्य ।) आः कथं सत्यमेव सारिका । (सरोषं दण्डकाष्ठमुद्यम्य ।) आः दास्याः पुत्रि किं त्वया ज्ञातं सत्यमेव वसन्तको बिभेतीति । तत्तिष्ठ मुहूर्तम् । यावदनेन पिशुनजनहृदयकुटिलेन दण्डकाष्ठेन परिपक्वमिव कपित्थफलमस्माद्बकुलपादपादाहत्य भूमौ त्वां पातयिष्यामि । (इति हन्तुमुद्यतः ।) (ग)

राजा—(निवारयन् ।) मूर्ख किमप्येषा रमणीयं व्याहरति । तत्किमेनां त्रासयसि । शृणुवस्तावत् ।

(**क**) एअस्सिं वउलपाअवे कोवि भूदो पडिवसदि । (**ख**) भो एसो क्खु फुडक्खरं एव मन्तेदि । ता जइ मम वअणं न पत्तिआअसि ता अग्गदो भविअ सअं एव्व दाव आअण्णेहि । (**ग**) आः कथं सच्चं एव्व सारिआ । आः दासीएं धीए किं तुए जाणिदं सच्चं ज्जेव्व वसन्तओ भाआदित्ति । ता चिठ्ठ मुहुत्तअम् । जाव इमिणा पिसुणजणहिअअकुडिलेण दण्डकठ्ठेण परिपक्कं विअ कइत्थफलं इमादो वउलपाअवादो आहणिअ भूमीए तुमं पाडयिस्सम् ।

स्पष्टाक्षरमिति । इदं स्पष्टानि अक्षराणि यस्य तत्स्पष्टाक्षरं मन्त्रणं यस्मात्स्त्रीस्वभावतः मधुरम् । अल्पाङ्गत्वात् अल्पं लघु अङ्गं यस्याः सा अल्पाङ्गा तस्या भावः अल्पाङ्गत्वं तस्मात् अनिर्ह्रादि अनुच्चैः श्रूयमाणं तस्मात्सारिका वदति इति मन्ये ॥ ६ ॥ अधिकपाठे—भयालुकः भयशीलः । अत्र आलुच् चिन्त्यः । भीलुक इति साधीयः । दास्याः पुत्रीति षष्ठ्या आक्रोशे इति अलुग्वा । पिशुनः दुर्जनस्तस्य हृदयमिव कुटिलेन

---

१ ईदृशानामत्र प्रभावः. २ आकर्ण्य. ३ तावत्. ४ उपसृत्योर्ध्वमवलोक्य, निरूप्य-निपुणमवलोक्य-स्मितं कृत्वा. ५ विचार्य, ऊर्ध्वं निरूप्य. ६ मन्त्रयते. ७ अस्सिं क्खु लकुच०. ८ भो एसो क्खु इति नास्ति पुस्तकान्तरे. ९ अस्मात्पूर्वं—राजा—(विहस्य) एवम् । विदू०—भो वअस्स तुमं भआलुओ जेण सारिअं भूदेत्ति मन्तेसि । राजा—धिङ् मूर्ख यदात्मना कृतं तन्मयि सम्भावयसि । विदू०—भो जइ एव्वं मा क्खु मं णिवारेसि । इत्यधिको ग्रन्थः केषुचित्पुस्तकेषु. १० दासीए मे...मम वस०. ११ सुपरिक्किविअ फलं...लकुचपा० भूमीए सीसं (शीर्षं).

(उभावाकर्णयतः ।)

विदूषकः—(आकर्ण्य ।) भो वयस्य श्रुतं त्वया यदेतया मन्त्रितम् । एषा भणति सखि क एष त्वयात्रालिखितः । सखि प्रवृत्तमदनमहोत्सवे भगवाननङ्ग इति । पुनरप्येषा भणति सखि कस्मात्त्वयाहमत्रालिखिता । सखि किमकारणं कुप्यसि । यादृशस्त्वया कामदेव आलिखितस्तादृशी मया रतिरालिखितेति । तदन्यथासंभाविनि किं तवैतेनालपितेन । कथय सर्वं वृत्तान्तम् । भो वयस्य किं न्विदम् । (क)

राजा—वयस्यैवं तर्कयामि । कयापि हृदयवल्लभोऽनुरागादालिख्य कामदेवव्यपदेशेन सखीपुरतोऽपह्नुतः । तत्सख्यापि प्रत्यभिज्ञाय वैदग्ध्यादसावपि तत्रैव रतिव्यपदेशेनालिखितेति ।

विदू०—(छोटिकां दत्वा ।) भो वयस्य युज्यते । एवं खल्वेतत् । (ख)

राजा—वयस्य तूष्णीं भव । पुनरप्येषा व्याहरति ।

विदू०—भो एषा भणति सखि मा लज्जस्व । ईदृशस्य कन्यारत्नस्यावश्यमेवेदृशे वरेऽभिलाषेण भवितव्यम् । भो वयस्य यैषा आलिखिता सा खलु कन्या दर्शनीया । (ग)

(क) भो वअस्सं सुदं तुए जं एदाए मन्तिदं । एसा भणादि सहि को एसो तुए एत्थ आलिहिदो । सहि पउत्तमअणमहूस्सवे भअवं अणङ्गोत्ति । पुणोवि एसा भणादि सहि कीस तुए अहं एत्थ आलिहिदा । सहि किं अआरणं कुप्पसि । जादिसो तुए कामदेओ आलिहिदो तादिसी मए रइ आलिहिदेत्ति । ता अण्णधासम्भाविणि किं तुए एदिणा आलविदेण । कहेहि सव्वं वुत्तान्तम् । भो वअस्स किं ण्णेदम् । (ख) भो वअस्स जुज्जेदि । एव्वं क्खु एदं । (ग) भो एसा भणादि सहि मा लज्ज । ईदिसस्स कण्णण्णारअणस्स अवस्सं एव्व ईदिसे वरे अहिलासेण होदव्वम् । भो वअस्स जा एसा आलिहिदा सा क्खु कण्णा दंसणीआ ।

वक्रेण । अधिके पाठे—उदरे प्रसितः औदरिक उदरपूरणपरः । तस्य अभ्यवहारे अन्ने । हृदयस्य वल्लभः हृदयवल्लभः । कामदेवो मदनः तस्य व्यपदेशेन व्याजेन । मदनत्वेन प्रतिपाद्येत्यर्थः । अपह्नुतः अपलपितः । वैदग्ध्यान्नैपुण्यात्तद् अपह्नवकरणं प्रत्यभिज्ञाय ज्ञात्वा । छोटिकामिति अङ्गुष्ठस्य मध्यमामाघट्य झटित्यपनयनाज्जायमानः शब्दः छोटिकासंज्ञः ।

---

१ विदू०—एवं भणादि । इमस्स बाम्हणस्स भोजणं दिज्जदि । राजा—सर्वमप्यौदरिकस्याभ्यवहार एव पर्यवस्यति तत्सत्यं वद किमालपति सारिका । इत्य०. २ श्रुत्वा. ३ कयाचिद्धृतवल्लभानु०. ४ अभिलि०. ५ शेन निह्नुतः. ६ ०दप्रतिभि–य–न्वान–तया. ७ तत्रालिख्य रतिव्य० दर्शितेति. ८ ददाति. ९ आस्त्व. १० भो वअस्स...अणङ्गोसि । पुणोवि एसा भणादि–इत्यस्य स्थाने किं भणादि इत्येव पठ्यते कैश्चित् । ११ सहि मा कुप्प मा कुप्प । जादि० अअं काम०...रइ त्ति. १२ जुज्जदि. १३ किं क्खु. १४ एतन्नास्ति पुस्त०.

राजा—यद्येवमवहितौ शृणुवस्तावत्। अस्त्यत्रावकाशो नः कुतूहलस्य। (इत्युभावाकर्णयतः।)

विदूषकः—भो वयस्य श्रुतं त्वया यदेतया मन्त्रितम्। सखि अपनयेमानि नलिनीपत्राणि मृणालवलयानि च। अलमेतेन। कथमकारण आत्मानमायासयसि। (क)

राजा—वयस्य न केवलं श्रुतमभिप्रायोऽपि लक्षितः।

विदूषकः—भो मा त्वं पाण्डित्यगर्वमुद्वह। अहं त एतस्या मुखाच्छ्रुत्वा सर्वं व्याख्यास्यामि। तच्छृणुवः। अद्यापि कुरकुरायत एव एषा सारिका दास्याः पुत्री। (ख)

राजा—युक्तमभिहितम्। (पुनराकर्णयतः।)

विदूषकः—भो वयस्य एषा खलु सारिका दास्या दुहिता चतुर्वेदी ब्राह्मण इव ऋचः पठितुं प्रवृत्ता। (ग)

राजा—वयस्य कथय किमप्यन्यचेतसा मया नावधारितं किमनयोक्तमिति।

विदूषकः—भो एतदेतया पठितम्। (घ)

दुर्लभजनानुरागो लज्जा गुर्वी परवश आत्मा।
प्रियसखि विषमं प्रेम मरणं शरणं न वरमेकम्॥ ७॥

(क) भो वअस्स सुदं तुए जं एदाए मन्तिदम्। सहि अवणेहि इमाइं णलिणीवत्ताइं मुणालवलआइं अ। अलं एदिणा। कीस अआरणे अत्ताणं आआसेसि। (ख) भो मा तुमं पण्डिअव्वगव्वं उव्वह। अहं दे एदाए मुहादो सुणिअ सव्वं वाक्खाणइस्सम्। ता सुणम्ह। अज्ज वि कुरकुराअदि एव्व एसा सारिआ दासीए धीआ। (ग) भो वअस्स एसा क्खु सारिका दासीए दुहिदा चतुव्वेदी बम्हणो विअ रिचाइं पठिदुं पवुत्ता। (घ) भो एदं एदाए पढिदम्।

दुल्लहजणाणुराओ लज्जा गुरुई परव्वसो अप्पा।
पिअसहि विसमं पेम्मं मरणं सरणं न वरमेक्कम्॥

कुरकुरायते—कुरकुरेति ध्वनेरनुकरणवाचि पदम्। ततः अव्यक्तानुकरणाद्यजवरार्धादिति डाचि लोहितादिडाज्भ्यः क्यष् इति क्यष्। महाब्राह्मणेत्यत्र कुत्सायां महच्छब्दः।

---

१ तदवहितैः श्रोतव्यम्. २ ज्ञात एव. ३ तत्किम...क्तम्. ४ मे. ५ मुणालिआओ अ। एदाइं अआरणे अत्ताणअं सहि किं आआ०. ६ पण्डिअग०. ७ कं वि कुर०. ८ चतुव्वेदो विअ ब०. ९ एवं भणादि.

राजा—(सस्मितम् ।) साधुं भवन्त महाब्राह्मणं मुक्त्वा कोऽन्य एवंमृचामभिज्ञः ।

विदूषकः—ततः किं नु खल्विदम् । (क)

राजा—ननु गाथेयम् ।

विदूषकः—किं गाथा । (ख)

राजा—कयापि श्लाघ्ययौवनया प्रियतममनासादयन्त्या जीवितनिरपेक्षयोक्तम् ।

विदूषकः—(उच्चैर्विहस्य ।) भोः किमेतैर्वक्रभणितैः । ऋज्वेव किं न भणासि यथा मामनासादयन्त्येति । अन्यथा कोऽन्यः कुसुमचापव्यपदेशेनैवं निह्नूयते । (हस्ततालं दत्वोच्चैर्विहसति ।) (ग)

राजा—(ऊर्ध्वमवलोक्य ।) धिङ् मूर्ख किमुच्चैर्हसता त्वयेयमुत्रासिता येनोड्डीयान्यत्र क्वापि गता ।

(उभौ निरूपयतः ।)

विदूषकः—(विलोक्य ।) भो एषा खलु कदलीगृहमेव गता । तदेहि । लघ्वनुसरावः । (घ)

राजा—

दुर्वारां कुसुमशरव्यथां वहन्त्या
कामिन्या यदभिहितं पुरः सखीनाम् ।

(क) तदो किं णु क्खु एदं । (ख) किं गाथा । (ग) भो किं एदेहिं वक्कभणिदेहिं । उज्जु एव्व किं ण भणासि जहा मं अणासादयन्तीएत्ति । अण्णहा को अण्णो कुसुमचावव्ववदेसेण एवं णिण्हवीअदि । (घ) भो एसा क्खु कअलीघरं एव्व गदा । ता एहि । लहुं अणुसरम्ह ।

तदुक्तम्—शंखे तैले तथा मांसे वैद्ये ज्योतिषिके द्विजे । यात्रायां पथि निद्रायां महच्छब्दो न दीयते । इति । गाथा प्राकृतभाषापद्यम् । अत्रार्या । गाथा श्लोके संस्कृतान्यभाषायां गेयवृत्तयोः । इति मेदिनी । श्लाघ्यं लोभनीयमित्यर्थः । अर्हार्थे ण्यत् । यौवनं यस्यास्तया । प्रियतममभिमतवल्लभम् । वक्रभणितैः कुटिलभाषणैः । ऋजु सरलं स्पष्टमित्यर्थः । अन्यथा एवं न चेत् । **दुर्वारामिति** । दुःखेन वार्यते इति दुर्वारा तां

---

१ विहस्य. २ साधु महाब्राह्मण साधु । कोऽन्यः; एवंविधं भवन्तं ब्राह्मणं; अहो महाब्राह्मणं वसन्तकं त्यक्त्वा; अहो महाब्राह्मणः खल्वसि; राजा—साकूतं शृणोति । ३ एवंविधानां. ४ मूर्ख. ५ वयस्य कथा. ६ ०वनफल–रमण–मनासादयन्त्या; प्रियजनमासादयितुमपारयन्त्या. ७ (उच्चैर्विहस्य) अहह. ८ विह०. ९ त्वया तपस्विनी त्रासितेयं. १० इति. ११ मदनकृतां. १२ किं क्खु दाव तए जाणिदं. १३ उज्जुअं. १४ भो वअस्स अण्णधा मा संभावेहि । एसा.

तद्भूयः शिशुशुकसारिकाभिरुक्तं
धन्यानां श्रवणपथातिथित्वमेति ॥ ८ ॥

विदूषकः—एत्वेतु भवान् । (परिक्रामतः ।) (क)

विदूषकः—भोः एतत्खलु कदलीगृहम् । यावत्प्रविशावः । (ख)

(उभौ प्रविशतः ।)

विदूषकः—भोः गता दास्याः पुत्री । अत्र तावन्मन्दमारुतोद्वेल्लद्बालकदलीदलशीतले शिलातल उपविश्य मुहूर्तं विश्राम्यावः । (ग)

राजा—यदभिरुचितं भवते ।

(इत्युपविशतः ।)

राजा—(निःश्वस्य । दुर्वारामित्यादि पुनः पठति ।)

विदूषकः—(पार्श्वतोऽवलोक्य ।) भोः एतेन खलूद्घाटितद्वारेण तस्याः सारिकायाः पञ्जरेण भवितव्यम् । एषोऽपि स चित्रफलकः । यावदेनं गृह्णामि । (फलकं गृहीत्वा निरूप्य च सहर्षम् ।) भो वयस्य दिष्ट्या वर्धसे । (घ)

(क) एदु एदु भवं । (ख) भो एदं क्खु कअलीघरअम् । जाव पविसम्ह । (ग) भो गदा दासीए धीआ । एत्थ दाव मन्दमारुदुव्वेल्लन्तबालकअलीदलसीदले सिलातले उपविसिअ मुहुत्तअं वीसम्ह । (घ) भो एदेण क्खु उग्घाडिअदुवारेण ताए सारिआए पञ्जरेण होदव्वम् । एसो वि सो चित्तफलओ । जाव णं गेण्हामि । भो वअस्स दिट्ठिआ वड्ढसि ।

दुर्वारां दुष्परिहराम् । ईषद्दुःसुषु कृच्छ्राकृच्छ्रार्थेषु खल् इति खल् । कुसुमशरस्य कामस्य व्यथां वहन्त्या धारयन्त्या कामिन्या सुन्दर्या सखीनां पुरः यदात्मनोऽनुरागस्य व्यञ्जकमुक्तं तद् भूयः पुनः शिशवः च शुकाश्च सारिकाश्च ताभिः उक्तं धन्यानां भाग्यशालिनां श्रवणस्य पन्थाः श्रवणपथः श्रोत्रविवरं तस्य अतिथित्वं गोचरत्वमेति । धन्या एव तत् शृण्वन्तीत्यर्थः । सामान्येन विशेषसमर्थनरूपोऽर्थान्तरन्यासोऽलंकारः । अनुप्रासश्च । प्रहर्षिणी वृत्तम् । तल्लक्षणं तु—म्नौ ज्रौ गस्त्रिदशयतिः प्रहर्षिणीयम् । इति ॥ ८ ॥ **मन्देति** । मन्देन मारुतेन वायुना उद्वेल्लन्ति कम्पमानानि यानि बालकदलीनां दलानि पत्राणि तैः शीतले । उद्घाटितद्वारेण दुष्टवानरेण इति पाठे दुष्टवानरेण उद्घाटितं द्वारं यस्य तेन इति योजनीयम् । किमेतदिति किं ते हर्षकारणं

---

१ शुकशिशु. २ पार्श्वाणि. ३ हर्षं नाटयति । ४ एदं तं... । ता पविसदु भवं. ५ भो अलं दाव ताए दासीए धीआए सारिआए अण्णेसिदेण । (अन्वेषितेन)—अण्णेसणपअत्तेण. ६ दुव्वेलिद...कदलीघरअं पविसिअ; मलअमारुदवेवमाण; सीअलिदसिला.

राजा—(सकौतुकम् ।) वयस्य किमेतत् ।

विदू०—भोः एतत्खलु तद्यन्मया भणितम् । त्वमेवात्रालिखितः । कोऽन्यः कुसुमचापव्यपदेशेन निह्नूयत इति । (क)

राजा—(सहर्षं हस्तौ प्रसार्य ।) सखे दर्शय दर्शय ।

विदूषकः—न ते दर्शयिष्यामि । सापि कन्यकात्रैवालिखिता तिष्ठति । तत्किं पारितोषिकेण विनेदृशं कन्यारत्नं दृश्यते । (ख)

राजा—(कटकमर्पयन्नेव बलाद् गृहीत्वा विलोक्य सविस्मयम् ।)

लीलावधूतपद्मा कथयन्ती पक्षपातमधिकं नः ।
मानसमुपैति केयं चित्रगता राजहंसीव ॥ ९ ॥

अपि च ।

विधायापूर्वपूर्णेन्दुमस्या मुखमभूद् ध्रुवम् ।
धाता निजासनाम्भोजविनिमीलनदुःस्थितः ॥ १० ॥

(**क**) भो एदं क्खु तं जं मए भणिदम् । तुमं ज्जेव एत्थ आलिहिदो । को अण्णो कुसुमचावव्ववदेसेण णिह्नवीअदित्ति । (**ख**) णं दे दंसइस्सम् । सा वि कण्णआ एत्थ ज्जेव आलिहिदा चिट्ठदि । ता किं पारितोसिएण विणा ईदिसं कण्णारअणं दंसीअदि ।

किमिति मां दिष्ट्या वर्धयसि इति भावः । विदू०—भो वयस्य दिष्ट्या वर्धसे । राजा–(सकौतुकम् ।)...कोऽन्यो...व्यपदिश्यते इत्यादिना तत्रावकाशो भवतः किमु स्यात् (श्लो. १५) इत्यन्तेन राजविदूषकसागरिकासुसङ्गतानामन्योन्यवचनेनोत्तरोत्तरानुरागबीजोद्घाटनात्प्रगमनमिति प्रतिमुखसन्धेरङ्गमुक्तम् । परितोषः प्रयोजनमस्य इति पारितोषिकं तेन । ठञ् । **लीलेत्यादि** । लीलया विलासेन अवधूता तिरस्कृता पद्मा लक्ष्मीः यया सा लीलावधूतपद्मा । लीलया हेलया अवधूतं भ्रमितं पद्मं कमलं यया इति केचित् । किं त्वेतदसङ्गतमत्रेति भाति । राजहंसीपक्षे लीलया लीलाभ्रमणेनेत्यर्थः अवधूतानि कम्पितानि पद्मानि यया सा तथोक्ता । चित्रगता चित्रं गता आलिखितेत्यर्थः । पक्षे चित्रं विविधं गतं गमनं यस्याः सा तथा । इयं का नः अस्माकं अस्मत्सम्बद्धमधिकं सविशेषं पक्षे पातः पक्षपातः तं पक्षपातमनुकूलतामित्यर्थः । पक्षे पक्षयोः पातः विधूननं पक्षपातस्तं कथयन्ती ख्यापयन्ती । राजहंसीव मानसं मनः पक्षे मानसाख्यं सरः । उपैति । श्लेषोपमे अलंकारौ । आर्या वृत्तम् ॥ ९ ॥ **विधायेति** । धाता ब्रह्मा अस्याः कन्यायाः मुखं । मुखरूपामित्यर्थः ।

---

१ (हस्तं प्रसारयति ।) सखे उपनय-समर्पय; (अधोमुखः सहर्षमुत्थाय हस्तं प्रसारयति). २ बलाद् गृहीत्वा सविस्मयं पश्यति; गृहीत्वा पश्यति; सवि० वयस्य पश्य पश्य । ३ ०चावसमाणरूवोत्ति; अण्णहा (अन्यथा)को. ४ भो ण दे; भो एदं दं०; ना परितोसेण देइस्सं. ५ कण्णआ–हत्थिआ०.

(ततः प्रविशति सागरिका सुसंगता च ।)

सुसं०—सखि न समासादितावाभ्यां सारिका । तच्चित्रफलकमपि तावदस्मात्कदलीगृहाद् गृहीत्वा लघ्वागच्छावः । (क)

साग०—सखि एवं कुर्वः । (ख)

(उभे परिक्रामतः ।)

विदूषकः—भो वयस्य कस्मात्पुनरेषावनतमुख्यालिखिता । (ग)

सुसंगता—(आकर्ण्य ।) सखि यथा वसन्तको मन्त्रयते तथा तर्कयामि भर्त्राप्यत्रैव भवितव्यम् । तत्कदलीगुल्मान्तरिते भूत्वा प्रेक्षावहे तावत् । (घ)

(उभे पश्यतः ।)

राजा—वयस्य पश्य पश्य । (विधायापूर्वपूर्णेन्दुमित्यादि पुनः पठति ।)

सुसं०—सखि दिष्ट्या वर्धसे । एष ते हृदयवल्लभस्त्वामेव निर्वर्णयंस्तिष्ठति । (ङ)

साग०—(सलज्जम् ।) कस्मात्परिहासशीलतयेमं जनं लघुं करोषि । (च)

विदू०—(राजानं चालयित्वा ।) ननु भणामि । कस्मादेषावनतमुख्यालिखितेति । (छ)

(क) सहि ण समासादिदा अम्हेहिं सारिआ । ता चित्तफलअं पि दाव इमादो कदलीघरादो गेण्हिअ लहुं आगच्छम्ह । (ख) सहि एवं करेम्ह । (ग) भो वअस्स कीस उण एसा अवणदमुही आलिहिदा । (घ) सहि जहा वसन्तओ मन्तेदि तहा तक्केमि भट्टिणा वि एत्थ ज्जेव्व होदव्वम् । ता कअलीगुम्मन्तरिदाओ भविअ पेक्खम्ह दाव । (ङ) सहि दिट्ठिआ वड्ढसि । एसो दे हिअअवल्लहो तुमं ज्जेव्व णिव्वण्णअन्तो चिट्ठदि । (च) कीस परिहासशीलदाए इमं जणं लहुं करेसि । (छ) णं भणामि । कीस एसा अवणदमुही आलिहिदेत्ति ।

पूर्वः पूर्वं निर्मितः न भवतीत्यपूर्वः । पूर्णश्चासौ इन्दुश्च पूर्णेन्दुः तम् । कलंकराहित्यात्सदैव पूर्णत्वादपूर्वत्वम् । विधाय सृष्ट्वा ध्रुवं निश्चितं निजं यदासनाम्भोजं आसनभूतं पद्मं तस्य विनिमीलनेन संकोचनेन । पूर्णेन्दोः सतताविर्भावादिति भावः । दुःस्थितः असुखमापन्नः अभूत् । दुःखितः इति पाठः साधीयान्भवेत् । उत्प्रेक्षालंकारः ॥ १० ॥ अवनतं नम्रं मुखं यस्याः सा । भर्त्रा वत्सराजेन । कदलीनां गुल्मः स्तम्बः तेनान्तरिते । **चालयित्वा**—एतदन्यत्र व्यासक्तचित्तस्य राजा स्वभाषणश्रवणपरत्वापादनार्थम् ।

---

१ साग०—सहि सुसं०. २ सुसं०. ३ उपसर्पतः. ४ आकर्णयतः. ५ उद्दिश्य. ६ सहि साअरिए; ०दिदा सा. ७ वअस्स...एसा उण रुण्ण(रुदित)मुही. ८ घरगु०. ९ सुणम्ह. १० वण्ण०. ११ किं एव्वं परिहासलीलाणं. १२ भो अण्णं भ० कीस उण एसा रुण्णमुही.

राजा—ननु सारिकयैव सकलमावेदितम् ।

सुसं०—सखि दर्शितं खलु मेधाविन्यात्मनो मेधावित्वम् । (क)

विदू०—भो वयस्य अपि सुखयति ते लोचनम् । (ख)

साग०—(ससाध्वसमात्मगतम् ।) किमेष भणिष्यतीति यत्सत्यं जीवितमरणयोरन्तरे वर्ते । (ग)

राजा—सुखयतीति किमुच्यते । पश्य ।

कृच्छ्रादूरुयुगं व्यतीत्य सुचिरं भ्रान्त्वा नितम्बस्थले
मध्येऽस्यास्त्रिवलीतरङ्गविषमे निस्पन्दतामागता ।
मद्दृष्टिस्तृषितेव संप्रति शनैरारुह्य तुङ्गौ स्तनौ
साकाङ्क्षं मुहुरीक्षते जललवप्रस्यन्दिनी लोचने ॥ ११ ॥

सुसंगता—सखि श्रुतं त्वया । (घ)

सागरिका—(विहस्य ।) त्वमेव शृणु यस्या आलेख्यविज्ञानमेवं वर्ण्यते । (ङ)

(क) सहि दंसिदं क्खु मेहाविणीए अत्तणो मेहावित्तणम् । (ख) भो वअस्स अवि सुहाअदि दे लोअणम् । (ग) किं एसो भणिस्सदित्ति जं सच्चं जीविदमरणाणं अन्तरे वट्टामि । (घ) सहि सुदं तुए । (ङ) तुमं एव्व सुणु जाए आलेहविण्णाणं एवं वण्णीअदि ।

मेधाविनीत्वं बुद्धौ धारणपाटवम् । मेधावित्वमिति पाठे मेधाविनो भावो मेधावित्वमिति सामान्यनपुंसकत्वमाश्रित्य समाधेयम् । सुखयतीत्यत्र सुखशब्दात्तत्करोतीति णिच् । लोचनयोरिति पाठे कर्मणः शेषत्वविवक्षायां षष्ठी । जीवितमरणयोरिति । न सुखयतीत्युक्ते जीवितधारणासम्भवान्मरणमेव शरणं भवेदन्यथा जीवितमिति भावः । कृच्छ्रादिति । मद्दृष्टिः मम नयने अस्याः ऊर्वोः युगं ऊरुयुगं सक्थिद्वयं कृच्छ्रात्प्रयासेन व्यतीत्य अतिक्रम्य । तद्दर्शनलोभात्तत्त्यागे प्रयासः । एवमितरत्रापि । नितम्बस्थले कट्याः पश्चाद्भागे सुचिरं भ्रान्त्वा । अनेन तस्य विशालतोक्ता । ततः तिस्रः वल्यः त्रिवली । दिक्संख्ये संज्ञायामिति समासः । तस्याः तरंगैः विषमे दुरतिक्रमे मध्ये निस्पन्दतां निश्चलत्वमागता सती सम्प्रति तृषितेव संजाततृष्णा इव तुङ्गौ उन्नतौ स्तनौ शनैः आरुह्य जलस्य अश्रुजलस्य लवान् प्रस्यन्दत इति जललवप्रस्यन्दिनी लोचने आकांक्षया स्पृहया सहितं यथा तथा साकांक्षं मुहुः वारंवारमीक्षते । उत्प्रेक्षालंकारः । शार्दूलविक्रीडितं वृत्तम् ॥ ११ ॥ विशिष्टं ज्ञानं विज्ञानम् ।

---

१ वयस्य...सर्वम् ; अभिहितम्. २ तथा हि. ३ कृच्छ्रेणो०. ४ मे दृष्टिः. ५ अस्मात्परं-सुखयतीति किमुच्यते । इत्य०. ६ सहि इदं क्खु दं०. ७(राजानं चालयन् ।) भो. ८ लोअणाणं, ०णं ण वेत्ति. ९ हद्धी किं; हद्धी हद्धी ण आणे किं. १० अस्मात्परं-विदू०-(राजानं चालयन् ।) भो अण्णं भणामि । अवि सुहाअदि दे लोअणाणम् । इत्य०. ११ तुए जं भट्टिणा मन्तिदं ।

विदूषकः—भो वयस्य यस्य पुनरीदृश्योऽप्येवं समागमं बहु मन्यन्ते तस्याप्यात्मन उपरि कः पराभवः येनात्रैव तयालिखितमात्मानं न प्रेक्षसे। (क)

राजा—(निर्वर्ण्य।) वयस्य अनया लिखितोऽहमिति यत्सत्यं ममात्मन्येव बहुमानस्तत्कथं न पश्यामि। पश्य—

भाति पतितो लिखन्त्यास्तस्या बाष्पाम्बुशीकरकणौघः।
स्वेदोद्गम इव करतलसंस्पर्शादेष मे वपुषि॥ १२॥

साग०—(आत्मगतम्।) हृदय समाश्वसिहि समाश्वसिहि। मनोरथोऽपि त एतावतीं भूमिं न गतः। (ख)

सुसं०—सखि त्वमेवैका श्लाघनीया यया भर्ताप्येवं मन्यते। (ग)

विदूषकः—(पार्श्वतोऽवलोक्य।) भो वयस्य एतत् सरसकमलिनीदलमृणालविरचितं तस्या एव मदनावस्थासूचकं शयनीयं लक्ष्यते। (घ)

राजा—वयस्य निपुणमुपलक्षितम्। तथा हि।

परिम्लानं पीनस्तनजघनसङ्गादुभयत-
स्तनोर्मध्यस्यान्तः परिमिलनमप्राप्य हरितम्।

(क) [4]भो वअस्स जस्स उण ईदिसीओ वि ऐवं समागमं बहुं मण्णन्ति तस्स वि अत्तणो उवरिं को परीहवो जेण एत्थ एव्व ताए आलिहिदं अत्ताणअं ण पेक्खसि। (ख) हिअअ समस्सस समस्सस। मणोरथो वि दे एत्तिअं भूमिं ण गदो। (ग) सहि तुमं एव्व एका सलाहणीआ जाए भट्टा वि एवं मन्तीअदि। (घ) भो वअस्स एदं सरसकमलिनीदलमुणालविरइदं ताए एव्व मअणावत्थासूअअं सअणीअं लक्खीअदि।

आलेख्यस्य चित्रकर्मणो विज्ञानमालेख्यविज्ञानम्। ईदृश्यः याभिस्त्वयापि कुतूहलमुत्पाद्यते तादृश्यः। आत्मन उपरि स्वात्मविषये। परिभवोऽनादरः। **भातीति**। लिखन्त्याः तस्याः मे वपुषि पतितः एष बाष्पाम्बुशीकरकणौघः बाष्पाम्बूनां शीकराः तेषां कणाः सूक्ष्मावयवाः तेषामोघः समूहः तस्याः करतलसंस्पर्शाद् हेतोः स्वेदस्य घर्मस्य उद्गम इव भाति। उत्प्रेक्षालंकारः। आर्या वृत्तम्॥ १२॥ मनोरथोऽपि ते इति। मनोरथादपि भर्ता मयि अधिकमनुरक्त इति भावः। सरसानि आर्द्राणि यानि कमलिनीनां दलानि पत्राणि मृणालानि बिसानि च तैः विरचितम्। मदनावस्था कामजनितसन्ताप इत्यर्थः तस्याः सूचकम्। निपुणं सूक्ष्मदृष्ट्येत्यर्थः। **परिम्लानमिति**। पीनस्तनजघनसङ्गात् स्तनौ च जघनं च स्तनजघनम्। पीनं पुष्टं च तत्स्तनजघनं च तस्य

---

१ ०नि बहु०. २ यतः. ३ भरितं. ४ (फलकं निर्वर्ण्य।) भोः. ५ फलगे आलिहिअ एवं. ६ जा उण ईरिसीए पिअस्स बहुमाणअंतीए आलिखिदो तस्स दे अत्तणो परिहवो. ७ परिहवो जेण इमाए. ८ भूमिं ग०. ९ सन्तोसीअदि. १० अवरं स०.

इदं व्यस्तन्यासं श्लथभुजलताक्षेपवलनैः[1]
कृशाङ्ग्याः संतापं वदति नलिनीपत्रशयनम्[2] ॥ १३ ॥

अपि च ।

स्थितमुरसि विशालं पद्मिनीपत्रमेत-
त्कथयति न तथान्तर्मन्मथोत्थामवस्थाम्[3][4] ।
अतिगुरुपरितापम्लापिताभ्यां[5][6] यथास्याः
स्तनयुगपरिणाहं मण्डलाभ्यां ब्रवीति ॥ १४ ॥

विदूषकः—(नाट्येन मृणालिकां गृहीत्वा ।) भो वयस्य अयमपरस्तस्या एव पीनस्तनोष्माक्लिश्यमानकोमलमृणालहारः । तत्प्रेक्षतां भवान् । (क)

राजा—(गृहीत्वोरसि विन्यस्य ।) अयि जडप्रकृते—

(क) भो वअस्स अँअं अवरो ताए एव्व पीणत्थणुम्हाकिलिसन्तकोमलमुणालहारो[7] । ता पेक्खदु भवं ।

सङ्गात्संपर्कात् उभयतः उभयभागयोः परिम्लानं तन्निष्ठतापादिति भावः । तनोर्मध्यस्य अन्तः मध्यभागे परिमिलनं संपर्कमप्राप्य हरितं क्लेषाभावाद् हरिद्वर्णम् । तथा च मनसिजसन्तापात् श्लथे भुजौ लते इव भुजलते तयोः आक्षेपाः वलनानि चलनानि च तैः व्यस्तः विक्षिप्तः न्यासः रचना यस्य तत् । नलिनीपत्रशयनं कृशाङ्ग्याः कृशमङ्गं यस्यास्तथोक्तायाः सन्तापं वदति कथयति सूचयतीत्यर्थः । शिखरिणी वृत्तम् । रसै रुद्रैश्छिन्ना यमनसभलागः शिखरिणी । इति तल्लक्षणम् ॥ १३ ॥ **स्थितमिति** । अस्या उरसि स्थितं विशालमेतत् पद्मिनीपत्रम् । अतिगुरुरतिमहांश्चासौ परितापश्च तेन म्लापिताभ्यां म्लानिं नीताभ्याम् । पाठान्तरे अतिशयश्चासौ परितापश्च तेन ग्लापितानि निःसहतां नीतानि अङ्गानि अवयवा यस्या इति अस्याः इत्यस्य विशेषणम् । मण्डलाभ्यां मन्मथोत्थां कामपीडाजन्यामवस्थां दशां तथा न ब्रवीति कथयति यथा स्तनयुगस्य परिणाहं विशालतां ब्रवीति । मालिनीवृत्तम् । तल्लक्षणं—ननमयययुतेयं मालिनी भोगिलोकैः इति ॥ १४ ॥ मृणालिकां मृणालमालामित्यर्थः । पीनस्तनयोः ऊष्मा तेन पाठान्तरे पीनस्तनाभ्यां यत्स्खलनं तेन क्लिश्यमानश्चासौ मृणालहारश्च । पाठान्तरे क्लिश्यमानानि म्लायमानानीत्यर्थः कमलानि यत्र तादृशः । जडा मन्दा प्रकृतिः स्वभावो

---

१ चलनैः. २ बिसिनी. ३ तथा मे. ४ मान्मथीयाम॰. ५ अतिशय. ६ ग्लापि॰.
७ अअं क्खु उवलद्धो अवरो ॰त्थणजोग्गो किल॰; ॰त्थणक्खलण॰; ॰सन्तकमलो; त्थणुण्णाहकि॰

परिच्युतस्तत्कुचकुम्भमध्या-
त्किं शोषमायासि मृणालहार ।
न सूक्ष्मतन्तोरपि तावकस्य
तत्रावकाशो भवतः किमु स्यात् ॥ १५ ॥

सुसं०—(स्वगतम् ।) हा धिक् हा धिक् । गुर्वनुरागोत्क्षिप्तहृदयो भर्ताऽसंबद्धमपि मन्त्रयितुं प्रवृत्तः । तन्न युक्तमतः परमुपेक्षितुम् । भवतु । एवं तावत् । (प्रकाशम् ।) सखि यस्य कृते त्वमागता सोऽयं ते पुरतस्तिष्ठति । (क)

साग०—(सासूयम् ।) सुसंगते कस्य कृतेऽहमत्रागता । (ख)

सुसं०—(विहस्य ।) अयि अन्यशङ्किते ननु चित्रफलकस्य । तद् गृहाणैतम् । (ग)

(क) हद्धी हद्धी । गुरुआणुराओखित्तहिअओ भट्टा असंबद्धं पि मन्तेदुं पउत्तो । तों ण जुत्तं अदो वरं उवेक्खिदुम् । भोदु । एव्वं दाव । सहि जस्स किदे तुमं आगदा सो अअं ते पुरदो चिट्ठदि । (ख) सुसंगदे कस्स किदे अहं एत्थ आगदा । (ग) अइ अण्णसङ्किदे णं चित्तफलअस्स । ता गेण्ह एदम् ।

यस्य स जडप्रकृतिः तत्सम्बुद्धिः जडप्रकृते इति । **परिच्युत इति** । हे मृणालहार तत्कुचकुम्भमध्यात् कुचौ कुम्भौ इव कुचकुम्भौ । उपमितं व्याघ्रादिभिः सामान्याप्रयोगे इति समासः । तस्याः कुचकुम्भौ तत्कुचकुम्भौ तयोः मध्यात् परिच्युतः स्खलितः इति किं शोषं शुष्कतामायासि गच्छसि । खिद्यसे इत्यर्थः । अकारणं खिद्यसे इत्यहो ते जडप्रकृतित्वमित्यर्थः । यतः तावकस्य तवायमिति तावकस्तस्य सूक्ष्मतन्तोः अपि तत्र तस्याः स्तनान्तरे अवकाशः स्थानं नास्ति भवतः तदपेक्षयातिमहतः किमु स्यात् कथं स संभवेत् । उपजातिश्छन्दः । तदुक्तं—स्यादिन्द्रवज्रा यदि तौ जगौ ग उपेन्द्रवज्रा जतजास्ततो गौ । अनन्तरोदीरितलक्ष्मभाजौ पादौ यदीयावुपजातयस्ताः ॥ इति ॥ १५ ॥ गुरुश्चासौ अनुरागश्च तेन उत्क्षिप्तमाकुलितं हृदयं यस्य स तथोक्तः । असम्बद्धमसमञ्जसम् । जडेऽपि हारे चेतनवद्व्यवहारादित्यर्थः । उक्तं च कालिदासेन—कामार्ता हि प्रकृतिकृपणाश्चेतनाचेतनेषु । इति । न युक्तमुपेक्षितुं सागारिकार्थमुत्ताम्यतोऽस्य तस्या दर्शनेऽलं विलम्बेनेति भावः । शङ्का अस्या संजातासौ शङ्किता । अन्येन शङ्किता अन्यशङ्किता । यद्वा अन्यस्य शङ्का अन्यशङ्का सा संजाताऽस्याः । तत्संबोधनम् ।

१ स्तन. २ आत्म० ३ अस्मात्परं—कहिं मुणालहारो कहिं तस्स उवालम्भो इत्य० ४ ता अदो अवरं उण ण जुत्तं अपेक्खिदुं (अपेक्षितुम्). ५ इदं. ६ ०गदा को वा एत्थ चिट्ठदि.

साग०—(सरोषम् ।) अकुशलास्मि तवेदृशानामालापानाम् । तदन्यतो गमिष्यामि । (इति गन्तुमिच्छति ।) (क)

सुसं०—(सागरिकां हस्ते गृहीत्वा ।) अयि असहने इह तिष्ठ तावन्मुहूर्तं यावदस्मात्कदलीगृहाच्चित्रफलकं गृहीत्वागच्छामि । (ख)

साग०—सखि एवं कुरु । (ग)

(सुसंगता कदलीगृहाभिमुखं परिक्रामति ।)

विदू०—(सुसंगतां दृष्ट्वा ससंभ्रमम् ।) भो वयस्य प्रच्छादयैतं चित्रफलकम् । एषा खलु देव्याः परिचारिका सुसंगतागता । (घ)

(राजा पटान्तेन फलकं प्रच्छादयति ।)

सुसं०—(उपसृत्य ।) जयतु जयतु भर्ता । (ङ)

राजा—सुसंगते स्वागतम् । इहोपविश्यताम् ।

(सुसंगतोपविशति ।)

राजा—सुसंगते कथमहमिहस्थो भवत्या ज्ञातः ।

सुसं०—(विहस्य) भर्तः न केवलं त्वमयमपि चित्रफलकेन सह सर्वो वृत्तान्तो मया विज्ञातः । तद्गत्वा देव्यै निवेदयिष्यामि । (च)

विदू०—(अपवार्य सभयम् ।) भो वयस्य सर्वं संभाव्यते । मुखरा खल्वेषा गर्भदासी । पारितोषिकेण संप्रीणयैनाम् । (छ)

(क) अउसलम्हि तुह ईदिसाणां आलावाणम् । ता अण्णदो गमिस्सम् । (ख) अइ असहणे इह चिट्ठ दाव मुहुत्तअं जाव इमादो कदलीघरादो चित्तफलहं गेण्हिअ आअच्छामि । (ग) सहि एव्वं करेहि । (घ) भो वअस्स पच्छादेहि एदं चित्तफलअम् । एसा क्खु देवीए परिचारिआ सुसंगदा आगदा । (ङ) जअदु जअदु भट्टा । (च) भट्टा ण केवलं तुमम् अअं पि चित्तफलएण सह सव्वो वुत्तन्तो मए विण्णादो । ता गदुअ देवीए णिवेदयस्सम् । (छ) भो वअस्य सव्वं संभावीअदि । मुहरा क्खु एसा गब्भदासी । ता पारितोसिएण संपीणेहि णम् ।

वत्सराजो मेऽभिप्रेत इति सञ्जातशङ्के इति नर्मोक्तिः । ईदृशानामालापानां वक्रभाषणानामित्यर्थः । ससंभ्रमं सत्वरम् । संभ्रमकारणमुक्तमेषा खलु इत्यनेन । मुखरा दुर्मुखा । अप्रियकथनतत्परेत्यर्थः । गर्भदासी गर्भे दासी गर्भादारभ्य दासीति वा निन्दावचनम् ।

---

१ प्रस्थिता पदद्वयं ददाति. २ गृहप्रवेशं नाटयति. ३ सभयम्. ४ सुसंगदे अउ०; सहि अणिउणाम्हि—अइ णिउणा क्खु तुमं वि ईदि०. ५ पडिवालेहि. ६ अस्मात्परं—सुसं०—एवं करेम्हि इत्य०. ७ ण के० देवो. ८ ता जाव. ९ परितोसेहि णं.

राजा—[1]युक्तमुक्तं भवता । (सुसंगतां हस्ते गृहीत्वा ।) सुसंगते क्रीडामात्रमेवैतत् । [2]अकारणे त्वया देवी न खेदयितव्या । [3]इदं ते पारितोषिकम् । (कर्णाभरणं प्र[4]यच्छति ।)

सुसं०—(प्रण[5]म्य सस्मितम् ।) भर्तः अलं शङ्कया । मयापि भर्तुः प्रसादेन क्रीडितमेव । तत्किं कर्णाभरणेन । एष एव मे गुरुः प्रसादो यत्कस्मात्त्वयाहमत्र चित्रफलक आलिखितेति कुपिता मे प्रियसखी सागरिका । तद्गत्वा प्रसादयत्वेनां भर्ता । (**क**)

राजा—(स[6]संभ्रममुत्थाय ।) क्वासौ क्वासौ ।

सुसं०—इत इतो भर्ता । (**ख**)

विदू०—भो गृह्णामि एतं चित्रफलकम् । कदापि पुनरप्येतेन कार्यं भविष्यति । (**ग**)

सुसं०—भर्तः इयं सा । (**घ**)

(सर्वे कदलीगृहान्नि[7]ष्क्रामन्ति ।)

साग०—(राजानं [8]दृष्ट्वा सहर्षं ससाध्वसं सकम्पं च स्वगतम् ।) हा

(**क**) भट्टा अलं [9]संङ्काए । मए वि भट्टिणो पसाएण कीलिदं एव्व । तां किं कण्णाभरणेण । एसो ज्जेव मे गुरुओ पसाओ जं कीस तुए अहं एत्थ चित्तफलए आलिहिदत्ति कुविदा मे पिअसही साअरिआ । ता गदुअ [10]पसादेदु णं भट्टा । (**ख**) इदो इदो भट्टा । (**ग**) [11]भो गेण्हामि एदं चित्तफलम् । कदा वि पुणो वि एदिणा कज्जं भविस्सदि । (**घ**) भट्टा इअं सा ।

क्रीडामात्रं न तु वास्तवमत्र किंचिदिति भावः । भर्तुः प्रसादेन क्रीडितं भर्तुः प्रसादमवलम्ब्य विनोद एष कृतः इति भावः । एष एव गुरुकः प्रसादः अयमेव महाननुग्रहो भवेदित्यर्थः । सुसं०-भट्टा...ता पसादीअदु इत्यनेन सुसंगतावचसा सागरिका मयालिखिता सागरिकया च त्वमिति सूचयता प्रसादोपन्यासेन बीजोद्भेदनाद् उपन्यास इति प्रतिमुखसन्धेरङ्गमिदम् । क्वासौ क्वासौ इति-अत्र सागरिकानुरागबीजस्य दृष्टनष्टस्य वत्सराजेनानुसरणात्परिसर्प इति प्रतिमुखसन्धेरङ्गमुक्तम् । **सहर्षमिति** ।

---

१ युक्तमभिहितम् । (सुसंगताया अलकान्संवृत्य ।). २ अकारणं, तथापि नाकारणे...देवी खे०; व्यथयितव्या-कोपयितव्या. ३ एतन्नास्ति पुस्त०. ४ समर्पयति; इति कर्णादवतार्याभरणं दातुमिच्छति; हस्तादवतार्य कटकं कर्णाभरणं चात्मन उपनीय सुसंगतायै दत्वा. ५ स० प्र० गृह्णाति. ६ (सहसो०) दर्शय दर्शय । क्वा०. ७ निष्क्रमणं नाटयन्ति; निष्क्रान्ताः. ८ सस्पृहं दृष्ट्वा ससाध्वसं चात्मगतम्. ९ अलं सङ्काए एदिणा भट्टुणो पसादेण अ । कीलिदं जेव्व । भट्टिणीए पसादेण बहुतरं कीलिदं जेव्व । एसो उण मे गुरुओ पसादो करीअदु जं कीस ०दोत्ति भणिअ कुविदा साग० पसादीअदु (प्रसाद्यताम्). १० एसा पसादीअदु. ११ (आत्मगतम् ।) गे०; इदस्स कज्जं; इमिणा...होदि.

धिक् हा धिक् । एतं प्रेक्ष्यातिसाध्वसेन न शक्नोमि पदात्पदमपि गन्तुम् । तत्किमिदानीमत्र करिष्यामि । (क)

विदू०—(सागरिकां दृष्ट्वा ।) ही ही भोः आश्चर्यमाश्चर्यम् । ईदृशं रूपं मनुष्यलोके न पुनर्दृश्यते । तत्तर्कयामि प्रजापतेरप्येतन्निर्माय्य विस्मयः समुत्पन्न इति । (ख)

राजा—वयस्य ममाप्येवं मनसि वर्तते ।

दृशः पृथुतरीकृता जितनिजाब्जपत्रत्विष-
श्चतुर्भिरपि साधु साध्विति मुखैः समं व्याहृतम् ।
शिरांसि चलितानि विस्मयवशाद् ध्रुवं वेधसा
विधाय ललनां जगत्रयललामभूतामिमाम् ॥ १६ ॥

साग०—(सासूयं सुसंगतामालोक्य ।) सखि ईदृशः चित्रफलकस्त्वया आनीतः । (इति गच्छति ।) (ग)

राजा—

दृष्टिं रुषा क्षिपसि भामिनि यद्यपीमां
स्निग्धेयमेष्यति तथापि न रूक्षभावम् ।
त्यक्त्वा त्वरां व्रज पदैस्स्खलितैरयं ते
खेदं करिष्यति गुरुर्नितरां नितम्बः ॥ १७ ॥

(क) हद्धी हद्धी । एदं पेक्खिअ अतिसद्धसेण न सक्कणोमि पदादो पदं वि गन्तुम् । ता किं दाणिं एत्थ करिस्सम् । (ख) ही ही भोः अच्चरिअं अच्चरिअम् । ईदिसं रूवं माणुसलोए ण पुणो दीसदि । ता तक्केमि पआवइणो वि एदं णिम्माविअ विम्हओ समुप्पण्णोत्ति । (ग) सहि ईदिसो चित्तफलओ तुए आणीदो ।

अभीष्टजनदर्शनाद्धर्षः । आकस्मिकदर्शनात्साध्वसं कम्पश्च । कन्यारत्नमिति पाठे कन्यानां रत्नं कन्यारत्नमिति सम्बन्धसामान्यषष्ठ्या समासः । दृश इति । जगतां त्रयं जगत्रयं तस्य ललामं भूता तां ललामभूतां भूषणस्वरूपामिमां ललनां विधाय सृष्ट्वा वेधसा ब्रह्मणा ध्रुवं निश्चितं विस्मयस्य वशादधीनत्वाद्विस्मयवशात् । जिता निजस्य अब्जस्यासनभूतस्य कमलस्य पत्राणां त्विट् शोभा याभिस्ताद्दृश्यः दृशः दृष्टयः पृथुतरीकृताः विस्फारिताः । तथा चतुर्भिरपि मुखैः समं युगपत्साधु साधु इति व्याहृतं भाषितम् । शिरांसि चलितानि चालितानि च । उत्प्रेक्षालंकारः । पृथ्वी वृत्तम् । जसौ जसयला वसुग्रहयतिश्च पृथ्वी गुरुः इति लक्षणात् ॥ १६ ॥ दृष्टिमिति । हे भामिनि कोपने । कोपना सैव भामिनी इत्यमरः । यद्यपि इमां दृष्टिं रुषा क्रोधेन क्षिपसि तथापि स्निग्धा स्नेहपूर्णेयं रूक्षभावं रूक्षतां न एष्यति यास्यति । त्वरां त्यक्त्वा व्रज गच्छ । यतः त्वरागमने पदस्खलितैः पदानां विसंष्ठुलैः पातैः अयं तव गुरुः पृथुः

---

१ प्येतदेव. २ वेधसः. ३ राजानं दृष्ट्वा सरोषम्. ४ कोपाद्गच्छति; गन्तुमिच्छति. ५ तव; पदैः. ६ हि. ७ गमिष्यति. ८ नियतम्. ९ उरुत्थम्भेण...०णोमि इदो गन्तुं; चलिदुम्. १० वा. ११ कण्णआरअणं, पि णाम रू०; मणुस्स०. १२ सुसंगदे ईदिसो सो.

सुसं०—भर्तः अतिकोपना खल्वेषा। तद्धस्ते गृहीत्वा प्रसादयैनाम्। (क)

राजा—(सानन्दम्।) यथाह भवती। (सागरिकां हस्ते गृहीत्वा स्पर्शसुखं नाटयति।)

विदू०—भोः एषा खलु त्वयाऽपूर्वा श्रीः समासादिता। (ख)

राजा—वयस्य सत्यम्।

> **श्रीरेषा पाणिरप्यस्याः पारिजातस्य पल्लवः।**
> **कुतोऽन्यथा स्रवत्येष स्वेदच्छद्मामृतद्रवः॥ १८॥**

सुसं०—सखि अतिनिष्ठुरेदानीमसि त्वं यैवं भर्त्रा हस्ते गृहीतापि कोपं न मुञ्चसि। (ग)

साग०—(सभ्रूभङ्गम्।) अयि सुसंगते अद्यापि न विरमसि। (घ)

राजा—अयि प्रसीद। न खलु युक्तः सखीजन एवंविधः कोपानुबन्धः।

(क) भट्टा अदिकोवणा क्खु एसा। ता हत्थे गेह्णिअ पसादेहि णम्। (ख) भो एसा क्खु तुए अपुव्वा सिरी समासादिदा। (ग) सहि अदिणिट्ठुरा दाणिं सि तुमं जा एवं भट्टिणा हत्थे गिहीदा वि कोवं ण मुञ्चसि। (घ) अइ सुसङ्गदे अज्ज वि ण विरमेसि।

नितम्बः ते नितरामत्यन्तं खेदं श्रमं करिष्यति जनयिष्यति। वसन्ततिलकं वृत्तम्। लक्षणमुक्तम्॥ १७॥ कोपना कोपशीला कुप क्रोधे इत्यस्मात् क्रुधमण्डार्थेभ्यश्च इत्यनेन ताच्छील्ये युच्। **श्रीरेषेति**। एषा इयं सुन्दरी श्रीः लक्ष्मीः। अस्याः पाणिश्च पारिजातस्य कल्पवृक्षस्य पल्लवः किसलयः। अत्र हेतुमाह—अन्यथा एवं न चेत् कुतः एष स्वेदः छद्म व्याजः यस्य स स्वेदच्छद्मा घर्मरूपः अमृतद्रवः अमृतरसः स्रवति। ०द्रवमिति पाठे एष पाणिः ०द्रवं स्रवति इति योज्यम्। रूपकालंकारः॥ १८॥ अत्र राजा सागरिकां हस्ते गृहीत्वा इत्यादिना स्वेदच्छद्मामृतद्रव इत्यन्तेन नायकयोः साक्षादन्योन्यदर्शनादिना सविशेषानुरागोद्घाटनात्पुष्पाख्यं प्रतिमुखसन्धेरङ्गम्। अतिनिष्ठुरा अतिकठोरहृदया। इतरा मानिन्यः प्रियेण हस्तग्रहे मानं मुञ्चन्ति त्वं तु तथा न करोषि इति निष्ठुरत्वम्। सभ्रूभङ्गं भ्रुवोर्भङ्गः उन्नयनं तेन सहितं यथा तथा। न विरमसि एवंविधभाषणादिति शेषः। अत्र सखि अतिनिष्ठुरासीत्यादिना विरमसीत्यन्तेन अनुरागबीजोद्घाटनान्वयेन धृतिः(नर्मजा द्युतिः) इत्यङ्गं दर्शितम्। कोपानुबन्धः

---

१ सानन्दं तथा करोति। हस्ते गृहीत्वा स्पर्शं ना०. २ पतत्ये०...द्रवम्. ३ ०ङ्गमीषद्विहस्य. ४ प्रिये सागरिके न खलु सखीजने युक्त एवं कोपा० ...कर्तुम् युज्यते. ५ अस्मादनन्तरं—विदू०—बुभुक्खिदो बम्हणो विअ किं कुप्पसि। सुसं०—सहि तुए सह ण बोल्लइस्सं (वक्ष्यामि). राजा—अयि कोपने नेतद्युक्तं समानप्रतिपत्तिषु सखीषु। इत्यधि० क्वचित्. ६ अदिउच्चसिरी. ७ अदिकोपणा क्खु. ८ हत्थे-त्था-वलम्बिदा; अज्ज वि. ९ दाणिं.

विदू०—एषा खल्वपरा देवी वासवदत्ता । (क)

(राजा सचकितं सागरिकाया हस्तं मुञ्चति ।)

साग०—(ससंभ्रमम् ।) सुसंगते किमिदानीमत्र करिष्ये । (ख)

सुसं०—सखि एतां तमालवीथिकामन्तरयित्वा निष्क्रामावः । (ग)

(निष्क्रान्ते ।)

राजा—(पार्श्वतोऽवलोक्य ।) वयस्य कैं सा देवी वासवदत्ता ।

विदू०—भो न जानामि क्व सा । मया एषा खल्वपरा देवी वासवदत्तातिदीर्घरोषतयेति भणितम् । (घ)

राजा—धिङ् मूर्ख ।

प्राप्ता कथमपि दैवात्कण्ठमनीतैव सा प्रकटरागा ।
रत्नावलीव कान्ता मम हस्ताद्भ्रंशिता भवता ॥ १९ ॥

(ततः प्रविशति वासवदत्ता काञ्चनमाला च ।)

वासवदत्ता—हञ्जे काञ्चनमाले अथ कियद्दूरं इदानीं सार्यपुत्रेण परिगृहीता नवमालिका । (ङ)

काञ्चनमाला—भर्त्रि एतत्कदलीगृहमतिक्रम्य दृश्यत एव । (च)

वासव०—तदादेशाय मार्गम् । (छ)

(क) एसा क्खु अवरा देवी वासवदत्ता । (ख) सुसंगदे किं दाणिं एत्थ करिस्सम् । (ग) सहि एदं तमालवीथिअं अन्तरिअ णिक्कमम्ह । (घ) भो ण जाणामि क्व सा । मए एसा क्खु अवरा देवी वासवदत्ता अदिदीहरोसदाए ति भणिदं । (ङ) हञ्जे कञ्चणमाले अध केत्तिअ दूरे दाणिं सा अज्जउत्तेण परिगिहीदा णोमालिआ । (च) भट्टिणि एदं कददीघरअं अदिक्कमिअ दीसदि एव्व । (छ) ता आदेसेहि मग्गम् ।

अविरतः कोपः दीर्घरोष इत्यर्थः । एषा सागरिका । राज्ञावगतार्थस्तु एषा इयमागतापरा देवी वासवदत्तेति । अत्र वासवदत्तागमने । **प्राप्तेति** । कथमपि दैवात्सुदैवात्प्राप्ता । सागरिका रत्नावली च । प्रकटरागा प्रकटः स्पष्टं दृश्यमानः रागः अनुरागः पक्षे प्रभा यस्याः सा । कान्ता हृदयंगमा । उभयत्र समानम् । सा रत्नावली रत्नमालेव कण्ठमनीता एव भवता त्वया मम हस्ताद् भ्रंशिता प्रच्याविता । श्लेषोपमयोरङ्गाङ्गिभावरूपः संकरः । आर्यावृत्तम् ॥ १९ ॥ अत्र राजा धिङ् मूर्ख इत्यारभ्य भ्रंशिता भवता

---

१ सभ्रूभङ्गम्. २ पार्श्वाणि, समन्तादव० सविस्मयम्. ३ क्वासौ. ४ अनीत्वैव. ५ ०दत्ता मे पडिभादि; अवरा वास०. ६ तमालविडवं, कदलीवीटिआए णि०. ७ भो सा एदम् । सा क्खु; वअस्स एदं क्खु मए भणिदं एसा क्खु...अदिकोवणदाए; एसा वास० अवरा दीग्घरोसदाए संवुत्तात्ति. ८ एव्व । ता एदु एदु देवी. ९ मग्गं । तत्थ एव्व गच्छम्ह.

काञ्चन०—एतु एतु भर्त्री। (क)

राजा—वयस्य क्वेदानीं प्रिया द्रष्टव्या।

काञ्चन०—भर्त्रि यथा समीपे भर्ता मन्त्रयते तथा तर्कयामि भर्त्रीमेव प्रतिपालयंस्तिष्ठतीति। तदुपसर्पतु भर्त्री। (ख)

वासव०—(उपसृत्य।) जयतु जयत्वार्यपुत्रः। (ग)

राजा—(अपवार्य।) वयस्य प्रच्छादय चित्रफलकम्।

(विदूषकः कैक्षायां फलकं प्रक्षिप्योत्तरीयेण प्रच्छादयति।)

वासव०—आर्यपुत्र अथ कुसुमिता नवमालिका। (घ)

राजा—देवि प्रथममिहागतैरप्यस्माभिस्त्वं चिरयसीति नैव दृष्टा। तदेहि। सहितावेव तां पश्यावः।

वासव०—(निर्वर्ण्य।) आर्यपुत्र मुखरागादेव मया ज्ञातं यथा कुसुमिता नवमालिकेति। तन्न गमिष्यामि। (ङ)

विदू०—ही ही भोः जितं जितमस्माभिः। (इति बाहू प्रसार्य नृत्यति। नृत्यतः कक्षान्तरात्फलकः पतति।) (च)

(राजा अपवार्य विदूषकमङ्गुल्याँ तर्जयति।)

विदू०—(अपवार्य।) भो मा कुप्य। तूष्णीकास्तिष्ठ। अहमेवात्र ज्ञास्यामि। (छ)

(क) एदु एदु भट्टिणी। (ख) भट्टिणि जहा समीवे भट्टा मन्तेदि तह तक्केमि भट्टिणीं एव्व पडिवालअन्तो चिट्ठदित्ति। ता उवसप्पदु भट्टिणी। (ग) जअदु जअदु अज्जउत्तो। (घ) अज्जउत्त अंह कुसुमिदा णोमालिआ। (ङ) अज्जउत्त मुहराआदो एव्व मए जाणिदं जहा कुसुमिदा णोमालिआत्ति। ता ण गमिस्सम्। (च) ही ही भो जिदं जिदं अम्हेहिं। (छ) भो मा कुप्प। तुण्हीओ चिट्ठ। अहं एव्व एत्थ जाणिस्सम्।

इत्यन्तेन वत्सराजस्य सागरिकासमागमरूपहितस्य वासवदत्ताप्रवेशसूचकेन विदूषकवचसा निरोधात् निरोधनाख्यं प्रतिमुखसन्धेरङ्गं दर्शितम्। उत्तरीयेण उपरिवस्त्रेण। उत्तरस्मिन्देहभागे भवमुत्तरीयम्। मुखरागात्त्वन्मुखकान्तिविशेषात्। आर्यपुत्रमुखरागादिति समस्तं वा पदम्। **नृत्यत** इत्यादि एवंविधा विदूषकस्यानवधानता सर्वश्रुतैव।

---

१ प्रियतमा. २ अस्मात्परं–देवि स्वागतम्। इत आस्यताम्. ३ गृहीत्वा कक्षे निक्षिपति. ४ राजा—(सस्मितम्). ५ न सा दृष्टा; दृष्टा नवमालिका; समेतावेव. ६ अस्मात्परं–तद् दृष्ट्वा विषादं नाटयति। इत्य०. ७ ०ल्यग्रेण; ०ल्या दर्शयन्वसंतकमुखं पश्यति. ८ तुमं. ९ देवी. १० अध सच्चकं जेव्व. ११ ०राएण...सा णो०. १२ भोदि जह एव्वं ता जिदं. १३ भो तुण्हीओ; तुमं–वं चि०.

काञ्चन०—(फलकं गृहीत्वा निरूप्यापवार्य ।) भर्त्रि प्रेक्षस्व तावत्किमत्र चित्रफलके आलिखितम् । (क)

वासव०—(निरूप्यापवार्य ।) काञ्चनमाले अयं आर्यपुत्रः । इयं पुनः सागरिका । किं न्वेतत् । (ख)

काञ्चन०—भर्त्रि अहमप्येतदेव चिन्तयामि । (ग)

वासव०—(सकोपहासम् ।) आर्यपुत्र केनेदमालिखितम् । (घ)

राजा—(सवैलक्ष्यस्मितम् । अपवार्य ।) वयस्य किं ब्रवीमि ।

विदू०—(अपवार्य ।) भो मा चिन्तय । अहमुत्तरं दास्यामि । (प्रकाशं वासवदत्तां प्रति ।) भवति मान्यथा संभावय । आत्मा किल दुःखेनालिख्यत इति मम वचनं श्रुत्वा प्रियवयस्येनैतदालेख्यविज्ञानं दर्शितम् । (ङ)

राजा—यथाह वसन्तकस्तथैवैतत् ।

वासव०—(फलकं निर्दिश्य) आर्यपुत्र एषापि यापरा तव समीप आलिखिता तत्किमार्यवसन्तकस्य विज्ञानम् । (च)

राजा—(सस्मितम् ।) देवि अलमन्यथा शङ्कया । इयं हि कापि कन्यका स्वचेतसैव परिकल्प्यालिखिता । न तु दृष्टपूर्वा ।

विदू०—भवति सत्यं सत्यम् । शपे ब्रह्मसूत्रेण यदीदृशी कदाप्यस्माभिर्दृष्टपूर्वा । (छ)

(क) भट्टिणि पेक्ख दाव किमेत्थ चित्तफलए आलिहिदं । (ख) कञ्चणमाले अअं अज्जउत्तो । इअं उण साअरिआ । किं ण्णेदम् । (ग) भट्टिणि अहं पि एदं एव्व चिन्तेमि । (घ) अज्जउत्त केण एदं आलिहिदम् । (ङ) भो मा चिन्तेहि । अहं उत्तरं दाइस्सम् । भोदि मा अण्णथा संभावेहि । अप्पा किल दुक्खेण आलिहीअदि त्ति मम वअणं सुणिअ पिअवअस्सेण एदं आलेक्खविण्णाणं दंसिदम् । (च) अज्जउत्त एसावि जा अवरा तुह समीवे आलिहिदा ता किं अज्जवसन्तअस्स विण्णाणम् । (छ) भोदि सच्चं सच्चम् । सवामि वम्हसुत्तेण जइ ईदिशी कदावि अम्हेहिं दिट्ठपुव्वा ।

मा कुप्येत्यत्र निषेधार्थो माशब्दो न तु माङ्यम् । सवैलक्ष्यस्मितमिति । विलक्षस्य भावः वैलक्ष्यम् । विलक्षो विस्मयान्विते । इत्यमरः । वैलक्ष्यद्योतकं स्मितं वैलक्ष्यस्मितं तेन सहितं यथा तथा सवैलक्ष्यस्मितम् । आत्मा स्वस्याकृतिः । ब्रह्मसूत्रेण यज्ञोपवीतेन ।

---

१ (फ० गृहीत्वा) भट्टिणि. २ (निर्वर्ण्य स्वगतम् ।) अअं...रिआ । (प्रकाशं राजानं प्रति ।) अज्जउत्त । किं णिवदम्. ३ ०स्मितं कृत्वाप०; सवैलक्ष्यं विदूषकं संज्ञापयति । विदू०—अप्पा किल इ०. ४ स्मितं कृत्वा; सवैलक्ष्यस्मितम्. ५ संभावितेन । इयं हि मया स्वचेतसा विकल्प्य कन्यामिलि०. ६ पेक्खदु पेक्खदु भट्टिणी किमित्थ० आलि० ति. ७ भोदि अप्पाथ किल इ०. ८ सच्चं सवामि; ९ बम्हणत्तणेण (ब्राह्मण्येन).

काञ्च०—(अपवार्य ।) भर्त्रि घुणाक्षरमपि कदापि संभवत्येव । (क)

वास०—(अपवार्य ।) अयि ऋजुके वसन्तकः खल्वेषः । न जानासि त्वमेतस्य वक्रभणितानि । (प्रकाशम् ।) आर्यपुत्र मम पुनरेतच्चित्रफलकं प्रेक्षमाणायाः शीर्षवेदना समुत्पन्ना । तद्गमिष्याम्यहम् । (प्रस्थिता ।)(ख)

राजा—(पटान्तेन गृहीत्वा ।) देवि[3] ।

प्रसीदेति ब्रूयामिदमसति कोपे न घटते
करिष्यामेवं नो पुनरिति भवेदभ्युपगमः ।
न मे दोषोऽस्तीति त्वमिदमपि च ज्ञास्यसि मृषा
किमेतस्मिन्वक्तुं क्षममिति न वेद्मि प्रियतमे ॥ २० ॥

वासवदत्ता—(सविनयं पटान्तमाकर्षन्ती ।) आर्यपुत्र मान्यथा संभावय । सत्यमेव मां शीर्षवेदना बाधते । तद्गमिष्यामि । (ग)

(क) भट्टिणि घुणक्खरं पि कदावि संभवदि ज्जेव । (ख) अइ उजुँए वसन्तओ क्खु एसो । ण जाणासि तुमं एअस्स वक्कभणिदाइं । अज्जउत्त मम उणे एदं चित्तफलअं पेक्खन्तीए सीसवेअणा समुप्पण्णा । तां गमिस्सं अहम् । (ग) अज्जउत्त मा अण्णधा संभावेहि । सेच्चं ज्जेव मं सीसवेअणा बाधेदि । ता गमिस्सम् ।

घुणाक्षरमिति । घुणाख्यः कीटविशेषः दारुणि लिखन् यदृच्छयाऽक्षराकारं रेखाविशेषं जनयति । अतः यदृच्छया अन्यवस्तुसंवादि किंचिदपि घुणाक्षरमित्युच्यते । यथात्र तथा प्रतिपादिता राज्ञालिखिता आकृतिः । ऋजुके सरले । कपटमजानति इत्यर्थः । वक्रभणितानि व्याजोक्तीः । शीर्षवेदना राज्ञः परगतचित्तत्वादिति भावः । अत्र वास० (फलकं निर्दिश्य) अज्जउत्त इत्यादिना सीसवेदणा समुप्पण्णा इत्यन्तेन वासवदत्तया वत्सराजस्य सागरिकानुरागोद्भेदनात्प्रत्यक्षनिष्ठुराभिधानं वज्रमित्यङ्गम् । **प्रसीदेति** । हे देवि प्रसीद मयि प्रसन्ना भव इति ब्रूयां चेद् इदं क्रोधे असति अविद्यमाने । त्वया क्रोधो न दर्शित इति । न घटते । न युक्तमित्यर्थः । एवं पुनः नो करिष्यामि इति ब्रूयां चेद् अभ्युपगमः अकृतस्याङ्गीकारः भवेत् । मे दोषो नास्ति इति ब्रूयां चेद् इदमपि त्वं मृषा मिथ्याभाषितं इति ज्ञास्यसि । एवं हे प्रियतमे अस्मिन्प्रस्तावे किं वक्तुमुचितमिति न वेद्मि । काव्यलिङ्गमलंकारः । शिखरिणी वृत्तम् । लक्षणमुक्तं (२१२) अत्र । चित्रगतयोर्नायकयोर्दर्शनात्कुपिताया वासवदत्ताया

---

१ इत्युत्थाय गच्छति, गन्तुमिच्छति. २ पटान्ते. ३ देवि प्रसीद प्रसीद. ४ करिष्येऽहं नैवं. ५ हि. ६ कदावि ईदिसं घु० संभ० ता अलं कोपेण. ७ अज्ज एव. ८ ०णीदीओ (भणितीः). ९ ममावि. १० ता सुहं चिट्ठदु अज्जउत्तो । अहं गमि०. ११ सच्चं...मे.

(उभे निष्क्रान्ते ।)

विदूषकः—(पार्श्वाण्यवलोक्य ।) भो दिष्ट्या वर्धसे । क्षेमेणास्माकमतिक्रान्ताऽकालवातावली । (क)

राजा—धिङ् मूर्ख कृतं परितोषेण । यान्त्या आभिजात्यान्निगूढो न लक्षितस्त्वया देव्याः कोपानुबन्धः ।

भ्रूभङ्गे सहसोद्गतेऽपि वदनं नीतं परां नम्रता-
मीषन्मां प्रति भेदकारि हसितं नोक्तं वचो निष्ठुरम् ।
अन्तर्बाष्पजडीकृतं प्रभुतया चक्षुर्न विस्फारितं
कोपश्च प्रकटीकृतो दयितया मुक्तश्च न प्रश्रयः ॥ २१ ॥

तदेहि । देवीमेवं प्रसादयितुं गच्छावः ।

(इति निष्क्रान्ताः सर्वे ।)

इति कदलीगृहो नाम द्वितीयोऽङ्कः ।

(क) भो दिट्ठिआ वड्ढसि । क्खेमेण अम्हाणं अदिक्कन्ता अआलवादावली ।

अनुनयनात्पर्युपासनमित्यङ्गमिदम् ॥ २० ॥ अयुक्तः कालः अकालः तत्र वातावली इव । **भ्रूभङ्ग** इति । भ्रुवोर्भङ्गः भ्रूभङ्गः भ्रुकुटिबन्धस्तस्मिन्सहसा उद्गतेऽपि । क्रोधस्य द्योतकमेतत् । दयितया वदनं परां नम्रतां नीतम् । मां प्रति मामुद्दिश्य भेदं करोतीति भेदकारि हृदयस्पर्शि हसितम् । तथापि निष्ठुरं वचो नोक्तम् । अन्तः मध्ये यद्बाष्पं तेन जडीकृतमपि चक्षुः न विस्फारितं विकासितम् । एवं दयितया कोपः प्रकटीकृतः च प्रश्रयः विनयः न मुक्तश्च । शार्दूलविक्रीडितं वृत्तम् ॥ २१ ॥ इति रत्नावलीटीकायां द्वितीयोऽङ्कः ॥ २ ॥

---

१ इति. २ अस्मात्परं–विदू०—कहं कुविदा गता. राजा—वयस्य आभिजात्यविनिगूढः...बन्धः । तथा हि. ३ सहसोत्थिते. ४ तस्याः संप्रति. ५ अस्मात्परं–विदू०–गदा देवी वा० ता कीस तुमं अरण्णरुदिअं करेसि. ६ देवीसकाशमेव ग०; देवीं प्रसादयितुमभ्यन्तरमेव; देवीं गत्वा प्रसादयामि; सर्वथा देवीप्रसादनं मुक्त्वानान्यत्रोपायमाकलयामि. ७ निष्क्रान्तौ. ८ रत्नावलीनामप्रधाननाटिकायां द्वि०. ९ भो वअस्स एसा क्खु अदि० अम्हाणं अकालभासकारिणी.

तृतीयोऽङ्कः ।

(ततः प्रविशति मदनिका ।)

मदनिका—(आकाशे ।) कौशाम्बिके कौशाम्बिके अपि दृष्टा त्वया भर्तुः सकाशे काञ्चनमाला न वा । (कर्णं दत्वा ।) किं भणसि । कोऽपि कालस्तस्या आगत्य गताया इति । तत्कुत्रेदानीं प्रेक्षिष्ये । (अग्रतोऽवलोक्य ।) कथमेषा खलु काञ्चनमालेत एवागच्छति । तद्याव-देनामुपसर्पामि । (क)

(ततः प्रविशति काञ्चनमाला ।)

काञ्चनमाला—(सोत्प्रासम् ।) साधु रे अमात्यवसन्तक साधु । अतिशयितस्त्वयामात्ययौगन्धरायणोऽनया संधिविग्रहचिन्तया । (ख)

मद०—(उपसृत्य सस्मितम् ।) हला काञ्चनमाले किमार्यवसन्तकेन कृतं येन स एवं श्लाघ्यते । (ग)

काञ्चन०—हला मदनिके किं तवैतेन ज्ञातेन । त्वमिदं रहस्यं रक्षितुं न पारयसि । (घ)

(क) कोसम्बिए कोसम्बिए अवि दिट्ठा तुए भट्टिणो सआसे कञ्चणमाला ण वा । किं भणासि । कोवि कालो ताए आअच्छिअ गदाए त्ति । ता कहिं दाणिं पेक्खिस्सम् । कहं एसा क्खु कञ्चणमाला इदो एव्व आगच्छदि । ता जाव णं उवसप्पापि । (ख) साहु रे अमच्चवसन्तअ साहु । अदिसइदो तुए अमच्चजोगन्धराअणो इमाए संधिविग्गहचिन्ताए । (ग) हला काञ्चणमाले किं अज्जवसन्तएण किदं जेण सो एवं सलाहिअदि । (घ) हला मअणिए किं तव एदिणा जाणिदेण । तुमं इमं रहस्सं रक्खिदुं ण पारेसि ।

इत आरभ्य गर्भसन्धिः यत्र प्रतिमुखसन्धौ स्तोकोद्भिन्नस्य बीजस्य मुहुरन्वेषणं क्रियते। अथ वत्सराजस्य सागरिकायामनुरागं वर्णयितुं प्रवेशकमवतारयति ततः प्रविशतीत्यादिना । **आकाशे** इति । एतदेवाकाशभाषितमित्युच्यते-किं ब्रवीष्येवमित्यादि विना पात्रं ब्रवीति यत् । श्रुत्वेवानुक्तमप्येकस्तत्स्यादाकाशभाषितम् ॥ इति तल्लक्षणम् । कोऽपि कियानपि। सोत्प्रासं सोल्लुण्ठनं सोपहासमिति यावत्। अमा सह भवः अमात्यः । सन्धिश्च विग्रहश्च सन्धिविग्रहौ तयोश्चिन्तया विचारेण । विदूषकपक्षे सन्धिविग्रहौ नायिकयोः संयोगविप्रयोगौ । अत्र साधु रे इत्यारभ्य प्रवेशकेन अभूताहरणाख्यं

---

१ दत्वाकर्ण्य, आकर्ण्य. २ परिक्रम्याग्र०. ३ सोल्लासम्. ४ कौमौदिए. ५ पिअसहिं पे० ६ अणो वि. ७ सहि तव किं एदिणा पुच्छिदेण पओजणम्. ८ ण मे इमं ...०दुं पारेसि०

मद०—शपे देव्याश्चरणाभ्यां यदि कस्यापि पुरतः प्रकाशयामि। (क)

काञ्च०—यद्येवं तच्छृणु। अद्य खलु मया राजकुलात्प्रतिनिवर्तमानया चित्रशालिकाद्वारे वसन्तकस्य सुसंगतया सममालापः श्रुतः। (ख)

मद०—(सकौतुकम्।) सखि कीदृशः। (ग)

काञ्च०—यथा सुसंगते न खलु सागरिकां वर्जयित्वा अन्यत्किमपि प्रियवयस्यस्यास्वस्थताया कारणम्। तच्चिन्तयात्र प्रतीकारमिति। (घ)

मद०—ततः सुसंगतया किं भणितम्। (ङ)

काञ्च०—एवं तया भणितम्। अद्य खलु देव्या चित्रफलकवृत्तान्तशङ्कितया सागरिकां रक्षितुं मम हस्ते समर्पयन्त्या यन्नेपथ्यं मे प्रसादीकृतं तेनैव विरचितभर्तृनीवेषां सागरिकां गृहीत्वाहमपि काञ्चनमालावेषधारिणी भूत्वा प्रदोष इहागमिष्यामि। त्वमपीहैव चित्रशालिकाद्वारे मां प्रतिपालयिष्यासि। ततो माधवीलतामण्डपे तया सह भर्तुः समागमो भविष्यतीति। (च)

(क) सवामि देवीऐ चलणेहिं जदि कस्स वि पुरदो पआसेमि। (ख) जइ एवं ता सुणु। अज्ज क्खु मए राअउलाओ पडिणिउत्तमानाए चित्तसालिआदुआरे वसन्तअस्स सुसंगदाए समं आलावो सुदो। (ग) सहि कीदिसो। (घ) जह सुसंगदे ण क्खु साअरिअं वज्जिअ अण्णं किं पि पिअवअस्सस्स असच्छदाए कारणं। ता चिन्तेहि एत्थ पडिआरंत्ति। (ङ) तदो सुसंगदाए किं भणिदम्। (च) एवं ताए भणिदम्। अज्ज खु देवीए चित्तफलअवुत्तन्तसङ्किदाए साअरिअं रक्खिदुं मम हत्थे समप्पन्तीए जं णेवत्थं मे पसादीकिदं तेण ज्जेव विरचिदभट्टिणीवेसं साअरिअं गिण्हिअ अहं पि कञ्चणमालावेसधारिणी भविअ पओसे इह आगमिस्सम्। तुमं पि ईहं एव्व चित्तसालिआदुआरे मं पडिवालइस्ससि। तदो माहवीलदामण्डवे ताए सह भट्टिणो समागमो भविस्सदित्ति।

गर्भसन्धेः अङ्गमुक्तम्। चित्राणां शाला चित्रशाला सैव चित्रशालिका। स्वार्थे कः। सागरिकां वर्जयित्वा सागरिकानुरागनिमित्तमेवेदमस्वास्थ्यम्। चित्रफलकसम्बधी वृत्तान्तः चित्रफलकवृत्तान्तस्तेन संजातशङ्कया। नेपथ्यं वस्त्राभरणादि। वत्सोऽस्या

---

१ भट्टिणीए...जादि अमुं...प्पकासइस्सम्। २ कहिस्सम्. ३ पडि–णि–वुत्तन्तीए, णिक्कमन्तीए. ४ सह अअं. ५ सहि कधेहि कीदिसो सो आलावो. ६ एवं वसन्तएण भणिदं जह. ७ तदो अइ. ८ फलअदंसणसं०. ९ साअरिअं मम. १० जहापरिहिदं (यथापरिहितं); जह पिणद्धं भत्तणो सव्वं मंडणं मह पसादीकिदं ता तेण एव्व देवीपसादलद्धेण अलंकरणेन विर०. ११ पदोसकाले भट्टिणो आ०, भट्टिणो आ०; भट्टिणो सआसं. १२ इह आट्ठिदा पडि०; इह ज्जेव पडिवालेहि. १३ संगमो० ०गमं करिस्सामोत्ति.

मद०—(सरोषम् ।) सुसंगते हतासि खलु त्वं यैवं परिजनवत्सलां देवीं वञ्चयसे । (क)

काञ्चन०—हला त्वमिदानीं कुत्र प्रस्थिता । (ख)

मद०—अहं खल्वस्वस्थशरीरस्य भर्तुः कुशलवृत्तान्तं ज्ञातुं गता त्वं चिरयसीत्युत्ताम्यन्त्या देव्या तव सकाशं प्रेषितास्मि । (ग)

काञ्चन०—अतिऋजुकेदानीं सा देवी यैवं प्रत्येति । एष खलु भर्ताऽस्वस्थतामिषेणात्मनो मदनावस्थां प्रच्छादयन्दन्ततोरणवलभ्यां तिष्ठति । तदेहि । एतं वृत्तान्तं भर्त्र्यै निवेदयावः । (घ)

(इति निष्क्रान्ते ।)

प्रवेशकः ।

(ततः प्रविशति मदनावस्थां नाटयन्नुपविष्टो राजा ।)

राजा—(निःश्वस्य ।)

(क) सुसंगदे हदा असि क्खु तुमं जा एवं परिअणवच्छलं देविं वञ्चेसि । (ख) हलाँ तुमं दाणिं कहिं पत्थिदा । (ग) अहं खु अस्सत्थसरीरस्स भट्टिणो कुसलवुत्तन्तं जाणिदुं गदा तुमं चिरअसीति उत्तमन्तीए देवीएँ तुह सआसं पेसिदम्हि । (घ) अदिउज्जुआ दाणिं सा देवी जा एवं पत्तीअदि । एसो क्खु भट्टा अस्सत्थदामिसेण अत्तणो मअणावत्थं पच्छादअन्तो दन्ततोरणवलभीए चिट्ठदि । ता एहि । एदं वुत्तन्तं भट्टिणीए णिवेदम्ह ।

अस्तीति वत्सला प्रेमवती । परिजनेषु वत्सला परिजनवत्सला ताम् । हतासि कृतघ्नेत्यर्थः । निन्दाव्यञ्जकमिदं । वञ्चयसे प्रतारयसि । गृधिवञ्च्योः प्रलम्भने इत्यात्मनेपदम् । चिरं करोति चिरयति । उत्ताम्यन्त्या चिन्ताव्याकुलचित्तया । अतिशयेन ऋजुका सरला अतिऋजुका । दन्तस्य तोरणं दन्तनिर्मितं बहिर्द्वारं यस्याः सा । तोरणोऽस्त्री बहिर्द्वारम् इत्यमरः । दन्ततोरणा वलभी सौधोर्ध्ववेश्म तस्मिन् । प्रवेशकलक्षणमुक्तम् । सोत्कण्ठं निःश्वस्येति क्वचित्पाठः । तत्र उत्कण्ठा उत्कलिका तया सहितं यथा तथेति विग्रहः । किं तु निःश्वासेनैवोत्कण्ठा व्यज्यतेऽतो हेयोऽयं पाठः ।

---

१ आसनस्थो–मदनावस्थो रा०. २ सोत्कण्ठं नि०. ३ हदा असि सुसं० तुमं हदा असि...पिअप्पसादवत्सलं; हदा क्खु तुमं सुसं० जा एव्वं वच्छलां वि भट्टिणीं व०. ४ हला मअणिके; सहि तुमं वि दाणिं कहिं. ५ पवुत्तिं. ६ भट्टिणीए पे०; तुए समीवे. ७ अइ उ० दाणिं; काञ्च०—(विहस्य) अदि०. ८ पत्तिआअदि ९ दन्तव०; ०भीए उवरि. १० अस्मात्परं—मद०—हला एवं करेम्ह । ता लहु गच्छम्ह; जं ते रोअदि.

संतापो हृदय स्मरानलकृतः संप्रत्ययं सह्यतां
नास्त्येवोपशमोऽस्य तां प्रति पुनः किं त्वं मुधा ताम्यसि ।
यन्मूढेन मया तदा कथमपि प्राप्तो गृहीत्वा चिरं
विन्यस्तस्त्वयि सान्द्रचन्दनरसस्पर्शो न तस्याः करः ॥ १ ॥

अहो महदाश्चर्यम् ।

मनश्चलं प्रकृत्यैव दुर्लक्ष्यं च तथापि मे ।
कामेनैतत्कथं विद्धं समं सर्वैः शिलीमुखैः ॥ २ ॥

(ऊर्ध्वमवलोक्य ।) कुसुमधन्वन् ।

बाणाः पञ्च मनोभवस्य नियतास्तेषामसंख्यो जनः
प्रायोऽस्माद्विध एव लक्ष्य इति यल्लोके प्रसिद्धिं गतम् ।

संताप इति । हे हृदय यद् यस्मात्कारणात् तदा कदलीगृहाभ्यासे सागरिका-समागमसमये कथमपि दैवात् प्राप्तः । सान्द्रः घनश्चासौ चन्दनरसश्च तस्य इव सुख-शीतलः स्पर्शः यस्य स सान्द्रचन्दनरसस्पर्शः तस्याः करः । गृहीत्वा करेण धृत्वेत्यर्थः । मूढेन अकार्यज्ञेन मया त्वयि चिरं बहुकालं न निहितः स्थापितः । तत् तस्माद् [अध्या-हार्यमेतत्] संप्रत्यधुना स्मरः कामः अनल इव स्मरानलः तेन कृतः स्मरानलकृतः अयं सन्तापः दाहः सह्यताम् । अस्य उपशमः शान्तिः नास्ति एव । तां प्रति तस्याः प्राप्तिमुद्दिश्येत्यर्थः । त्वं पुनः मुधा व्यर्थं किं किमर्थं ताम्यसि ग्लायसि । व्यर्थ एव ते ताप इत्यर्थः । अनुप्रासालंकारः । शार्दूलविक्रीडितं वृत्तम् ॥ १ ॥ महदाश्चर्यमेव दर्शयति—**मन**इत्यादिना । मनः अन्तःकरणं प्रकृत्या स्वभावेनैव चलं चञ्चलमस्थिर-मित्यर्थः । तदुक्तं भगवद्गीतायां—असंशयं महाबाहो मनो दुर्निग्रहं चलम् । इति । दुःखेन लक्ष्यते ज्ञायते इति दुर्लक्ष्यं चक्षुरग्राह्यमिति यावत् । च । अणुत्वादिति भावः । तथापि एवं तस्य दुर्वेध्यत्वेऽपि मे एतन्मनः कामेन सर्वैः शिलीमुखैः बाणैः समं तुल्यकालं कथं विद्धम् । प्रथमं वेध एव दुःसाध्यः । तत्रापि न एकेन बाणेन किं तु सर्वैरपि । तत्रापि न यथाकथंचिदवसरं प्राप्य किं तु समकालमित्यहो महदाश्चर्यमिति भावः । अत्र वेधस्य स्थैर्यत्वलक्ष्यत्वरूपहेत्वोरसत्त्वेऽपि वेधस्य कार्यस्य वर्णनाद्विभावनालंकारः । अनुष्टुप् छन्दः ॥ २ ॥ कुसुमधन्वन् कुसुमानि धनुरस्य असौ कुसुमधन्वा तत्सम्बो-धनम् । धनुषश्च । वा संज्ञायाम् इति वानङ् । **बाणा** इति । मनसि भव उत्पत्तिर्यस्य स मनोभवस्तस्य मनोभवस्य कामस्य पञ्च बाणा नियताः नियमितसंख्याकाः । तेषां बाणानाम् । नास्ति संख्या यस्यासौ असंख्यः । अस्माकमिव विधा प्रकारो यस्य सः अस्मद्विधः प्रियाविप्रयुक्तः जनः एव प्रायः बाहुल्येन लक्ष्यः वेध्यः । इति यद् लोके

---

१ संप्रति; ०शमो हि. २ तथा. ३ ०त्वादरात्. ४ आश्चर्यं, आ० आश्च०, ०र्यम् । तथा हि. ५ मनः प्रकृत्यैव चलं. ६ अपि च भो भो विषमायुध. ७ लक्ष्यमिति.

दृष्टं तत्त्वयि विप्रतीपमधुना यस्मा[1]दसंख्यैरयं
विद्धः कामिजनः शरैरशरणो नीतस्त्वया[2] पञ्चताम् ॥ ३ ॥

(विचिन्त्य[3] ।) न तथाहमेवंविधावस्थ[4]मात्मानमनुचिन्तयामि यथान्तर्निगूढ-कोप[5]संरम्भाया देव्या[6] लोचनगोचरगतां तपस्विनीं सागरिकाम् । तथा हि ।

ह्रिया सर्वस्या[7]सौ हरति विदितास्मीति वदनं
द्वयोर्दृष्ट्वालापं कलयति कथा[8]मात्मविषयाम् ।
सखीषु स्मेरासु प्रकटयति वैलक्ष्य[9]मधिकं
प्रिया प्रायेणास्ते हृदयनिहितातङ्कविधु[10]रा ॥ ४ ॥

तद्[11]वार्तान्वेषणाय गतः कथं चिरयति वसन्तकः ।

(तत[12]ः प्रविशति हृष्टो वसन्तकः ।)

विदू०—(सपरितोष[13]म् ।) ही ही भोः कौशाम्बीराज्यलाभेनापि न तादृशः प्रियवयस्यस्य परितोष आसीद्यादृशोऽद्य मम सकाशात्प्रियवचनं श्रुत्वा भविष्यतीति तर्कयामि । तद्यावद् गत्वा प्रियवयस्यस्य निवेदयिष्यामि । (परिक्रम्यावलोक्य च ।) कथमेष प्रियवयस्य इमामेव दिशमवलोकयंस्तिष्ठति तथा तर्कयामि मामेव प्रतिपालयतीति । तदुपसर्पा-

---

प्रसिद्धिं गतं तदधुना त्वयि विप्रतीपं विपरीतं दृष्टम् । तत्र हेतुमाह—यस्माद् असंख्यैः गणनारहितैः शरैः त्वया विद्धः अयं मादृशः कामिजनः कामुकवर्गः अशरणः नास्ति शरणं रक्षिता यस्य तादृशः सन् त्वया पञ्चतां पञ्चसंख्यावत्तां पक्षे पञ्चभूतात्मकतां । मरणमिति यावत् । नीतः प्रापितः । शार्दूलविक्रीडितं छन्दः ॥ ३ ॥

एवं विधा यस्याः सा एवंविधा तादृशी अवस्था यस्य स एवंविधावस्थः । अन्तः हृदये निगूढः संवृतः कोपस्य संरम्भ आवेशो यस्याः सा तस्याः । तपस्विनीं दीनाम् । **ह्रियेति** । विदिता अस्मि मम चेष्टितं राज्ञा रहसि संगमादि ज्ञातमिति हेतोः ह्रिया लज्जया असौ सर्वस्य जनस्य । सर्वस्माज्जनादिति यावत् । वदनं हरति व्यावर्तयति । द्वयोः आलापं भाषणं दृष्ट्वा आलपन्तौ द्वौ जनौ दृष्ट्वेत्यर्थः । आत्मविषयामात्मसम्बन्धिनीं कथां कलयति । सखीषु स्मेरासु सहासासु अधिकं वैलक्ष्यं लज्जां प्रकटयति । एवं प्रिया प्रायेण बाहुल्येन हृदये निहितः स्थापितः यः आतङ्कः भयं पीडा वा । आतङ्को भयपीडयोः इति कोशः । तेन विधुरा व्याकुला आस्ते । शिखरिणी वृत्तम् ॥ ४ ॥

---

१ यत्तैर०. २ त्वयेमां दशाम्. ३ नि:श्वस्य. ४ एवमव०, एतदव०; ०त्मानं चिन्त०. ५ रोष०, ०संभारायाः. ६ देव्या गो०, तामेव तप०. ७ स्याचो नयति, स्याग्रे न०. ८ कथां नात्म०. ९ क्ष्यमिति मे. १० विधुरम्. ११ प्रेषितश्च मया तद्वार्तान्वेषणाय वस० तत्कथं चिरयति. १२ (प्रविश्य) वसं०. १३ सहर्षम्.

म्येनम् । (उपसृत्य ।) जयतु जयतु प्रियवयस्यः । भो वयस्य दिष्ट्या वर्धसे समीहिताभ्यधिकया कार्यसिद्ध्या । (क)

राजा—(सहर्षम् ।) वयस्य अपि कुशलं प्रियायाः ।

विदू०—(सगर्वम् ।) भो अचिरेण स्वयमेव प्रेक्ष्य ज्ञास्यसि । (ख)

राजा—(सपरितोषम् ।) वयस्य दर्शनमपि भविष्यति प्रियायाः ।

विदू०—(साहंकारम् ।) भोः कस्मान्न भविष्यति यस्य ते उपहसितबृहस्पतिबुद्धिविभवोऽहममात्यः । (ग)

राजा—(विहस्य ।) न खलु चित्रम् । किं न संभाव्यते त्वयि । तत्कथय विस्तरतः श्रोतुमिच्छामि ।

विदूषकः—(कर्णे ।) एवमेवम् ।

राजा—(सहर्षम् ।) साधु वयस्य साधु । इदं ते पारितोषिकम् । (इति हस्तादपनीय कटकं ददाति ।)

विदूषकः—(कटकं परिधाय आत्मानं निर्वर्ण्य ।) भो इमं तावच्छुद्धसुवर्णकटकमण्डितहस्तमात्मनो ब्राह्मण्यै गत्वा दर्शयिष्यामि । (घ)

(क) ही ही भोः कौसम्बीरज्जलाहेणावि ण तादिसो पिअवअस्सस्स परितोसो आसि जादिसो अज्ज मह सआसादो पिअवअणं सुणिअ भविस्सदित्ति तक्केमि । ता जाव गदुअ पिअवअस्सस्स णिवेदइस्सम् । कधं एसो पिअवअस्सो इमं ज्जेव दिसं अवलोकअन्तो चिट्ठदि तहा तक्केमि मं एव्व पडिवालेदित्ति । ता उवसप्पामि णम् । जअदु जअदु पिअवअस्सो । भो वअस्स दिट्ठिआ वड्ढसि समीहिदब्भधिकाए कज्जसिद्धीए । (ख) भो अचिरेण सअं ज्जेव पेक्खिअ जाणिस्ससि । (ग) भो कीस ण भविस्सदि जस्स दे उवहसिदविहप्पदिबुद्धिविहवो अहं अमच्चो । (घ) भो इमं ताव सुद्धसुवण्णकडअमाण्डिअहत्थं अत्तणो बम्भणीए गदुअ दंसइस्सम् ।

प्रियवचनं अभीष्टसिद्धेः दर्शकं वचनम् । अत्र ही ही भो इत्यारभ्य भविष्यतीति तर्कयामि इत्यनेन रत्नावलीप्राप्तिवार्तापि कौशाम्बीराज्यलाभादतिरिच्यते इत्युत्कर्षाभिधानाद् उदाहृतिरिति गर्भसन्धेरङ्गम् । समीहिताभ्याधिकया समीहितं सागरिकायाः कुशलवार्तालाभः तस्मादभ्यधिका सागरिकासमागमसंघटनरूपा सिद्धिः तया । उपहसितः

---

१ ०याः सागरिकायाः. २ वयस्य न खलु किंचिन्न सं०. ३ ०मेवं कथयति. ४ सपरितोषम्. ५ ०भोः ही ही भोः...कम्भेण ण तादिसो ०स्सो सपरितोसो आसी. ६ तक्केमि । मं एव्व पडिपालअन्तो चिट्ठदि । ता उप० । (उपसृत्य ।) जअदु जअदु भवं समीहिदसहिदाए कज्ज०. ७ ०हिदकज्ज०. ८ ०स्सादि । जस्स पिअवअस्सो दे उव० वो अहं वट्टामि. ९ ताव सअं सोवण्ण० मण्डिअं अत्ताणअं कदुअ; भोदु एव्वं दाव । इमं सुहसी०; इदं दाव अणअरअणभूसिदसोवडअ धूसिदं अप्पाणं गदुअ मे बम्ह०.

राजा—(हस्ते गृहीत्वा निवारयन् ।) सखे पश्चाद् दर्शयिष्यसि । ज्ञायतां तावत्किमवशिष्टमह्न इति ।

विदूषकः—(विलोक्य ।) भोः प्रेक्षस्व प्रेक्षस्व । एष खलु गुर्वनुरागोत्क्षिप्तहृदयः संध्यावधूदत्तसंकेत इवास्तगिरिशिखरकाननमनुसरति भगवान्सहस्ररश्मिः । (क)

राजा—(विलोक्य सहर्षम् ।) सखे सम्यगुपलक्षितम् । पर्यवसितमहः । तथा हि ।

अध्वानं नैकचक्रः प्रभवति भुवनभ्रान्तिदीर्घं विलङ्घ्य
प्रातः प्राप्तुं रथो मे पुनरिति मनसि न्यस्तचिन्तातिभारः ।
संध्यामृष्टावशिष्टस्वकरपरिकरस्पष्टहेमारपङ्क्ति
र्व्याकृष्यावस्थितोऽस्तक्षितिभृति नयतीवैष दिक्चक्रमर्कः ॥ ५ ॥

अपि च ।

(क) भो पेक्ख पेक्ख । एसो क्खु गरुआणुराओक्खित्तहिअओ संज्झावधूदिण्णसंकेदो विअ अत्थगिरिसिहरकाणणं अणुसरदि भअवं सहस्सरस्सी ।

बृहस्पतेः वाचस्पतेः बुद्धेः विभवो येन । ततोऽप्याधिककुशाग्रबुद्धिः इत्यर्थः । कर्णे एवमेवमिति–अत्र तत्त्वार्थकथनात् मार्गाख्यं गर्भसन्धेरङ्गमुक्तम् । शुद्धं यत्सुवर्णं तस्य कटकेन मण्डितः हस्तः तम् । ब्राह्मण्यै स्वपत्न्यै । गुरुश्चासावनुरागश्च तेन उत्क्षिप्तं व्याक्षिप्तं हृदयं यस्य । सन्ध्या एव वधूः तया दत्तः संकेतः अमुकसमये त्वया अमुकस्थल आगन्तव्यमित्येवंरूपः यस्य । अस्तगिरेः शिखरमस्तगिरिशिखरं तत्र यत्काननं तत् । सहस्रं रश्मयः किरणा यस्य स सहस्ररश्मिः सूर्यः । पर्यवसितमवसन्नम् । **अध्वानमिति** । एकं चक्रं यस्यासौ एकचक्रः मे रथः भुवनभ्रान्तिदीर्घं भुवने भ्रान्तिः भ्रमणं तेन दीर्घमध्वानं विलङ्घ्य पुनः प्रातः प्रातःकाले प्राप्तुम् । उदयाचलमिति शेषः । न प्रभवति शक्ष्यति इति मनसि न्यस्तः चिन्ताया अतिभारः येन स न्यस्तचिन्तातिभारः एषः अर्कः सूर्यः अस्तक्षितिभृति अस्ताचले अवस्थितः सन् । सन्ध्यया आमृष्टा विलुप्ताः तेभ्योऽवशिष्टो यः स्वकिरणानां परिकरः समूहः स एव स्पष्टा प्रकटं भासमाना हेमारपङ्क्तिः हेम्नः अराणां नेम्यवष्टम्भकदण्डानां पङ्क्तिः यस्य तत् । दिक्चक्रमाकृष्य द्वितीयचक्रस्थाने योजयितुमिति शेषः । नयति इव । उत्प्रेक्षालंकारः ।

---

१ (विधृत्य) सखे. २ पुनः. ३ अवसितमहः. ४ विदू०—किं ण पेक्खदि भवं; जं पिअवअस्सो-भट्टा-आणवेदि. ५ परिक्रम्याव० च सहर्षम्. ६ राजा—अये पर्य०. ७ कृष्टा०. ८ स्पृष्ट, करैः स्प०, ०पंक्तिः. ९ वारुणीव०. १० गिरिकाण०; गिरिकुहरका० अहिस०.

यातोऽस्मि पद्मनयने समयो ममैषं
सुप्ता मयैव भवती प्रतिबोधनीया ।
प्रत्यायनामयमितीव सरोरुहिण्याः
सूर्योऽस्तमस्तकनिविष्टकरः करोति ॥ ६ ॥

तदुत्तिष्ठ माधवीलतामण्डपं गत्वा प्रियतमासंकेतावसरं प्रतिपाल्यावः ।

विदूषकः—भोः शोभनं भणितम् । (इत्युत्तिष्ठतः ।) (क)

विदूषकः—(विलोक्य ।) भो वयस्य प्रेक्षस्व प्रेक्षस्व । एष खलु बहलीकृतविरलवनराजिसनिवेशो गृहीतघनपङ्कपीवरवनवराहमहिषकृष्णच्छविः प्रसरति पूर्वदिशं प्रच्छादयंस्तिमिरसंघः । (ख)

(क) भो सोहंणं भणिदं । (ख) भो वअस्स पेक्ख पेक्ख । एसो क्खु बहलीकिदविरलवणराइसंनिवेसो गँहीदघणपङ्कपीवरवनवराहमाहिसाकिसिणछवी पसरदि पूव्वदिसं पच्छादअन्तो तिमिरसंघा ओ ।

स्रग्धरा वृत्तम् ॥ ५ ॥ **यातोऽस्मी**ति । हे पद्मनयने पद्मं नयनं यस्यास्तत्सम्बुद्धिः । यातोस्मि गतोस्मि । एष मम समयः नियतः अस्तस्य कालः । एष सुप्तेत्यादिना वक्ष्यमाणः मम समयः संकेतः इत्यपि ध्वनिः । मयि गतेपि न चिरविरहचिन्ता कार्या इत्याह—सुप्ता । कमलनयननिमीलनात् तथोक्तिः । भवती मयैव प्रतिबोधनीया विकासयितव्या सान्त्वयितव्या च । इति उक्तप्रकारेण अस्तमस्तकनिविष्टकरः अस्तमस्तके निविष्टाः कराः किरणा यस्य स तथोक्तः । पक्षे अस्तं शोकादधोनिहितं यन्मस्तकं शिरः अर्थान्नायिकायाः तत्र निविष्टः सान्त्वनार्थं निहितः करो हस्तो यस्य । सुवति कर्मणि लोकं प्रेरयति इति सूर्यः । राजसूयसूर्य—इत्यादिना निपातनात्क्यप् रुडागमश्च । सरोरुहिण्याः नायिकायाः प्रत्यायनां विश्वासोत्पादनं करोतीव । अत्रेदमपि अर्थान्तरं प्रतीयते—हे पद्मनयने कमलनेत्रे अधुना यातोस्मि यतोयं मम गमनकालः । सुप्ता भवती संकेतं पालयता मयैवागत्य प्रतिबोधनीया जागरयितव्या । इति सूरिषु बुधेषु साधुः सूर्यः कश्चिन्नायकः सरोरुहं लीलार्थमलंकारार्थं वा कमलमस्या विद्यते इति सरोरुहिणी । तादृश्या नायिकायाः । शेषं समानम् । श्लेषाश्रया समासोक्तिरुत्प्रेक्षा च तयोः संकरः । वसन्ततिलका वृत्तम् ॥ ६ ॥ प्रियासंकेतावसरं प्रियागमनं यावदित्यर्थः । न बहलः अबहलः अबहलः बहलः घनः सम्पद्यमानः कृतः बहलीकृतः । बहलीकृतः स्थगितान्तरालः कृत इत्यर्थः । विरलः वनराजीनां संनिवेशः संस्थानं येन स तथोक्तः । गृहीतः घनः बहलः पङ्कः कर्दमः यैः ते गृहीतघनपङ्काः । पीवराः स्थूला वनवासिनः वराहाश्च महिषाश्च वनवराहमहिषाः । शाकपार्थिवादिः । गृहीतघन-

---

१ वदने. २ ममैव. ३ वयस्य तदु०; ०त्तिष्ठ तत्रैव ०मण्डपे. ४ प्रियासंकेतसमयं ५ ०ष्ठति. ६ भो सोहणं भणासि. ७ तक्खणगहिर...वनमाहिस...विसणिद्धो (स्निग्धो) ओदरदि पुरत्थिमि० (अवतरति पुरस्ति०).

राजा—([1]समन्ताद्विलोक्य ।) [2]सखे साधु दृष्टम् । तथा हि ।

[3]पुरः पूर्वामेव स्थगयति ततो[4]ऽन्यामपि दिशं
क्रमात्क्रामन्नद्रिद्रुमपुरवि[5]भागांस्तिरयति ।
उपेतः पीनत्वं तदनु भुव[6]नस्येक्षणफलं
तमःसंघातोऽयं हरति हरकण्ठद्युतिहरः ॥ ७ ॥

[7]तदादेशय मार्गम् ।

विदू०—एत्वेतु प्रियवयस्यः । (क)

(परिक्रामतः ।)

विदू०—(निरूप्य ।) भो वयस्य एतत्खलु समासन्नं संसक्तबहलपत्रपादपलताभिः पिण्डीकृतान्धकारमिव मकरन्दोद्यानम् । तत्कथमत्र मार्गो लक्ष्यते । (ख)

राजा—(गन्धमाघ्राय ।) [8]वयस्य गच्छाग्रतः । ननु सुपरि[9]ज्ञात एवात्र मार्गः । तथा हि ।

[10]पालीयं च[11]म्पकानां नियतमयमसौ सुन्द[12]रः सिन्दुवारः
सान्द्रा वीथी तथेयं बकुलविटपिनां पाटलापङ्क्तिरेषा ।

(क) एदु एदु पि[13]अवअस्सो । (ख) भो वअस्स एदं क्खु समासण्णं संस[14]त्त-बहलपत्तपादवलदाहिं पिण्डीकिदान्धआरं विअ मअरन्दुज्जाणम् । ता कहं एत्थ मग्गो लक्खीअदि ।

पङ्काश्च ते पीवरवनवराहमहिषाश्च तेषामिव कृष्णा छविः कान्तिर्यस्य । **पुर** इति । अयं पुरो दृश्यमानः हरकण्ठद्युतिहरः हरस्य कण्ठः तस्य द्युतिः कान्तिः तां हरति अनुकरोतीति तथोक्तः । कृष्णवर्ण इत्यर्थः । तमःसंघातः पुरः प्रथमं पूर्वामेव दिशं स्थगयति । क्रामन् क्रमादद्रीणां द्रुमाणां पुराणां च विभागान् भिन्नानवयवान् तिरयति आच्छादयति । तदनु तत्पश्चात पीनत्वं घनतामित्यर्थः उपेतः भुवनस्य लक्षणया तद्वर्तिलोकस्य ईक्षणानां लोचनानां फलं पदार्थावलोकनरूपं हरति विलुम्पति । स्वभावोक्तिः । शिखरिणी वृत्तम् ॥ ७ ॥ समासन्नं समीपस्थितम् । संसक्तानि अन्योन्यानुविद्धानि बहलानि पत्राणि यासां ताः पादपाश्च लताश्च ताभिः । पिण्डीकृतः पुञ्जीकृतः । **पालीयमिति** । नियतमियं चम्पकानां पाली श्रेणिः । अयमसौ सुविज्ञातः सुन्दरः सिन्दुवारः निर्गुडीवृक्षः । तथा इयं बकुलविटपिणां केसरवृक्षाणां सान्द्रा निबिडा वीथी

---

१ सहर्षं सम०. २ वयस्य सम्यग्दृ०, सम्यगुपलक्षितम्. ३ पुरा. ४ ततोऽप्यापि विशदः-विदिशः. ५ विभागं. ६ च जनस्येक्षणपथं. ७ तदेहावतरावः. ८ वयस्य सुविज्ञातमेतत् । पश्य. ९ सुपरिचितः. १० आलीयं. ११ चन्दनानां सुरभिरयमसौ. १२ सिन्दुरः. १३ मर्ष. १४ बहलपादवदाए (बहलपादपतया).

आघ्रायाघ्राय गन्धं विविधमधिगतैः पादपैरेवमस्मि-
न्व्यक्तिं पन्थाः प्रयाति द्विगुणतरतमोनिह्नुतोऽप्येष चिह्नैः ॥८॥

(इति परिक्रामतः ।)

विदू०—भो एतं खलु निपतन्मत्तमधुकरं कुसुमामोदवासितदशदिशं मसृणमरकतमणिशिलाकुट्टिमसुखायमानचरणसंचारसूचितं तमेव माधवीलतामण्डपं संप्राप्तौ स्वः। तदिहैव तिष्ठतु भवान् यावदहं देवीवेषधारिणीं सागरिकां गृहीत्वा लघ्वागच्छामि। (क)

राजा—वयस्य तेन हि त्वर्यतां त्वर्यताम्।

विदू०—भोः मा उत्ताम्य। एष आगतोऽस्मि। (इति निष्क्रान्तः।) (ख)

राजा—यावदहमप्यस्यां मरकतशिलावेदिकायामुपविश्य प्रियायाः संकेतसमयं प्रतिपालयामि। (उपविश्य सचिन्तम्।) अहो कोऽपि कामिजनस्य स्वगृहिणीसमागमपरिभाविनो जनमभिनवं प्रति पक्षपातः। तथा हि।

(क) भो एदं क्खु णिवडन्तमत्तमहुअरं कुसुमामोदवासिददसदिसं मसिणमरअदमणिसिलाकुट्टिमसुहाअन्तचलणसंचारसूचिदं तं एव्व माहवीलदामण्डपं संपत्तम्ह। ता इह ज्जेव्व चिट्ठदु भवं जाव अहं देवीवेसधारिणं साअरिअं गेण्हिअ लहुं आअच्छामि।
(ख) भो मा उत्तम्म। एस आगदोम्हि।

आवलिः। एषा पाटलानां पाटलीनां पंक्तिः। अस्मिन्नुद्याने अतिशयेन द्विगुणं द्विगुणतरं तच्च तत्तमश्च तेन निह्नुतः तिरस्कृतः अपि एष मार्गः। एवं विशिष्टा विधाः प्रकारा यस्य स विविधः तं विविधं गन्धमाघ्रायाघ्राय अधिगतैः ज्ञातैः पादपैः चिह्नैः व्यक्तिं प्रयाति स्फुटो भवति। स्रग्धरा वृत्तम् ॥८॥ निपतन्तः मधुकरा यस्मिन्। कुसुमानामामोदः अतिमनोहरः गन्धस्तेन वासिताः। सुरभीकृता इत्यर्थः। दश दिशो येन तत्। मसृणा याः मरकतमणीनां शिलाः तासां कुट्टिमं निबद्धभूमिः तस्मिन् सुखं वेदयते अनुभवतीति सुखायमानः। सुखादिभ्यः कर्तृवेदनायाम् इति क्यङ्। यः चरणसंचारः। सञ्चारकवेद्यसुखस्य सञ्चारे उपचारः। तेन सूचितम्। देव्या वेषमवश्यं धरतीति देवीवेषधारिणी। धृधातोः आवश्यकाधमर्ण्ययोर्णिनिः इति णिनिः। उपपदसमासः। भूयान् कामोस्य इति कामी। भूम्नि इनिप्रत्ययः। कोपि अनिर्वचनीयः। स्वस्य स्वा वा गृहिणी तया तस्या वा समागमः तं परिभवतीति तस्य। ताच्छील्ये णिनिः।

---

१ रेव य०. २ तो ह्येष. ३ संकेतं. ४ किमपि. ५ समागमं परित्यज्य. ६ ०अरबहुल-बकुल-कुसुमा-सिददिसामुहं. ७ चिट्ठ तुमं जाव पि देवीए.

प्रणयविशदां दृष्टिं वक्त्रे ददाति न शङ्किता
घटयति घनं कण्ठाश्लेषे रसान्न पयोधरौ ।
वदति बहुशो गच्छामीति प्रयत्नधृताप्यहो
रमयतितरां संकेतस्था तथापि हि कामिनी ॥ ९ ॥

अये कथं[1] चिरयति वसन्तकः । तत्[2] किं नु खलु विदितः स्यादय वृत्तान्तो देव्याः[3] ।

(ततः प्रविशति वासवदत्ता काञ्चनमाला च ।)

वासव०—हञ्जे काञ्चनमाले सत्यमेव मम वेषं कृत्वा सागरिकार्यपुत्रमभिसरिष्यति । (**क**)

काञ्चन०—कथमन्यथा भट्टिन्यै निवेद्यते । अथ वा चित्रशालिकाद्वारे स्थितो वसन्तक एव ते प्रत्ययमुत्पादयिष्यति । (**ख**)

वासव०—तेन हि तत्रैव गच्छावः । (**ग**)

काञ्चन०—एत्वेतु भट्टिनी । (**घ**)

(उभे परिक्रामतः ।)

(**क**) हञ्जे काञ्चनमाले सच्चं ज्जेव्व मह वेसं कदुअ साअरिआ अज्जउत्तं अहिसैरिस्सदि । (**ख**) कधं अण्णधा भट्टिणीएँ णिवेदीअदि । अथ वा चित्तसालिआदुआरे ठ्ठिदो[7] वसन्तओ ज्जेव्व दे पच्चअं उप्पादइस्सदि । (**ग**) तेण हि तहिं ज्जेव्व गच्छम्ह । (**घ**) एदु एदु भट्टिणी ।

अभिनवं जनं नवस्त्रीरूपम् । पक्षपातः गाढाभिलाष इति यावत् । **प्रणयविशदामिति** । संकेते संकेतस्थाने तिष्ठतीति संकेतस्था कामिनी कामवती नायिका । परेण विदिता स्यां कोपि मां पश्यति किमिति वा शङ्का जाता अस्याः सा शङ्किता सती प्रणयविशदां प्रणयेन प्रेम्णा विशदां प्रसन्नां दृष्टिं न ददाति । विश्रब्धं न पश्यतीत्यर्थः । कण्ठाश्लेषे आलिङ्गनविधौ रसात्प्रीत्या स्तनौ घनं दृढं न घटयति । स्तनोपपीडं नालिङ्गतीत्यर्थः । प्रयत्नेन धृता प्रयत्नधृता अपि गच्छामीति बहुशः वदति । तथापि एवमरतिहेतुषु सत्स्वपि । अहो इत्याश्चर्ये । रमयतितरां हि नायकमतिशयेन रमयत्येव । अत्र कारणाभावेप्यतिशयरमणरूपकार्यस्य वर्णनाद्विभावनालंकारः । हरिणी वृत्तम् ॥ ९ ॥ किं नु खल्विति वितर्के । अन्यथा अलीकमित्यर्थः । प्रत्ययं विश्वासम् ।

---

१ तद्वार्तान्वेषणाय गतः कथं. २ न खलु. ३ देव्या वासवदत्तया; देव्याः. ४ ०सरदि. ५ ०धा वा. ६ देवीए. ७ उवट्ठिदो, संनिहिदो.

(ततः प्रविशति कृतावगुण्ठनो वसन्तकः ।)

वसन्तकः—(कर्णं दत्त्वा ।) यथा चित्रशालिकाद्वारे पदशब्दः श्रूयते तथा तर्कयाम्यागता सागरिकेति । (क)

काञ्चन०—भट्टिनि इयं सा चित्रशालिका । तद्यावद्वसन्तकस्य संज्ञां करोमि । (इति छोटिकां ददाति ।) (ख)

विदू०—(सहर्षमुपसृत्य सस्मितम् ।) सुसंगते सुष्ठु खलु कृतस्त्वया एष काञ्चनमालाया वेषः । अथ सागरिकेदानीं कुत्र । (ग)

काञ्चन०—(अङ्गुल्या दर्शयन्ती ।) नन्वेषा । (घ)

विदू०—(दृष्ट्वा सविस्मयम् ।) एषा स्फुटमेव देवी वासवदत्ता । (ङ)

वासव०—(साशङ्कमात्मगतम् ।) कथं ज्ञातास्मि । (च)

विदू०—(छोटिकां ददाति ।) भवति सागरिके इत आगच्छ । (वासवदत्ता विहस्य काञ्चनमालामवलोकयति ।) (छ)

काञ्चन०—(अपवार्य अङ्गुल्या तर्जयन्ती ।) हताश स्मरिष्यस्येतदात्मनो वचनम् । (ज)

विदू०—त्वरतां त्वरतां सागरिका । एष खलु पूर्वदिश उद्गच्छति भगवान्मृगलाञ्छनः । (परिक्रामति ।) (झ)

(क) जधा चित्तसालिआदुआरे पदसद्दो सुणीअदि तधा तक्केमि आगदा साअरिअत्ति । (ख) भट्टिणि इअं सा चित्तसालिआ । ता जाव वसन्तअस्स सण्णं करेमि । (ग) सुसंगदे सुट्ठु क्खु किदो तुए एसो कञ्चणमालाए वेसो । अध साअरिआ दाणिं कहिं । (घ) णं एसो । (ङ) ऐसा फुडं एव्व देवी वासवदत्ता । (च) कधं जाणिदम्हि । (छ) भोदि साअरिए इदो आअच्छ । (ज) हआस सुमरिस्ससि एदं अत्तणो वअणम् । (झ) तुरअदु तुरअदु साअरिआ । एसो क्खु पुव्वदिसादो उग्गच्छदि भअवं मिअलञ्छणो ।

कृतावगुण्ठनः कृतमवगुण्ठनं मुखावेष्टनं येन स तथा । अत्र वासवदत्ताकाञ्चनमालाभ्यां सागरिकासुसङ्गतावेषाभ्यां राजविदूषकयोरभिसंधीयमानत्वादधिबलमिति गर्भसन्धेरङ्गम् । तर्जयन्ती भर्त्सयमाना । मृगः लाञ्छनं यस्य स मृगलाञ्छनः चन्द्रः ।

---

१ उपविष्टः कृता०. २ निदर्शयति. ३ ससंभ्रममा०-मपवार्य. ४ पश्यति. ५ विदूषकं त०. ६ सर्वे परिक्रामन्ति. ७ पडिसद्दो (प्रतिश०). ८ देमि. ९ एसा सा. १० इअं... देवी. ११ पच्चभिणादम्हि एदेण (प्रत्यभिज्ञातास्म्ये०) । ता गमिस्सम् । (इति गन्तुमिच्छति ।). १२ इदो इदो एहि एहि. १३ सुमरेसि. १४ भोदी सा०. १ अस्मात्परं—(ससंभ्रममपवार्य-ससाध्वसम्) भअवं मिअलञ्छण णमो दे । मुहुत्तअं दाव ओवारिदसरीरो (अपवारितशरीरः) होहि जेण पेक्खामि से भावाणुबन्धम् इत्य० क्वचित्.

राजा—अये[1] उपस्थितप्रियासमागमस्यापि[2] किमिदमत्यर्थमुत्ताम्यति[3][4] मे चेतः[5]। अथ वा[6]।

तीव्रः स्मरसंतापो न तथादौ[7] बाधते यथासन्ने[8]।
तपति प्रावृषि नितरामभ्यर्णजलागमो दिवसः ॥ १० ॥

विदू०—(कर्णं दत्त्वा[10]।) भवति सागरिके एष खलु प्रियवयस्यस्त्वामेवोद्दिश्योत्कण्ठानिर्भरं मन्त्रयते। तन्निवेदयाम्यस्मै तवागमनम्। (क)

वासव०—(शिरः[11]संज्ञां ददाति।)

विदू०—(राजानमुपसृत्य[12]।) भो वयस्य दिष्ट्या वर्धसे। एषा खलु मयानीता सागरिका। (ख)

राजा—(सहर्षं सहसोत्थाय।) वयस्य क्वासौ क्वासौ।

विदूषकः—नन्वेषा। (ग)

राजा—(उपसृत्य।) प्रिये सागरिके।

शीतांशुर्मुखमुत्पले तव दृशौ पद्मानुकारौ करौ
रम्भागर्भनिभं तथोरुयुगलं बाहू मृणालोपमौ।
इत्याह्लादकराखिलाङ्गि रभसान्निःशङ्कमालिङ्ग्य मा-
मङ्गानि त्वमनङ्गतापविधुराण्येह्येहि निर्वापय ॥ ११ ॥

(क) भोदि साअरिए एसो खु पिअवअस्सो तुमं ज्जेव उद्दिसिअ उक्कण्ठाणिब्भरं मन्तेदि। ता णिवेदेमि से तुहागमणं[13]। (ख) भो वअस्स दिट्ठिआ वड्ढसि। एसा क्खु मए आनीदा साअरिआ। (ग) णं एसा।

उपस्थितः आसन्नः प्रियासमागमः यस्य। **तीव्र इति**। तीव्रः कठोरः स्मरस्य संतापः कामकृतो दाहः आदौ प्रियादर्शने जाते तथा न बाधते यथा आसन्ने प्रियासमागमे बाधते। तत्र दृष्टान्तमाह—प्रावृषि वर्षासु अभ्यर्णजलागमः अभ्यर्णः समीपः जलागमः वृष्टिरिति यावत् यस्मिन् तादृशः दिवसः नितरां तपति। न तु प्रावृडारम्भदिवसस्तथा। दृष्टान्तालंकारः। आर्या ॥ १० ॥ उत्कण्ठानिर्भरं उत्कण्ठा सस्पृहं चिन्तनं सा निर्भरा यस्मिन्कर्मणि तद्यथा तथा। अत्र राजा अये उपनतप्रियासमागमस्य इत्यत आरभ्य निवेदयामि तवागमनमित्यन्तेन वत्सराजस्य सागरिकासमागममभिलषतः एव भ्रान्तसागरिकाप्राप्तिरिति क्रमो नाम गर्भसन्धेरङ्गमुक्तम्। प्रिये सागरिके। **शीतांशुरिति**। तव मुखं शीतांशुः हिमकिरणः चन्द्रः। तद्वत्तापहरणादाह्लाद-

१ (सोत्कण्ठमात्मगतम्।) उप०. २ संगमोत्सुकोऽपि. ३ अकारणम्. ४ उत्तपति. ५ मनः. ६ अथ वा साधुरयं जनापवादः—प्रवादः. ७ तथासौ. ८ प्राप्त, ०सन्नः. ९ सुतरां. १० आकर्ण्य. ११ शिरश्चालयति. १२ उपसर्पन्. १३ ०गमणम्। (सहसोपसृत्य।) भो एसा आअदा साअरिआ।

वासव०—(सबाष्पमपवार्य ।) काञ्चनमाले एवमपि मन्त्रयित्वार्यपुत्रः पुनरपि मामालपिष्यतीत्यहो आश्चर्यम् । (क)

काञ्च०—(अपवार्य ।) भर्त्रि एवं न्विदम् । किं पुनः साहसिकानां पुरुषाणां न सम्भाव्यते । (ख)

विदूषकः—भवति सागरिके विश्रब्धा भूत्वा प्रियवयस्यमालप । अद्यापि तावदस्य नित्यरुष्टाया देव्या वासवदत्ताया दुष्टवचनैः कटुकिते श्रोत्रे साम्प्रतं सुखयतु तव मधुरवचनोपन्यासः । (ग)

वासव०—(अपवार्य सरोषस्मितम् ।) काञ्चनमाले अहमीदृशी कटुभाषिणी । आर्यवसन्तकः पुनः प्रियंवदः । (घ)

(क) काञ्चनमाले ऍव्वं पि मन्तिअ अज्जउत्तो पुणो वि मं आलविस्सदित्ति अहो अच्चरिअं । (ख) भट्टिणि एव्वं ण्णेदम् । किं उण साहसिआणं पुरुषाणं ण सम्भावीअदि । (ग) भोदि साअरिऍ[3] वीसद्धा भविअ पिअवअस्सं आलावेहि । अज्जवि दाव से णिच्चरुट्ठाए देवीए वासवदत्ताए दुव्वअणेहिं कडुइदाइं सोत्ताइं सम्पदं सुहावेदु तुह म[3]हुरवअणोवण्णासो । (घ) कञ्चणमाले अहं ईदिसी कडु[4]अभासिणी । अज्ज वसन्तओ उण पिअंवदो ।

करमित्यर्थः । एवं शीतलस्पर्शत्वादाह्लादकरत्वं सर्वत्रोन्नेयम् । तवेति सर्वत्र सम्बध्यते । तव दृशौ नयने उत्पले कुवलये । करौ पद्ममनुकुरुत इति पद्मानुकारौं । कर्मण्यण् । तथा ऊरुयुगलं सक्थियुग्मं रम्भायाः कदल्याः गर्भः रम्भागर्भः अपहृतबहिरावरणः रम्भाकाण्डः तेन निभं तुल्यम् । बाहू मृणालं बिसं उपमा ययोः ते तथा । यद्वा मृणालेन सदृशौ मृणालोपमौ । इति एवं प्रकारेण हे आह्लादकराखिलाङ्गि आह्लादकराणि आनन्दनानि अखिलानि अङ्गानि यस्यास्तथाविधे । एह्येहि । सम्भ्रमार्था द्विरुक्तिः । रभसाद्वेगान्मां निर्गता शङ्का यस्मात्तन्निःशङ्कं यथा तथा आलिङ्ग्य त्वमनङ्गः कामस्तस्य यस्तापस्तेन विधुराणि विवशानि मे अङ्गानि निर्वापय सुखय । रूपकमुपमा चालङ्कारौ । शार्दूलविक्रीडितं वृत्तम् ॥ ११ ॥ अत्र **राजा** उपसृत्य प्रिये इत्यादिना इह तदप्यस्त्येव बिम्बाधरे इत्यन्तेन येषां मते भावज्ञानं क्रमस्तन्मतेन वासवदत्तया वत्सराजभावस्य ज्ञातत्वात्क्रम इत्यङ्गमुक्तम् । कथं अन्यसंक्रान्तप्रेमा सन्नित्यर्थः । सहसा वर्तन्त इति साहसिकाः । ओजःसहोम्भसा वर्तते इति ठक् । साहसमत्र नायिकान्तरानु-

---

१ एव्वं सअं मन्तेदि अज्ज०...वि मं कहं आलविस्सादि. २ रिए वासवदत्तावअणेहिं कडुइकिदा कण्णा सुहावीअन्तु तव वअणेहिं. ३ मउ(मृदु)महुर०. ४ ईदिसी । वसन्त०.

काञ्च०—([1]अपवार्य ।) हताश स्मरिष्यस्येतद्वचनम् । (क)

विदू०—(विलोक्य ।) भो वयस्य प्रेक्षस्व प्रेक्षस्व । एष खलु कुपितकामिनीकपोलसंनिभः [3]पूर्वदिशं प्रकाशयन्नुदितो भगवान्मृगलाञ्छनः । (ख)

राजा—[2]प्रिये सागरिके पश्य ।

आरुह्य शैलशिखरं त्वद्वदनापहृतकान्तिसर्वस्वः ।
[4]प्रतिकर्तुमिवोर्ध्वकरः स्थितः पुरस्तान्निशानाथः ॥ १२ ॥

[5]अपि च । दर्शितमनेनोद्गच्छता प्रकृतिजडत्वम् । कुतः ।

किं पद्मस्य [6]रुचं न हन्ति नयनानन्दं विधत्ते न किं
वृद्धिं वा झषकेतनस्य कुरुते नालोकमात्रेण किम् ।
वक्त्रेन्दौ तव सत्ययं यदपरः शीतांशुरभ्युद्[7]गतो
दर्पः स्यादमृतेन चेदि[8]ह तदप्येवास्ति बिम्बाधरे ॥ १३ ॥

(क) हदास सुमरिस्ससि एदं वअणम् । (ख) भो वअस्स पेक्ख पेक्ख । एसो क्खु कुविदकामिणी[9]कपोलसण्णिहो पुव्वदिसं पआसन्तो उदिदो भअवं मिअलञ्छणो ।

रागप्रवृत्तिः । साहसिकैः सर्वमुचितमनुचितं क्रियते इति भावः । विश्रब्धा वीतशङ्का । कटुकिते कट्वेव कटुकं तत्सञ्जातमनयोरिति । यद्वा कटुके कृते । णिच् कर्मणि क्तः । मधुराणि च तानि वचनानि च तेषामुपन्यासः प्रस्तावनम् । कुपितकामिनीकपोलसंनिभः कुपिता क्रुद्धा चासौ कामिनी च तस्याः कपोलस्तत्संनिभस्तत्तुल्यः । आरक्तवर्ण इत्यर्थः । **आरुह्येति** । तव वदनं त्वद्वदनं तेनापहृतं कान्तिरेव सर्वस्वं यस्य स त्वद्वदनापहृतकान्तिसर्वस्वः निशानाथः चन्द्रः शैलशिखरमारुह्य ऊर्ध्वकरः ऊर्ध्वं करौ यस्य । पक्षे कराः किरणा यस्य स तथोक्तः । प्रतिकर्तुमिव त्वन्मुखकृतकान्तिस्तेयरूपापराधस्य प्रतिक्रियार्थं पुरस्तात्पुरतः पक्षे पूर्वस्यां दिशि स्थितः । श्लेषाश्रयोपमालङ्कारः समासोक्तिरपि ॥१२॥ जडत्वं बुद्धिमान्द्यं विचाररहित्यमिति यावत् । तदेव विशदयति—**किं पद्मस्ये**त्यादिना । अयं तव वक्त्रेन्दुः मुखचन्द्रः पद्मस्य रुचं कान्तिं न हन्ति प्रत्यादिशति किमिति काकुः । अपि तु प्रत्यादिशत्येव । प्रेक्षितुर्नयनानन्दं न विधत्ते करोति किं । अपि तु विधत्ते एव । वा अथ वा आलोकमात्रेण आलोकः दर्शनं स एव आलोकमात्रस्तेन । झषः मीनः केतनं यस्य स झषकेतनः कामः पक्षे समुद्रो वा तस्य वृद्धिं न करोति किम् । अपि तु करोत्येव । यद् यस्मात्कारणादयं शीतांशुः उक्तकार्यकरण-

---

१ अपवार्याङ्गुल्या तर्जयन्ती. २ प्रिये पश्य. ३ उदयाद्रिस्थित—उदयोर्वीभृत एषः. ४ फूत्कर्तुमिव. ५ ननु प्रिये—दर्शित०, किं न दर्शि०...अनेन जडत्वं; उद्यता जडत्वं प्रकटितमनेन. ६ रुचिं. ७ अभ्युद्यतः; उज्जृम्भते. ८ वे तदाखिलं नन्वास्ति; तथाप्यस्त्येव. ९ कवोलसप्पभो सव्वं ज्जेव; ०सादिसो सच्चं ज्जेव दिसं [illegible]—पआसीकरन्तो; उदिदो-उट्ठिदो.

वासव०—(सरोषमवगुण्ठनमपनीय ।) आर्यपुत्र सत्यमेवाहं सागरिका । त्वं पुनः सागरिकोत्क्षिप्तहृदयः सर्वमेव सागरिकामयं प्रेक्षसे । (क)

राजा—(सवैलक्ष्यमपवार्य ।) कथं देवी वासवदत्ता । वयस्य किमेतत् ।

विदू०—(सविषादम् ।) भो वयस्य किमपरम् । अस्माकं जीवितसंशयो जात एषः । (ख)

राजा—(उपविश्याञ्जलिं बद्ध्वा ।) प्रिये वासवदत्ते प्रसीद प्रसीद ।

वासव०—(तन्मुखाभिमुखं हस्तौ प्रसार्याश्रूणि विधारयन्ती ।) आर्यपुत्र मैवं भण । अन्यगतानीमान्यक्षराणि । (ग)

विदू०—(आत्मगतम् ।) किमिदानीमत्र करिष्यामि । भवत्वेवं तावत् । (प्रकाशम् ।) भवति महानुभावा खलु त्वम् । तत्क्षम्यतां तावदेकोऽपराधः प्रियवयस्यस्य । (घ)

वासव०—आर्य वसन्तक ननु प्रथमसंगमे विघ्नं कुर्वत्या मयैवैतस्यापराद्धम् । (ङ)

(क) अज्जउत्त सच्चं एव्व अहं साअरिआ । तुमं उण साअरिओक्खित्तहिअओ सव्वं एव्व साअरिआमअं पेक्खसि । (ख) भो वअस्स किं अवरं । अम्हाणं जीविअसंसओ जादो एसो । (ग) अज्जउत्त मा एवं भण । अण्णगदाइं इमाइं अक्खराइं । (घ) किं दाणिं एत्थ करिस्सं । भोदु एवं दाव । भोदि महाणुभावा क्खु तुमम् । ता खमीअदुं दाव एक्को अवराहो पिअवअस्सस्स । (ङ) अज्ज वसन्तअ णं पढमसंगमे विग्घं करन्तीए मए एव्व एदस्स अवरद्धम् ।

समर्थे तव वक्त्रेन्दौ सति विद्यमाने अभ्युद्यतः । अतः जडोयऽमिति भावः । अथ ब्रूयान्मयावश्यमुदेतव्यं यतोऽहममृतमयो न च मत्कार्यं वक्त्रेन्दुः कुर्यादिति तदपि नेत्याह । अमृतेन दर्पः स्यादहमेवामृतं धारयामि इति गर्वः स्याच्चेत्तदपि अस्मिन् बिम्बाधरे बिम्बं बिम्बीफलं तदिव अधरः तस्मिन्नस्त्येव । अतः व्यर्थोऽयमस्योदयः । इति प्रसिद्धस्योपमानस्य तिरस्कारफलकव्यर्थतोक्त्या प्रतीपमलङ्कारः । शार्दूलविक्रीडितं वृत्तम् ॥ १३ ॥ अस्माकं मम सागरिकायाः सुसङ्गतायाः च । अन्यगतानि सागरिकागतानि इत्यर्थात् । महानुभावा महाननुभावः पराक्रमो यस्याः सा । अत एव बहुक्षमा । प्रत्यक्षं दृष्टं व्यलीकं अप्रियकरणम् । अपराध इति यावद् यस्य ।

---

१ अस्य स्थाने (१३ श्लोकादनन्तरं)—(विलोक्य वासवदत्ताया मुखं—मुखमुन्नमय्य—दृष्ट्वा सविषादम् ।) कथं देवी वास० । वयस्य इ०. २ हा धिक् कष्टम् । कथं. ३ सभयम्. ४ तदभिमुखमश्रूणि निपातयन्ती. ५ ०काणुरत्त, ०हिअअओ भविअ; साअरिआसरिसं. ६ सकन्ना क्खु इदाणिं एदे अक्खरा. ७ ०अदु सो अअं...राधो. ८ ०मसंकेअस्स...अवराधं कदं (अपराधः कृतः).

राजा—देवि एवं प्रत्यक्षदृष्टव्यलीकः किं ब्रवीमि । तथापि विज्ञापयामि ।

(पादयोः पतति ।)

आताम्रतामपनयामि विलक्ष एष
लाक्षाकृतां चरणयोस्तव देवि मूर्ध्ना ।
कोपोपरागजनितां तु मुखेन्दुबिम्बे
हर्तुं क्षमो, यदि परं करुणा मयि स्यात् ॥ १४ ॥

वासव०—(हस्तेन वारयन्ती ।) आर्यपुत्र उत्तिष्ठोत्तिष्ठ । निर्लज्जः खलु स जनो य आर्यपुत्रस्येदृशं हृदयं ज्ञात्वा पुनरपि कुप्यति । तत्सुखं तिष्ठत्वार्यपुत्रः । गमिष्याम्यहम् । (इति गन्तुमिच्छति ।) (क)

काञ्चन०—भर्त्रि कुरु प्रसादम् । एवं चरणपतितं महाराजमुज्झित्वा गताया देव्या अवश्यं पश्चात्तापेन भवितव्यम् । (ख)

वासव०—अपेहि अपण्डिते किमत्र प्रसादस्य पश्चात्तापस्य वा कारणम् । तदेहि गच्छावः । (ग)

राजा—देवि प्रसीद प्रसीद । (आताम्रतामपनयामि इत्यादि पुनः पठति ।)

(क) अज्जउत्त उट्ठेहि उट्ठेहि । णिल्लज्जो खु सो जणो जो अज्जउत्तस्स ईदिसं हिअअं जाणिअ पुणो वि कुप्पदि । ता सुहं चिट्ठदु अज्जउत्तो । गमिस्सं अहम् । **(ख)** भट्टिणि करेहि पसादम् । एवं चलणपडिदं महाराअं उज्झिअ गदाए देवीए अवस्सं पच्छादावेण होदव्वम् । **(ग)** अवेहि अपण्डिदे कुदो एत्थ पसादस्स पच्चादावस्स वा कारणम् । ता एहि गच्छम्ह ।

आताम्रतामिति । हे देवि विलक्षः स्वाप्रियाचरणेन लज्जितः अहं तव चरणयोः लाक्षया जतुरागेण कृतामाताम्रतामीषद्रक्ततामेष मूर्ध्ना तत्र शिरःसंघर्षणेन अपनयामि । पादपतनेनापराधपरिमार्जनं करोमीति भावः । मुखेन्दुबिम्बे मुखमेवेन्दुबिम्बं चन्द्रमण्डलं तत्र कोप एव उपरागः राहुग्रहः तेन जनितां आताम्रतां हर्तुं तु क्षमः स्यां यदि मयि तव परं करुणा स्यात् । वसन्ततिलकं वृत्तम् ॥ १४ ॥ अपण्डिते मूढे । पण्डा बुद्धिः अस्याः सञ्जाता पण्डिता । न पण्डिता अपण्डिता । अत्र विषये

---

१ एवमपि प्रत्यक्षमपि...किं विज्ञा०. २ विवर्णः, एष–एव. ३ गच्छति. ४ ता विसत्थो (विश्वस्तः) भोदु अ०. ५ चलणवन्दिदं...०दावो भविस्सदि. ६ को एत्थ पसादकालो; गदो क्खु पच्चादावस्स कालो.

विदू०—भो उत्तिष्ठ । गता देवी । तत्किमत्रारण्यरुदितं करोषि । (क)

राजा—(मुखमुन्नमय्य[1] दृष्ट्वा ।) कथमकृत्वैव प्रसादं गता देवी ।

विदू०—कथं न कृतः प्रसादो यदद्याप्यक्षतशरीरौ तिष्ठावः । (ख)

राजा—धिङ् मूर्ख किमेवं मामुपहससि[2] । ननु त्वत्कृत एवायमापतितोऽस्माकं महाननर्थः[3] । कुतः ।

> **समारूढा प्रीतिः प्रणयबहुमानादनुदिनं**
> **व्यलीकं वीक्ष्येदं कृतमकृतपूर्वं खलु मया ।**
> **प्रिया मुञ्चत्यद्य स्फुटमसहना[4] जीवितमसौ**
> **प्रकृष्टस्य प्रेम्णः स्खलितमविषह्यं हि भवति ॥ १५ ॥**

विदू०—भो रुष्टा देवि किं करिष्यतीति न जानामि । सागरिका पुनर्दुष्करं जीविष्यतीति तर्कयामि । (ग)

राजा—वयस्य[5] अहमप्येवं चिन्तयामि । हा प्रिये सागरिके ।

(ततः प्रविशति वासवदत्तावेषधारिणी सागरिका ।)

साग०—(सोद्वेगम् ।) दिष्ट्या नाहमनेन विरचितदेवीवेषेणास्याश्चि-

---

(**क**) भो उत्तिहि । गदा देवी । ता कीस एत्थ अरण्णरुदिदं करेसि । (**ख**) कहं ण किदो पसादो जं अज्ज वि अक्खदसरीरा चिट्ठम्ह । (**ग**) भो[6] रुठ्ठा देवी किं करइस्सदित्ति ण जाणामि । साअरिआ[7] उण दुक्करं जीविस्सदित्ति तक्केमि ।

कर्तव्यमजानति इत्यर्थः । अक्षतमपीडितं शरीरं ययोस्तौ । **समारूढेति** । प्रणयस्य प्रेम्णः बहुमानादत्यादृतत्वात्प्रीतिः स्नेहः समारूढा प्रचयं गता । अतः खलु पूर्वं कृतं कृतपूर्वं न कृतपूर्वमकृतपूर्वमिदं व्यलीकं अकार्यमन्यस्त्रीप्रार्थनरूपमद्य मया कृतं वीक्ष्य दृष्ट्वा असहना अमर्षणशीला असौ वासवदत्ता अद्य स्फुटमसंशयं जीवितं मुञ्चति त्यक्ष्यति । हि यस्मात्प्रकृष्टस्य प्रेम्णः अनुरागस्य विषये स्खलितं विपरीतकरणमविषह्यं सोढुमशक्यं भवति । सामान्येन विशेषसमर्थनरूपोऽर्थान्तरन्यासोऽलङ्कारः । शिखरिणी वृत्तम् ॥ १५ ॥ **राजा** धिङ् मूर्खे त्वत्कृत इत्यादिना सागरिका पुनः दुष्करं जीविष्यतीति तर्कयामि इत्यत्र प्रकृष्टप्रेमस्खलनेन सागरिकानुरागजन्येन वासवदत्ताया मरणास्याभ्यूहनादनुमानं नाम गर्भसन्धेः अङ्गम् ।

---

१ उत्तानीकृत्य. २ किं मामुप-परिह०; कृतं परिहासेन. ३ ०र्थक्रमः, ०र्थकन्दः. ४ ध्रुवम्...मही. ५ एवमेतत्. ६ भो किं पुनः. ७ ०रिआ उण अज्ज दुक्करं जीवदित्ति, ०रिआए उण जीविदं दुक्करंति.

ऋशालिकाया निष्क्रामन्ती केनापि लक्षितास्मि । तदिदानीं किं करिष्यामि । (सास्रं चिन्तयति ।) (क)

विदू०—भोः किं मूढ इव तिष्ठसि । चिन्तयात्र प्रतीकारम् । (ख)

राजा—ननु तमेव चिन्तयामि । वयस्य देवीप्रसादनं मुक्त्वा नान्यमत्रोपायं पश्यामि । तदेहि । तत्रैव गच्छावः ।

(इति परिक्रामतः ।)

सागरिका—(विमृश्य ।) वरमिदानीं स्वयमेवात्मानमुद्बध्योपरता न पुनर्ज्ञातसंकेतवृत्तान्तया देव्या परिभूतास्मि । तद्यावदहमशोकपादपं गत्वा यथासमीहितं करिष्यामि । (ग)

विदू०—(आकर्ण्य ।) तिष्ठ तावत्तिष्ठ भोः पदशब्दः श्रूयते । जानामि कदापि गृहीतपश्चात्तापा पुनरपि देव्यागता भवेत् । (घ)

राजा—वयस्य महानुभावा खलु देवी । कदाचिदेवमपि स्यात् । तत्त्वरितं निरूप्यताम् ।

विदूषकः—यद्भवानाज्ञापयति । (इति परिक्रामति ।) (ङ)

(क) दिट्ठिआ णाहं इमिणा विरइददेवीवेसेण इमादो चित्तसालीआदो णिक्कमन्ती केणावि लक्खिदह्मि । ता इदाणिं किं करइस्सम् । (ख) भोः किं मूढो विअ चिट्ठसि । चिन्तेहि एत्थ पडिआरं । (ग) वरं दाणिं सअं ज्जेव्व अप्पाणं उब्बन्धिअ उवरदा न उण जाणिदसंकेतवुत्तन्ताए देवीए परिभूदम्हि । ता जाव अहं असोअपादवं गदुअ जहासमीहिदं करिस्सम् । (घ) चिट्ठ दाव चिट्ठ भो पदसद्दो सुणीअदि । जाणामि कदावि गहिदपच्छादावा पुणोवि देवी आगदा भवे । (ङ) जं भवं आणवेदि ।

मूढः प्रतिपत्तिशून्यः । नान्यमत्रोपायं पश्यामि—अत्र अनन्तराङ्कार्थबिन्दुनाऽनेन देवीलक्षणापायस्य प्रसादनेन निवारणान्नियता फलप्राप्तिः सूचिता । सास्रमस्रैः सहितं यथा तथा । । उपरता मृता । ज्ञातः संकेतस्य वासवदत्तावेषधारिणी तव समीपमागमिष्यामीत्येवंरूपस्य वृत्तान्तो यया तया । परिभूता अपमानिता । यथासमीहितं

---

१ सास्रा विचि०. २ वयस्य ननु. ३ मूर्ख उत्तिष्ठ. ४ उत्तिष्ठतः. ५ कर्णं दत्वा. ६ निरूपय. ७ दिट्ठा (दृष्टा)...भट्टिणीवेसेण अविणीदा केणावि इ० लिआदो णिग्गदा; विरइदेण देवी० संगीदसालादो. ८ जाणीहि दाव को अस्स उवावोत्थि. ९ ०रदा भविस्सं । ०देवीए सुसंगदा विअ परि०, विदितसंकेत० सुसङ्गदाए सह देवीए परिभूदा चिट्ठामि. १० जाव माहवीलदाए पासं विरइअ जहा०; असोअपादअदले ग०. ११ पिट्ठे एसो क्खु पडिसद्दो. १२ तक्केमि...भविस्सदि ।

सागरिका—(उपसृत्य ।) तद्यावदेताया माधवीलतायाः पाशं विरचय्याशोकपादप आत्मानमुद्बध्य व्यापादयामि । (इति लतापाशं रचयन्ती ।) हा तात हा अम्ब एषेदानीमहमनाथाऽशरणा विपद्ये मन्दभागिनी । (इति कण्ठे लतापाशमर्पयति ।) (क)

विदूषकः—(विलोक्य ।) का पुनरेषा । कथं देवी वासवदत्ता । (ससंभ्रममुच्चैः ।) भो वयस्य परित्रायस्व परित्रायस्व । एषा खलु देवी वासवदत्तोद्बध्यात्मानं व्यापादयति । (ख)

राजा—(ससंभ्रममुपसृत्य ।) क्वासौ क्वासौ ।

विदूषकः—नन्वेषा । (ग)

राजा—(उपसृत्य कण्ठात्पाशमपनयन् ।) अयि साहसकारिणि किमिदमकार्यं क्रियते ।

मम कण्ठगताः प्राणाः पाशे कण्ठगते तव ।
अतः स्वार्थः प्रयत्नोऽयं त्यज्यतां साहसं प्रिये ॥ १६ ॥

सागरिका—(राजानं दृष्ट्वा ।) अम्मो कथमेष भर्ता । (सहर्षमात्मगतम् ।) यत्सत्यमेनं प्रेक्ष्य पुनरपि मे जीविताभिलाषः संवृत्तः । अथवैनं

(क) ता जाव इमाए माहवीलदाए पासं विरइअ असोअपादवे अप्पाणअं उब्बन्धिअ वावादेमि । हा ताद हा अम्ब एसा दाणिं अहं अणाधा असरणा विवज्जामि मन्दभाइणी । (ख) का पुण एसा । कहं देवी वासवदत्ता । भो वअस्स परित्ताहि परित्ताहि । एसा क्खु देवी वासवदत्ता उब्बन्धिअ अत्ताणअं वावादेदि । (ग) णं एसा ।

समीहितमभीष्टं तदनतिक्रम्य वर्तेते तत् । उद्बन्धनेन मरणमित्यर्थः । नास्ति नाथः स्वामी यस्याः सा अनाथा । नास्ति शरणं रक्षिता यस्याः सा अशरणा । विपद्ये म्रिये । साहसकारिणि साहसं करोतीति साहसकारिणी तत्सम्बोधनम् । कर्तुमर्हं कार्यम् । अर्हे कृत्यतृचश्चेति अर्हार्थे ण्यत्प्रत्ययः । न कार्यमकार्यमयोग्यं कर्म । ममेति । हे प्रिये साहसं प्राणत्यागरूपं त्यज्यताम् । यतः पाशे तव कण्ठगते कण्ठे स्थिते मम प्राणाः कण्ठं गताः कण्ठगताः । बहिर्गमनोन्मुखा इत्यर्थः । अतः कारणादयं मम प्रयत्नः त्वन्निवारणे इति शेषः । स्वस्माययमिति स्वार्थः । असङ्गत्यलंकारः । कार्यकारणयोर्भिन्नदेशत्वे स्यादसङ्गतिः इति लक्षणात् ॥ १६ ॥ अम्मो इत्याश्चर्ये ।

---

१ पश्यन्नुच्चैः ससंभ्रमम्. २ ०सर्पन्. ३ ०नयति. ४ कण्ठस्थिते. ५ स्वार्थप्र०; स्वार्थाय यत्नो. ६ आत्मगतम्. ७ णं एदाए...पासं करइस्सम् । (कण्ठे पाशं निक्षिप्य ।) हा ताद हा अज्ज एसा क्खु असरणा वि०. ८ इह ज्जेव पासं.

प्रेक्ष्य कृतार्था भूत्वा सुखेनैव जीवितं परित्यक्ष्यामि । (प्रकाशम् ।) मुञ्चतु मुञ्चतु मां भर्ता । पराधीनः खल्वयं जनः न पुनरीदृशमवसरं मर्तुं प्राप्नोति । (इति पुनः पाशं कण्ठे दातुमिच्छति ।) (क)

राजा—(निर्वर्ण्य सहर्षमात्मगतम् ।) कथं प्रिया मे सागरिका । (कण्ठात्पाशमाक्षिप्य ।)

अलमलमतिमात्रं साहसेनामुना ते
त्वरितमयि विमुञ्च त्वं लतापाशमेतम् ।
चलितमपि निरोद्धुं जीवितं जीवितेशे
क्षणमिह मम कण्ठे बाहुपाशं निधेहि ॥ १७ ॥

(इति बाहुमाक्षिप्य कण्ठे कृत्वा स्पर्शं नाटयन् ।) सखे इयमनभ्रा वृष्टिः ।

विदू०—भो एवं न्विदं यद्यकालवातावली भूत्वा नायाति देवी वासवदत्ता । (ख)

(क) अम्मो कथं एसो भट्टा । जं सच्चं एणं पेक्खिअ पुणोवि मे जीविदाहिलासो संवुत्तो । अह वा एणं पेक्खिअ कदत्था भविअ सुहेण एव्व जीविदं परिच्चइस्सम् । मुञ्चदु मुञ्चदु मं भट्टा । पराहीणो खु अअं जणो न उण ईदिसं अवसरं मरिदुं पाँवेदि ।
(ख) भो एवं ण्णेदं जदि अआलवादावली भविअ न आआदि देवी वासवदत्ता ।

जीविताभिलाषो जीवितार्थमाशा । पराधीनः परतन्त्रः । अवसरं युक्तं कालम् । निर्वर्ण्य सम्यगालोक्य । **अलमलमिति** । अयि सागरिके अमुना ते अतिमात्रं अतिक्रान्ता मात्रा यस्मिन्कर्मणि तद्यथा तथा साहसेन अलमलम् । एवंरूपमतिसाहसं सर्वथा मा कुरु इत्यर्थः । त्वमेतं लतापाशं त्वरितं विमुञ्च । हे जीवितेशे चलितमपि त्वत्साहसं दृष्ट्वा गमनोन्मुखमपि जीवितम् । अर्थान्मम । निरोद्धुं प्रतिबद्धुं इह अस्मिन्मम कण्ठे क्षणं बाहुपाशं बाहू एव पाशस्तं निधेहि । मामालिङ्ग्य मज्जीवितं धारय यतस्त्वं तस्येशासीति पर्यायेणोक्तत्वात्पर्यायोक्तमलंकारः । मालिनी वृत्तम् । ननमयययुतेयं मालिनी भोगिलोकैः इति तल्लक्षणम् ॥ १७ ॥ न विद्यते अभ्रं यस्यां सा अनभ्रा अतर्कितोपनता इत्यर्थः । अकाले वातावलीव अकालवातावली । मुग्धसुपेति

---

१ कण्ठे ददाति; करोति, अर्पयति. २ निरूप्य; आत्मगतमिति नास्ति पुस्तकान्तरे. ३ लतापाशमाक्षिपन्; शीघ्रं लतापाशमाक्षिपति. ४ मयि. ५ एवम्. ६ मिव. ७ विधेहि. ८ बाहुपाशमाक्षिप्य कण्ठे गृहीत्वा स्पर्शसुखमभिनीय विदूषकं प्रति. ९ अज्जउत्तो । एदं पेक्खिअ इदाणीं कदत्था भ० ०स्सम् । (प्रकाशं ।) अज्जउत्त मुञ्च । पराहीणो इ०. १० अस्मात्परं—तुमं पि देवीए मा अप्पाणं अवराहिणं करेसि (कुरुष्व). ११ वली विव देवी वा० आगच्छिअ अण्णदो ण णइस्सदि; भविअ देवी आअच्छिअ–अण्णदो ण णइस्सदि–अण्णधा न करिस्सदि.

(ततः प्रविशति वासवदत्ता काञ्चनमाला च ।)

वासव०—हञ्जे काञ्चनमाले तं तथा चरणनिपतितमार्यपुत्रमवधीर्यागच्छन्त्या मयातिनिष्ठुरं कृतम् । तदिदानीं स्वयमेव गत्वार्यपुत्रमनुनेष्यामि । (क)

काञ्चन०—कोऽन्यो देवीं वर्जयित्वैवं भणितुं जानाति । वरं स एव देवो दुर्जनो भवतु न पुनर्देवी । तदेत्वेतु भट्टिनी । (ख)

(परिक्रामतः ।)

राजा—अयि मुग्धे किमद्यापि मध्यस्थतया वयं विफलमनोरथाः क्रियामहे ।

काञ्च०—(कर्णं दत्त्वा ।) भट्टिनि एष खलु यथा समीपे भर्ता मन्त्रयते तथा तर्कयामि त्वामेवानुनेतुमित एवागच्छति । (ग)

वासव०—(सहर्षम् ।) तेन ह्यलक्षितैव पृष्ठतो गत्वा कण्ठे गृहीत्वा प्रसादयिष्यामि । (घ)

विदू०—भवति सागरिके विश्वस्ता भूत्वा प्रियवयस्यमालप । (ङ)

(क) हञ्जे कञ्चणमाले तं तहा चलणणिवडिदं अज्जउत्तं अवधीरिअ आअच्छन्तीए मए अतिणिठ्ठुरं किदम् । ता इदाणिं सअं जेव्व गदुअ अज्जउत्तं अणुणइस्सम् । (ख) को अण्णो देवीं वज्जिअ एव्वं भणिदुं जाणादि । वरं सो ज्जेव्व देवो दुज्जणो भोदु ण उण देवी । ता एदु एदु भट्टिणी । (ग) भट्टिणि एसो खु जहा समीवे भट्टा मन्तेदि तदा तक्केमि तुमं एव्व अणुणेदुं इदो एव्वागच्छदि । (घ) तेण हि अलक्खिदा एव्व पुठ्ठदो गच्छुअ कण्ठे गेण्हिअ पसादइस्सम् । (ङ) भोदि साअरिए वीसत्था भविअ पिअवअस्सं आलवेहि ।

समासः । देवीं वर्जयित्वा देव्या महानुभावत्वादेव एतद्भण्यते इत्यर्थः । स एव देवो दुर्जनो भवतु इति देव्या स्वयं गत्वा राज्ञः प्रसादनात्तस्या एव सौजन्यप्रकटनादिति भावः । मध्यस्थतया उदासीनतया । सागरिकाया भावप्रकटनाभावादियमुक्तिः । मध्यस्थस्य भावो मध्यस्थता । सामान्ये नपुंसकात्तल्प्रत्ययः । अन्यथा मध्यस्थातयेति स्यात् । त्वतलोर्गुणवचनस्य इति वचनान्मध्यस्थाशब्दस्य पुंवद्भावाप्राप्तेः ।

---

१ मध्यस्थितया. २ हला. ३ मह च०; तह चलणे पडिदं अज्जउत्त आअच्छ गच्छन्तीए मए; ०उत्तं अवधीरिअ गच्छन्तीए अदिणिठुरं ज्जेव्व मए किदम्. ४ सच्चं. ५ का अण्णा धण्णा. ६ ईदिसं मन्तेदि; देवीं तुमं...ईदिसं चिन्तेदि. ७ ज्जेव्व दुज्जणो भोदु मा भट्टिणी । ८ अतः परं—ता उवसप्पदु भट्टिणी । इत्य०. ९ ०खिदं एव गच्छिअ कण्ठे गहिस्सम्. १० ०ए कीस...स्सं न आलवसि (आलपसि.)

वासव०—(आकर्ण्य सविषादम् ।) काञ्चनमाले कथं सागरिकेत एवागता । तच्छ्रोष्यामि तावत्पश्चादुपसर्प्स्यामि । **(क)** (तथा करोति ।)

साग०—भर्तः किमेतेनालीकदाक्षिण्येन जीवितादपि वल्लभतराया देव्या आत्मानमपराधिनं करोषि । **(ख)**

राजा—अयि मिथ्यावादिनी खल्वसि । कुतः ।

श्वासोत्कम्पिनि कम्पितं कुचयुगे मौने प्रियं भाषितं
वक्त्रेऽस्याः कुटिलीकृतभ्रुणि तथा यातं मया पादयोः ।
इत्थं नः सहजाभिजात्यजनिता सेवैव देव्याः परं
प्रेमाबन्धविवर्धिताधिकरसा प्रीतिस्तु या सा त्वयि ॥ १८ ॥

वासव०—(सहसोपसृत्य सरोषम् ।) आर्यपुत्र युक्तमेतत् सदृशमेतत् । **(ग)**

(क) कंचणमाले कधं साअरिआ इदो एव्वागदा । ता सुणिस्सं दाव पच्छा उपसप्पिस्सम् । **(ख)** भट्टं किं एदिणा अलीअदाक्खिण्णेण जीविआदोवि वल्लहतराए देवीए अप्पाणं अवराहिणं करेसि । **(ग)** अज्जउत्त जुत्तं एदं सरिसं एदम् ।

अलीकदाक्षिण्येनेति दक्षिणस्य भावो दाक्षिण्यं परच्छन्दानुवर्तित्वम् । ब्राह्मणादित्वाद्भावे ष्यञ् । अलीकं मिथ्या च तद्दाक्षिण्यं च तेन । तदेव प्रकटयति–जीवितादपीत्यादिना । मिथ्यावादिनि अवश्यं मिथ्या वदतीति मिथ्यावादिनी तत्सम्बोधनम् । आवश्यकाधमर्ण्ययोर्णिनिः इति णिनिः । तत्र हेतुं दर्शयति–**श्वासोत्कम्पिनीति** । अस्या देव्याः कुचयोः युगं तस्मिन्कुचयुगे श्वासेन कोपसंवृद्धेन । अभीक्ष्णमुत्कम्पते इति उत्कम्पि । तस्मिन् श्वासोत्कम्पिनि सति मया कम्पितं कम्पः प्रदर्शितः । अस्या मौने मौनमास्थितायामस्यां मया तस्याः संतोषार्थं प्रियं भाषितम् । अस्या मुखे कुटिलीकृते वक्रीकृते भ्रुवौ यस्मिन् तस्मिन् सति । कुटिलशब्दात् कृभ्वस्तियोगे सम्पद्यकर्तरि च्विः इति च्विः । कुगतीति कृतशब्देन समासः । मया तथा तेन प्रकारेण तस्याः पादयोः यातं तत्प्रसादनार्थं पादपतनं कृतम् । इत्थं नः मम परं केवलं यत्स्वाभाविकमाभिजात्यं कुलीनता तेन जनिता कारिता देव्याः सेवैव । यत्कृतं तदौपचारिकं देव्याः सेवार्थमेवेति भावः । या तु प्रेम्ण आबन्धेन विवर्धिता उत्कर्षं नीता अधिको रसो यस्यां सा अधिकरसा प्रीतिः सा त्वयि एव । शार्दूलविक्रीडितं वृत्तम् ॥ १८ ॥ सदृशं यत्त्वया

---

१ सविषादं कर्णं दत्वा. २ कुरुतः; इति तथा स्थिते. अस्मात्परं क्वचित्—राजा—आकर्णायतलोचने शशिमुखि प्रोत्सृज्य लज्जां प्रिये स्वाङ्गैरङ्गमनङ्गतापविधुरं गाढं [illegible]ालिङ्ग मे । किं त्वं माममृतोपमेन वचसा प्रीत्या न सं (च नो) भाषसे पीनैरम्बुधरैरिवोन्नतकुचैर्वक्षःस्थलं ह्लादय ॥ इत्य०. ३ स्तनयु०. ४ भ्रुवि. ५ रुषा; कुटिलभ्रुणि प्रणतयः सद्यो मुहुः पादयोः. ६ प्राणाबन्ध. ७ ०कतरा. ८ उपसृत्य स०. ९हञ्जे कञ्च०. साअ० वि एत्थ एव्व चिट्ठदि । ता सुणम्ह । जाणिअ पच्छा. १० अज्जउत्त किं इमिणा; ०ण्णेण जीविदोवि अधिअवल्लभाए देवीए पुणोवि अत्ताणअं अव० किं करेसि.

राजा—(दृष्ट्वा सवैलक्ष्यम् ।) देवि न खल्वकारणे मामुपालब्धुमर्हसि । सत्यं त्वामेव मत्वा वेषसादृश्यविप्रलब्धा वयमिहागताः । तत्क्षम्यताम् । (इति पादयोः पतति ।)

वासव०—(सरोषम् ।) आर्यपुत्र उत्तिष्ठ उत्तिष्ठ । किमद्यापि सहजाभिजातायाः सेवया दुःखमनुभूयते । (**क**)

राजा—(स्वगतम् ।) कि[3]मेतदपि श्रुतं देव्या । तत्सर्वथा देवीप्रसादनं प्रति निराशीभूताः स्मः । (अधोमुखस्तिष्ठति ।)

विदू०—भवति त्वं किमुद्बध्यात्मानं व्यापादयसीति वेषसादृश्यमोहितेन मया प्रियवयस्योऽत्रानीतः । यदि मम वचनं न प्रत्येषि तत्प्रेक्षस्वैतं लतापाशम् । (इति लतापाशं दर्शयति ।) (**ख**)

वासव०—(सकोपम् ।) काञ्चनमाले एतेनैव लतापाशेन बद्ध्वा गृहाणैनं ब्राह्मणम् । एतां च दुर्विनीतां कन्यकामग्रतः कुरु । (**ग**)

काञ्चन०—यद्देव्याज्ञापयति । (लतापाशेन विदूषकं बध्नती ।) हताश अनुभवेदानीमात्मनो दुर्नयस्य फलम् । सागरिके त्वमप्यग्रतो भव । (**घ**)

(**क**) अज्जउत्त उट्ठेहि उट्ठेहि । किं अज्जवि सहजाभिजादाए सेवाए दुक्खं अणुहवीअदि । (**ख**) भोदि तुमं किं उब्बन्धिअ अत्ताणअं वावादेसित्ति वेससारिस्समोहिदेण मए पिअवअस्सो इत्थ आणिदो । जइ मम वअणं ण पत्तिआअसि ता पेक्ख एदं लदापासम् । (**ग**) कञ्चणमाले एदेण ज्जेव लदापासेण बन्धिअ गेण्ह एणं बम्भणम् । एदं च दुव्विणीदं कण्णकं अग्गदो करेहि । (**घ**) जं देवी आणवेदि । हदास अणुहव दाणिं अत्तणो दुण्णअस्स फलम् । सागरिए तुमं वि अग्गदो होहि ।

पूर्वोक्तं तस्य योग्यमित्यर्थः । सवैलक्ष्यं सविस्मयम् । उपालब्धुं जुगुप्सितुम् । विप्रलब्ध वञ्चिताः । सहजमभिजाता तस्याः सेवया । व्यापादयसि मारयसि । मोहितेन जातभ्रमेण वञ्चितेनेत्यर्थः । प्रत्येषि विश्वसिषि । दुर्विनीतां धृष्टामित्यर्थः । अत्र वास०–(उपसृत्य) आर्यपुत्र युक्तमिदमित्यत आरभ्य एतामपि कन्यकामग्रतः कुरु इत्यन्तेन वासवदत्तासंरब्धवचसा सागरिकासमागमान्तरायभूतेन अनियतप्राप्तिकारणं तोटकं नाम गर्भसन्धे-

---

१ (सत्रासं; ०सं सागरिकां मुक्त्वा); (देवीं दृष्ट्वात्मगतम् ।) अहो सत्यमेवेदं सुखमसुखावसानं नामेति । किमिदानीं करिष्ये । (प्रकाशं) न खलु इ०. २ ०श्याद्विप्र०; ०याताः । तत्क्षन्तव्यं; तथा मे क्ष०. ३ कथमे० श्रुतम् । सर्वथा. ४ प्रसादनोपायं; निष्प्रत्याशाः, ०शीभूतोस्मि मन्दभाग्यः. ५ विदू०—(विषादं नाटयति ।). ६ हस्तेन गृहीत्वा द०. ७ वसन्तकं गले बद्ध्वा ताडयति; बद्ध्वा. ८ अज्जवि अभिजादाए;० भिजादाए; ०भिजादिसेवादुःखम्. ९ विवज्जासित्ति. १० ता किं ण पेक्खदि भोदी एवं. ११ आणेहि; ०णबडुअं, दुट्ठब. १२ अवि०; दुट्ठकण्णअं. १३ दाव अत्तणो अवि० । देवीए दुट्ठवअणेहिं कडुइका कण्णात्ति सुमरेहि तं वअणं । १४ अस्मात्परं—इति अग्रतः पश्यन्ती विदूषकमाकर्षन्ती प्रस्थिता ।.

सा ग०—(स्वगतम्।) हा धिक् कथमकृतपुण्यया मया मर्तुमप्यात्मन इच्छया न पारितम्। (क)

विदू[1]०—(सविषादं राजानमवलोक्य।) भो वयस्य स्मर मामनाथं देव्या बन्धनाद्विपद्यमानम्। (ख)

(सर्वा[2]नादाय निष्क्रान्ता वासवदत्ता।)

राजा—(सखेदम्।) क[3]ष्टं भोः कष्टम्।

किं देव्याः कृतदीर्घरोषमुषितास्निग्धास्मितं तन्मुखं
त्रस्तां सागरिकां [4]सुसंभृतरुषा किं त[5]र्ज्यमानां तया।
बद्ध्वा नीतमितो वसन्तकम[6]हं किं चिन्तयामीत्य[7]हो
सर्वा[8]कारकृतव्यथः क्ष[9]णमपि प्राप्नोमि नो निर्वृतिम्॥१९॥

तत्किमिदानीमिह स्थिते[10]न। देवीं प्र[11]सादयितुमभ्यन्तरमेव प्रविशामि।

(इति निष्क्रान्ताः सर्वे।)

इति संकेतो ना[12]म तृतीयोऽङ्कः।

(क) हद्धी कधं अकिदपुण्णाए मए मरिदुं पि अत्तणो इच्छए न पारिदम्।
(ख) भो वअस्स सुमरेहि मं अणाधं देवीए बन्धनादो विवज्जन्तं।

रङ्गमुक्तम्। दुर्विनयस्य कुचेष्टितस्य। अकृतपुण्यया दुर्भाग्ययेत्यर्थः। यतः पुण्यवानेव भाग्यवान्। पारितं पार्यते इति दशरूपकोद्धृतः पाठः। अत्र वासवदत्तायाः सागरिकाया भयमित्युद्वेगो नाम गर्भसन्धेरङ्गम्। यो हि यस्यापकारी स तस्यारिः इति दशरूपकम्। **किं देव्या** इति। देव्या वासवदत्तायाः तत्सुपरिचितं कृतः यः दीर्घः दृढ इत्यर्थः रोषः अर्थाद्देव्या तेन मुषितं विलोपितं स्निग्धं रुचिरं स्मितं यस्मिंस्तत्। मुखं चिन्तयामि किं स्मृत्वा शोचामि किमित्यर्थः। अथ वा सुष्ठु संभृता विवृद्धा रुट् क्रोधः यस्यास्तादृश्या देव्या तर्ज्यमानां भर्त्स्यमानामतः त्रस्तां भीतां सागरिकां चिन्तयामि किम्। किं वा बद्ध्वा पाशेन नियन्त्रितं कृत्वा इतो नीतं वसन्तकं चिन्तयामि। इति अनेन प्रकारेण। अहो इति खेदे। सर्वाकारेण सर्वप्रकारेण कृता व्यथा पीडा यस्य सोऽहं क्षणमपि निर्वृतिं चित्तस्वास्थ्यं न प्राप्नोमि लभे। शार्दूलविक्रीडितं वृत्तम्॥ १९॥ **तत्किमिदानीमित्यादि**। अत्र देवीप्रसादायत्ता सागरिकासमागमसिद्धिरिति गर्भबीजोद्भेदादाक्षेप इति गर्भसन्धेरङ्गम्॥ इति रत्नावलीटीकायां तृतीयोऽङ्कः॥ ३॥

---

१ विदू०—(विषादं नाटयति। नायकस्य मुखमवलोक्य।) भो वअस्स सु० मं बह्मणं; (सविषादं) भो वअ०...मं विवज्जन्तं। (इति राजानमालोकयति।). २ वास० राजानमालोकयन्ती सागरिकां वसन्तकं च गृहीत्वा काञ्चनमालया सह निष्क्रान्ता; राजानं मुक्त्वा सर्वे निष्क्रान्ताः. ३ अहो क०. ४ तु सं०, क्रमोद्धतरुपा. ५ संत०, संत्यज्यमानां. ६ महो, ०मिमं. ७ म्यद्य भोः. ८ रम्भ. ९ कथमपि. १० स्थितेन प्रयोजनम्. ११ देवीसकाशमेव गच्छामि; देवीमेव गत्वा प्रसादयामि. १२ ०तकं ना०, इति रत्नावल्यां—रत्नावलीनामप्रधाननाटिकायां तृ०.

चतुर्थोऽङ्कः ।

(ततः प्रविशति गृहीतरत्नमाला साम्रा सुसंगता ।)

सुसंगता—(सकरुणं निःश्वस्य ।) हा प्रियसखि सागरिके हा लज्जावति हा उदारशीले हा सखीजनवत्सले हा सौम्यदर्शने कुत्रेदानीं त्वं मया प्रेक्षितव्या । (इति रोदिति । ऊर्ध्वमवलोक्य निःश्वस्य च ।) अयि दैवहतक अकरुण असामान्यरूपशोभा तादृशी त्वया यदि निर्मिता तत्कस्मात्पुनरीदृशमवस्थान्तरं प्रापिता । इयं च रत्नमाला जीवितनिराशया तया कस्यापि ब्राह्मणस्य हस्ते प्रतिपादयेति भणित्वा मम हस्ते समर्पिता । तद्यावत्कमपि ब्राह्मणमन्विष्यामि । (परिक्रम्याग्रतो विलोक्य च ।) अये एष खल्वार्यवसन्तक इत एवागच्छति । तद्यावदेतस्मा एवैतां प्रतिपादयिष्यामि ।(क)

(ततः प्रविशति प्रहृष्टो वसन्तकः ।)

(क) हा पिअसहि साअरिए हा लज्जाउण्णि हा उदारशीले हा सहीजणवच्छले हा सोम्मदंसणे कहिं दाणिं तुमं मए पेक्खिदव्वा । अइ देव्वहदअ अअरुण असामण्णरूअसोहा तादिसी तुए जइ णिम्मिदा ता कीस उण ईदिसं अवत्थन्तरं पाविदा । इअं अ रअणमाला जीविदणिरासाए ताए कस्सवि बम्हणस्स हत्थे पडिवादेसुत्ति भणिअ मम हत्थे समप्पिदा । ता जाव कं पि बम्हणं अण्णेसामि । अए एसो खु अज्जवसन्तओ इदो ज्जेव आअच्छदि । तां जाव एदस्स ज्जेव एदं पडिवादइस्सम् ।

अथ चतुर्थाङ्केऽवशिष्टौ अवमर्शनिबर्हणसन्धी प्रतिपाद्येते । तत्रादौ तावदग्निविद्रवपर्यन्तो वासवदत्ताप्रसक्त्या निरपायरत्नावलीप्राप्त्यवसायात्माऽवमर्शो दर्शितः । अथ वत्सराजप्रवेशं सूचयितुं प्रवेशकमारभते—**ततः प्रविशती**त्यादिना । सकरुणमिति अत्र करुणा सख्या दुर्दशापन्नत्वात् । हा इति विषादे । हा विषादशुगर्तिषु इत्यमरः । लज्जालुके इति पाठे लज्जां लाति इति लज्जालुः । मितत्वादिल्वाल्लाधातोर्डु प्रत्ययः । आलुच् तु दुष्प्रापः स्पृहिग्रहिपतीत्याद्युक्तत्वात् । लज्जालुरेव लज्जालुका । स्वार्थे कः । तत्संबोधनम् । सौम्यं मनोज्ञं दर्शनं यस्याः सा । दैवहतक कुत्सितदैव । न सामान्या असामान्या रूपस्य शोभा यस्याः सा । जीवितनिराशया जीविते निर्गता

---

१ रत्नमालामादाय; ०शात्युद्विग्नमनाः सु०. २ ०क्रम्यावलोक्य, विलोक्य. ३ लज्जालुए (लुके). ४ गण. ५ कहिं गदा दाणिं पुणो;...देक्खिदव्वा. ६ दिव्व तुए जादि असा० सा णिम्माविदा; ०हदअ जइ उण अणण्णसाहारणरूवादिसोहा एदादिसी णिम्मिदा. ७ वि ०माला ताए बम्हणस्स कस्सवि पडिवादणीआत्ति; (रत्नमालां विलोक्य ।) इअं अ. ८ पेक्खामि. ९ ता इमास्सि; ज्जेव पडि०; ता इह ट्ठिदा एव्व.

वसन्तकः—ही ही भो अद्य खलु प्रियवयस्येन प्रसादितया तत्रभवत्या वासवदत्तया बन्धनान्मोचयित्वा स्वहस्तदत्तैर्मोदकैश्चिरस्य तावत्कालस्योदरं मे सुपूरितं कृतम्। अन्यच्चैतत्पट्टांशुकयुगलं कर्णाभरणं च दत्तम्। तद्यावदिदानीं गत्वा प्रियवयस्यं प्रेक्षे। (परिक्रामति।) (क)

सुसं०—(रुदती सहसोपसृत्य।) आर्य वसन्तक तिष्ठ तावन्मुहूर्तम्।(ख)

विदू०—(दृष्ट्वा।) कथं सुसंगता । सुसंगते किंनिमित्तं रुद्यते। न खलु सागरिकाया अत्याहितं किमपि संवृत्तम्। (ग)

सुसं०—आर्य वसन्तक एतदेव निवेदयिष्यामि। सा खलु तपस्विनी देव्या उज्जयिनीं नीयत इति प्रवादं कृत्वोपस्थितेऽर्धरात्रे न ज्ञायते कुत्र नीतेति। (घ)

विदू०—(सोद्वेगम्।) अतिनिर्घृणं खलु कृतं देव्या। (ङ)

सुसं०—इयं च रत्नमाला तया जीवितनिराशया आर्यवसन्तकस्य हस्ते प्रतिपादयेति भणित्वा मम हस्ते समर्पिता। तद्गृहाणेतामार्यः। (च)

(क) ही ही भो अज्ज क्खु पिअंवअस्सेण पसादिदाए तत्तभोदीए वासवदत्ताए बन्धणादो मोआविअ सहत्थदिण्णेहिं मोदएहिं चिरस्स दाव कालस्स उअरं मे सुपूरिदं किदम्। अण्णं च एदं पट्टंसुअजुअलं कण्णाभरणं अ दिण्णम्। ता जाव दाणिं गदुअ पिअवअस्सं पेक्खामि। (ख) अज्ज वसन्तअ चिट्ठ दावं मुहुत्तअम्। (ग) कधं सुसंगदा। सुसंगदे किंणिमित्तं रोदीअदि। णं क्खु साअरिआए अच्चाहिदं किंवि संवुत्तम्। (घ) अज्ज वसन्तअ एदं ज्जेव णिवेदइस्सम्। सा क्खु तवस्सिणी देवीए उज्जइणिं णीअदित्ति पवादं कदुअ उवत्थिदे अद्धरत्ते ण जाणीअदि कहिं णीदेत्ति। (ङ) अदिणिग्घिणं क्खु किदं देवीए। (च) इअं च रअणमाला ताए जीविदणिरासाए अज्जवसन्तअस्स हत्थे पडिवादेसुत्ति भणिअ मम हत्थे समप्पिदा। ता गेण्हदु एदं अज्जो।

आशा यस्याः सा तया। अतः परं न जीविष्यामीति मन्यमानयेत्यर्थः। प्रतिपादय देहि। पट्टांशुकयोर्युगलं पट्टांशुकयुगलम्। अत्याहितं महाभीतिः। महारिष्टमिति यावत्। तपस्विनी अनुकम्पार्हा। दीनेति यावत्। अर्धं रात्रेः अर्धरात्रः तस्मिन्। अतिनिर्घृण-

---

१ रुदत्यु०. २ ०स्सपसा०, ०स्सस्स पसण्णाए. ३ देवीए. ४ मोअअलड्डुएहिं उदरं मे. ५ दाणिं पिअ० पेक्खिस्सम्. ६ दाव तुमं. ७ कधं इअं. ८ एत्थ किं. ९ किं णु;...किंवि सुदं (श्रुतं). १० अज्जाहिदं एव्व. ११ पेसिद–नीदे–त्ति. १२ आदिणिट्ठुहुरं; हा भोदि साअ० हा असामाण्णरूवसोहे हा मिदुभासिणि अदिणिग्घिणं दाणीं देवीए किदं। तदो तदो.

विदू०—(सास्रम् ।) भवति न म ईदृशे प्रस्तावे हस्तौ ग्रहीतुं प्रसरतः । (क)

(उभौ रुदितः ।)

सुसं०—(अञ्जलिं बद्ध्वा ।) तस्या एवानुग्रहं कुर्वन्नङ्गीकरोत्वे-तामार्यः । (ख)

विदू०—(विचिन्त्य ।) अथ वोपनय । येनानयैव सागरिकाविरहदुः-खितं प्रियवयस्यं विनोदयिष्यामि । (ग)

(सुसंगतोपनयति ।)

विदू०—(गृहीत्वा निर्वर्ण्य सविस्मयम् ।) सुसंगते कुतः पुनस्तस्या ईदृशस्यालंकारस्य समागमः । (घ)

सुसं०—आर्य मयापि सा कौतूहलेन पृष्टैवासीत् । (ङ)

विदू०—ततस्तया किं भणितम् । (च)

सुसं०—ततः सोर्ध्वं प्रेक्ष्य दीर्घं निःश्वस्य सुसंगते किमिदानीं तवैतया कथयेति भणित्वा रोदितुं प्रवृत्ता । (छ)

(क) भोदि ण मे ईदिसे पत्थावे हत्था गेण्हिदुं पसरन्ति । (ख) ताए ज्जेव अणुग्गहं करन्तो अङ्गीकरेदु एदं अज्जो । (ग) अह वा उवणेहि । जेण इमाए ज्जेव्व साअरिआविरहदुक्खिदं पिअवअस्सं विणोदइस्सम् । (घ) सुसंगदे कुदो उण ताए ईदिसस्स अलंकारस्स समागमो । (ङ) अज्ज मए वि सा कोदुहलेण पुच्छिदा ज्जेवासि । (च) तदो ताए किं भणिदम् । (छ) तदो सा उद्धं पेक्खिअ दीहं णिस्ससिअ सुसंगदे किं दाणिं तुए एदाए कधाए त्ति भणिअ रोदिदुं पउत्ता ।

मतिनिर्देयं कृतम् । ईदृशे एवंविधे प्रस्तावे प्रसङ्गे । सागरिकायामेवंविधदुर्दशां गतायामित्यर्थः । अनुग्रहं कुर्वन्निति । अस्या अङ्गीकारे तस्यामेवानुग्रहः कृतः स्यादिति भावः । सागरिकाया विरहस्तेन दुःखितम् । दुःखमस्य संजातमिति दुःखितः तम् । तदस्य संजातमिति तारकादिभ्य इतच् इति इतच् । ननु इत्याक्षेपे । सामान्यश्चासौ

---

१ सकरुणं, सास्रं सकरुणं कर्णौ पिधाय. २ कृताञ्जलिः. ३ सु० वसन्तकस्य हस्ते-वसन्तकाय-रत्नमालां ददाति; सु० तस्य हस्ते समर्पयति. ४ गृहीत्वा निरूप्य, ०त्वा रत्नमालां. ५ एदं वोढुं हत्थो पसरदि; अहह भवदि कधं मम ईदिसे पत्थावे एदं गे०. ६ अह (अथ); भोदु गेण्हामि एदं. ७ ०रिआए विरहदुक्खं अवणेमि (अपनयामि) पिअवअस्सस्स; विरहकुण्ठिदं; विरहुक्कंठिदं. ८ संभावेदि; विणोदेमि. ९ कुदो ईदिसस्स ०स्सागमो. १० अज्ज दीहं णिस्ससिअ किं दाणिं इमाए चिन्ताए त्ति भ०

विदू०—ननु कथितमेव सामान्यजनदुर्लभेनानेन परिच्छदेन सर्वथा महाकुलप्रसूतया तया भवितव्यमिति। सुसंगते प्रियवयस्य इदानी कुत्र। (क)

सुसं०—आर्य एष खलु भर्ता देवीभवनान्निष्क्रम्य स्फटिकशिलामण्डपं गतः। तद्गच्छत्वार्यः। अहमपि देव्याः पार्श्ववर्तिनी भविष्यामि। (ख)

विदू०—एवम्। (ग)

(इति निष्क्रान्तौ।)

प्रवेशकः।

(ततः प्रविशत्यासनस्थो राजा।)

राजा—(विचिन्त्य।)

सव्याजैः शपथैः प्रियेण वचसा चित्तानुवृत्त्याधिकं
वैलक्ष्येण परेण पादपतनैर्वाक्यैः सखीनां मुहुः।
प्रत्यापत्तिमुपागता नै हि तथा देवी रुदत्या यथा
प्रक्षाल्येव तयैव बाष्पसलिलैः कोपोऽपनीतः स्वयम्॥ १॥

(क) [4]णं कहिदं ज्जेव सामण्णजणदुल्लहेग इमिणा परिच्छदेण सव्वहा महाकुलप्पसूदाए ताए होदव्वंत्ति। सुसङ्गदे पिअवअस्सो दाणिं कहिं। (ख) अज्ज एसो खु भट्टा देवीभवणाओ णिक्कमिअ फडिअसिलामण्डवं गदो। ता गच्छदु अज्जो। अहं वि देवीए पासवत्तिणी भविस्सम्। (ग) एव्वम्।

जनश्च तेन दुर्लभस्तेन। परिच्छदेनालंकारेण। महच्च तत्कुलं च महाकुलं तत्र प्रसूतया। महाभिजनसमुत्पन्नयेति पाठे अभिजायते अस्मिन्नित्यभिजनः कुलम्। अधिकरणे घञ्। तस्मिन्समुत्पन्नया। स्फटिकशिलानां स्फटिकशिलानिर्मितो वा मण्डपः स्फटिकशिलामण्डपस्तम्। अभीक्ष्णं परितः वर्तते इति पार्श्ववर्तिनी। बहुलमाभीक्ष्ण्ये इति णिनिः। देवीमुपचरितुं गमिष्यामीत्यर्थः। **सव्याजैरिति**। व्याजेन कपटेन युक्तयेति यावत् सहिताः सव्याजाः तैः सव्याजैः शपथैः। आत्मनः मिथ्याभाषणदोषो यथा न स्याद्देवी च विश्वासमियात्तथा वाचोयुक्त्या कृतैः शपथैरित्यर्थः। प्रियेण संतोषकारिणा वचसा अधिकं चित्तस्य। अर्थाद् देव्याः। अनुवृत्त्या अनुकूलाचरणेन। छन्दो-

१ उभौ. २ प्रत्यासत्तिं. ३ मम. ४ भो दिण्णं...ज्जेव ताए–इमाए लज्जाए; परिच्छदेण परिअणसंकासंवुत्तघणेवअणेण हिअअभावेण. ५ महाहिजणाए. ६ एतदादि नास्ति पुस्तकान्तरे. ७ (दृष्ट्वा) अज्ज...सिलाअलं ज्जेव पत्थिदो। ता गच्छ तुमम्. ८ परिचारिणी. ९ होमि.

(सोत्कण्ठं निःश्वस्य ।) इदानीं देव्यां प्रसन्नायां सागरिकाचिन्तैव केवलं मां बाधते । कुतः ।

अम्भोजगर्भसुकुमारतनुस्तथासौ
कण्ठग्रहे प्रथमरागघने विलीय ।
सद्यःपतन्मदनमार्गणरन्ध्रमार्गै-
र्मन्ये मम प्रियतमा हृदयं प्रविष्टा ॥ २ ॥

(विचिन्त्य ।) योऽपि मे विश्वासस्थानं वसन्तकः सोऽपि देव्या संयतस्तिष्ठति । तत्कस्याग्रे बाष्पमोक्षं करिष्ये । (इति निःश्वसिति ।)

(ततः प्रविशति वसन्तकः ।)

वस०—(राजानं दृष्ट्वा ।) एष खलु निर्भरोत्कण्ठापरिक्षामामपि श्लाघनीयलावण्यां तनुं समुद्वहन्नुदित इव द्वितीयाचन्द्रोऽधिकतरं शोभते

नुवृत्त्येत्यर्थः । परेणात्यर्थेन वैलक्ष्येण लज्जाप्रदर्शनेन इति यावत् । पादपतनैः क्षमायाचनार्थं चरणपातैः । यद्वा परेण वैलक्ष्येण हेतुभूतेन कृतैः पादपतनैः इति योज्यम् । मुहुः उक्तैः सखीनां प्रियाप्रसादनचतुराणामित्यर्थात् । वाक्यैः वचनैः । देवी वासवदत्ता तथा प्रत्यापत्तिं प्रकृतिभावम् । प्रसन्नतामिति यावत् । न हि नैव नीता यथा रुदत्या तया स्वयमेव बाष्पाण्येव सलिलानि जलानि तैः प्रक्षाल्येव कोपः अपनीतः दूरीकृतः । अयं भावः-मत्कृतैः सान्त्वोपायैः सा रोदनपरा बभूव । रुदत्याश्च तस्या हृदयं तथा मृदुतामगच्छद्यथा तस्याः कोपो बाष्पसलिलैः प्रक्षालित इव विलयं गतः । उत्प्रेक्षालंकारः । शार्दूलविक्रीडितं वृत्तम् ॥ १ ॥ अत्र सागरिकालाभविरोधिवासवदत्ताकोपोपशमनात् शक्तिर्नाम विमर्शसन्धेरङ्गं प्रदर्शितम् । उत्कण्ठया सहितं सोत्कण्ठम् । **अम्भोजेत्यादि** । अम्भोजस्य कमलस्य गर्भः मध्यभागः स इव सुकुमारा तनुर्यस्याः सा अम्भोजगर्भसुकुमारतनुः असौ प्रियतमा सागरिका तदा मकरन्दोद्यानसंमेलनसमये । प्रथमरागघने प्रथमः अभिनवः रागः अनुरागः तेन घने निबिडे । दृढे इत्यर्थः । कण्ठग्रहे कण्ठाश्लेषे विलीय विलयं प्राप्य विशीर्णा भूत्वेत्यर्थः । सद्यः तत्क्षणं पतन्तो ये मदनस्य मार्गणाः सायकाः तेषां यानि रन्ध्राणि तान्येव अन्तःप्रवेशार्थं मार्गाः तैः मम हृदयं प्रविष्टा इति मन्ये । मन्येशब्दप्रयोगादुत्प्रेक्षालंकारः । वसन्ततिलकं वृत्तम् ॥ २ ॥ विश्वासस्थानमित्यत्र विश्रामस्थानमिति केषांचित्पाठः । तत्र विश्राम इति शब्दः अपाणिनीयोऽपि बहुलं कविभिः प्रयुज्यते । निर्भरा अतिशयिता या उत्कण्ठा

---

१ प्रसादितायां; इदानीं प्रसन्ना देवी. २ तथा हि. ३ ग्रहैः...रागघनैः. ४ ०धगर्भैः. ५ विश्राम०. ६ संयतः । तत्कस्याग्रतः.

प्रियवयस्यः । तद्यावदेनमुपसर्पामि । (उपसृत्य ।) स्वस्ति भवते । दिष्ट्या दृष्टोऽसि देवीहस्तगतेनापि मया पुनरप्येताभ्यामक्षिभ्याम् । (क)

राजा—(दृष्ट्वा सहर्षम् ।) अये वसन्तकः प्राप्तः । सखे परिष्वजस्व माम् ।

विदू०—(परिष्वजति ।)

राजा—वयस्य वेषेणैव निवेदितस्ते देव्याः प्रसादः । तत्कथ्यतामिदानीं सागरिकायाः का वार्तेति ।

(विदूषकः सवैलक्ष्यमधोमुखस्तिष्ठति ।)

राजा—वयस्य किं न कथयसि ।

विदू०—अप्रियं ते निवेदयितुं न पारयामि । (ख)

राजा—(सोद्वेगम् ।) वयस्य कथमप्रियम् । व्यक्तमुत्सृष्टं जीवितं तया । हा प्रिये सागरिके । (इति मूर्च्छति ।)

विदू०—(ससंभ्रमम् ।) समाश्वसितु समाश्वसितु प्रियवयस्यः । (ग)

राजा—(समाश्वस्य । सास्रम् ।)

प्राणाः परित्यजत काममदक्षिणं मां
　रे दक्षिणा भवत मद्वचनं कुरुध्वम् ।
शीघ्रं न यात यदि तन्मुषिताः स्थ नूनं
　याता सुदूरमधुना गजगामिनी सा ॥ ३ ॥

(**क**) एसो क्खु णिब्भरोक्कण्ठापरिक्खीमं वि सलाघणिज्जलावण्णं तणुं समुव्वहन्तो उदिओ विअ दुदिआचन्दो अहिअअरं सोहदि पिअवअस्सो । ता जाव णं उवसप्पामि । सोत्थि भवदे । दिट्ठिआ दिट्ठोसि देवीहत्थगदेणावि मए पुणोवि एदेहिं अच्छीहिं । (**ख**) अप्पिअं ते णिवेदिदुं न पारेमि । (**ग**) समस्ससदु समस्ससदु पिअवअस्सो ।

तया परिक्षामां कृशाम् । श्लाघनीयं मनोज्ञं लावण्यं यस्याः ताम् । सोद्वेगमुद्वेगेन मनोव्यथया सहितं यथा तथा । **प्राणा** इति । हे प्राणा दक्षिणा अनुकूला भवत । मम वचनं मद्वचनं कुरुध्वम् । किं तदित्याह काममत्यन्तम् । अदक्षिणं दक्षिणः परच्छन्दानुवर्ती स न भवति तादृशम् । मां परित्यजत । यदि शीघ्रं न यात गच्छत तर्हि

---

१ माम् । (विदूषकं परिष्वज्य) वयस्य...दितस्त्वया. २ (परिष्वज्य) भो वअस्स देवीए अणुग्गहीदोम्हि. ३ को वृत्तान्तः; ०रिका किं वर्तते. ४ णक्खं, क्षणमात्रम्. ५ अयि वयस्य. ६ ०गं ससंभ्रमं; साशंकम्. ७ ०सृष्टजीविता सा, व्यक्तमेवो०; मोहं नाटयति; मोहमुपगतः. ८ काममकामदक्षं; मा मम सत्पथोर्य हे दक्षि०. ९ शृणुध्वं. १० मूढाः. ११ ०क्खामताए सअंवेसेण सलावण्णतणुं. १२ भो दिट्ठिआ वड्ढासि देवीह० अच्छीहिं जं दिट्ठोसि, देवीसहत्थ०...एदेहिं एव. १३ भो पिअवअस्स ण सक्कुणोमि आचक्खिदुम्.

विदू०—भो वयस्य मान्यथा संभावय । सा खलु तपस्विनी देव्योज्जयिनीं प्रेषितेति श्रूयते । अतो मयाऽप्रियमिति भणितम् । (क)

राजा—कथमुज्जयिनीं प्रेषिता । अहो निरनुरोधा मयि देवी । वयस्य केन तवैतदाख्यातम् ।

विदू०—(सास्रं निःश्वस्य ।) भोः सुसंगतया । अन्यच्च मम हस्ते तया किमपिनिमित्तमियं रत्नमाला प्रेषिता । (ख)

राजा—किमपरं मां समाश्वासयितुम्[3] । तद्वयस्योपनय ।

(विदूषक उपनयति ।)

राजा—(गृहीत्वा रत्नमालां निर्वर्ण्य हृदये निधाय ।) अहह ।

कण्ठाश्लेषं समासाद्य तस्याः प्रभ्रष्टयानया ।
तुल्यावस्था सखीवेयं तनुराश्वास्यते मम ॥ ४ ॥

(क) भो वअस्स मा अण्णधा संभावेहि[6] । सा क्खु तवस्सिणी देवीए उज्जेणिं पेसिदेत्ति[7] सुणीअदि । अदो मए अप्पिअं त्ति भणिदम् । (ख) भो सुसंगदाए । अण्णं च मम हत्थे ताएं किंविणिमित्तं इअं रअणमाला पेसिदा ।

नूनं ध्रुवं मुषिता वञ्चिता इति यावत् स्थ भविष्यथ । यतः सा गजगामिनी गज इव गन्तुं शीलं यस्याः सा अधुना सम्प्रति सुदूरं विप्रकृष्टान्तरं याता गता । वसन्ततिलका वृत्तम् ॥ ३ ॥ अन्यथा अन्यप्रकारेण मा संभावय मनसि कुरु । मृतेति मा मन्यस्वेत्यर्थः । सुसं०—सा खलु तपस्विनी कुत्रापि नीतेति । विदू० (सोद्वेगं ।) अतिनिर्घृणं खलु कृतं देव्या । पुनः—भो वयस्य मा खलु अन्यथा संभावय''' अतोऽप्रियमिति भणितम् । राजा—अहो निरनुरोधा मयि देवी इत्यनेन वासवदत्तादोषप्रख्यापनाद् अपवादः नाम अविमर्शसन्धेरङ्गं दर्शितम् । निरनुरोधा निर्गतः अनुरोधः अनुवर्तनं यस्याः सा । पाठान्तरे निरनुक्रोशा निष्कृपा । कृपा दयानुकम्पा स्यादनुक्रोशोऽपि । इत्यमरः । अत्र वासवदत्तयेष्टासम्पादनाद्वत्सराजस्यावमाननाच्छलमिति अवमर्शसन्धेरङ्गम् । अन्यच्च अन्यदपि कथनीयमस्तीत्यर्थः । किमपिनिमित्तं केनापि हेतुना । **कण्ठाश्लेषमिति** । तस्याः सागरिकायाः कण्ठाश्लेषं कण्ठस्याश्लेषमालिङ्गनं प्राप्य प्रभ्रष्टया च्युतया अनया रत्नमालया तुल्या समाना अवस्था यस्याः सा तुल्यावस्था ।

---

१ ०रनुक्रोशा; ०रोधिता मयि देव्याः. २ वसन्तक. ३ ०यितुम् । (गृहीत्वा रत्नमालां हृदये निवेश्य) अहह. ४ विन्यस्य, ददाति. ५ आश्लिष्यते. ६ आसंक. ७ पेसिदा । अदो मए विप्पिअंत्ति भणिअ ण कथिदम्. ८ ताए एव्व;–एव्व सुसंगदाए; इअं रअणमाला वसन्तअस्स पडिवालेदित्ति भणिअ ताए सुसंगदाहत्थे समप्पिदा ताए वि मम हत्थे दिण्णा । ९ कज्जेण.

वयस्य त्वं परिधत्स्वैताम्। येन वयमेनां तावद् दृष्ट्वा धृतिं करिष्यामः।

विदू०—यद्भवानाज्ञापयति। (परिदधाति।) (क)

राजा—(सास्रम्।) वयस्य दुर्लभं पुनः दर्शनं प्रियायाः।

विदू०—(दिशोऽवलोक्य सभयम्।) भो वयस्य मैवमुच्चैर्मन्त्रयस्व। कदापि कोऽपि देव्या इह संचरति। (ख)

(ततः प्रविशति वेत्रहस्ता वसुंधरा।)

वसु०—(उपसृत्य।) जयतु जयतु भर्ता। भर्तः एष खलु रुमण्वतो भागिनेयो विजयवर्मा प्रियं किमपि निवेदयितुकामो द्वारे तिष्ठति। (ग)

राजा—वसुंधरे अविलम्बितं प्रवेशय।

प्रतीहारी—यद्देव आज्ञापयति। (इति निष्क्रम्य विजयवर्मणा सह पुनः प्रविश्य।) विजयवर्मन् एष खलु भर्ता। तदुपसर्पत्वार्यः। (घ)

विजय०—(उपसृत्य।) जयतु जयतु देवः। देव दिष्ट्या वर्धसे रुमण्वतो विजयेन।

राजा—साधु रुमण्वन् साधु। अचिरान्महत्प्रयोजनमनुष्ठितम्। विजयवर्मन् इत आस्यताम्।

(विजयवर्मोपविशति।)

(क) जं भवं आणवेदि। (ख) भो वअस्स मा एव्वं उच्च मन्तेहि। कआवि को वि देवीए इह संचरदि। (ग) जअदु जअदु भट्टा। भट्टा एसो क्खु रुमण्वदो भाइणेओ विजयवम्मा पिअं किंपि णिवेदिदुकामो दुआरे चिट्ठदि। (घ) जं देवो आणवेदि। विजअवम्म एसो खु भट्टा। ता उवसप्पदु अज्जो।

इयं मम तनुः शरीरं सखीव आश्वास्यते सान्त्व्यते। उपमालङ्कारः ॥ ४ ॥ धृतिं धैर्यं संतोषं वा। वेत्रं वेत्रयष्टिः हस्ते यस्याः सा। वसुंधरा एतन्नाम्नी प्रतीहारी। भागिनेयः भगिन्याः पुत्रः। स्त्रीभ्यो ढक् इति अपत्यार्थे ढक्। निवेदयितुं कामो यस्य स निवेदयितुकामः। तुंकाममनसोरपि इति मलोपः। कतिपयैः अहोभिः

---

१ तद्वयस्य परिधत्स्व; त्वमेवैनां परि०. २ एनामपि दृष्ट्वा तावद्वृत्तिं; विरहवदनादेस्त्यागं; हृदयविनोदम्. ३ सास्रं निःश्वस्य. ४ सागरिकाया दर्शनम्. ५ खड्ग०, ०शति प्रतीहारी. ६ राजानमुप०. ७ ०धरे गच्छ. ८ ०धर्मणा. ९ राजा—(सपरितोषम्।) विजयवर्मन् अपि जिता कोसलाः। विज०—देवस्य प्रभावेण। राजा—साधु रुम०...ष्ठितम्। विजयवर्मन् तत्कथय कथाम्। अतिविस्तरतः श्रोतुमिच्छामि। १० एव्वं भण। कोवि इह; कदावि वासवदत्तापरिआरिणी एत्थ संचरे। (कर्णं दत्वा) चिट्ठ कोवि पदसद्द विअ. ११ पिअमिअ. १२ ०दिदुं. १३ ०वम्म.

राजा—विजयवर्मन् जितः कोसलाधिपतिः[1]।

विजय०—देवस्य[2] प्रभावेण।

राजा—विजयवर्मन् तत्कथय कथमिति। विस्तरतः श्रोतुमिच्छामि।

विजय०—देव श्रूयताम्। वयमितो[3] देवादेशात्कतिपयैरेवाहोभिरनेककरितुरगपत्तिदुर्निवारेण महता बलसमूहेन गत्वा विन्ध्यदुर्गावस्थितस्य कोसलाधिपतेर्द्वारमवष्टभ्य सेनाः समावेशयितुमारब्धाः।

राजा—ततस्ततः।

विजय०—ततः कोसलाधिपतिरपि दर्पात्परिभवमसहमानो[4] हास्तिकप्रायमशेषमात्मसैन्यं सज्जीकृतवान्।

विदू०—भो लघ्वाचक्ष्व। वेपत इव मे हृदयम्। (क)

राजा—ततस्ततः।

विजय०—देव कृतनिश्चयश्चासौ[5]।

योद्धुं निर्गत्य विन्ध्यादभवदभिमुखस्तत्क्षणं दिग्विभागा-
न्विन्ध्येनेवापरेण द्विपपतिपृतनापीडबन्धेन[7] रुन्धन्।
वेगाद्बाणान्विमुञ्चन्समदकरिघटा[8]त्पिष्टपत्तिर्निपत्य
प्रत्यैच्छद्वाञ्छितात्तिद्विगुणितरभसस्तं रुमण्वान्क्षणेन[10] ॥ ५ ॥

(क) [11]भोः लहुं आचक्ख। वेवदि विअ मे हिअअम्।

अल्पैर्दिनैः। करिणश्च तुरगाश्च पत्तयश्च करितुरगपत्ति। सेनाङ्गत्वात्समाहारद्वंद्वः। अनेकेन करितुरगपत्तिना दुर्निवारं दुःखेन निवारयितुं शक्यं तेन। विन्ध्यस्य विन्ध्यस्थं वा यद् दुर्गं तत्रावस्थितस्य। अवष्टभ्य निरुध्य। समावेशयितुं व्यवस्थापयितुम्। परिभवं द्वाररोधरूपमपमानम्। हास्तिकप्रायं हस्तिनां समूहो हास्तिकम्। अचित्तहस्तिधेनोष्ठक् इति समूहे ठक्। तत्प्रायं यस्मिन्। **योद्धुमिति**। कृतः निश्चयः येन स कृतनिश्चयः असौ योद्धुं निर्गत्य तत्क्षणं स चासौ क्षणश्च तत्क्षणस्तम्। अपरेण अन्येन विन्ध्येन इव। द्वाभ्यां पिबन्तीति द्विपाः। सुपि इति कः। तेषां पतयः महागजा इत्यर्थः। तेषां या पृतना सेना तस्या आपीडबन्धः घनव्यूहाकारेण रचना तेन

१ कोसलेश्वरः २ देवप्रसादेन,—सादात्; देव एवम्. ३ इतो...रेव दिनै० तुरगरथदुर्निवारपत्तिसमुदायेन गत्वा...तेर्द्वारि समा०; सेनाः समावासयितुं—०ब्धवन्तः; देवपादादेशाद्यथा निर्दिष्टः कतिपयैरेव दिवसैः...गत्वा रुमण्वान्...समारब्धवान्. ४अमृष्यमाणः. ५ चासौ कोसल-लाधि-पतिः. ६ मुखो दक्षिणादिग्विभागम्. ७ पीठब०, द्विरदपतिघटापीड०. ८ गज०; ०श्चन्नथ समदगजो०; ०पार्त्ति. ९ प्रत्यागात्; संप्रैच्छत्; वाञ्छिताधि०. १० जवेन. ११ विजयवर्मन् लहुं आचक्खदु.

अपि च ।

> अस्त्रव्यस्तशिरस्त्रशस्त्रकषणोत्कृत्तोत्तमाङ्गे क्षणं
> व्यूढासृक्सरिति स्वनत्प्रहरणे वर्मोद्वलद्वह्निनि ।
> आहूयाजिमुखे सकोसलपतिर्भग्नप्रतीपीभव-
> न्नेकेनैव रुमण्वता शरशतैर्मत्तद्विपस्थो हतः ॥ ६ ॥

विदू०—जयतु जयतु भवान् । जितमस्माभिः । (इत्युत्थाय नृत्यति ।) (क)

राजा—साधु कोसलपते साधु । मृत्युरपि ते श्लाघ्यो यस्य शत्रवोऽप्येवं पुरुषकारं वर्णयन्ति । ततस्ततः ।

विजय०—देव ततो रुमण्वानपि कोसलेषु मद्भ्रातरं ज्यायांसं जयवर्माणं स्थापयित्वा समरव्रणितमशेषबलमनुवर्तमानः शनैः शनैरागच्छत्येव ।

राजा—वसुंधरे उच्यतां यौगन्धरायणः दीयतां मत्प्रसादोऽस्येति ।

(क) जअदु जअदु भवं । जितं अम्हेहिं ।

दिग्विभागान्दिक्प्रान्तान् निरुन्धन् व्याप्नुवन् । अभिमुखः अभवत् पुरः स्थितः । क्षणेन तत्क्षणं बाणान् विमुञ्चन् । समदानां करिणां घटाः समूहाः ताभिः उत्पिष्टाः चूर्णिताः पत्तयो येन यस्य वा स तथोक्तः । वाञ्छितस्य अभीष्टस्य कोसलपतिना सह द्वंद्वस्य या आप्तिः प्राप्तिस्तया द्विगुणितः रभसो वेगो हर्षो वा यस्य स वाञ्छिताप्तिद्विगुणितरभसः । रुमण्वान् वेगात् निपत्य तं प्रत्यैच्छत् प्रतियातः । वीरो रसः । उत्प्रेक्षालंकारः । स्रग्धरा वृत्तम् ॥ ५ ॥ **अस्त्रव्यस्तेति** । अस्त्रैः शस्त्रैः व्यस्तानि व्याक्षिप्तानि शिरस्त्राणि यैस्तादृशानि शस्त्राणि तेषां कषणैः प्रहारैरिति यावत् । उत्कृत्तानि छिन्नानि उत्तमाङ्गानि शिरांसि यस्मिन् । क्षणं व्यूढा वृद्धा असृजः रक्तस्य सरित् यस्मिन् । पुनश्च स्वनन्ति शब्दायमानानि प्रहरणानि यस्मिन् तथाभूते । तथा च वर्मभ्यः कवचेभ्यः उद्वलन् प्रादुर्भवन्वह्निः अग्निर्यस्मिन् तादृशे आजिमुखे रणशिरसि भग्नप्रतीपीभवन् भङ्गस्य स्वपराभवस्य प्रतीपीभवन् तं वारयन् इत्यर्थः । पाठान्तरे प्रधाने मुख्यबले भग्ने पराभूते सति । मत्तद्विपस्थः स कोसलपतिः आहूय आकार्य एकेन एव रुमण्वता शरशतैर्हतः । अनुप्रासोऽलंकारः । शार्दूलविक्रीडितं वृत्तम् ॥ ६ ॥ पुरुषकारं पराक्रमम् । समरे व्रणितं सञ्जातव्रणम् । अनुवर्तमानः अनुसरन् । तेन

---

१ अस्त. २ कषणैः कृत्तो०. ३ ०र्मोद्गल०; ०रणोद्रेगोद्गम०. ४ भग्ने प्रधाने बले; भग्नप्रतीपः; अस्मात्परं—राजा—कथमस्मदीयान्यपि बलानि भग्नानि । विज०—एकेनैव इ. ५ राजा—कोसलपते मृ०. ६ स्वभ्रा०। कोसलेशज्यायांसं भ्रा०. ७ ०प्रहारव्रणितहास्तिकप्रायमशेषसैन्यं; गाढ-समर-प्रहार०. ८ मन्दं मन्दं. ९ प्रदर्श्यताम्;-मत्प्रसादस्य विभवः इति; प्रियकथानुरूपेण दीय०. १० भवदा.

वसुं०—यद्देव आज्ञापयति । (इति विजयवर्मणा सह निष्कान्ता ।) (क)

(ततः प्रविशति काञ्चनमाला ।)

काञ्चन०—आज्ञप्तास्मि देव्या यथा—हञ्जे काञ्चनमाले गच्छ । एतमैन्द्रजालिकमार्यपुत्राय दर्शय । (परिक्रम्यावलोक्य च ।) । एष खलु भर्ता । तद्यावदुपसर्पामि । (उपसृत्य ।) जयतु जयतु भर्ता । देवी विज्ञापयति—एष खलूज्जयिनीतः सर्वसिद्धिर्नामैन्द्रजालिक आगतः । तत्प्रेक्षतामेनमार्यपुत्र इति । (ख)

राजा—अस्ति नः कौतुकमिन्द्रजाले । तच्छीघ्रं प्रवेशय ।

काञ्चन०—यद्देव आज्ञापयति । (ग)

(निष्क्रम्य पुनः पिच्छिकाहस्तेनैन्द्रजालिकेन सह प्रविशति ।)

ऐन्द्रजालिकः—(पिच्छिकां भ्रमयन् ।)

प्रणमत चरणाविन्द्रस्येन्द्रजालकपिनद्धनाम्नः ।
तथैव शम्बरस्य मायासुप्रतिष्ठितयशसः ॥ ७ ॥ (घ)

(क) जं देवो आणवेदि । (ख) आणत्तम्हि देवीए जह हञ्जे काञ्चणमाले गच्छ । एदं इन्दजालिअं अज्जउत्तस्स दंसेहि । एसो क्खु भट्टा । ता जाव उवसप्पामि । जअदु जअदु भट्टा । देवी विण्णवेदि एसो खु उज्जेणीदो सव्वसिद्धि णाम इन्दआलिओ आगदो । ता पेक्खदु णं अज्जउत्तोत्ति । (ग) जं देवो आणवेदित्ति ।

(घ) पणमह चलण इन्दस्स इन्दजालअपिणद्धणामस्स ।
तह ज्जेव्व संबरस्स माआसुपरिट्ठिदजसस्स ॥

सहेत्यर्थः । प्रसादः लक्षणया प्रसादानुरूपं पारितोषिकम् । ऐन्द्रजालिकः मायिकः । इन्द्रजालं शिल्पमस्य । शिल्पम् इति ठक् । इन्द्रजालिक इति पाठे इन्द्रजालमस्त्यस्य । अत इनिठनौ इति मत्वर्थे ठन् । पिच्छिका मयूरपिच्छकूर्चः । सा हस्ते यस्य तेन । **प्रणमतेति** । इन्द्रजालके पिनद्धं बद्धं नाम यस्य तस्य इन्द्रजालकपिनद्धनाम्नः इन्द्रस्य चरणौ प्रणमत । तथैव मायायामिन्द्रजालविद्यायां सुप्रतिष्ठितं यशो यस्य तस्य मायासुप्रतिष्ठितयशसः शम्बरस्य तन्नामकासुरस्य च चरणौ प्रणमत ॥ ७ ॥

---

१ ऐन्द्रजालिके. २ प्रविष्टा. (प्रविश्य)–एदु एदु अज्जो । (ऐन्द्रजालिकः परिक्रामति ।) काञ्चन०—एसो भट्टा । ता उपसप्पदु अज्जो । ऐन्द्र०—(उपसृत्य) जअदु. ३ ०कां भ्रामयित्वा बहुधा-विधं हास्यं कृत्वा. ४ इन्दजालम्हिलद्धसक्खस्स । ०जाले लब्धसाक्ष्यस्य । तह अज्ज सं० सुपरिच्छिदसव्वजगस्स (सुपरीक्षितसर्वजगतः); तहा संबरे सम्ब०; जालिआत्ति लद्धणामस्स । तह एव्व अज्ज (अद्य) असुरस्स–सम्बरस्स सुपरि०.

काञ्चन०—(उपसृत्य ।) भर्तः एष खल्वैन्द्रजालिकः । (क)

ऐन्द्र०—जयतु जयतु देवः । देव ।

किं धरण्यां मृगाङ्क आकाशे महीधरो जले ज्वलनः ।
मध्याह्ने प्रदोषो दर्श्यतां देह्याज्ञप्तिम् ॥ ८ ॥

अथ वा किं बहुना जल्पितेन ।

मम प्रतिज्ञैषा यद्यद् हृदयेनेहसे संद्रष्टुम् ।
तत्तद्दर्शयाम्यहं गुरोर्मन्त्रप्रभावेण ॥ ९ ॥ (ख)

विदूषकः—भो वयस्य अवहितो भव । ईदृशोऽस्यावष्टम्भो येन सर्वं संभाव्यते । (ग)

राजा—भद्र तिष्ठ तावत् । काञ्चनमाले उच्यतां देवी । युष्मदीय एवायमैन्द्रजालिको विजनीकृतश्चायमुद्देशः । तदेहि । सहितावेवैनं पश्याव इति ।

(क) भट्टा एसो क्खु इन्दिजालओ । (ख) जअदु जअदु देवो । देवं ।

किं धरणिए मिअङ्को आआसे महिहरो जले जलणो ।
मज्झण्हम्मि पओसो दाविज्जइ देहि आणत्तिम् ॥

अहं वा किं वहुणा जप्पिदेण ।

मज्ज पइण्णा एसा जं जं हिअएण इहसि संदट्ठुम् ।
तं तं दंसेमि अहं गुरुणो मन्तप्पभावेण ॥

(ग) भो वअस्स अवहिदो होहि । ईदिसो से अवट्टम्भो जेण सव्वं संभावीअदि ।

किं धरण्यामिति । धरण्यां किं मृगः अङ्कः यस्य स मृगाङ्कः चन्द्रः प्रदर्श्यताम् तथा च आकाशे महीधरः पर्वतः जले ज्वलनः अग्निः मध्याह्ने प्रदोषः रजनीमुखं प्रदर्श्यताम् । आज्ञप्तिं देहि । यदादिशसि तद्भवेदित्यर्थः ॥ ८ ॥ **ममेति** । मम प्रतिज्ञा एषा । यद्यद् हृदयेन मनसा संद्रष्टुमीहसि इच्छसि तत्तद्गुरोः मन्त्रस्य प्रभावेण सामर्थ्येन दर्शयामि ॥ ९ ॥ अत्र श्लोकद्वयेनैन्द्रजालिको मिथ्याग्निसंभ्रमोत्थापनेन वत्सराजस्य हृदयस्थसागरिकादर्शनानुकूलां निजशक्तिमाविष्कृतवानिति व्यवसायाख्यमङ्गमिदम् । अवष्टम्भः उत्साहभरः । युष्माकमयं युष्मदीयः । त्यदादीनि चेति वृद्धसंज्ञायां वृद्धाच्छः इति तस्येदमित्यर्थे छः । विगता जना अस्मादिति विजनः । न

---

१ यदि युष्मदीयोयं. २ देव किं—धरणीए मिअअङ्को. ३ सिज्जउ (सिध्यतु) तह , दाव सिजउ. ४ महाराअ कोसम्बीपते किं; अह वा-किं जप्पिएण बहुणा जं जं हिअएण इच्छसि. द० ५ एसा भणामि हिअएण जं-सि दट्ठव्वम् (द्रष्टव्यं); महसि (वाञ्छसि) दट्ठुम्. ६ दावमि. ७ प्पसादेण. ८ भो ईदिसो दे.

काञ्चन०—यद्भर्ताज्ञापयति । (इति निष्क्रान्ता ।) (क)

(ततः प्रविशति वासवदत्ता काञ्चनमाला च ।)

वासव०—काञ्चनमाले उज्जयिनीत आगत इत्यस्ति मे तस्मिन्नैन्द्रजालिके पक्षपातः । (ख)

काञ्चन०—ज्ञातिकुलबहुमानः खल्वेष भर्त्र्याः । तदेत्वेतु भर्त्री । (इति परिक्रानतः ।) (ग)

वासव०—(उपसृत्य ।) जयतु जयत्वार्यपुत्रः । (घ)

राजा—देवि बहुतरमनेन गर्जितम् । तदिहोपविश्यताम् । पश्यामस्तावत् ।

(वासवदत्तोपविशति ।)

राजा—भद्र प्रस्तूयतामिन्द्रजालम् ।

ऐन्द्रजा०—यद्देव आज्ञापयति । (इति बहुविधं नाट्य कृत्वा पिच्छिका भ्रमयन् ।)

हरिहरब्रह्मप्रमुखान्देवान्दर्शयामि देवराजं च ।
गगने सिद्धचारणसुरवधूसार्थं च नृत्यन्तम् ॥ १० ॥

तत्प्रेक्षतां देवः । (ङ)

(क) जं भट्टा आणवेदि । (ख) कञ्चणमाले उज्जइणीदो आअदोत्ति अत्थि मे तस्सिं इन्दजालिए पक्खवादो । (ग) णादिकुलबहुमाणो क्खु एसो भट्टिणीए । ता एदु एदु भट्टिणी । (घ) जेदु जेदु अज्जउत्तो । (ङ) जं देवो आणवेदि ।

हरिहरबम्हप्पमुहे देवे दंसेमि देवराअं च ।
गगणम्मि सिद्धचारणसुरवहुसत्थं च णच्चन्तम् ॥

तं पेक्खदु देवो ।

विजनः अविजनः । अविजनः विजनः संपद्यमानः कृतः विजनीकृतः । पक्षे पातः पक्षपातः । अभिमान इत्यर्थः । बहुतरं गर्जितं स्वपाटवमधिकृत्य अतीव विकत्थितम् । प्रस्तूयतामारभ्यताम् । **हरिहरेति** । हरिहरब्रह्माणः प्रमुखाः प्रमुखे वा येषां तान् । देवराजमिन्द्रं च दर्शयामि । सिद्धचारणा देवयोनिविशेषाः । सुरवध्वो देवाङ्गनाः तासां सार्थं समूहं च नृत्यन्तं दर्शयामि ॥ १० ॥ श्लोकचतुष्टयस्य गाथाच्छन्दः ।

---

१ इति निष्क्रम्य वासवदत्तया सह प्रविशति । वास०— २ बहुतरेन; अनेन विस्फूर्जितम्. ३ तदितः स्थीयताम्,; तदेहि उप०. ४ तामिदानीं व; ०तां बहुविधमिन्द्र०. ५ अत्थि तहिं इन्द० बहुमाणो. ६ माइ (मातृ) ढल०, णाभि (नाभि)०; ०कुल-पक्खवादो भ०. ७ अस्य स्थाने-सर्वं सन्निरमयं पश्यन्ति.

राजा-(ऊर्ध्वमवलोक्यासनादवतरन् ।) आश्चर्यमाश्चर्यम् । देवि पश्य ।

एष ब्रह्मा सरोजे रजनिकरकलाशेखरः शंकरोऽयं
दोर्भिर्दैत्यान्तकोऽसौ सधनुरसिगदाचक्रचिह्नैश्चतुर्भिः ।
एषोऽप्यैरावतस्थस्त्रिदशपतिरमी देवि देवास्तथान्ये
नृत्यन्ति व्योम्नि चैताश्चलचरणरणन्नूपुरा दिव्यनार्यः ॥ ११ ॥

वासव०—आश्चर्यमाश्चर्यम् । (क)

विदूषकः—(अपवार्य ।) आः दास्याः पुत्र ऐन्द्रजालिक किमेतैर्देवैरप्सरोभिश्च दर्शितैः । यदि तेऽनेन परितुष्टेन कार्यं तत्सागरिकां दर्शय । (ख)

(ततः प्रविशति वसुंधरा ।)

वसुंधरा—(राजानमुपसृत्य ।) जयतु जयतु भर्ता । अमात्यो यौगन्धरायणो विज्ञापयति—एष खलु विक्रमबाहोः प्रधानामात्यो वसुभूतिर्बाभ्रव्येन कञ्चुकिना सहागतः । तदर्हति देवोऽस्मिन्नेव सुन्दरमुहूर्ते प्रेक्षितुम् । अहमपि कार्यशेषं समाप्यागत एवेति । (ग)

(क) अच्चरिअं अच्चरिअम् । (ख) ओः दासीए पुत्त इन्दजालिअ किं एदेहिं देवेहिं अच्छाराहिं च दंसिदाहिं । जइ दे इमिणा परितुट्ठेण कज्जं ता साअरिअं दंसेहि । (ग) जेदु जेदु भट्टा । अमच्चो जोगन्धराअणो विण्णवेदि—एसो क्खु विक्कमबाहुणो पहाणामच्चो वसुभूदी बब्भव्वेण कञ्चुइणा सह आगदो । ता अरुहदि देवो इमस्सिं ज्जेव सुन्दरमुहुत्तए पेक्खिदुम् । अहंपि कज्जसेसं समाविअ आगदो एव्वत्ति ।

एष इति । व्योम्नि आकाशे सरोजे आसनभूते कमले एष ब्रह्मा दृश्यते । अयं रजनिकरस्य चन्द्रस्य कला शेखरः शिरोभूषणं यस्य स रजनिकरकलाशेखरः शंकरः । असौ दूरे दृश्यमानः धनुः शार्ङ्गं असिः नन्दकाख्यः गदा कौमोदकी नाम्ना चक्रं सुदर्शनं तानि चिह्नानि तैः सहितैः सधनुरसिगदाचक्रचिह्नैः चतुर्भिः दोर्भिः उपलक्षितः दैत्यान्तको विष्णुः । एष समीपतरवर्ती ऐरावते तिष्ठतीति ऐरावतस्थः । अपि शब्दं कः । त्रिदशपतिः इन्द्रः । तथा च हे देवि अमी अन्ये देवाः । दृश्यन्ते इति शेषः । एताः च चलेषु चरणेषु रणन्तः नूपुरा मञ्जीरा यासां तादृश्यः दिवि भवा दिव्याः । दिगादित्वाद्यत् । दिव्याश्च ता नार्यश्च दिव्यनार्यः सुराङ्गनाः । अप्सरस इत्यर्थः । नृत्यन्ति । तान्सर्वानेतान्पश्येति पूर्वेण सम्बन्धः ॥ स्रग्धरा वृत्तम् ॥ ११ ॥ दास्याः

---

१ ऊर्ध्वं दृष्ट्वा; ०रन्सविस्मयम्. २ अहो आश्चर्यम्; अस्मात्परं—वसन्त०—अच्चारिअं अच्चरिअं । राजा—देवि. ३ अयं. ४ त्रिदिव. ५ वसं०; विदू० साहु रे एन्दजा० साहु । दंसिदं क्खु तुए आत्तणो विण्णाणं । (अप०). ६ अस्मात्परं—राजा-भद्र भवतु तथा । ७ प्रविश्य वसु०. ८ नास्त्येतत्क्वचित्. ९ हा इन्द०. १० ०अणो देवस्स चलणजुअलं इदं. ११ पहाणो अमच्चवसुभूदी बब्भव्वक०... । ता पेक्ख भट्टं । इमे एव्व सुन्दरं मुहुत्तं (अयमेव सुन्दरो मुहूर्तः); सिंहलेश्वरामात्यो०; ०बाहुणा पहाणामच्चो अणुप्पेसिदो. १२ अरिहसि देव.

वासव०—आर्यपुत्र तिष्ठतु तावदिन्द्रजालम् । मातुलगृहात्प्रधानामात्यो वसुभूतिरागतः । तं तावत्प्रेक्षतामार्यपुत्रः । (क)

राजा—यथाह देवी । (ऐन्द्रजालिकं प्रति ।) भद्र विश्रम्यतामिदानीम् ।

ऐन्द्रजालिकः—यद्देव आज्ञापयति । (पुनः पिच्छिकां भ्रमयति ।) (निष्क्रामन् ।) एकः पुनर्मम खेलोऽवश्यं देवेन प्रेक्षितव्यः । (ख)

राजा—भद्र द्रक्ष्यामः ।

वासव०—काञ्चनमाले गच्छ त्वं देह्यस्य पारितोषिकम् । (ग)

काञ्चन०—यद्देव्याज्ञापयति । (ऐन्द्रजालिकेन सह निष्क्रान्ता ।) (घ)

राजा—वसन्तक प्रत्युद्गम्य प्रवेशयैतां वसुभूतिः ।

विदू०—यद्देव आज्ञापयति । (इति वसुंधरया सह निष्क्रान्तः ।) (ङ)

(ततः प्रविशति वसन्तकेनानुगम्यमानो वसुभूतिर्बाभ्रव्यश्च ।)

वसुभूतिः—(समन्तादवलोक्य ।) अहो वत्सेश्वरस्यानुभावः । इह हि

आक्षिप्तो जयकुञ्जरेण तुरगान्निर्वर्णयन्वल्लभा-
न्संगीतध्वनिना हृतः क्षितिभृतां गोष्ठीषु तिष्ठन्क्षणम् ।

(क) अज्जउत्त चिट्ठदु दाव इन्दआलं । माउलघैरादो पहाणामच्चो वसुभूदी आगदो । तं दाव पेक्खदु अज्जउत्तो । (ख) जं देवो आणवेदि । एक्को उण मह खेलओ अवस्सं देवेण पेक्खिदव्वो । (ग) कञ्चणमाले गच्छ तुमं देहि से पारितोसिकम् । (घ) जं देवी आणवेदि । (ङ) जं देवो आणवेदि ।

पुत्र । षष्ठ्या आक्रोशे इति अलुक् । शोभनः मुहूर्तः सुमुहूर्तस्तस्मिन् । इन्द्रजालं ऐन्द्रजालिकमायाप्रेक्षणमित्यर्थः । देह्यस्येत्यत्र सम्प्रदानस्य शेषत्वविवक्षायां षष्ठी । प्रत्युद्गम्यादरदर्शनार्थमभिमुखं गत्वा । अनुभावः प्रभावः विभूतिरिति यावत् आक्षिप्त इति । वल्लभान्राज्ञोऽभीष्टान् । मनोज्ञान् इत्यर्थः । तुरगान् निर्वर्णयन्सावधानेन पश्यन् अहम् । कुञ्जः हस्तिनो हनुर्दन्तो वा सोऽस्यास्तीति कुञ्जरः । जयस्य जयावहः कुञ्जरः जयकुञ्जरः नेन आक्षिप्तः आकृष्टः । दर्शनीयाश्वबद्धदृष्टिरपि दर्शनीयतरकुञ्जरेणाकृष्टदृष्टिरस्मीत्यर्थः । क्षितिभृतां वत्सेश्वरोपासनार्थं प्राप्तानां सामन्तानां

---

१ नास्त्येतत्क्वचित्. २ एवम् । द्रक्ष्यामि. ३ प्रवेशय वसुभूतिम्. ४ प्रत्युद्गम्यमानः, प्रविशति वस०, बा०, वसन्तकश्च । ५ अस्मात्प्राक्—वसन्त०—एदु एदु अमच्चो वसुभूदी । इत्य. ६ ०लोक्य सविस्मयम्. ७ भवनद्वारभासः. ८ आक्षिप्तान्नवकु०. ९ क्षितिभुजां. १० पेक्खणं, इन्दजा०. ११ कुलादो अज्जो अम०. १२ परं एक्को खिड्डको.

सद्यो विस्मृतसिंहलेन्द्रविभवः कक्षाप्रदेशेऽप्यहो
द्वाःस्थेनैव कुतूहलेन महता ग्राम्यो यथाहं कृतः ॥ १२ ॥

बाभ्रव्यः—[1]वसुभूते अद्य खलु चिरात्स्वामिनं द्रक्ष्यामीति यत्सत्यमानन्दातिशयेन किमप्यवस्थान्तरमनुभवामि[2] । कुतः ।

विवृद्धिं कम्पस्य प्रथयतितरां साध्वसवशा-
दविस्पष्टां दृष्टिं तिरयतितरां बाष्पपटलैः[3] ।
स्खलद्वर्णां व[4]र्णां जडयतितरां गद्गदतया
जरायाः साहाय्यं मम हि परितोषोऽद्य कुरुते ॥ १३ ॥

विदूषकः—([5]अग्रे भूत्वा ।) एत्वेत्वमात्यः । (क)

वसुभू०—(विदूषकस्य कण्ठे रत्नमालां दृष्ट्वाऽपवार्य ।) बाभ्रव्य [7]जाने सैवेयं रत्नमाला या देवेन राजपुत्र्यै प्रस्थानकाले दत्ता ।

(क) एदु एदु अमच्चो ।

सभासु मण्डलेषु क्षणं तिष्ठन् संगीतस्य ध्वनिः स्वरः तेन संगीतध्वनिना हृतः प्रसभमाकृष्ट इत्यर्थः । अहो इत्याश्चर्ये । एवं कक्षाप्रदेशे प्रकोष्ठे अपि । कक्षाप्रदेशस्थस्य मे एवमत्रस्था । मुख्यगृहस्थितस्य का भवेदिति अपेरर्थः । सद्यः तत्क्षणं विस्मृतसिंहलेन्द्रविभवः विस्मृतः सिंहलनृपतेः विभव ऐश्वर्यं येन तथाभूतोऽहं द्वारि तिष्ठतीति द्वाःस्थं तेन महता कुतूहलेन । कुतूहलकारिणा वैभवेनेति यावत् । ग्राम्यो यथा ग्रामे भवः ग्राम्यः । दिगादित्वाद्यत् । स इव कृतः । नगरं गतो ग्राम्यो नरो यथा तत्रस्थवैभवं दृष्ट्वा आश्चर्यचकितो भवति तथाहं भूतोस्मीत्यर्थः । उदात्तालंकारः । उपमा च । शार्दूलविक्रीडितं वृत्तम् ॥ १२ ॥ किमप्यनिर्वचनीयम् । अन्या अवस्था अवस्थान्तरम् । अन्यार्थकेनान्तरशब्देन मयूरव्यंसकादित्वात्समासः । **विवृद्धिमिति** । अद्य मम परितोषः स्वामिदर्शनं भविष्यतीति आनन्दः जरायाः । सहायस्य भावः साहाय्यम् । सहायाद्वा इति ष्यञ् । कुरुते हि । तदेव विशदयति—साध्वसवशाद् राज्ञः पुरोगमनभयहेतोः कम्पस्य विवृद्धिं प्रथयतितरामतिशयेन वर्धयति । बाष्पपटलैः अश्रुजलजालकैः अविस्पष्टां मन्दां दृष्टिं तिरयतितरामतिशयेन छादयति । तिरश्शब्दात्तत्करोतीति णिच् । ततस्तिङश्चेति तरप् किमेत्तिङव्ययेति तरबन्तादाम् । तथा च स्खलन्तोऽस्पष्टं निर्गच्छन्तः वर्णा यस्यां तां स्खलद्वर्णां वाणीं गद्गदतया वाक्स्खलनेन जडयतितरामतिशयेन जडां करोति । पूर्ववज्जडशब्दाण्णिच् । तिङन्तात्तरबन्तादाम् । अत्र जरोत्पन्नकम्पादेः प्राक्सिद्धस्य परितोषजन्यसाध्वसादिना गुणोत्कर्षवर्णनादनुगुणालंकारः । तदुक्त—प्राक्सिद्धस्वगुणोत्कर्षोऽनुगुणः परसंनिधेः । इति । शिखरिणी वृत्तम् ॥ १३ ॥

१ (सहर्षम् ।) वसु०. २ नान्यदवस्था०... ३ तिरयति पुनर्बाष्पसलिलैः. ४ वर्णा वाणी भवति नितरां. ५ अग्रतः ६ अवलोक्य निःश्वस्याप०. ७ ज्ञायते, अपि प्रत्यभिज्ञायते. ८ ०च्चो वसुभूदी.

बाभ्रव्यः—अमात्य अस्ति सादृश्यम् । तत्किं वसन्तकं पृच्छामि प्राप्तिमस्याः ।

वसुभू०—बाभ्रव्य मा मैवम् । महति राजकुले रत्नबाहुल्यान्न दुर्लभो भूषणानां संवादः । (इति परिक्रामति ।)

विदू०—भो एष खलु महाराजः । तदुपसर्पत्वमात्यः । (क)

वसु०—(उपसृत्य ।) विजयतां महाराजः ।

राजा—(उत्थाय ।) आर्य अभिवादये ।

वसु०—आयुष्मान्भव ।

राजा—आसनमासनमार्याय ।

विदू०—एतदासनम् । उपविशत्वमात्यः । (ख)

(वसुभूतिरुपविशति ।)

बाभ्रव्यः—देव बाभ्रव्यः प्रणमति ।

राजा—(पृष्ठे हस्तं दत्वा ।) बाभ्रव्य इत आस्यताम् । (बाभ्रव्य उपविशति ।)

विदू०—अमात्य एषा देवी वासवदत्ता प्रणमति । (ग)

वासव०—आर्य प्रणमामि । (घ)

वसुभू०—आयुष्मति वत्सराजसदृशं पुत्रमाप्नुहि ।

(सर्वे उपविशन्ति ।)

राजा—आर्य वसुभूते अपि कुशलं तत्रभवतः सिंहलेश्वरस्य ।

(**क**) भो एसो क्खु महाराओ । ता उपसप्पदु अमच्चो । (**ख**) एदं आसणम् । उपविसदु अमच्चो । (**ग**) अमच्च एसा देवी वासवदत्ता पणमदि । (**घ**) अज्ज पणमामि ।

देवेन विक्रमबाहुना । प्रस्थानसमये अर्थात्सिंहलद्वीपात् । संवादः सादृश्यम् । अन्यत्सदृशं भूषणं संभवेदित्यर्थः । **उत्थायेति**–प्रवयसो वसुभूतेरादरदर्शनार्थमुत्थानम् । आयुष्माम्

---

१ सत्यमस्त्येव. २ वसन्तकादवगच्छामि–मः प्रभवमस्याः. ३ रत्नमालाबा० ४ सादरम् ; राजा–वसुभूते इदमासनमास्यताम् । विदू०—इदमासणमुपविशदु अमच्चो । राजा–(सादरमुत्थाय ।) आर्य अभि०. ५ ०दये । वयस्य आसनमासनम् ; दीयतामासनमार्याय । विदू०--एदमास०. ६ अतिश्रेयांस्त्वं भूयाः. ७ राजा—वसुभूते उपविश । ८ कञ्चुकी. ९ राजा—बाभ्रव्य... । (पृष्ठे हस्तं ददाति । सर्वे उपविशन्ति ।) १० अस्मात्परं—कञ्चुकी-बाभ्रव्यः--देवि बाभ्रव्यः प्रणमति । ११ अमात्य. १२ (राजानमुद्दिश्य ।) भो. १३ (आसनमादाय ।) भो एदं. १४ एसा क्खु देवी पणामं करेदि.

वसुभू०---(ऊर्ध्वमवलोक्य निःश्वस्य च ।) देव न जाने किं विज्ञापयामि । (अधोमुखस्तिष्ठति ।)

वासव०---(सविषादमात्मगतम् ।) हा धिक् हा धिक् । किमिदानीं वसुभूतिः कथयिष्यति । (क)

राजा---कथय किमेतत् । आर्य आकुल इव मेऽन्तरात्मा ।

बाभ्रव्यः---(अपवार्य ।) अमात्य चिरमपि स्थित्वा कथनीयम् । तत्कथ्यताम् ।

वसु०---(सास्रम् ।) देवं न शक्यं निवेदयितुं तथाप्येष कथयामि मन्दभाग्यः । यासौ सिंहलेश्वरेण स्वदुहिता रत्नावली नाम आयुष्मतीं वासवदत्तां दग्धामुपश्रुत्य देवाय पूर्वं प्रार्थिता सती दत्ता---

राजा---(अपवार्य ।) देवि किमेतदलीकमेव त्वन्मातुलामात्यः कथयति ।

वासव०---(स्मित्वा ।) आर्यपुत्र न ज्ञायते कोऽलीकं मन्त्रयत इति । (ख)

विदू०---ततस्तस्याः किं वृत्तम् । (ग)

वसु०---सा च युष्मदन्तिकमानीयमाना यानभङ्गात्सागरे निमग्ना । (इति रुदन्नधोमुखस्तिष्ठति ।)

(क) हद्धी हद्धी । किं दाणिं वसुभूदी कधइस्सदि । (ख) अज्जउत्त ण जाणीअदि को अलिअं मन्तेदित्ति । (ग) तदो ताए किं वुत्तम् ।

अतिश्रेयसीति पाठे अतिशायितं श्रेयः कल्याणं यस्य सः । आकुलः पर्याकुलः । अलीकमसत्यम् । त्वन्मातुला०--तव मातुलो विक्रमबाहुः तस्य । यानभङ्गान्नौकाया भग्नत्वात् ।

---

१ जानामि । किमपि वि०. २ रुदन्नधो०. ३ पर्याकुल एवास्मि; वसुभूते कथय किमेवं पर्याकुलयसि; ०भूते कथं पर्याकुल इवासि. ४ यत्कथ० तदिदानीमेव कथ्यताम् । ५ एष मन्दो दुर्भाग्यो विज्ञापयामि । यासौ तत्रभवता सिंह० ०ली नाम वासवदत्तामायुष्मतीमुपसृत्य देवाय प्रार्थिता सती न दत्ता; तत्रभवतः ०रस्य...नामायुष्मती सिद्धादेशेनादिष्टा योऽस्याः पाणिग्रहणं करिष्यति स सार्वभौमो राजा भविष्यतीति । राजा---ततस्ततः । वसु०---तत्प्रत्ययादार्यार्थं यौगन्धरायणेन बहुशः प्रार्थ्यमानापि सा सिंहलेश्वरेण वासवदत्तायाश्चित्तखेदं परिहरता न दत्ता. ६ किमिदमलीकं त्व०,-मिदमिदानीमलीकं त्वदीयमा०; प्रलपति. ७ ततो युष्म० माना सती वाहनभं०; ततो लावाणकेन वह्निना देवी दग्धेति वार्तामुत्पाद्य देवेन तदन्तिकं बाभ्रव्यः प्रहितः । पुनरपि प्रार्थिता च । ततस्तत्रभवता सिंहलेश्वरेण चिन्तितम् । देवेन सहास्माकं सम्बन्धलोपो मा भूदिति । दत्ता च सा रत्नावली देवाय प्रतिपादयितुमस्माभिरानीयमाना समुद्रे यानभङ्गान्निमग्ना; सा च युष्मदन्तिकं प्रहिता ततश्चास्माभिरानीयमाना वाहनभ०

वासव०—(सास्रम् ।) हा हतास्मि मन्दभागिनी । हा भगिनि रत्नावलि कुत्रेदानीमसि । देहि मे प्रतिवचनम् । (क)

राजा—देवि समाश्वसिहि समाश्वसिहि । दुरवगाहा गतिर्दैवस्य । यौगन्धरायणः क्षणात्पतितोत्थितौ नन्वेतावेव ते निदर्शनम् । (इति वसुभूतिबाभ्रव्यौ दर्शयति ।)

वासव०—आर्यपुत्र युज्यत एतत् । परं कुतो ममैतावद्भागधेयम् । (ख)

(नेपथ्ये महान्कलकलः ।)

हर्म्याणां हेमशृङ्गश्रियमिव निचयैरर्चिषामादधानः
सान्द्रोद्यानद्रुमाग्रग्लपनपिशुनितात्यन्ततीव्राभितापः ।
कुर्वन्क्रीडामहीध्रं सजलजलधरश्यामलं धूमपातै-
रेष प्लोषार्तयोषिज्जन इह सहसैवोत्थितोऽन्तःपुरेऽग्निः ॥ १४ ॥

अपि च ।

देवीदाहप्रवादोऽसौ योऽभूल्लावाणके पुरा ।
करिष्यन्निव तं सत्यमयमग्निः समुत्थितः ॥ १५ ॥

(सर्वे संभ्रान्ताः पश्यन्ति ।)

(क) हा हदम्हि मन्दभाइणी । हा बहिणि रअणावलि कहिं दाणिं सि । देहि मे पडिवअणम् । (ख) अज्जउत्त जुज्जदि एदं । परं कुतो मम एत्तिअं भाअहेअम् ।

दुरवगाहा दुर्ज्ञेया । दैवं किं घटयेदिति न ज्ञायते । इमाविव सापि कदाचिज्जीवन्ती तीरं प्राप्ता भवेदिति भावः । **हर्म्याणामिति** । अर्चिषां ज्वालानां निचयैः निवहैः हर्म्याणां हेमशृङ्गाणां सुवर्णशिखराणामिव श्रियं आदधानः कुर्वाणः । सान्द्राणां निबिडानामुद्यानद्रुमाणां यानि अग्राणि तेषां ग्लपनेन म्लानतापादनेन पिशुनितः सूचितः अत्यन्ततीव्रः अभितापः यस्य तादृशः । पुनश्च धूमपातैः धूमावतरणैः क्रीडामहीध्रं क्रीडापर्वतं जलेन सहितः सजलः यः जलधरस्तद्वच्छ्यामलं कुर्वन् । प्लोषेण दाहेन आर्तः योषिज्जनः स्त्रीसमूहो यस्मादेतादृशः इह अन्तःपुरे शुद्धान्ते एषः अग्निः सहसा अतर्कितमेवोत्थितः । उत्प्रेक्षालंकारः । भयानकरसः । स्रग्धरा वृत्तम् ॥ १४ ॥ **देवीति** । पुरा लावाणके ग्रामे देव्याः दाहप्रवादः अभूत् तं सत्यं करिष्यन्निवाधुना तत्त्वतो देवीं दग्ध्वेति भावः । अयमग्निः समुत्थितः ॥ १५ ॥

---

१ नास्त्येतत्क्वचित्. २ अस्मादनन्तरं-इति मूर्च्छिता पतति । इत्य०. ३ वाहनभङ्गान्निपतितौ...वेव निद०. ४ अस्मात्परं—राजा (अपवार्य ।) कथय किमेतदिति नावगच्छामि । बा०—देव श्रूयतामित्य० क्वचित्. ५ निवहैः. ६ श्यामलैः. ७ देव्या... दोयं. ८ तमसत्यं मन्ये वह्निः-त्यमत्राग्निरयमु०. ९ हा देव्व । बहिणीए कहिं तुमं चिक्खुदन्ना । ता देहि. १० इत्तिअ. भागधेअ-एत्तिआणि-भाअधेआणि.

राजा—(ससंभ्रममुत्थाय ।) कथमन्तःपुरेऽग्निः । कष्टं देवी वासवदत्ता दग्धा । हा प्रिये वासवदत्ते ।

वासव०—आर्यपुत्र परित्रायस्व परित्रायस्व । (क)

राजा—अये कथमतिसंभ्रमादिहस्थापि देवी नोपलक्षिता । देवि समाश्वसिहि समाश्वसिहि ।

वासव०—आर्यपुत्र मयात्मनः कृते न भणितम् । एषा खलु मया निर्घृणयेह निगडेन संयमिता सागरिका विपद्यते । तत्तां परित्रायतामार्यपुत्रः । (ख)

राजा—कथं देवि सागरिका विपद्यते । एष गच्छामि ।

वसु०—देव किमकारणमेव पतंगवृत्तिः क्रियते ।

बाभ्रव्यः—देव युक्तमाह वसुभूतिः ।

विदू०—(राजानमुत्तरीये गृहीत्वा ।) वयस्य मा खल्वेवं साहसं कुरु । (ग)

राजा—(उत्तरीयमुत्सृज्य ।) धिङ् मूर्ख सागरिका विपद्यते । किमद्यापि प्राणा धार्यन्ते । (इति ज्वलनप्रवेशं नाटयित्वा धूमाभिभवं नाटयन् ।)

विरम विरम वह्ने मुञ्च धूमानुबन्धं
प्रकटयसि किमुच्चैरर्चिषां चक्रवालम् ।
विरहहुतभुजाहं यो न दग्धः प्रियायाः
प्रलयदहनभासा तस्य किं त्वं करोषि ॥ १६ ॥

(क) अज्जउत्त परित्ताहि परित्ताहि । (ख) अज्जउत्त मए अत्तणो किदे ण भणिदम् । एसा क्खु मए णिग्घिणाए इध निअडेण संजमिदा साअरिआ विवज्जदि । ता तं परित्ताअदु अज्जउत्तो । (ग) वअस्स मा क्खु एवं साहसं करेहि ।

निगडेन शृंखलया संयमिता बद्धा । पतङ्गवृत्तिः पतङ्गवदग्नौ पातात्स्वशरीरनाशः । धूमाभिभवं धूमेनाभिभवः आवरणं तम् । **विरमेति** । हे वह्ने विरम विरम । झटिति शान्तो भव । धूमानुबन्धं धूमसान्तत्यं मुञ्च । उच्चैः उच्चगामि अर्चिषां चक्रवालं मण्डलं किं प्रकटयसि । व्यर्थं तदित्याह—योऽहं प्रलये यः दहनोऽग्निस्तस्य इव भाः दाहकं तेजो यस्य तेन प्रियाया विरहहुतभुजा विरहाग्निना न दग्धस्तस्य त्वं किं करोषि तं कथं

---

१ ज्वलनं दृष्ट्वा ससंभ्रममुत्तिष्ठन्. २ कथमिहस्थापि देवी विस्मृता । अलमतिसंभ्रमेण ।–देवी न लक्षिता । (कण्ठे गृहीत्वा) देवि अलं भयेन । ०लक्षिता । (देव्याः पाणिं गृहीत्वालिङ्ग्य ।) देवि समा०. ३ ०रण इदं क्रि०–रण एव. ४ ०मुक्तं ०तिना. ५ ०माक्षिप्य;–माकर्षन्–मुत्सृजन्. ६ दह्यते. ७ किमर्थम्, किमस्माभिः;...ध्रियन्ते–परिरक्ष्यन्ते. ८ नाटयति. ९ ०अदु ०अदु ०उत्तो. १० ण हि अत्तणो कारणे एवं भणामि । ...०णाए इध संयदा चिट्ठदि सा० । ११ भो मा क्खु सा०.

वासव०—कथं मम दुःखभागिन्या वचनादेवमध्यवसितमार्यपुत्रेण । तदहमप्यार्यपुत्रमेवानुगमिष्यामि । (क)

विदू०—(परिक्रम्याग्रतो भूत्वा ।) भवति अहमपि ते पथ्युपदेशको भवामि । (ख)

वसु०—कथं प्रविष्ट एव ज्वलनं वत्सराजः । तन्ममापि दृष्टराजपुत्रीविपत्तेरिहैव युक्तमात्मानमाहुतीकर्तुम् ।

बाभ्रव्यः—हा देव किमिदमकारणमेव भरतकुलं संशयतुलामारोपितम् । अथ वा किं प्रलापेन । अहमपि भक्तिसदृशमाचरामि ।

(सर्वेऽग्निप्रवेशं नाटयन्ति ।)

(ततः प्रविशति निगडसंयता सागरिका ।)

साग०—(दिशोऽवलोक्य ।) हा धिक् समन्ततः प्रज्वलितो हुतवहः । (विचिन्त्य सपरितोषम् ।) अद्य हुतवहो दिष्ट्या करिष्यति मम दुःखावसानम् । (ग)

राजा—अये इयमासन्नहुतवहा वर्तते सागरिका । तत्त्वरितमेनां संभावयामि । (त्वरितमुपसृत्य ।) अयि प्रिये किमद्यापि संभ्रमे स्वस्थयावस्थीयते ।

(क) कधं ममं दुक्खभाइणीए वअणादो एव्वं अज्झवसिदं अज्जउत्तेण । ता अहंपि अज्जउत्तं एव्व अणुगमिस्सम् । (ख) भोदि अहं वि दे पंथोवदेसओ होमि । (ग) हंद्धी समन्तदो पज्जलिदो हुतवहो । अज्ज हुतवहो दिट्ठिआ करिस्सदि मे दुःखावसाणम् ।

दहेः । रूपकालंकारः । मालिनी वृत्तम् ॥ १६ ॥ अध्यवसितं प्रतिपन्नम् । दृष्टा राजपुत्र्याः रत्नावल्या विपत्तिर्नाशो येन तस्य । आहुतीकर्तुमेकदैव प्रक्षेप्तुम् । संशयतुलामारोपितं संशये निक्षिप्तम् । भक्तिसदृशं स्वामिभक्तेरुचितम् । अग्निप्रवेशं करोमीत्यर्थः । दिष्ट्या मुदैवात् । दुःखावसानं देहदाहाद् दुःखसमाप्तिम् । आसन्नः हुतवहोऽग्निर्यस्याः सा आसन्नहुतवहा । संभावयामि अग्नेर्मध्यादुद्धरिष्यामीत्यर्थः । संभ्रमे त्वराकारणे ।

---

१ युक्तमिहैव राज्ञा सहात्मा०;-मिन्धनीकर्तुं. २ स्वामिन्, महाराज;...प्रलपितेन. ३ अस्मात्परं—राजा (दक्षिणबाहुस्पन्दं निरूप्य ।) एतदवस्थस्य मम कुत एतत्फलम् । (अग्रतोवलोक्य सहर्षोद्वेगम् ।) कथमासन्नहुतवहा वर्तते सागरिका । तत्त्वरितमेनां संभावयामि । इति पठ्यते कैश्चित्. ४ राजा—(त्वरितमुपसृत्य) अयि इय०. ५ त्वरितमिति नास्ति क्वचित्. ६ मध्यस्थतया वर्तसे. ७ कधं दुक्खकारिणीए वअणेण...। ता किं मए ठिआए । अहं वि. ८ अग्गदो—मग्गोवदेसओ. ९ दिट्ठिआ समं० ०लिदो अज्ज करि० दुःखावसाणं भअवं हुदासणो.

सागरिका—(राजानं दृष्ट्वा । स्वगतम् ।) कथमार्यपुत्रः । तदेतं प्रेक्ष्य पुनरपि मे जीविताभिलाषः संवृत्तः । (प्रकाशम् ।) परित्रायतां परित्रायतां भर्ता । (क)

राजा—भीरु अलं भयेन ।

मुहूर्तमपि सह्यतां बहल एष धूमोद्गमो (अग्रतोऽवलोक्य ।)
हहा धिगिदमंशुकं ज्वलति ते स्तनात्प्रच्युतम् ।
(विलोक्य ।)**मुहुः स्खलसि किं कथं निगडसंयतासि** (परिकरं बद्ध्वा ।) **द्रुतं**
नयामि भवतीमितः प्रियतमेऽवलम्बस्व माम् ॥ १७ ॥

(कण्ठे गृहीत्वा निमीलिताक्षः स्पर्शसुखं नाटयन् ।) अहो क्षणान्मेऽपगतोऽयं संतापः । प्रिये समाश्वसिहि समाश्वसिहि ।

व्यक्तं लग्नोऽपि भवतीं न दहत्येव पावकः ।
यतः संतापमेवायं स्पर्शस्ते हरति प्रिये ॥ १८ ॥

(उन्मील्याक्षिणी दिशोऽवलोक्य सागरिकां च मुक्त्वा ।) अहो महदाश्चर्यम् ।

क्वासौ गतो हुतवहस्तदवस्थमेत-
दन्तःपुरं (वासवदत्तां दृष्ट्वा ।) **कथमवन्तिनृपात्मजेयम् ।**

वासव०—(राज्ञः शरीरं परामृश्य सहर्षम् ।) दिष्ट्याऽक्षतशरीर आर्यपुत्रः । (ख)

(**क**) कधं अज्जउत्तो । ता एदं पेक्खिअ पुणोवि मे जीविदाहिलासो संवुत्तो । परित्ताअदु परित्ताअदु भट्टा । (**ख**) दिट्ठिआ अक्खतसरीरो अज्जउत्तो ।

मुहूर्तमिति । एष बहलः घनः धूमोद्गमः मुहूर्तं क्षणमपि सह्यताम् । हहा इति खेदे । धिक् । इदं ते स्तनात्प्रच्युतमंशुकं वस्त्रं ज्वलति । किं कस्मात्कारणान्मुहुः स्खलसि । कथं निगडेन शृंखलया संयतासि । इतः अस्मादग्नेः भवतीं द्रुतं शीघ्रं नयामि । अतः हे प्रियतमे मामवलम्बस्व ॥ १७ ॥ निमीलिते अक्षिणी येन यस्य वा । अहो इत्याश्चर्ये । **व्यक्तमिति** । हे प्रिये लग्नोपि पावकः भवतीं न दहत्येवेति व्यक्तं स्फुटमेव । तत्र हेतुमाह—यतः अयं ते स्पर्शः संतापमेव हरति ॥ १८ ॥ **क्वासाविति** । गद्यांशैर्भिन्नमेतत्पद्यं तान्विहाय पठनीयम् । असौ सम्प्रत्येवोत्थितः हुतवहः क्व गतः । एतदन्तःपुरं सा अग्निकालात्पूर्वा अवस्था यस्य तत् तदवस्थम् । अस्पृष्टाग्नि

---

१ आत्मग०. २ अयि प्रियतमे भीरु मुहूर्तमपि इ०; अलं संभ्रमेण—आवेगेन. ३ ०तमिव–मिह. ४ बहुल. ५ अहो. ६ स्वस्त०, ०नमच्यु०. ७ ता ते गतिर्न यामि भवतीं विना. ८ तीमहं. ९ ०यति. १० मे शोकाग्निसं०. ११ ०लिताक्षः. १२ क्वासौ प्रज्वलनहुता०–पुरम् । कथमचिन्त्यरूपमेवम् । १३ अज्जउत्त ०त्ताहि ०त्ताहि.

राजा—बाभ्रव्य एष—

बाभ्रव्यः—देव इदानीं प्रत्युज्जीविताः स्मः ।

राजा—   वसुभूतिरयं—

वसु०—विजयतां महाराजः ।

राजा—   वयस्यः

विदू०—जयतु जयतु भवान् । (क)

राजा—स्वप्ने मतिर्भ्रमति किं न्विदमिन्द्रजालम् ॥ १९ ॥

विदू०—भोः मा संदेहं कुरु । इन्द्रजालमेवेदम् । भणितं तेन दास्याःपुत्रेणैन्द्रजालिकेन यथैको मम पुनः खेलोऽवश्यं देवेन प्रेक्षितव्य इति । तत्तदेवैतत् । (ख)

राजा—देवि इयं त्वद्वचनादस्माभिरिहानीता सागरिका ।

वासव०—(सस्मितम् ।) आर्यपुत्र ज्ञातं मया । (ग)

वसु०—(सागरिकां दृष्ट्वापवार्य ।) बाभ्रव्य सदृशीयं राजपुत्र्या ।

बाभ्रव्यः—अमात्य ममाप्येतदेव मनसि वर्तते ।

वसु०—(राजानमुद्दिश्य) । देव कुत इयं कन्यका ।

राजा—देवी जानाति ।

वसु०—देवि कुतः पुनरियं कन्यका ।

(क) जअदु जअदु भवं । (ख) भो मा संदेहं करेहि । इन्दजालं एव्व एदम् । भणिदं तेण दासीए पुत्तेण इन्दजालिएण जहा एक्को उण मह खेलओ अवस्सं देवेण पेक्खिदव्वत्ति । ता तं ज्जेव्व एदम् । (ग) अज्जउत्त जाणिदं मए ।

इत्यर्थः । कथमियमवन्तिनृपात्मजा वासवदत्ता । एष बाभ्रव्यः । एष वसुभूतिः । अयं वयस्यः वसन्तकः । सर्वे यथापूर्वमविकृता एव दृश्यन्ते । अतो मे मतिः स्वप्ने भ्रमति किम् । किं नु स्वप्ने इदमभिदर्शनम् । अथ वा इन्द्रजालमिदं मायेयम् । वसन्ततिलकं वृत्तम् ॥ १९ ॥ अक्षतमग्निनाऽकृतापकारं शरीरं यस्य । **वसु०**- सागरिकां दृष्ट्वा इत्यादि । इत आरभ्य निर्वहणसन्धिः । अत्र वसुभूतिबाभ्रव्याभ्यां नायिकाबी-

---

१ विजयतां महाराजः । देव दिष्टया वर्धसे पुनरुच्छ्वसिताः स्मः. २ देव दिष्टया वर्धसे. ३ विदूषकोऽयम्, वसन्तक एषः. ४ स्वप्नोऽयमिति भाति; किमिदमिन्द्र०. ५ कन्यका. ६ निर्वर्ण्य. ७ प्रकाशं राजा०, निर्वर्ण्य. ८ वसु. ९ एदं अ तेण दासीपुत्तेण इन्दिआलिएण कहिदं जधा एक्को अवस्सं खेडुको तुम्हेहिं पेक्खिदव्वोत्ति । ता एदं तम् ।

वासव०—अमात्य एषा खलु सागरात्प्राप्तेति भणित्वामात्ययौगन्धरायणेन मम हस्ते निक्षिप्ता। अत एव सागरिकेति शब्द्यते। (क)

राजा—(स्वगतम्।) यौगन्धरायणेन न्यस्ता। कथमसौ मामनिवेद्य किंचित्करिष्यति।

वसु०—(अपवार्य।) बाभ्रव्य यथा सुसदृशी वसन्तकस्य कण्ठे रत्नमाला अस्याश्च सागरात्प्राप्तिः तथा व्यक्तं सिंहलेश्वरस्य दुहिता रत्नावलीयम्। (प्रकाशम्।) आयुष्मति न खलु राजपुत्री रत्नावली त्वमेनामवस्थामुपगता।

साग०—(वसुभूतिं विलोक्य सास्रम्।) कथममात्यो वसुभूतिः। (ख)

वसु०—(सास्रम्।) हा हतोऽस्मि मन्दभाग्यः। (भूमौ निपतति।)

साग०—हा तात हा अम्ब कुत्रासि देहि मे प्रतिवचनम्। (इति वसुभूतेरुपरि पतन्ती मोहमुपगता।) (ग)

वास०—(ससंभ्रमम्।) आर्य कञ्चुकिन् इयं सा मम भगिनी रत्नावली। (घ)

बाभ्र०—देवि इयमेव सा।

वास०—(रत्नावलीमालिङ्ग्य।) भगिनि समाश्वसिहि समाश्वसिहि। (ङ)

राजा—कथमुदात्तवंशस्य सिंहलेश्वरस्य विक्रमबाहोरात्मजेयम्।

(क) अमच्च एसा क्खु सागरादो पाविदेत्ति भणिअ अमच्चजोअन्धराअणेण मम हत्थे णिक्खिदा। अदो एव्व साअरिआत्ति सद्दावीअदि। (ख) कहं अमच्चो वसुभूदी। (ग) हा ताद हा अम्ब कहिं सि देहि मे पडिवअणम्। (घ) अज्ज कञ्चुइं इअं सा मम बहिणी रअणावली। (ङ) बहिणि समस्सस समस्सस।

जोपगमात्संधिनामकं निर्वहणसंधेरङ्गम्। **सागरिकेति**-सागरोऽस्ति अस्याः प्राप्तिस्थानत्वेनेति मत्वर्थे अत इनिठनौ इति ठन्। स्त्रियां टाप्। वसुभूतिः देव कुत इयं कन्यका इत्यारभ्य कथमसौ मामनिवेद्य किंचित्करिष्यतीत्यन्तेन रत्नावलीलक्षणकार्यान्वेषणाद्विबोधाख्यं निर्वहणसन्धेरङ्गम्। मन्दभाग्यः मन्दभाग्यत्वं कष्टां दशामापन्नाया राजपुत्र्या दर्शनात्। उदात्तः महान् वंशो यस्य तस्य। सामान्यजनस्य प्राकृतजनस्य।

---

१. कथं यौ० न्यस्तेयम्. २ (सागरिकां निर्दिश्य) अस्या अपि......सैवेयं सिंहलराजपुत्री-लेश्वरदुहिता. ३ ०ष्मति रत्नावलि, त्वमीदृशीमवस्थां गतासि. ४ दृष्ट्वा सा० ५ (वसुभूतेरुपरि निपत्य) हा. ६ आस्मानं पातयन्ती. ७ अज्जउत्त. ८ हा हदम्हि मन्दभाइणी। हा ताद इ०.

विदू०—(रत्नमाला स्पृशन् स्वगतम् ।) प्रथममेव मया ज्ञातं न खलु सामान्यजनस्येदृशः परिच्छदो भवतीति । (क)

वसु०—(उत्थाय ।) आयुष्मति समाश्वसिहि समाश्वसिहि । नन्वियं ज्यायसी ते भगिनी दुःखमास्ते । तत्परिष्वजस्वैनाम् ।

साग०—(समाश्वस्य वासवदत्तां दृष्ट्वा स्वगतम् ।) कृतापराधा खल्वहं देव्या न शक्नोमि मुखं दर्शयितुम् । (इत्यधोमुखी तिष्ठति ।) (ख)

वास०—(सास्रं बाहू प्रसार्य ।) एह्येह्यतिनिष्ठुरे इदानीमपि तावत्स्नेहं दर्शय । (इति कण्ठे गृह्णाति । रत्नावली स्खलितं नाटयति ।) । (अपवार्य ।) आर्यपुत्र लज्जे खल्वनेनात्मनो नृशंसत्वेन । तदपनयाम्या बन्धनम् । (ग)

राजा—(सपरितोषम् ।) यथाह देवी । (इति तथा करोति ।)

वास०—आर्यपुत्र अमात्ययौगन्धरायणेनैतावन्तं खलु कालं दुर्जनीकृतास्मि । येन जानतापि न निवेदितम् । (घ)

(ततः प्रविशति यौगन्धरायणः ।)

यौगन्ध०—

देव्या मद्वचनाद्यदाभ्युपगतः पत्युर्वियोगस्तदा
सा देवस्य कलत्रसंघटनया दुःखं मया स्थापिता ।

(क) पढमं जेव्व मए जाणिदं ण क्खु सामण्णजणस्स ईदिसो परिच्छओ होदित्ति । (ख) किदावराहा क्खु अहं देवीए ण सक्कुणोमि मुहं दंसिदुम् । (ग) एहि एहि अदिणिट्ठुरे इदाणिं पि दाव सिणेहं दंसेहि । अज्जउत्त लज्जेमि क्खु इमिणा अत्तणो णिसंसत्तणेन । ता अवणेहि से बन्धणम् । (घ) अज्जउत्त अमच्चयौगन्धराअणेण एत्तिअं क्खु कालं दुज्जणीकिदम्हि । जेणं जाणंतेण वि ण णिवेदिदम् ।

परिच्छदोऽलंकारः । अतिनिष्ठुरे तावत्कालं स्वयथार्थनामादरप्रकटनादुपेत्यालिङ्गनं वा विलम्बकरणादेवमुक्तिः । एतावन्तम् । अत्यन्तसंयोगे द्वितीया । दुर्जनीकृतास्मि अज्ञानात्सागरिकां प्रति नैष्ठुर्याचरणादिति भावः । **देव्या** इति । पुरा यौगन्धरायणेन–एवं कृते वत्सराजस्य पृथ्वीलाभः स्यादित्यादिवचनैः प्रबोधिता स्वपति-

---

१ आत्मगतम् । रत्न० स्पृशन् । २ अस्मात्परं—इति रत्नमालां–रत्नावली–कण्ठे समर्पयति । इत्य. ३ उत्थाय रत्नावलीं प्रति. ४ राजपुत्रि. ५ अस्मात्परं–वास०—समस्सह (इति परिष्वजते ।) इत्य. ६ राजानमप०. ७ इति सागरिकां मुञ्चति; सागरिकाया बन्धनमपनयति. ८ ०नात्तथाभ्यु; त्पथामु०. ९ परं प्रापिता. १० रअणाअलीं दिट्ठिअ पढमं; मए भणिदं. ११ बन्धुसि०. १२ जाणिअ ण आचक्खिदं.

तस्याः प्रीतिमयं करिष्यति जगत्स्वामित्वलाभः प्रभोः
सत्यं दर्शयितुं तथापि वदनं शक्नोमि नो लज्जया ॥ २० ॥

(क्षणं विचिन्त्य ।) अथ वा किं क्रियते । ईदृशमत्यन्तमाननीयेष्वपि निरनुरोधवृत्ति स्वामिभक्तिव्रतम् । (विलोक्य ।) अयं देवः । याव-दुपसर्पामि । (उपसृत्य ।) जयतु जयतु देवः । देव क्षम्यतां यन्मया देवस्यानिवेद्य कृतम् ।

राजा—यौगन्धरायण कथय किमनिवेद्य कृतम् ।

यौगन्ध०—करोत्वासनपरिग्रहं देवः । सर्वं विज्ञापयामि ।

(सर्वे यथास्थानमुपविशन्ति ।)

यौगन्ध०—(कृताञ्जलिः ।) देव श्रूयताम् । इयं सिंहलेश्वरदुहिता सिद्धेनादिष्टा यथा योऽस्याः पाणिं ग्रहीष्यति स सार्वभौमो राजा भवि-ष्यति । ततस्तत्प्रत्ययादस्माभिः स्वाम्यर्थं बहुशः प्रार्थ्यमानेनापि सिंह-लेश्वरेण देव्या वासवदत्तायाश्चित्तखेदं परिहरता यदा न दत्ता—

राजा—तदा किम् ।

हितैकपरा देवी पत्युः कञ्चित्कालमात्मनो वियोगं तस्य पत्न्यन्तरग्रहणं चानुमेने । तथा च कथासरित्सागरे—यौगन्धरायणो धीमान्सरुमण्वद्वसन्तकः । देव्या वासवदत्ताया विजनं निकटं ययौ ॥ तत्र तां राजकार्येऽत्र साहाय्ये तत्तदुक्तिभिः । प्रह्वामभ्यर्थयामास भ्रात्रा पूर्वं प्रबोधिताम् ॥ सानुमेने च विरहक्लेशदायि तदात्मनः । इति ॥ इति पूर्ववृत्तं स्मरन्नाह—यदा लावाणकग्रामेऽग्निप्रयोगकाले मद्वचनान्मदुक्तिमनुरुध्य देव्या पत्युर्वियोगः अभ्युपगतोऽङ्गीकृतस्तदा सा मया देवस्य अन्यकलत्रेण संघटना संयोगस्तया हेतुना दुःखं स्थापिता क्लेशे नियुक्ता । प्रभोः अयं जगत्स्वामित्वलाभस्तस्याः प्रीतिं करिष्य-तीति सत्यम् । तथापि लज्जया मत्सम्बन्धेनास्याः दाहप्रवादः उत्पन्नः सपत्नी च जातेति त्रपया वदनं दर्शयितुं न शक्नोमि । अत्र यौगन्धरायणेन स्वगुणानुकीर्तनाद् विचल-नाख्यमविमर्शसंधेरङ्गम् । शार्दूलविक्रीडितं वृत्तम् ॥ २० ॥ अत्यन्तं यथा तथा माननी-येषु आदरणीयेषु । देवीसदृशेषु । सुप्सुपेति समासः । निरनुरोधवृत्ति निर्गतः अनुरोधः अपेक्षा यस्याः सा निरनुरोधा तादृशी वृत्तिरस्य इति । स्वामिनः भक्तिरेव व्रतं स्वामि-

---

१ लाभात्, ०भात्प्रभुः. २ शमिदम०...निरुपरोध० स्वामिनो भक्तव्र०; निरनुरोध-प्रवृत्ति, निरनुक्रोशवृत्तिः स्वामिभक्तिवृत्तिर्नाम. ३ निरूप्य. ४ देवो महाराजः. ५ (पादयोर्निपत्य) देव. ६ एतन्नास्ति क्वचित्; यौग० सर्वमेव नावगच्छामि । तत्क-थय किमनाख्याय त्वया कृतम् । ७ सर्वे राज्ञा सह; राजा तथा करोति. ८ यत्तं सिंह० सा स्वामिनोऽर्थे; अस्माभिर्युष्मदर्थं बहु याच्यमानेनापि-प्रार्थ्यमानेनापि देवेन.

यौगन्ध०—तदा लावाणकेन वह्निना देवी दग्धेति प्रसिद्धिमुत्पाद्य तदन्तिकं बाभ्रव्यः प्रहितः ।

राजा—ततः परं श्रुतं मया । अथेयं देव्या हस्ते किमनुचिन्त्य स्थापिता ।

विदू०—भो अनाख्यातमप्येतज्ज्ञायत एव यथा अन्तःपुरगता सुखेन ते नयनपथं गमिष्यतीति । (क)

राजा—(विहस्य ।) यौगन्धरायण गृहीतोऽभिप्रायोऽसि वसन्तकेन ।

यौगन्ध०—यदाज्ञापयति देवः ।

राजा—ऐन्द्रजालिकवृत्तान्तोऽपि मन्ये त्वत्प्रयोग एव ।

यौगन्ध०—देव एवम् । अन्यथान्तःपुरे बद्धाया अस्याः कुतो देवेन दर्शनम् । अदृष्टायाश्च वसुभूतिना कुतः परिज्ञानम् । (विहस्य ।) परिज्ञातायाश्च भगिन्याः संप्रति यथाकरणीयं तत्र देवी प्रमाणम् ।

वासव०—(सस्मितम् ।) आर्य स्फुटमेव किं न भणसि यथा प्रतिपादयास्मै रत्नावलीमिति । (ख)

(क) भो अणाचक्खिदं वि एदं जाणीअदि जेव जधा अन्तेउरगदा सुहेण दे णअणपधं गमिस्सदित्ति । (ख) अज्ज फुडं जेव किं ण भणासि जहा पडिवादेहि से रअणावलिं त्ति ।

भक्तिव्रतम् । अत्र देव क्षम्यतां यन्मयेत्यादिना वत्सराजस्य रत्नावलीप्रापणकार्योपक्षेपाद् ग्रथनाख्यमङ्गम् । तथा च देव क्षम्यतामित्यादि प्रसादाख्यमङ्गं च । विज्ञापयामि कथयामि इत्यर्थः । स्थानमनतिक्रम्येति यथास्थानम् । स्वस्वोचितस्थाने इत्यर्थः । चित्तखेदं सपत्नीभावजन्या पीडा । अत्र देव श्रूयतामित्यारभ्य बाभ्रव्यः प्रहितः इत्यन्तेन यौगन्धरायणेन स्वानुभूतार्थकथनान्निर्णयाख्यमङ्गम् । गृहीतः अभिप्रायो यस्य । वसन्तकेन यथा ते आशयो ज्ञातस्तथैव स किमित्यर्थः । अन्यथा । ऐन्द्रजालिकप्रयोगेणाग्निसंरम्भजननाभावे । देवी प्रमाणं सर्वं देव्यधीनमित्यर्थः । अत्र भगिन्याः संप्रति यत्करणीयं तत्र देवी प्रमाणमित्यारभ्य वासव०–प्रतीच्छ रत्नावलीम् इत्यन्तेन वत्सराजाय रत्नावली दीयतामिति कार्यस्य यौगन्धरायणाभिप्रायानुप्रविष्टस्य वासवदत्तया दर्शना-

---

१ (सलज्जम् ।) तदा. २ यौगन्धरायण ततः. ३ गृहीतस्तेऽभि०; वस० गृहीताभिप्राय एवासि. ४ त्वत्प्रयुक्तः. ५ ०करणीयं.. ६ ०चक्खिदो वि एदस्स अभिप्पाओ मए जाणिदो जेव्व । जधा ०उरगदस्स १० दंसणपथं, दिट्ठिगोअरं णिवडिस्सदि. ८ क्रअं.

विदू०—भवति सुष्ठु त्वया ज्ञातोऽमात्यस्याभिप्रायः । (क)

वासव०—(हस्तं प्रसार्य ।) एहि रत्नावलि एहि । एतावदपि तावन्मे भगिनिकानुरूपं भवतु । (रत्नावलीं स्वैराभरणैरलंकृत्य हस्ते गृहीत्वा राजानमुपसृत्य ।) आर्यपुत्र प्रतीच्छैनाम् । (ख)

राजा—(सपरितोषं हस्तौ प्रसार्य ।) को देव्याः प्रसादो न बहु मन्यते ।

वासव०—आर्यपुत्र दूरे खल्वेतस्याः पितृकुलम् । तत्तथा कुरु यथा न बन्धुजनं स्मरति । (इति समर्पयति ।) (ग)

राजा—यथाज्ञापयति देवी । (रत्नावलीं गृह्णाति ।)

विदू०—(नृत्यन् ।) ही ही भोः पृथ्वी खल्विदानीं हस्तगता प्रियवयस्यस्य । (घ)

वसु०—आयुष्मति स्थाने देवीशब्दमुद्वहसि ।

यौगन्ध०—इदानीं सफलपरिश्रमोऽस्मि संवृत्तः । देव तदुच्यतां किं ते भूयः प्रियमुपकरोमि ।

राजा—किमतःपरमपि प्रियमस्ति । यतः—

नीतो विक्रमबाहुरात्मसमतां प्राप्तेयमुर्वीतले
सारं सागरिका ससागरमहीप्राप्त्येकहेतुः प्रिया ।

(**क**) भोदी सुट्ठ तुए जाणिदो अमच्चस्साभिप्पाओ । (**ख**) एहि रअणावलि एहि । एत्तिअंवि दाव मे बहिणिआणुरूवं भोदु । अज्जउत्त पडिच्छ एदं । (**ग**) अज्जउत्त दूरे क्खु एदाए पिदुकुलम् । ता तधा करेहि जधा ण बन्धुज्जणं सुमरेदि । (**घ**) ही ही भो पुहवी क्खु दाणि हत्थगदा पिअवअस्सस्स ।

त्पूर्वभावाख्यमङ्गम् । यथाह देवी । अत्र प्रार्थितरत्नावलीसमागमस्य । वत्सराजेन प्राप्तत्वादानन्दाख्यमङ्गम् । राजा को देव्या... । वास०–आर्यपुत्र...बन्धुजनं न स्मरति । इत्यन्योन्यवचसा लब्धायां रत्नावल्यां राज्ञः सुश्लिष्य उपशमनात् कृतिरित्यङ्गम् । सफलपरिश्रमः राज्ञो रत्नावलीलाभेनेति भावः । **नीत** इति । विक्रमबाहुः तत्कन्यायाः पत्नीत्वेन स्वीकारात् आत्मसमतां नीतः । उर्वीतले भूतले सारं

---

१ स्वकीयैरा०. २ सहर्षं. ३ अस्मात्परं–इति सागरिकां गृह्णाति इत्य० क्वचित्. ४ यदाज्ञा०. ५ सहर्षं नृ०. ६ राजपुत्रि वासवदत्तां प्रणामेनार्चय । (रत्नावली तथा करोति ।) बाभ्रव्यः—देवि स्थाने इ०. ७ बाभ्रव्यः—अमात्य इदानीं सफलपरिश्रमः संवृत्तः. यौग०—देव उच्यतां प्रियं करोमि. ८ यतः. ९ समस्तवसुधा, तथा च भुवन. १० आसओ. ११ एदं रअणावलिं; पडिच्छदु मम बहिणिअं रअणावलिं अज्जउत्तो. १२ णाभि–दि. १३ इह चिट्ठन्तीनं. १४ भोः । जअदु जअदु जअदु भवं । पु०.

देवी प्रीतिमुपागता च भगिनीलाभाज्जिताः कोसलाः
किं नास्ति त्वयि सत्यमात्यवृषभे यस्मै करोमि स्पृहाम् ॥२१॥

तथापीदमस्तु । (भरतवाक्यम् ।)

उर्वीमुद्दामसस्यां जनयतु विसृजन्वासवो वृष्टिमिष्टा-
मिष्टैस्त्रैविष्टपानां विदधतु विधिवत्प्रीणनं विप्रमुख्याः ।
आकल्पान्तं च भूयात्समुपचितसुखः संगमः सज्जनानां
निःशेषं यान्तु शान्तिं पिशुनजनगिरो दुर्जया वज्रलेपाः ॥२२॥

(इति निष्क्रान्ताः सर्वे ।)

इत्यैन्द्रजालिको नाम चतुर्थोऽङ्कः ।

इति श्रीहर्षदेवस्य कृतिः समाप्तेयं रत्नावली नाम नाटिका ।

रत्नभूता ससागराया मह्याः प्राप्तेः एकहेतुः प्रधानं कारणमियं सागरिका प्राप्ता । भगिनीलाभाद्देवी प्रसादं सन्तोषमुपगता । कोसला जिताः । एवं त्वयि अमात्यवृषभे मन्त्रिमुख्ये सति किमभीष्टं वस्तु मम नास्ति यस्मै स्पृहां करोमि । अत्र कामार्थमानादिलाभाद्भाषणमित्यङ्गम् । शार्दूलविक्रीडितं छन्दः ॥ २१ ॥ **उर्वीमिति** । वासव इन्द्रः इष्टामभिलषितां वृष्टिं विसृजन् उर्वीं महीमुद्दामं सस्यं यस्यां तथाविधां जनयतु । विप्रेषु मुख्याः विप्रमुख्या द्विजश्रेष्ठाः इष्टैः यज्ञैः । नपुंसके भावे क्तः । तृतीयं विष्टपं त्रिविष्टपं स्वर्गः । तत्र भवाः त्रैविष्टपा देवाः । तत्र भवः इत्यण् । तेषां विधिवत्प्रीणनं प्रीतिं विदधतु कुर्वन्तु । समुपचितं वृद्धिं प्राप्तं सुखं यस्मात्तादृशः सज्जनानां संगमः संगतिः आकल्पान्तं प्रलयपर्यन्तं भूयाद्भवतु । तथा च वज्रस्य इव लेपः प्रसक्तिर्यासां ताः । वज्रलेपाः अतिकठिनाः दुर्जया जेतुमशक्याः दुष्परिहरा इत्यर्थः । पिशुनजनानां खलानां गिरो वाचः निःशेषं यथा तथा शान्तिं यान्तु नश्यन्तु । अत्र आशीर्नाम नाट्याङ्गमुक्तम् । स्रग्धरा वृत्तम् ॥२२॥ इति रत्नावलीटीकायां चतुर्थोऽङ्कः ॥

---

१ किं नामास्ति विधेयमत्र भुवने यस्मिन्, यस्मिन्क॰. २ विकिरन्. ३ विविध. ४ राजमुख्याः. ५ क्रियासु. क्रममुपरचितं संगतं सज्जनाश्च निर्विश्लेषावकाशं...जनवचोवर्जनाद्वज्रलेपम्; सूक्तिकीर्तिर्विलसतु सुकवेर्हृद्यसद्वृत्तरत्ना नाम्ना रत्नावलीयं सकलजनमनोनाटिका नाटिकास्तु; भूयास्थिरसमुपचितं संगतं. ६ नाशं; यातु...वचो दुःसहो वज्रलेपः. ७ इतिश्रीहर्षदेवकृतायां रत्नावलीलाभो नाम; रत्नावलीप्रधाननाटिकायां च॰. ८ श्रीपण्डितशिरोमणिकविराजेन श्रीहर्षेण विरचिता रत्नावली नाम नाटिका समाप्ता.

श्लोकानुक्रमः ।

TRANSLATION.

Act I.

May the handful of flowers, thrown by Girijà (Pàrvatî) at the time of worshipping (waiting on) Sambhu, protect you (and us)!—that handful, which was intended to fall on his head, but which, giving way in the middle, fell between, as she, standing on tiptoe, but repeatedly brought to a stooping posture by the weight of her breasts, became nervous (*lit.* was overcome with shame), having come within the range of his three wistful eyes, and manifested tremor, accompanied by horripilation and the appearance of perspiration. (1)

Moreover—

May Gaurî, who at the time of her first meeting (with her husband), hastened forth through eagerness but turned back through inborn bashfulness, who was again led before (made to face) him by the various persuasive words of her kinswomen, but who on beholding her husband in front of her, displayed a leaning towards shyness (*lit.* fright), and who was embraced, her hair standing on end, by S'iva, smiling, (at her embarrassment), be for your good! (2)

Again,

May he grant protection to you whom the daughter of the mountain (-lord) and Lakshmî thus addressed in wrath—

(*a*) For me formerly did the fish-bannered god (Madana) meet his destruction from thee; it is meet then, O shameless one, that thou shouldst bear the many coursed one (Gangâ, on thy head) in my presence. Do then conciliate her alone who is crooked by nature, and let go thy hold (*or* embrace), O dark-necked one, of me.

(*b*) For (that thou shouldst obtain) me, did the fish-bannered (sea) formerly suffer churning at thy hands; so it is meet, O shameless one, that thou shouldst, in my very presence, keep company with one who leads a many-coursed (loose) life: do then conciliate, O Krishna, her who is of a cunning mind, and let go thy hold (embrace) of my neck.

And further:

May Śiva protect you! who laughed (heartily) when thus narrating to the goddess (Pârvatî) his destruction of Daksha's sacrifice—the three fires were extinguished by glances from the three eyes blazing with ire; the panic-stricken priests, with the cloth of their turbans snatched away by the *gaṇas* (attendants) actively moving about, fell down; Daksha began to praise, while his spouse wept piteously; and the gods took to flight. (3)

And again—

Triumphant is the Lord of the stars (moon); reverence to the gods; may the eminent Brâhmaṇas be free from molestation; may the Earth yield plentiful corn; and may the illustrious King (Śrîharsha) with a body (lovely) like the moon, shine pre-eminently! (4)

(*After the recital of the* Nàndî).

MANAGER—Enough of protraction. To-day, on the occasion of the Spring-festival, being called with great respect by the multitude of kings, dependent on the lotus-like feet of our King, the illustrious Śrî-Harsha, arrived here from regions in the various quarters, I was thus addressed—"Our master, Śrî-Harshadeva, has composed a Náṭiká, entitled Ratnávalî, graced with a novel arrangement of the plot. We have heard about it from hearsay, but have not seen it acted. Out of respect, therefore, for that very King, the gladdener of the hearts of all people, and with a mind to favour us, the same should be enacted on the stage by you with proper acting (or representation)." I will then arrange the tiring-room now (or make my toilet) and then do as desired. (*Walking about and looking on.*) Ah! I am quite sure, the minds of all the spectators have been won over (or favourably disposed towards us). For,

Śrîharsha is an eminent poet, and this audience here is capable of appreciating merits; the story of Vatsarája is an attractive one in the world, and we are masters of the histrionic art: each one of these circumstances is, even by it self, the source of the attainment of the desired object; what to say then, when there has come about this combination of all advantages through the accumulation (greatness) of my luck. (5)

I will then go home, call my wife, and begin the music. (*Turning round and looking towards the tiring-room.*) This is my house; let me enter. (*Entering*) Lady, (come) here for a while.

(*Entering.*)

THE ACTRESS—Here I am, my dear. Let Your Honour command what business is to be executed.

MANAGER—Lady, this assembly of kings is eager to see the Ratnâvalî (represented on the stage); so attire yourself (for it).

ACTRESS—(*Heaving a sigh, with dejection*). Dear husband, you are now free from anxiety; so why should you not dance? But I, hapless that I am, have an only daughter; and even she has been betrothed by you (to some one) in some distant country. With (being lost in) the thought as to how her marriage with a bridegroom living in a distant country could be accomplished, I am not cognizant even of myself. What of dancing then!

MANAGER—Lady! away with uneasiness as to (the bridegroom) being at a distant place; just see—

Propitious fate brings at once the desired object, even from a different isle, or from the ocean's depths, or from the extreme limit of a quarter, and puts one in possession of that. (6)

(*Behind the scenes.*)

Well said, son (or, follower) of Bharata, thus it is; where is the doubt (about that)? (He repeats *Propitious fate &c.*)

MANAGER—(*Hearing and looking towards the tiring-room, with joy*). Lady, here has just come my younger brother, assuming the character of Yaugandharâyana. Come away then; we become ready for putting on our costumes. (*Exeunt both.*)

(*End of the Prelude.*)

(*Enter* Yaugandharàyana.)

YAUGA.—So it is; what doubt is there? (He repeats *Propitious fate &c.*) Else, where (how incongruous) is the finding of a plank by the daughter of the King of Siṃhala sought (by me) through confidence in the words of a Seer, as she rose up after being submerged in the sea owing to ship-wreck, and where the rescue of her found in that plight by a merchant of Kauśāmbî returning from Siṃhala, and her being brought here, through recognition, as she was distinguished by the gem necklace. (*With joy*) Prosperity attends our master in every way (*Reflecting*) I too acted very properly in respectfully delivering her into the hands (entrusting her to the keeping) of the Queen. I have also heard that Bàbhravya, the Chamberlain, along with Vasubhùti, the Minister of the King of Siṃhala, having somehow got to land from the sea, has joined Rumanvat, who has gone to uproot the King of the Kosalas. My master's purpose, though almost accomplished in this way, does not bring me mental ease: so, painful, indeed, is the position of a servant. For—

In this undertaking, the source of my master's advancement, to which a helping hand has thus been given by fate, there is no doubt as to its success; this is true: yet, acting of my own accord, I am quite afraid of my master. (7)

(*A mixed noise behind the curtains*).

YAUGA.—(*Hearing*) Ah, since there is swelling, in front, the noise of the clapping of the hands of the citizens, sweet on account of the songs, accompanied by the mellow sound of the tabors gently beaten, I conjecture that His Majesty has started for the palace to witness the merriment of the citizens, heightened by the Madana Festival. (*Looking up*) Ah, how now! The King has ascended the palace! He,

The lord of Vatsa, like the flower-bowed god (Madana) in person, as it were, with all talk of Vigraha (the war-body) ceased, having Rati (love of the people, —his wife), living in the hearts of the people, and one to whom Vasantaka (his companion—Spring), is dear, is advancing, eager to behold his own great festival. (8)

I will then go to my residence and give thought to what remains of the business to be accomplished. (*Exit*).

End of the Vishkambhaka.

(*Enter the* KING. *seated, in a dress suited to the spring festival, and* VIDU'SHAKA.)

KING—(*With a look of delight.*) Friend, Vasantaka.

VIDU'SHAKA—Your commands, sire.

KING—The kingdom has all its enemies entirely vanquished; the burden (of government) is placed on (entrusted to) a worthy (competent) minister; the people, with all their troubles warded off, are tended with proper protection; (and further—) Pradyota's daughter (for my wife), the Vernal season and yourself.—With all these (advantages to complete my happiness), let Káma have ample satisfaction by its name: but I, on my part, regard the great festival as mine. (9)

VIDU'.—(*With jubilation*) O friend, so indeed, it is. I, however, feel that this great festival is neither yours nor Káma's; it is of me alone, a Bráhmana, of whom my dear friend has thus spoken. (*Looking on.*) But what have we to do with this? Just behold the beauty of this great Madana-festival, in which curiosity is excited by the citizens (or gallants), dancing as they are struck by the water from the syringes taken up, of their own accord, by the amorous women intoxicated with wine; which is attractive on account of the openings of the streets resounding with the sound of the *charchari* songs (or clappings of hands) deepened by the tabors beaten all round, and which has rendered the faces of the ten directions yellowish-red by means of the heaps of *patavàsa* scattered about.

KING—(*Casting a glance all round*) Oh, the gaiety of the citizens has reached its highest point! For,

By the heaps of scented powder scattered about, yellow with saffron dust and imparting to the day the appearance of the dawn, by the glitter of gold ornaments and by the wreaths of Aśoka flowers that cause the heads to bend low by their weight, this Kauśámbî, which has surpassed all the treasures of the Lord of wealth by its oppulence apparent from the dresses (of the people), and which seems to have its inhabitants covered with liquid gold as it were, appears all yellow. (10)

Moreover,

In the courtyard which is flooded all over with the continuous streams of water ejected by the fountains and where sport is carried on in the mud caused by the simultaneous and close treadings, the yon pavement is reddened by the people with the imprints (*lit.* plantings) of their feet, red with the colour of the vermillion dropping from the cheeks of the females (moving about) without restraint. (11)

VIDU'—(*Looking forth*) Let my dear friend enjoy the sight of the sporting of the courtesans, charming on account of the hissing-sounds uttered, on their being struck by the (jets of) water from syringes discharged by the very expert gallants.

KING—(*Marking*) Well observed by you, friend! For,

The multitude of gallants (also, *nágas*), with uplifted syringes of the form of hoods (syringes like hoods) and dimly seen by the glitter of the jewel-ornaments in this gloom caused by the fragrant powder scattered about, puts me in mind of the nether world. (12)

VIDU'.—(*Observing*) Ho, here is Madaniká coming just hitherwards, along with Chûtalatikà, dancing with gesticulations indicative of spring and with steps falling unevenly owing to excited passion.

(*Enter the* TWO MAIDS *exhibiting love-sport and singing the dvipadi ditty*).

MAIDS—(*Sing*)

Now is blowing the South-wind, the loved messenger of the flower-weaponed god, causing many a mango tree to blossom and slackening the jealous pride of women. (13)

Multitudes of young females that have caused the blossoming of the *Bakula* and the *As'oka* trees and that have been eagerly waiting for the company of their beloveds, are pining, unable to wait. (14)

Now the month of Madhu first makes the hearts of persons soft; and then Káma pierces them with his flower-arrows that have (thus) found scope. (15)

KING—(*Marking closely, with astonishment*) Oh the excess of passion for sport of the servant-girls! For,

Of this intoxicated maid, sporting, regardless of the breaking of her waist bending under the weight of her breasts, the mass of hair, loosened and dishevelled, is giving up, in pain as it were, the beauty imparted by the wreath of flowers; here her two anklets, clinging to her feet, are crying, through uneasines as it were, with a double force; and this her necklace, tossed about by the continuous shaking, is, through constraint as it were, ceaselessly striking her bosom. (16)

VIDU.—O friend, I too shall go and honour the Madana festival by dancing and singing in their midst.

KING—(*Smiling*) Friend, do so.

VIDU'.—(*Rising and dancing between the two*) Honoured Madaniká, honoured Chûtalatika, teach me too this *Charcharí*.

BOTH—(*Laughing*) Fool, this is not a *Charcharí*.

VI'DU'.—What, indeed, is this then!

MADA.—This, to be sure, is a *dvipadí khaṇḍa*.

VIDU'.—(*Joyfully*). What, are *modukas* or balls made with it?

MADA.—(*Laughing*) You hapless chap, not at all; it is (a poem that is) recited.

VIDU'.—(*Dejectedly*) It is a thing to be chanted! Then I have nothing to do with it. To my friend's presence I will retire. (*Wishes to go.*)

BOTH—(*Seizing him by the hand*) Come, let us play. Vasantaka, where would you go? (*They pull him in many ways*).

VIDU'.—(*Pulling off his hand, running away and approaching the* KING) Friend, I was made to dance; no, no; I sped away, after having sported.

KING—Well done.

CHU'TA.—Friend Madaniká, we have, indeed sported for a long time. Come, then; let us communicate the queen's message to His Majesty.

MADA.—Friend, let us do so.

BOTH—*(Walking forth and approaching)* Victory, victory to Your Majesty! Sire, the Queen commands–*(Gesticulating shame at this half uttered)* No, no; respectfully submits—

KING—*(Smiling, with respect)* Madaniká, 'commands' itself is, indeed, pleasing, especially to-day, on the occasion of Madana's festival. So pray, tell what the Queen commands.

VIDU'.—Ho, slave's daughter, sayest thou—the Queen commands!

BOTH—This is Her Majesty's request—"To-day, I have to go to the Makaranda garden and offer worship to (the image of) the god of Love, placed at the root of the red Asóka tree. My husband should be present there".

KING—*(With delight)* Friend, surely it should be said that one festival is followed by another yet greater.

VIDU'.—Friend, get up then. There we shall go, so that, gone there, I, too, a Bráhmana, may get some present.

KING—Madaniká, go and tell the Queen that I am just gone to the Makaranda garden.

BOTH—As master commands. *(Exeunt).*

KING—Friend, come, let us descend.

BOTH—*(Gesticulate descent from the palace).*

KING—Friend, lead the way to the Makaranda garden.

VIDU'.—As Your Honour commands. Come, your Honour, come.

(BOTH *Walk on*).

VIDU'—*(Looking in front)* Friend, here is the Makaranda garden. Come then, let us enter. *(They enter).*

VIDU'.—(*Looking about with wonder*) Look, O friend, look. With a canopy formed by means of the mass of the pollen from the full-blown blossoms of the mango trees shaken by the Malaya wind, and gratifying to the ear by the music of the sweet notes of the cuckoos, mingled with the hums of intoxicated bees; this Makaranda garden appears, indeed, to be honouring your visit (by thus preparing to receive you). So let Your Highness honour it with a look.

KING—(*Looking all round*) Oh the loveliness of the Makaranda garden! For, here,

Wearing a ruddy appearance by their sprouts that possess the lustre of shooting corals, displaying the fun of uttering unintelligible words by means of the sweet indistinct hums of the rows of bees, and reeling ever and anon, with the clusters of their branches waving as they are struck by the Malaya breeze, these trees now appear to be tipsy as it were by their being touched by the influence of Madhu (the season-wine).(17)

Moreover,

The wine sprinkled in mouthfuls (and collected) at the root, is, as if, being scented with the shower of their flowers by the Bakula trees; the Champaka flowers smile to-day after a long time, while the moon-like faces of young females are yet red with the flush of wine; and hearing the jingle of the anklets loudly resounding in the act of giving strokes (by ladies) to the Aśoka trees, an imitation of it is begun, as it were, by swarms of bees with their responsive songs. (18)

VIDU'.—(*Listening*) O friend, these are not the bees imitating the sound of anklets; it is the sound itself of the anklets of the Queen's attendants.

KING—Friend, you have rightly marked.

(*Then enter* VA'SAVADATTA', KA'NCHANAMA'LA', SA'GARIKA' *with the materials of worship in her hands, and in order of their status*).

VA'SAVADATTA'—Show me the way to the Makaranda garden.

KA'NCH.—This way, this way, mistress.

VA'SA.—(*Walking about*) O Kànchanamálá, how far from here is the *red As'oka* tree where I have to offer worship to the god of Love?

KA'NCH.—Quite close at hand, mistress. Does not Your Highness see it? This is, indeed, Your Highness' favourite Mādhavî creeper, lovely by its ever, (or, close,) grown flowers. And this other is the Navamálika creeper, believing in the untimely flowering of which the master has been worrying himself day and night. Beyond this is just seen the red Aśoka, where Your Majesty is to perform the worship.

VA'SAV.—Come then, there let us go quickly.

KA'NCH.—This way, mistress, this way

(*All walk round.*)

KA'NCH.—Mistress, here is the red Aśoka tree where Your Majesty is to offer worship.

VA'SAV.—Then bring me the materials of worship.

SA'GARIKA'—(*Approaching*) Mistress, here is everything ready.

VA'SAV.—(*Observing, to herself*). Oh the carelessness of my servants! She will fall within the view of him from whose range of sight she has been assiduously kept away. Well, I will say this much:—(*Aloud*) Maid, Sāgariká, why have you come here, leaving away the Sàrikà (canary bird) when all attendants are entirely occupied with the Madana-festival? So, go you there quickly. Deliver all these materials of worship into the hands of Kàñchanamālā.

SA'GARIKA'—As Your Majesty commands. (*Doing accordingly and going a few steps, to herself*) I have delivered Sārikà into the hands of Susaṃgatâ. I have also a desire to see this—whether the Bodiless one (Káma) is worshipped here in the same way as in the female apartments of my father, or otherwise. So being concealed I shall watch. Until it is time here to offer the worship I, too, will gather flowers to worship the Divine Ananga himself. (*Gesticulates the collecting of flowers*).

VA'SAV.—Kāñchanamálā, place (the image of) Pradyumna at the root of the As'oka.

KA'NCH.—As mistress commands. *(Does as ordered).*

VIDU'.—O friend, as the jingling of the anklets has ceased, I guess the Queen has arrived at the foot of the As'oka.

KING—*(Looking on)* Rightly ascertained, friend. Mark the Queen, she, who, surely,

Standing by the side of the shark-bannered one (Káma), appears like his bow-staff, possessing a form delicate like a flower and a waist attenuated by the observance of a vow. (19)

Come then; we approach her. *(Advancing).* Dear Vâsavadattā.

VA'SAV.—*(Seeing)* How now! My husband! Victory, victory, to my lord! Here is a seat; let my lord sit down.

(The KING *shows that he sits down.)*

KA'NCH.—Mistress, let the divine Pradyumna be worshipped (by you) after having decorated the red As'oka with finger-applications of saffron made with your own hand.

VA'SAV.—Bring me the materials of worship.

(KA'NCHANAMA'LA *brings them,* VA'SAVADATTA *does as requested.)*

KING—My darling,

With your complexion rendered specially clear (brighter) by the fresh bath, and with the fringe of your garment shining beautifully with its red *Kusumbha* dye, you, while worshipping the god of Love, appear like a twig grown on a tree, having tender new leaves, with its form made cleaner by being sprinkled over with a shower and charming by its shining tints, agreeable like those of the *Kusumbha* flowers. (20)

Moreover,

O dear one, this As'oka, touched by you with your hand engaged in the worship of Smara (Káma.) appears to have another more delicate sprout, as it were, sprung (from it). (21)

Also,

This Bodiless god will certainly deplore his bodilessness to-day, since he has not experienced the joy of the touch of your hand. (22)

KA'NCH.—Mistress, the divine Pradyumna is worshipped. Now offer suitable worship to your husband.

VA'SAV.—Then bring me the flowers and sandal.

KA'NCH.—Mistress, here is everything ready.

(Vásavadattâ *acts worshipping the* KING.)

SA'GARIKA'—(*With flowers taken*) O fie! O fie! How have I tarried long, my heart (thoughts) being entirely taken up by the greed of flowers! I will then observe, with my person concealed by this cluster of the twigs of the *Sindhuvâra* tree. (*Doing so and observing, with wonder*). How now! The flower-arrowed god is accepting worship here in a visible form. In my father's house, however, he is worshipped being represented in a picture. I, too, just standing here, will then offer worship to the divine Kàma. (*Offering the flowers*) My salutation to thee, O flower-armed god! Mayest thou be of a sight not-unproductive (of bliss) unto me now! (*With this, bowing*) Whatever was to be seen has been seen. I will then go away before any one notices me. (*Walks forth a few steps*).

KA'NCH.—Revered Vasantaka, come, you too accept an auspicious present now. (Vidû. *approaches*).

VA'SAV.—(*After offering sandal unguent, flowers and ornaments*) Noble one, accept this auspicious present. (*Presents it*).

VIDU'.—(*Joyfully taking it.*) My blessing to your ladyship.

(*A* Bard *sings behind the scenes.*)

The Sun having entirely gone to the end of the sky, with all his radiant light cast on the setting-mountain, now at the time of dusk this assemblage of princes, pouring all together into the audience-hall, is eagerly waiting to pay homage to the feet, that rob (resemble) the lustre of lotuses, of thee Udyana, that givest excessive delight to the eyes, as they would to the rays, that deprive the day-lotus of its tints, of the rising moon, the bringer of a fund of joy to the eyes. (23).

SA'GARIKA'—(*Hearing and turning back with joy, and looking longingly at the* KING) How now! This is king Udyana, to whom I was betrothed by my father. (*Sighing deeply*). So my life, although degraded being in another's service, has become highly estimable now, by (my having obtained) his sight.

KING—What! With our mind engrossed by the festival, even the lapse of the evening twilight was not noticed by us. The day has drawn to its close now Behold, my Queen,

This Eastern—quarter, with her pale aspect, indicates (the presence of) the lord of night (moon) screened by the slopes of the rising-mountain, as a lovely woman does, by her pale face, that of her husband dwelling in the heart. (24).

Queen, get up then; let us enter inside the palace (*All rise and walk on.*)

SA'GARIKA'.—Ah, the Queen has started. Well, I too will quickly go then. (*Looking longingly at the* KING *with a sigh*) O fie, O fie!

This person could not be even seen for a long time by me, a hapless person! (*Exit, gazing at the* KING).

KING.—(*Walking about*)

Queen, behold—surpassed by the lotus of your face that eclipses the splendour of the moon, the lotuses suddenly grow pale (lose their lustre); and hearing the songs of the courtezans forming your train, the female bees are slowly lurking in the interiors of buds, as if smitten with shame. (25).

(*Exeunt Omnes.*)

End of Act I, styled 'Madana-great-festival.'

Act II.

(Enter SUSANGATA', *with her hand occupied with the cage of a Starling).*

SUSANGATA'—O fie, O fie! Where has my dear friend, Sâgariká gone, having delivered the starling's cage into my hand? Where, then, can I find her? (*Looking in front*) How now! Here is Nipunikâ coming this very way. I will then enquire of her.

(*Then enter* NIPUNIKA'.)

NIPUNIKA'—*(With wonder)* Oh, what wonder! Extraordinary I think is the power of a deity. I have indeed got the information regarding the King; so I will go and communicate it to the Queen. *(Walks about).*

SUSAN.—*(Approaching)* Friend Nipunikä, where are you going, disregarding me, standing here, and passing on like one with a mind distracted with wonder?

NIP.—Oh, Susangatá! Friend, you have rightly guessed. This is the cause of my wonder. To-day, it was said, Master would learn the secret formula of causing an untimely production of flowers, from a pious man, named Śrikanthadâs, who has come from Sriparvata, and would make his favourite creeper, Navamàlikā smile with a profusion of flowers; and I was sent by Her Majesty to ascertain the truth about this matter. But whither have you set out?

SUSA.—To search for my dear friend Sàgarikà.

NIPU.—Friend, I saw your dear friend, Sàgariká, entering the plantain-arbour, as if distracted, carrying with her a picture-board. a brush and a paint-box. Go then, you. I too will repair to the presence of the Queen.

(Exeunt Both.)

End of the Interlude.

(Enter SA'GARIKA' *with a picture-board and brush* in hand *and exhibiting love-sickness.)*

SA'GA.—*(Heaving a sigh)* My heart, take cheer; take cheer. What is the use of this persistent yearning after a person difficult to obtain, the only result of which is anguish? Moreover, you wish to see again the very person at whose sight your distress increases: so woeful is your stupidity! Again, O you exceedingly cruel heart, how don't you blush to follow a person known to you only after a moment's sight, forsaking this person brought up with you from birth? Or what is your fault (here)! You have thus acted to-day, being afraid of the descent of Ananga's shafts. *(Tearfully)* Well, I will rebuke Anañga. *(Joining the hollowed palms)* Divine wearer of flower-weapons, being one who has conquered all the gods and the demons, how are you not ashamed to strike at womankind! *(Reflecting)* Or why, you are without a body (and hence also feelings). *(Heaving a long sigh)* In fact death itself has approached me, a luckless person, as indicated by this evil omen. *(Looking at the picture-board)* Then so long as no one comes here, I will gaze upon that coveted person drawn in a picture and then do as desired. *(Firmly concentrating her mind and gesticulating the taking up of the picture-board, with a sigh)* Though on account of extreme nervousness this my fore-hand tremble very much, still as there is no other means of seeing that person, I will paint, just as I can, and behold him. *(Acts drawing him)*.

(Enter SUSANGATA'.*)*

SUSAN.—This is that plantain-bower. I will enter *(Entering and looking in front, wonderingly)*. Here is my dear friend, Sāgarikà. But why does she not look at me, engaged in painting something as though her heart were overpowered by deep love? Well. In the meantime avoiding the range of her eye-sight. I will see what she has been painting. *(With gentle steps standing at her back and seeing, with joy)* How now! She has painted our master. Noble, Sāgarikà, noble! Or rather, how can a female royal swan find pleasure except in a tank full of lotuses!

SA'GA.—I have drawn him, indeed. But again, my sight is not able to see him, owing to the water of tears ceaselessly falling down. *(Raising her face and wiping off the tears then covering the board with her upper garment on noticing* SUSANGATA, *with a smile)* Ah, my dear friend, Susangatà! Friend, sit here.

SUSAN.—(*Sitting down and forcibly taking the board*) O friend, who is this that is drawn by you here?

SA'GAR.—(*Blushingly*) Friend, god Anaṅga, now that the Madana-festival is being celebrated.

SUSAN.—(*Smiling*) Oh your skill! But how is it then that the picture appears like one that is solitary. So I, too, will draw, and make it have Rati by its side.

(*Takes the brush and while acting portraying* RATI, *paints* Sàgariká).

SA'GAR.—(*Looking at the picture and with an air of fault-finding*) Susangatà, why have you painted me here?

SUSAN.—(*Laughing*) Friend, why do you get angry without cause! As is the god of love painted by you, so is Rati painted by me. So, O you perverter of things, what is the use of your talking in this wise? Tell me at once the whole story.

SA'GAR.—(*Blushiing, to herself*) Surely I am found out by my friend. (*Taking* Susangatà *by the hand, aloud*) Dear friend, great, indeed, is the shame I feel. So act in such a way that no one will know of this affair.

SUSAN.—Friend, be not ashamed. Such a jewel of a girl must necessarily have a desire for such a husband. Still I shall so manage it that no one will know any thing about this matter. But this intelligent starling may be the cause (of disclosure) in this case. Catching up the words of this conversation, she might, perchance, reproduce them before any one else.

SA'GA.—What shall I do then in this matter? My torment grows yet more. (*Gesticulates love-torment.*)

SUSANG.—(*Placing her hand on* Ságariká's *bosom.*) Be composed, friend, be composed. In the meanwhile I shall take lotus-leaves and lotus-stalks from this tank and come back quickly. (*Going out and coming back, represents the forming of a bed with lotus-leaves and the making of bracelets with the stalks and puts the remaining lotus-leaves on* Ságariká's *bosom.)*

SA'GARIKA'—Friend, remove these lotus-leaves and the bracelets of the lotus-stalks. Away with these. Why do you trouble yourself in vain ? Just I say—

Love for a person unattainable, (the sense of) shame very great, and self under the power of another: (thus) dear friend, this love is unequal ; is not death the only best refuge then ? (or death alone is the best refuge). (1)

(Faints.)

SUS.—*(Pitifully)* Friend Ságariká, take heart, take heart.

(Behind the scenes.)

Dragging under him the remaining part of the golden chain tied round his neck, after it was snapped, and with the circle of small bells gingling on account of the wanton movement of the feet, this monkey here, broken loose from his stable, having crossed the gates, is entering the King's palace, causing fright to the ladies, with his path followed in haste and confusion by the stable-keepers. (2)

Moreover,

The eunuchs, casting off shame not being reckoned among men, have fled away ; this dwarf through terror is entering the inside of the Chamberlain's robe ; the *Kirátas*, betaking themselves to the outskirts of the harem, have acted in a manner befitting their name ; and the hunch-backs are slinking off in a low posture, fearing lest they might be noticed. (3)

SUS.—*(Hearing, looking forward, then rising in haste and taking* Ságariká *by the hand)* Friend, get up. This wicked monkey is, indeed, making in this very direction. Hiding ourselves, unnoticed in the gloom of the *tamála trees*, let us have him pass off. *(Doing accordingly they remain watching.)*.

SA'GA.—Susangatá, how have you left behind the picture-board ? Perchance some one may see it.

SUS.—O you who are quite at ease, what have you still to do with the picture-board? Here has the wicked monkey, fond of rice with curds, opened the cage of the starling and gone away; and Medhavinî (or, the sharp-talented bird) has flown up and is going away. Come, then; let us quickly follow her. She has caught the words of our conversation and might utter them before anyone else.

SA'GA.—Friend, let us do so. *(They walk round.)*

(Behind the scenes.)

Ah, Ho! Marvellous, marvellous!

SA'GA.—*(Looking forth, with fear)* Susaṅgatà, methinks the wicked monkey is coming up again.

SUS.—*(Seeing the* Vidú., *and smiling.)* Ah, you timid girl, don't you fear; this is the noble Vasantaka, our master's companion.

SA'GA.—*(Looking at him eagerly.)* Susaṅgatá, worthy of sight is this person, indeed!

SUS.—O you careless girl, why tarry to see him? The Sáriká, indeed, is covering a longer distance. Come away then; let us follow her.

(Exeunt BOTH. *)*

(Then enters VIDU'. *in high glee.)*

VIDU'.—What wonder, Ho! How marvellous! Bravo, O pious S'rîkhaṇḍadâsa, bravo. For the very moment the *desideratum* was supplied, the Navamâlikâ was so changed that, with its twigs decked with the thick-grown bunches of flowers, it appears to be laughing disdainfully, as it were, at the Màdhavì creeper, the Queen's favourite. I will then go and congratulate my dear friend. *(Walking round and looking)* Here, indeed, is my dear friend coming this very way, with his eyes dilated through joy, and through confindence in the *dohada* beholding, as it were before him, the Navamâlikâ in blossoms, though out of his sight. So I will approach him.

(Enter the KING *as described.)*

KING—*(Joyfully.)*

To-day I shall certainly make the Queen's face purple with anger, gazing upon this garden-creeper, as upon another woman in love, that in a moment has displayed a profusion of buds (a powerful longing), has a pale complexion, has its buds opening up (has commenced to yawn), and has been manifesting the disturbance (anguish) felt by it (her) by the ceaseless puffs of wind (by means of the constant heavings of sighs). (4)

But Vasantaka, gone to learn the tidings about that, does not come back yet!

VIDU'.—*(Entering suddenly)* Prosperity, prosperity to my dear friend! Friend, my congratulations to you. (*He repeats—The very moment the desideratum was supplied &c.*)

KING—What doubt is there, friend? Incomprehensible is the potency of gems, charms and herbs. Behold—

The enemies of Lord Vishṇu vanished, when in a battle they saw the gem (Kaustubha) in his neck; the serpents live in the nether region, humbled by the power of charms; and in the days of yore the hero Lakshmaṇa, and the monkey-warriors that were struck down by Meghanâda (Indrajit) were restored to life when they inhaled the odour of the great herb, the repository of potent virtue. (5)

Show me the way then, that I too may enjoy the fruit of my eyes by looking at it.

VIDU'.—(*With dignity*) This way, Your Highness.

KING—Lead the way.

(BOTH *walk with pride.*)

VIDU'.—(*Hearing, turning back in fright, and taking hold of the* KING, *in agitation*) O friend, come, let us run away.

KING—What for?

VIDU'.—Some ghost lives in this *Bakula tree.*

KING—Fie upon you, fool; go fearlessly. Whence can there be the possibility of such existing here?

VIDU'.—Oh, here he is speaking in distinct terms. If you do not believe in what I say, then step in front and listen yourself.

KING—(*Doing so and hearing*).

This (speech) has its syllables distinct; it is sweet as is natural from a female; and it is not resonant owing to the smallness of body: so I think it is a Sáriká that is speaking. (6)

(*Looking up and observing carefully*) How now! *it is a Sáriká.*

VIDU'.—(*Looking up*) Ah, strange! it is really a Sárikà. (*Angrily raising his staff*) Ha, you slave's daughter! Did you think that Vasantaka really feared (you)! Wait a moment; so that striking you with this staff, which is as crooked as a wicked man's heart, I will knock you down from this Bakula tree like a ripe Kapittha fruit. (*Prepares to strike*).

KING—(*Preventing him*). Fool, she is saying something pleasant; why do you trouble her then?' Let us just listen.

(*Both listen*).

VIDU'.—(*Having listened*). O friend, did you hear what was said by her? She says—Friend, who is this that is drawn by you here? Friend, God Ananga, now that the Madana festival is being celebrated. She again says—Friend, why have you painted me here? Friend, why do you get angry without cause? As is the God of love painted by you, so is Rati painted by me. So, O you perverter of things, what is the use of your talking in this wise? Tell me at once the whole story! O friend, what can this be?

KING—Friend, I conjecture thus—By some one her heart's darling was painted through love, and concealed before her friend under the guise of (being passed off as) the God of love; and that she too was drawn there by her friend, having cleverly guessed the truth.

VIDU'.—(*With a fillip*) Friend, it is reasonable; it must be so.

KING—Friend, keep quiet, she speaks again.

VIDU'—O, she says—Friend, be not ashamed. Such a jewel of a girl must necessarily have a desire for such a husband. O friend, she who is drawn here must be a maiden worth looking at.

KING—If so let us listen attentively; there is scope for our curiosity here. (*They both listen*).

VIDU'.—Friend, remove these lotus-leaves and the bracelets of the lotus-stalks. Away with those; why do you trouble yourself in vain?

KING—Friend, I heard and knew its import also.

VIDU'.—Friend, do not boast of your skill at interpretation. I will explain everything to you having heard it from her mouth. Let us hear. This Sârikâ, the slave's daughter, yet continues to jabber.

KING—Well said. (*They listen again*).

VIDU'.—O friend, this rascally Śarikà has now begun to chant Ṛiks, like a Bràhmaṇa, knowing the four Vedas,

KING—Friend, tell me; with my mind engaged somewhere else, I did not comprehend what she said.

VIDU'.—O, she says this—Love for a person &c. (See S'loka 1.) (7)

KING—Ah! leaving the great Bráhmaṇa, Vasantaka, who else can know (recognize) such Ṛiks?

VIDU'.—Then, what is this?

KING—Why? it is a Gáthá.

VIDU'.—What do you say? A Gáthá?

KING—This is spoken by some one, in excellent youth, despairing of life, not having obtained her beloved.

VIDU'.—(*Laughing loudly*). Why adopt these circumlocutory speeches! Why don't you say straight—not having obtained *me*. Who else could be concealed under the guise of the flower-weaponed god? (*Claps his hands, and laughs loudly*).

KING—(*Looking up)* Fie, blockhead! Why have you frightened her laughing loudly, so that having flown up she has gone somewhere else.

(BOTH *look for her*).

VIDU′.—(*Observing)* Oh, she has surely gone to the plantain-arbour; come then; let us quickly follow her.

KING—

That which is said before her friends by a love-stricken maiden, suffering irresistible love-torment, the same, repeated by children, parrots and starlings, (unexpectedly) comes within the hearing of fortunate persons only. (8)

VIDU′.—Come, come, your Honour. (*They walk round.*)

VIDU′.—Oh, here is the plantain-arbour. Let us enter. (*Both enter*).

VIDU′.—Oh! That slave-girl has gone away. Let us rest here for a while, sitting on this stone-slab, cool by the plantain-leaves waved by a gentle breeze.

KING—As my friend likes. (BOTH *sit down*)

KING—(*Sighing*) *Repeats,*—That which is said &c. (S′loka 8.)

VIDU′.—(*Looking sideways*) Oh! This must be the Sáriká's cage, with its door thrown open. And this, too, is that picture-board. I will take it up. (*Taking the board and observing with joy*). O friend, fortune favours you!

KING—(*With curiosity)* Friend, what do you mean by this?

VIDU′.—Oh, this is what was said by me—You yourself are delineated here; who else can be concealed under the guise of the flower-weaponed god?

KING—(*Joyfully streching forth his hands*). Show it, friend, show it.

VIDU′.—I will not show you. That maiden, too, is delineated here. What then? Can such a gem of a girl be shown without a reward?

KING—*(Forcibly taking the board while offering his bracelet, and seeing, with wonder.)*

Who is this, committed to painting, outshining Lakshmî by her grace and declaring her great love for me, that enters (captivates) my heart, as a female royal swan enters the Mânasa (lake), agitating the lotuses in her sportive movements, and indicating to us the great flapping of her wings? (9)

Moreover,

Having formed the unique full moon of her face, the Creator must have surely become ill-placed on account of the closing-up of the lotus forming his seat. (10)

(Enter Ságarikà *and* Susangatá.*)*

SUS.—Friend, we have not secured the Sáriká. Let us at least take the picture-board from this plantain-bower and return quickly.

SA'GA.—Friend, let us do so.

(Both move about.)

VIDU'.—Friend, why has this one been painted with her face hung down.

SUS.—*(Hearing)*. Friend, since Vasantaka is speaking, I think Master also must be here. So we shall watch, hidden by the cluster of the plantain trees.

(Both look on.)

KING—Friend, look, look here. (*He repeats—Having formed lhe unique moon &c.*)

SUS.—Friend, fortune smiles upon you. Here is your heart's darling gazing upon you (your picture).

SA'GA.—*(Bashfully)* Friend, why do you lower this personage on account of your jocular disposition?

VIDU'.—*(Shaking the* KING*)*. Here, I say, why has she been drawn with her face hung down?

KING—Why, all has been told by the Sáriká herself.

SUS.—Friend, Medhavinī has shown her power of remembrance.

VIDU'.—O friend, does your eye feel delighted?

SA'GA.—*(With trepidation, to herself)* Thinking as to what he will say now, I really stand between life and death.

KING—Need it be said that it does? See—

My sight, having travelled beyond her pair of thighs with great difficulty and wandered for a long time over her expansive hips, remained fixed on her middle, uneven with the three wave-like folds; and now having eagerly (*lit.* as if it were thirsty) mounted her lofty breasts, it has been wistfully looking again and again at her eyes shedding drops of tears. (11)

SUS.—Friend, have you heard?

SA'GA.—Hear yourself, whose knowledge of (skill at) delineation is thus lauded.

VIDU'.—What is this disregard of even your own self, union with whom even such (beauties) highly esteem, that you do not notice your own self painted by her just here?

KING—*(Closely examining).* Friend, truly I regard myself as highly honoured inasmuch as I have been drawn by her; how shall I not see myself then? See—

This cluster of the particles of her tear-drops, fallen as she was delineating me, looks like the appearance of perspiration on my person caused by the touch of her palm. (12)

SA'GA.—*(To herself)* Cheer up my heart, do cheer up. Even your desire could not have reached such a height.

SUS.—Friend, you alone are worthy of praise by whom even Master is made to speak thus.

VIDU'.—*(Looking to his side).* Friend, here is seen a bed made of juicy lotus leaves and shoots, indicative of the love-sickness of that very girl.

KING—Cleverly marked, friend. For,

This bed of the lotus-leaves, withered on both sides owing to the contact of her stout breasts and hips, green (in the middle), not having come in close touch with her slender waist; and with its arrangement dis-ordered by the tossings and turning of her drooping creeper-like arms, tells of the torment of the slim-bodied one. (13)

Again—

This large lotus-leaf, that had lain on her bosom, does not, by its two circular parts parched by excessive heat, so much indicate her inward love-affection, as it does the expanse of her two breasts. (14)

VIDU'.—(*Acting the picking up of lotus-shoots*). O friend, here is another thing, a string of tender lotus-stalks fading by the heat of her plump breasts.

KING—(*Taking it and placing it on his chest*) Insentient by nature that you are, why do you, O garland of lotus-stalks, undergo pining, being dislodged from between her huge breasts? There is no room there even for a slender fibre of thine; how could there be any for you then? (15)

SUS.—(*To herself*) Oh fie, fie! With his heart tossed about by violent love, Master has begun to speak incoherently even; so it won't be proper to remain indifferent any more. Well, I shall do this. (*Aloud*) Friend, here is before you what you came here for.

SA'GA.—(*Chidingly*) For whom did I come here?

SUS.—(*Laughing*) O you apprehender of something else, I say, for the picture-board. take it then.

SA'GA.—(*Angrily*) I am not clever enough to understand such (enigmatical) speeches of yours. I will, therefore, go elsewhere. (*Wishes to go.*)

SUS.—(*Seizing* Sàgariká *by the hand*) You impatient (or irascible) girl, wait here for a short while till I come back, having taken the picture-board from the plantain-bower.

SA'GA.—Friend, do so.

(Susangatâ *walks towards the plantain-bower*).

VIDU'.—(*Seeing* Susangatà, *in confusion*). O friend, hide the picture-board. Here is the Queen's maid-servant, Susańgatá, coming.

(The King *covers the board with the end of his garment).*

SUS.—(*Advancing*). Victory, victory to your Majesty!

KING—Welcome, Susańgatá. Sit down here.

(Susańgatà *sits down*).

KING.—Susańgatà, how knew you that I was here?

SUS.—(*Smiling*) Sire, not only Your Highness, but the whole affair, together with the picture-board, has been known by me; so I will go and inform the Queen accordingly.

VIDU'.—(*Aside; with alarm*). O friend, everything is possible; this born-slave is a great tattler. So please her with a present.

KING—Properly said by you. (*Taking* SUSAMGATA' *by the hand*) Susangatá, this is merely a joke; you should not annoy the Queen for nothing. Here is a reward for you. (*Offers her the ear-ornament.*)

SUS.—(*Bowing, with a smile*)

Sire, away with fear. (Emboldened) by Your Majesty's favour, I. too, played a joke. So where is the need for the ear-ornament? This will be a high favour on me—My friend Ságariká is angry with me, saying—why am I painted here on this picture-board? So my lord should go there and appease her.

KING—(*Rising in haste*) Where is she, where is she?

SUS.—This way, this way, Your Majesty.

VIDU'.—O, I shall take this picture-board with me It may, perchance, be of use again.

SUS.—Sire, here she is.

(All issue forth from the plantain-bower).

SA'GA.—(*Seeing the* King, *with joy accompanied by nervousness and tremor, to herself)* Alas, pity! On seeing him I am not able to move forward a single step through excessive agitation. What, then, shall I do now (*lit.* in this case)?

VIDU'.—*(On seeing* SA'GARIKA'*).* Oh, bless me! What wonder! Such grace of form is not to be seen in the world of mortals. Methinks even the Creator must have been struck with wonder on creating it.

KING—Friend, I, too, have this in my mind—

Surely, by the Creator, overpowered by wonder at having created this beauty, the ornament of the three worlds, his eyes, surpassing in beauty the petals of his own lotus, were extended the more; the exclamations—Excellent, Excellent—must have been uttered simultaneously with all the four mouths, and the heads nodded (in satisfaction). (16)

SA'GA.—*(Looking reprovingly at* SUSAMGATA' *).* Such is the picture-board you have brought. *(Goes).*

KING—

Though you cast this glance (eyes) in anger, O passionate one, yet, it being naturally affectionate, will not assume harshness; go, giving up haste; your heavy hips will cause pain to you by the stumblings of your feet. (17)

SUS.—Master, this one is, indeed, greatly irascible; so pacify her by taking her by the hand.

KING—*(With joy).* As your ladyship says. *(Takes* SA'GARIKA' *by the hand and gesticulates the pleasure of touch.)*

VIDU'.—Oh, this, indeed, is Śrî, in a new form that you have obtained.

KING—Friend, it is true.

This is S'rî, and her arm, too, is the shoot of the Pârijâta; how else exudes this flow of ambrosia in the guise of perspiration? (18)

SUS.—You are extremly hard-hearted, dear, since you do not give up your anger though thus held by the hand by His Majesty.

SA'GA.—(*Knitting her eyebrows*) Ah, Susaṅgatá, you do not still desist!

KING—Be pleased, dear; such persistence of anger towards a friend is, indeed, not proper.

VIDU'.—This is, indeed, another queen, Vásavadattâ (Here is another, Queen Vásavadattâ).

(*The* KING *lets go* SA'GARIKA''S *hand in fright*).

SA'GA.—(*In flurry*) Susamgata', what shall I do now?

SUS.—Friend, hidden by this avenue of the *tamàla* trees, we shall depart. (*Exeunt*).

KING—(*Looking towards the sides*) Friend, where is that Queen Vâsavatdattâ?

VIDU'.—Oh! I do not know where she is. I said she (Sâga.) was another queen Va'savadattâ, owing to her cherishing anger for a long time.

KING—Fie upon you, fool,

That my beloved, somehow found by good luck, like a necklace of gems, with Râga (love, brilliancy) manifest, was made to fall off from my hand by you, even before she was taken to the neck (she was embraced, it was placed round). (19)

(Then *enter* VA'SAVADATTA' *and* Kâñchanamâla'.)

VA'SAV.—Maid Kâñchanamâla, how far yet is that Navamàliká received into his favour by my husband?

KA'NCH.—Mistress, it is, indeed, seen beyond this Banian—bower.

VA'SA.—Then lead the way.

KA'NCH.—This way, this way, Mistress.

KING—Friend, where can I see my beloved?

KA'NCH.—Mistress, as Master is talking near at hand, I think he has been waiting for Your Highness. So let my mistress approach.

VA'SAVA.—(*Advancing*). Pròsperity, prosperity, to my husband!

KING—(*Aside*). Friend, conceal the picture-board.

(VIDU'SHAKA *places the board under his armpit and conceals it with his upper garment)* ?

VA'SAVA.—My lord, has the Navamáliká blossomed!

KING—My Queen, though we came here first we did not see it, as you delayed. Come, then; let us see it together.

VA'SAVA.—*(Marking closely)*; My husband, from the very expression of your face I have known that the Navamâlikâ has flowered. So I will not go now.

VIDU'.—Holla! Ho! We have won!

(Stretches forth his hands and dances; while dancing the board falls down from his arm-pit).

KING—*(Aside; threatens* VIDU'. *with the finger).*

VIDU'.—*(Aside)* Ho, do not be angry; sit quiet. I will see to that.

KA'NCH.—*(Taking up the board, eyeing it, aside).* Mistress, just mark what is drawn here on the picture-board.

VA'SAVA.—(*Marking it, aside*) Kâñchanamàlà, this is my husband; and this again is Sàgariká. What can this be?

KA'NCH.—My mistress, I too was thinking of the same.

VA'SAVA.—(*With an angry smile*) My husband, who has drawn this?

KING—(*With a smile of embarrassment; aside*), Friend, what shall I say?

VIDU'.—(*Aside*). Oh, do not be anxious; I will give a reply. (*Aloud*, to VA'SAVADATTA') Madam, do not think it otherwise. On hearing my remark that one's own self is painted with difficulty, my friend thus displayed his skill in drawing.

KING—It is just as Vasantaka has said it.

VA'SAVA.—(*Pointing at the board*). My husband, and this other one that is drawn near you—is that the noble Vasantaka's skill ?

KING—(*Smiling*) Enough of misunderstanding, my Queen. This is some girl, drawn after being conceived by my own imagination, but never seen before.

VIDU'.—My lady, this is true; quite true. I swear by my sacred thread, if one like this was ever seen by us before.

KA'NCH.—*(Aside)* Mistress, such accidental resemblance is sometimes quite possible.

VA'SAVA.—*(Aside)* You simpleton, this is, indeed, Vasantaka; you do not understand his prevarications. *(Aloud)* My lord, I for myself have got headache while looking steadfastly at the board. So I will go. *(Departs)*.

KING—*(Taking her by the skirt of her garment)*.

Queen, should I say—'Be pacified', it would not suit as there is no anger (displayed); to say that I shall not do so again would be an admission (of a fault); if I say 'there is no fault on my part', you will know it to be false: so dearest, I do not know what would be proper to say in this case. (20)

VA'SAVA.—(*Respectfully pulling off the skirt of her garment)* My dear, do not take it otherwise. Headache has been really troubling me; so I will depart. (*Exeunt* BOTH.)

VIDU'.—*(Looking about himself*). Oh, fortune favours you! The untimely hurricane has passed, leaving us unharmed.

KING—Nonsense, blockhead! Away with gratification! The Queen's persistent anger, concealed by her, when passing, through high-breeding, was not marked by you.

Through power of self-control, though there was sudden knitting of the eye-brows, the face was hung down very low; she directed a gentle piercing smile at me but no harsh words were uttered; the eyes, though rendered dull by the tears gathered within, were not opened wide: (thus) by my darling, anger was manifested and yet propriety was not given up discarded. (21)

Come, then, let us go to propitiate the Queen herself. *(Exeunt omnes.)*

(End of Act II, styled 'the Plantain-Bower.')

ACT III.

(Enter MADANIKA'*).*

MADANIKA'—*(In the air)* Kauśâmbikâ, O Kauśâmbikâ, did you see Kâñchanamâlâ with Master or not? *(Listening)* What say you? 'She came and went away a long time since?' Well, where then can I find her? *(Looking in front)* How now? Here is Kâñchanamâlâ, coming this very way. I will then approach her.

(Then enter KA'NCHANAMA'LA'*).*

KA'NCH.—*(Sarcastically)* Bravo, minister Vasantaka, bravo! By this your attention to (planning of) union and discord you have surpassed even his Excellency Yaugandharâyaṇa.

MADANIKA'—*(Approaching, with a smile)* Dear Kâñchanamâlâ, what is done by the noble Vasantaka that he is thus extolled?

KA'NCHAN.—Friend Madanikà, what are you to gain by asking this question? You will not be able to keep the secret.

MADANIKA'—I swear by the feet of the Queen, if I disclose it before any one.

KA'NCHAN.—If so, then listen. To-day while coming back from the royal palace, I overheard Vasantaka's conversation with Susaṃgatâ.

MADA.—*(With curiosity)* Friend, of what sort?

KA'NCHAN.—Thus–Susaṅgatâ, excepting Sâgarikâ, there is no other cause of my friend's indisposition; therefore, think out some remedy for this.

MADA.—What did Susañgatâ say to that?

KA'NCHN.—This was said by her—To-day, indeed, I shall take Sâgarikâ with me, apparelled as the Mistress with the dress which was presented to me by the Queen, as she placed Sâgarikâ under my charge, her suspicion being roused by the incident of the picture-board, and myself, dressed as Kâñchanamâlà, will come here at dusk. You too shall wait for me just here, at the entrance to the picture-hall. Then the meeting of Master with her will take place in the Màdhavî bower.

MADA.—(*Angrily*) Susaṃgatá, condemned are you that thus deceive the Queen, who is, indeed, so kind to her attendants.

KA'NCHA.—Friend, whither have you set out now?

MADA.—I was sent to look for you by the Queen, getting anxious as you delayed, having gone to learn the tidings about the well-being of Master, who was bodily indisposed.

KA'NCH.—Very simple-minded now must be the Queen who has such a belief. Here is Master sitting in the balcony with the ivory-gate, concealing his love-sickness under the guise of indisposition. Come, then; let us communicate this news to our mistress.

(*Exeunt both*)

(*End of Praveśaka*)

(*Then enter the* KING *seated, gesticulating love-sickness.*)

KING—(*Sighing*)

Endure now, my heart, the fever caused by the fire of love; it cannot at all be allayed: why do you then pine for her in vain? Since by me, a fool that I was, her hand which was then somehow obtained and the touch of which was like that of thick sandal-paste, was not seized and put on you for a long time. (1)

Oh, a great wonder!

Mind, by nature, is unsteady and difficult to be hit; and yet how is it that the same of me has been equally pierced with all his arrows by Káma? (2)

(Looking heavenwards) O god of flowery bow,

The arrows of the mind-born god are fixed as five; and of them thousands of men, mostly of my type, form the mark—this that has got currency in the world is now seen to be the reverse in your case; for this body of lovers, pierced with innumerable arrows and helpless, has been reduced to the state of five (death). (3)

(Reflecting) I do not so much think of myself, reduced to a state of this sort, as of that poor Sāgarikā, come within the range of the sight of the Queen, whose vehemence of anger was suppressed within. For,

She turns away her face from all, feeling that she is known; seeing two persons conversing, she considers the talk as relating to herself; and when her companions smile, she manifests the greater confusion: thus my beloved is mostly disconsolate owing to anxiety cherished at heart. (4).

How does Vasantaka, sent to learn the news about her, delay?

(Then enter VASANTAKA *in high spirits.)*

VIDU'.—*(With satisfaction).* Ho, ho! Such entire satisfaction was not felt by my dear friend even on the acquisition of the kingdom of Kauśāmbī as I think he will feel to-day on hearing the agreeable news from me. I will then go to my dear friend and communicate it to him. (*Walking round and looking*) How now? This my dear friend is sitting, looking in this very direction; so I think he is waiting just for me. I will, then, approach him. (*Advancing*) Victory, victory, to my dear friend! O friend, I congratulate you on the more-than-expected success of your business.

KING—*(With joy)* Friend, is my darling all safe?

VIDU'.—*(With pride)* Oh, before long you will know it on seeing her yourself.

KING—*(With satisfaction)* Friend, will there be also a meeting with my beloved?

VIDU'.—*(With self-conceit)* Why should there not be, when I, who laugh at the intellectual powers of Bṛihaspati, am your counsellor?

KING—*(Smiling)* Not at all strange. What is not possible in your case? So tell it; I wish to hear in detail.

VIDU'.—*(Whispers in the ear)* Thus, thus.

KING—*(With joy)* Bravo, friend, bravo! Here is your reward. *(Taking off a bracelet from his hand presents it)*,

VIDU'.—*(Putting on the bracelet and looking at himself).* Oh, I will go and show my wife this my hand decked with the bracelet of pure gold.

KING—*(Restraining him by holding the hand)* Friend, you will show it afterwards. First ascertain how much of the day now remains.

VIDU'.—*(Observing)* Mark, O, Mark! The Lord of thousand rays (Sun), having as it were an appointment made to him by his bride, the eve, is proceeding, with his heart swayed by deep love, towards a wood on the top of the setting mountain.

KING—*(Marking with delight).* Well observed; friend! The day has drawn to its close. For,

With a heavy load of anxiety laid on his mind, at the thought that his one-wheeled car will not be able to come up again in the morning after having traversed the road (distance) long on account of the circuit of the world, this Sun, stationed on the Setting Mountain, has drawn off and is carrying away, as it were, the wheel of the directions, the array of the golden spokes of which is clearly seen in the form of the circle of the remnants of his own rays swallowed up by dusk. (5)

Moreover,

I am gone, O lotus-eyed one; this is my time (to depart); gone to sleep you are to be roused by me alone: thus does this Sun, with his rays focussed on the peak of the Setting Mountain (his hands placed on the drooping head) offer consolation to the lotus-plant. (6)

So get up; let us go to the very Mâdhavî creeper and await the time of the appointment of the dearest one.

VIDU'.—Oh, well spoken. (*Both rise*).

VIDU'.—(*Observing*) O friend, mark, mark. This mass of darkness that has extended (so as to appear connected-thickened) the thinly-spread rows of woods, and has the dark hue of the stout wild boars and bisons covered with deep mud, is moving onwards covering up the eastern direction.

KING—(*Looking about*) Friend, well observed; for,

This mass of darkness that steals (possesses) the hue of S'iva's neck first envelops the east and then the other quarters also; advancing, it obscures in succession mountains trees and the different parts of the town; thereafter acquiring thickness it deprives the fruit (use) of eyes. (7)

Show me the way, then.

VIDU'.—This, way come this way, dear friend. (*They walk round*).

VIDU'.—(*Observing carefully*) Friend, here at hand is the Makaranda garden, having, as it were, darkness rolled into a mass in it, on account of the trees and creepers, with their thick foliage closely interwoven. How then can the way be noticed here?

KING—(*Smelling the fragrance*) Friend, go ahead; the path here is surely very well known. For,

This is certainly the row of the Champaka trees; this is that beautiful Sinduvâra; so also here is the dense avenue of the Bakula trees, and this is the line of Páṭalà plants: thus in this garden the path, though obscured by the doubly dense darkness, becomes manifest by means of the signs of trees (as they become) revealed by severally inhaling their varied odour. (8)

(*They walk on*)

VIDU'.—Oh, here we are arrived at the bower of the Màdhavî creepers, to which the infatuated bees are flocking, which has scented the ten directions with its highly gratifying fragrance, and which is indicated by the ease experienced by the feet as they tread on the pavement of the polished emerald slabs. Your

Honour then should wait just here, while I come back quickly taking with me Sâgariká wearing the apparel of the Queen.

KING—Friend, make haste then, make haste.

VIDU'.—Oh, do not be impatient. Here I come back. *(Exit).*

KING—In the meantime I too shall sit on the dais formed of the emerald slabs and await the time of my darling's appointment. *(Sitting down and musing)* Oh, strange is the predilection for his new love of an amorous person, disregarding union with his own wife. For,

Full of fear she does not cast a glance bright with love on (her lover's) face * * *; and though held with effort she repeatedly says that she would go away : and yet an amorous girl that has been present at the rendezvous delights all the more. (9)

Ah, how does Vasantaka tarry ! What then? Has the matter been known by the Queen?

(Then enter VA'SAVADATTA' *and* KA'NCHANAMA'LA'*).*

VA'SAVA.—Káñchanamálà, is Ságariká really going to meet my husband, in my dress?

KA'NCHA.—How can Mistress be informed falsely? Or why, Vasantaka himself, waiting at the door of the picture-hall, will carry conviction to Your Highness.

VA'SAVA.—Thither then do we go.

KA'NCHA.—Come, come, my mistress. *(Both walk forth).*

(Enter VASANTAKA *covered with a veil).*

VIDU'.—*(Listening attentively)* Since the sound of foot-steps is heard at the door of the picture-hall, I think Sâgarikâ has come.

KA'NCHA.—Mistress, this is the picture-hall. I will then make a sign to Vasantaka. *(Snaps her finger).*

VIDU'.—*(Joyfully approaching, with a smile)* Susangatá, you have very well put on Kâñchanamâlâ's disguise. Now, where is Sâgarikâ?

KA'NCHA.—*(Pointing with the finger)* Why, this, here.

VIDU'.—*(Looking with wonder)* This is evidently Queen Vâsavadattâ herself!

VA'SAVA.—*(With apprehension, to herself)* What, am I known?

VIDU'.—*(Snaps his fingers)* Lady Sâgarikâ, come this way. (VA'SAVADATTA' *smiles and looks at* KA'NCHANAMA'LA').

KA'NCHA.—*(Aside, threatening with her finger)* Cursed one, you will have to remember these words of thine.

VIDU'.—Hasten, let Sâgarikâ hasten—Here, indeed, is rising from the eastern quarter, the divine moon. *(Walks about.)*

KING—Why does my mind feel such ardent longing when union with my beloved is at hand? Or rather,

The fierce heat of love does not cause so much burning at the beginning, as it does when (its object is) near; in the rainy season, the day oppresses the most when the downpour of water is at hand. (10)

VIDU'.—*(Directing his ear)* Lady Sâgarikâ, here is my dear friend speaking in a manner full of anxious thoughts with reference to your own self. I will, therefore, inform him of your arrival.

VA'SAVA.—*(Nods assent.)*

VIDU'.—*(Approaching the* KING*)* Friend, fortune smiles upon you. Here, indeed, have I brought Sâgarikâ.

KING—*(Rising hastily, in joy)* Friend, where is she? Oh, where?

VIDU'.—Why, here.

KING—*(Approaching)* My darling, Sàgarikâ,

Your face is the moon; your eyes are (but) two (blue) lotuses; your hands imitate the day-lotuses; your pair of thighs are like plantain-stocks and your arms bear resemblance to lotus-shoots; O you, all of whose limbs are thus delight-giving, come, come, and having quickly and without hesitation embraced me soothe my limbs languid on account of the fever of love. (11)

VA'SAVA.—*(With tears, aside)* Kâñchanamâlâ, my husband, having uttered such words, will again address me, this, Oh, is a wonder.

KA'NCHA.—*(Aside)* Mistress, it is certainly so. But what cannot be expected from adventurous men?

VIDU'.—Lady Sâgarikâ, be quite easy of mind and talk with my dear friend. Even now his ears are grated with the harsh words of the ever-irate Queen Vâsavadattâ; let the sweet cadence of your words regale them now.

VA'SAVA.—*(Aside, angrily)* Kâñchanamàlâ, I am thus harsh-tongued; worthy Vasantaka, again, is a sweet-speaker.

KA'NCHA.—*(Aside)* Cursed one, you will have to remember these words.

VIDU'.—*(Observing)* Friend, look, look. Here has risen the divine moon, lighting up the east and looking (reddish) like the cheek of an angry woman.

KING—Dear Sàgarikà, behold—

The lord of night, with the all-in-all of his brilliance robbed by your face, having ascended the mountain's peak now stands confronting you, with hands (rays) stretched up, as if to retaliate. (12)

Again, by him, rising, his natural dull-headedness is shown. For,

Does not the moon of your face cause to fade (eclipse) the beauty of the lotus; does it not bring delight to the eyes; or does it not by its mere appearance cause the fish-bannered (god of love—the sea) to swell?—that, notwithstanding its presence, this other moon has risen? If there be pride on account of (the presence of) nectar, that too is here in the Bimba-like lower lip. (13)

VA'SAVA.—*(Casting off the veil, angrily)* My husband, I am truly Sàgariká. But you, with your heart entirely taken up by Sâgariká, see everything as consisting of Ságarikâ,

KING—*(With confusion, aside)* How now? This is Queen Vàsavadattá. Friend, what means this?

VIDU'.—*(With despair)* What else, friend? Our life is jeopardized.

KING—*(Sitiing down and joining the hollowed palms)* Dear Vásavadattà, be pleased, be pleased.

VA'SAVA.—*(Turning towards him and stretching forth her hands, with suppressed tears)* My husband, say not so: these words are transferred to another.

VIDU'.—*(To himself)* What shall I do in this case? Well, I shall say this.—*(Aloud)* Madam, you are magnanimous, indeed. So let this one fault of my dear friend be forgiven.

VA'SAVA.—Noble Vasantaka, rather I myself have been guilty towards him, interposing an obstacle in his first meeting.

KING—Queen, with my offence thus clearly seen, what shall I say? Still I submit—

Here shall I, full of shame, O Queen, wipe off with my head the reddish tint of your feet caused by red lac; but that caused by the eclipse-like anger on the moon of your face I shall be able to remove only if compassion be shown to me. (14)

(Falls at her feet)

VA'SAVA.—*(Preventing him with her hand)* Rise, my husband, rise. Shameless, indeed, must be the person, who on knowing my husband's heart to be such, again becomes angry. Let then my husband be in the enjoyment of happiness. I will go.

(Wishes to go).

KA'NCHANA.—Mistress, be favourably disposed. Going away, leaving the great King thus fallen at the feet, Your Highness is sure to feel remorse.

VA'SAVA.—Away, you silly girl. Where is the reason either for favour or remorse in this case? So come away, let us go.

KING—Relent, my Queen, do relent.

(*He repeats*—I shall wipe off the reddish tint &c.)

VIDU'.—Get up, ho! The Queen has gone away; why do you cry in the wilderness then?

KING—(*Raising his head and seeing*) How is it that the Queen has gone even without showing favour?

VIDU'.—How has she not shown favour, when we stand yet with our persons uninjured (all safe)?

KING—Fie upon you, idiot! Why do you make fun of me thus? It is rather the result of your action that this great mishap has befallen us. For,

Our attachment has developed from day to day owing to the feeling of love being (mutually) highly esteemed. So seeing this slip on my part, never committed before, that intolerant darling of me will surely give up life to-day; for, a blundering, when love reaches its climax, becomes intolerable. (15)

VIDU'.—Oh, I do not konw what the Queen being angry will do; but Sâgarikâ I can guess will live a hard life.

KING.—Friend, I too think so. Alas, my dear Sagarikâ!

(*Then enter* SA'GARIKA' wearing the dress of VA'SAVADATTA').

SA'GAR.—(*Dejectedly*) Luckily, I have not been noticed by any one while coming out of the picture-hall, with the dress of the Queen put on. What shall I then do now (*Reflects tearfully*).

VIDU'.—Oh, why do you stand like one bewildered? Think of some remedy for this.

KING—Why, it is just the same that I am thinking about. Friend, I see no other remedy in this case save the Queen's propitiation. Come then, thither let us go.

(*They Walk forth*).

SA'GARIKA'—*(Musing)* Better I should cease to exist (die) by hanging myself up, than be disgraced by the Queen on coming to know about our engagement-affair. I will then go to the Aśoka tree and do as desired.

VIDU'.—*(Listening)* Stay, Oh, stay, for a while; the sound of footsteps is heard. I think the Queen, feeling repentant, might be coming.

KING—Friend, the Queen is, indeed, noble-minded; perchance it may be so also. So ascertain it.

VIDU'.—As Your Honour commands. *(He walks round).*

SA'GAR.—*(Advancing)* I will then make a noose of the Màdhavî creeper, and hanging myself from the Aśoka tree, will kill myself. *(Prepares a noose with the creeper).* Alas father, ho mother, here I, an unlucky creature, forlorn and helpless, die. *(With these words throws the noose round her neck).*

VIDU'.—*(Looking)* But who again can this be? How now? It is Queen Vásavadattâ! *(In alarm; aloud)* Save, save, O friend! Here is Queen Vásavadattà killing herself by hanging.

KING—*(Advancing, in great haste)* Where is she, where is she?

VIDU'.—Oh, here!

KING—*(Approaching and removing the noose from the neck)* O you acting rashly, why is this foul deed being done?

The noose being round your neck my life has come up to my throat (as it were); so this my attempt is (rather) in self-interest; give up this adventure, my darling. (16)

SA'GA.—*(Seeing the* KING*)* Ah! How now! It is the Master. *(Joyfully to herself).* Truly speaking, love of life (*lit.*, desire to live) has again sprung up in me on beholding him. Or rather, gazing on him and having become happy thereby. I shall quit life with quite an easy heart.

(Aloud) Leave me; let my lord leave me. This person is, indeed, in the power of another and will not get such an opportunity again to die.

(Wishes to throw the noose round her neck again.)

KING—*(Observing closely, with joy to himself)* How now! It is my darling Ságariká! *(Removing the noose from her neck)*.

Away, away with this extremely desperate act of thine; do then throw away quickly, this creeper-noose: for a moment, O mistress of my life, twine the noose of thy arms round my neck to stay my life though set out (to go). (17)

(Pulling her arm, throwing it round his neck and gesticulating the thrill of touch) Friend, this is a shower without (the presence of) clouds!

VIDU'.—Oh, it is just so, if Queen Vàsavadattâ does not come acting the part of an untimely gale.
(Then enter VA'SAVADATTA' *and* KA'NCHANAMA'LA'*)*.

VA'SAVADATTA'—Maid Kánchanamálâ, I acted very cruelly in coming away after having slighted my husband fallen at my feet in that manner. So, I will now go personally and conciliate my husband.

KA'NCH.—Who else but the Queen knows to speak in this way? Better be the King a bad person, but not the Queen. Let Your Hignness come then.

(They walk round).

KING—O you simple one, why am I even now foiled in my object by (such) indifference?

KA'NCH.—*(Listening)* Mistress, since Master is talking near at hand, I guess he is coming just to pacify you.

VA'SAVA.—*(Joyfully)* If so, I will go unobserved from behind and casting my arms round his neck will please him.

VIDU'.—Lady Ságarikâ, have an easy mind and talk with my dear friend.

VA'SAV.—*(Hearing with sorrow)* Káñchanamàlà, how is it that Sâgariká has come here? So I will listen and then advance. *(She does accordingly.)*

SA'GA.—My lord, why are you, with this false courtesy, making yourself guilty towards the Queen who is dearer (to you) than even life?

KING—O you, you are certainly the speaker of what is not true. For,

I quaked when the pair of her breasts throbbed through hard breathing; when she observed silence, I addressed sweet words; and when her face had its eye-brows bent (through anger) I fell prostrate at her feet in that way: thus all that was service on my part due to the Queen's inborn nobility of mind (and nothing more); but what is (true) love, which has its flavour heightened by steady affection—that I have for *you* (alone). (18)

VA'SAVA.—*(Advancing at once)* My husband, this is worthy of you; it befits you!

KING—*(Seeing; with confusion)* My Queen, it is not proper for you to blame me without cause. Misled by the resemblance of dress, we thought her to be yourself and came here.

VA'SAVA.—*(In anger)* Rise, my lord, rise. Why should you suffer trouble even now owing to the service of one naturally high-born?

KING—*(To himself)* What? is this also over-heard by the Queen? Then I have no hope whatsoever as regards the Queen's pacification. *(Remains with face hung down).*

VIDU'.—Madam, wrongly led to believe, by the similarity of dress, that you were destroying yourself by hanging, I brought my dear friend here. If you do not believe what I say, then see this creeper-noose (*Shows the creeper-noose*).

VA'SAVA.—*(Angrily)* Kâñchanamâlà, secure this Brâhmaṇa by binding him with this very creeper-noose; and place this ill-bred girl in the front.

KA'NCHA.—As the Queen commands. *(Fettering* VIDU'. *with the creeper-noose)* Hapless man, experience now the fruit of your own evil plan. Sâgarikâ, do you also step forward.

SA'GAR.—*(To herself)* Oh, fie; meritless that I am, I was not able to die even as I wished.

VIDU'.—*(Despairingly looking at the* KING*)* O friend. remember me—a helpless person—subject to misery owing to the Queen's captivity.

(Exit VA'SAVADATTA', *accompanied by all).*

KING—*(Sorrowfully)* Alas! Oh! Pity!

Shall I think of that face of the Queen robbed of its affectionate smile by long-cherished rage; or of Ságarikà frightened by being rebuked with intense (*lit.*, highly developed) wrath; or of Vâsantaka, bound and led away from here? Thus subjected to pain of every form, I do not experience ease even for a moment. (19)

What is the use of my staying here, then! In I will enter then to propitiate the Queen.

(Exuent Omnes).

END OF ACT III, STYLED "SAMKETA".

ACT IV.

(Enter SUSANGATA' *in tears, with a necklace of jewels).*

SUS.—*(Heaving a sigh, piteously)* Alas, dear friend Sâgariká! O bashful one, O you of noble disposition, O you so loving to your friends, O you of gentle aspect! Where can I see you now? *(Weeps; looking up and sighing)* Ah cursed fate, relentless, if one like that, of uncommon beauty and splendour, was created by you, why was she then reduced to such a change of condition? This necklace of jewels was placed in my hands by her, despairing of life, saying—'Give it to some Bràhmana'. I will then look out for a Bràhmana.

(Going round and looking) **Ah, here, indeed, is noble Vasantaka coming this very way. To him then I will give this.**

(Then enter the delighted VASANTAKA).

VAS.—Holla, holla, ho! To-day, indeed, I was set free by Her Majesty, appeased by my friend, and my belly well filled with *modakas* by her with her own hands. I will then go and see my dear friend. *(Walks round).*

SUS.—*(Advancing suddenly; weeping)* Noble Vasantaka, just stay a moment.

VAS.—*(Seeing)* Ah, Susañgatá! Susañgatá, why do you weep? Nothing disastrous, I hope, has befallen Ságarikà?

SUS.—Just *that* I am going to relate. That poor girl, indeed, was, at the approach of mid-night, transported, nobody knows where, by the Queen, having got a report circulated that she was to be taken to Ujjayinî.

VIDU'.—*(With pain)* A very cruel thing, indeed, was done by the Queen?

SUS.—And this jewel-necklace was delivered into my hands by her, despairing of life, saying—Give this to the noble Vasantaka. So let the noble one accept this.

VIDU'.—*(Weeping)* Lady, under such circumstances my hands do not proceed to receive it. *(Both weep).*

SUSAN.—*(Joining her palms)* Your noble self should accept it just favouring her.

VIDU'.—*(Musing)* Or bring it; so that with this itself I will divert my friend, grieved at the separation of Sâgarikâ.

SUS.—*(Presents it).*

VIDU'.—*(Taking it and examining it with wonder)* Susangatà, but whence could she come to possess such an ornament?

SUS.—Noble one, she was asked by me also (about that) through curiosity.

VIDU'.—What did she say then?

SUS.—Then she looked upwards, heaved a long sigh and saying 'Susangatà, what have you to do with this tale?' began to weep.

VIDU'.—Surely the ornament itself, which is out of the reach of ordinary persons, tells that she is, in every way, of high pedigree. Susangatá, where is my friend now?

SUS.—Noble one, having left the Queen's palace, Master has just now gone to the crystal-bower. Let Your Honour go then. I too will be by the side of the Queen.

VIDU'.—Just so. *(Exeunt* BOTH.*)*

End of the PRAVES'AKA.

(Then enter the KING *seated).*

KING—*(Reflecting)*

Not indeed, by equivocal oaths, by endearing words, by ministering to her desire all the more, by the (manifestation of) great sense of shame, by prostrations at her feet, and by the constant exhortations of her friends, did the Queen return to herself (her usual genial disposition) as she did, when by her, weeping, anger was removed, of her own motion, having washed it off, as it were, with the waters of her tears. (1)

(Sighing anxiously) Now that the Queen has been pleased, concern for Ságariká only troubles me. For,

That my darling, with a frame as delicate as the interior of a lotus, having melted away in that way at the first embrace at the neck, firm on account of the first fervour of passion, has entered my heart, I think, through the passages of the holes made by the shafts of Madana, falling the very moment. (2)

(Reflecting) Even that Vasantaka, who was the object of my confidence, he, too, has been imprisoned by the Queen. Before whom, then, shall I shed tears? *(Sighs).*

(Enter VASANTAKA*)*.

VIDU'.—*(Seeing the* KING *)* This my dear friend, bearing a body with commendable beauty though emaciated on account of excessive longing, appears, indeed, all the more splendid, like the second day-moon (in the bright half) risen. I will then approach him. *(Approaching)* Bliss to your Honour! Luckily are you seen again with these eyes by me though fallen into the Queen's hands.

KING—*(Seeing with joy)* Hey! Vasantaka comes! Embrace me, friend.

VIDU'.—*(Embraces him)*.

KING—Friend, by your dress itself is declared the Queen's favour unto you. Tell me, then, what the news is about Ságarikà.

VIDU'.—*(Stands confused with face downcast)*.

KING.—Friend, why don't you tell?

VIDU'.—I am not able to tell you what is unpleasant.

KING—*(With anguish)* Friend, how do you say, unpleasant? Clearly she has quitted life. Alas! my dear Ságarikà. *(He faints)*.

VIDU'.—*(With alarm)* Revive; revive, my friend.

KING—*(Having revived; with tears)*.

Life, quit me who am exceedingly ungenerous; O you, be courteous, and act according to my words: If you do not depart at once, then you are certainly robbed; for that one with an elephant's gait has gone very far now. (3)

VIDU'.—Friend, do not take it otherwise. The poor girl, it is rumoured, has been sent to Ujjayinî by the Queen. Hence I said it was unpleasant.

KING—How! Sent to Ujjayinî. Oh! The Queen's absence of regard for me! Friend, who told you this?

VIDU'.—*(Sighing, with tears)* Susañgatâ. And more; this necklace was sent by her my hands, with some object in view.

KING—What else; to console me. So bring it, friend.

VIDU'.—(*Presents it*).

KING—(*Taking the necklace, closely observing it and placing it on his bosom*) Alas!

By this (necklace) fallen off after having obtained the embrace of her neck, this similarly-circumstanced body of mine is comforted, like a friend. (4)

Friend, you put this on; so that beholding it I shall sustain myself (*lit.*, take courage).

VIDU'.—As Your Honour commands. (*Wears it*).

KING—(*Shedding tears*) Friend, the sight of my friend is difficult to obtain again.

VIDU'.—(*Looking in the quarters; in alarm*) Friend, speak not thus loudly. Perchance some one, connected with the Queen, may be passing about here.

(*Enter* VASUNDHARA' *with a cane-staff in her hand*).

VASUNDHARA'—(*Advancing*) Prosperity, prosperity, to Your Majesty! My lord, here, indeed, is Vijayavarman, Rumanvat's sister's son, waiting at the door, wishing to communicate some pleasant news.

KING—Vasundhará, usher him in without delay.

DOOR-KEEPER—As Your Majesty commands. (*Departing and entering again with* VIJAYAVARMAN) Vijayavarman, here, indeed, is Master; let Your Honour approach.

VIJAYA.—(*Having approached*) Prosperity, prosperity to Your Majesty! My Lord, congratulations to you on the victory obtained by Rumanvat.

KING—Commendable, Rumanvat, commendable! In a short time you have achieved a great end. Vijayavarman, sit down here.

VIJAYA.—(*Sits down*).

KING—Vijayavarman, is the King of the Kosalas vanquished.

VIJAY.—By Your Majesty's prowess.

KING.—Vijayavarman, then tell me, how it was. I wish to hear the full details.

VIJAYA.—My lord, listen—At Your Majesty's command we started from here with a large army, irresistible on account of the numerous elephants, horses and foot-soldiers, and going in a few days we began to encamp our battalions, having blocked up the outward passage of the King of the Kosalas stationed in a fort on the mountain Vindhya.

KING—What next?

VIJAYA.—Then the Kosala—King also, unable to bear the affront through pride, put into battle-array the whole of his army, mostly consisting of elephants.

VIDU'.—Finish (*lit.*, narrate) quickly, Oh, my heart trembles, as it were.

KING—And after that?

VIJA.—My lord, and he, whose resolution was formed,

Having issued forth for giving battle from the Vindhya mountain faced (us), blocking up, the very moment, the divisions of the quarters with the close and compact array of his army of lordly elephants, as if with another Vindhya mountain; Rumanvat, whose foot-soldiers were crushed by the arrays of elephants in rut, falling on him, rapidly discharging arrows, encountered him in an instant, his ardour being doubled by the obtainment of what was desired. (5)

And,

As the battle began, in which heads were severed by the strokes of weapons, their helmets being tossed off by missiles, wherein there swelled a momentary river of blood, and in which weapons clanged and fire flashed forth from armours, the King of the Kosalas, seated on a powerful (*lit.*, intoxicated) elephant was challenged, as he was keeping off his army from a break-down, and slain by Rumaṇvat, single-handed, with hundreds of arrows. (6)

VIDU'.—Prosperity, prosperity. to Your Honour. We have triumphed. *(With these words he rises and dances).*

KING—Bravo! Lord of the Kosalas, bravo! Even the death of you is commendable, whose prowess even enemies thus extol. What next?

VIJAY.—My lord, then Rumaṇvat too, posted my elder brother, Jayavarman, over the Kosala country and is himself now coming with slow marches, leading the whole of his army wounded in the fight.

KING—Vasundharà, tell Yaugandharàyaṇa that my favour be bestowed on this person.

VASUN.—As Your Majesty commands.

(Exit with VIJAYAVARMAN*).*

(Enter KA'NCHANAMA'LA'*).*

KA'NCHA.—I am ordered by the Queen thus—Maid Káñchanamàlâ, go you and present this magician to my husband. *(Walking about and looking on)* Here, indeed, is the master. I will then approach. *(Advancing)* Victory, victory, to the Lord! The Queen requests—Here is a magician, named Sarvasiddhi. come from Ujjayinî. May my husband, therefore, see him.

KING—I take pleasure in magic: quickly bring him in, then.

KA'NCH.—As Your Majesty commands. *(Exit and re-enter, accompanied by the Magician. with a bunch of peacock's feathers in his hand).*

MAGICIAN—*(Waving the bunch of feathers).*

Bow to the feet of Indra, whose name is closely associated with (the art of) magic, as also of Saṁbara. whose fame is well established in magic. (7)

KA'NCH.—*(Advancing)* Sire, here is the magician.

MAGICIAN—Prosperity, prosperity, to Your Majesty! My lord,

Should the moon be exhibited on earth, or a mountain in the sky, or fire in the ocean, or dusk at noon? Give the command. (8)

Or, why waste many words!

This is my solemn assertion.—Through power of my preceptor's incantations, I will show whatever you desire at heart to see. (9)

VIDU'.—O friend, be attentive. Such is (the display of) his self-confidence that everything can be possible.

KING—My good man, wait for a while. Káñchanamàlà, say to the Queen.—This magician is yours; and this place is cleared of the people. You should come then; together we shall see his performance.

KA'NCHA.—As Your Majesty commands. (*Exit*).

(*Enter* VA'SAVADATTA' *and* KA'NCHANAMA'LA'.)

VA'SAVA.—I have a leaning towards that magician, as he comes from Ujjayinî.

KA'NCH.—This is, indeed, the Queen's high regard for her kinsmen; so, my mistress, proceed. (*They walk about*).

VA'SAV.—(*Approaching*) Prosperity, prosperity to my lord!

KING.—My Queen, this man has vaunted a great deal; sit down here then; let us see.

(VA'SAVADATTA' *sits down.*)

KING—My good man, now begin your magical feats.

MAGICIAN—As Your Majesty commands.

(*Dancing in many ways and waving his bundle of feathers*).

I will exhibit, in the sky, the gods headed by Hari, Hara and Brahman, the lord of the gods (Indra), and the host of the Siddhas, Cháranas, and the heavenly nymphs, dancing. (10)

May Your Majesty behold.

KING—(*Looking up and descending from his seat.*) Oh, Wonder, wonder! See my Queen.

Here in the sky is Brahmâ, on his lotus, and this is Śañkara with the tiara of the digit of the moon; there is Hari, the destroyer of the demons, with (distinguished by) his four arms marked with the bow, the sword, the mace and the discus; this is (Indra), the lord of the gods, seated on the Airávata; and here, my Queen, are the other gods, and also the celestial nymphs dancing with their anklets jingling responsive to the movements of their feet. (11)

VA'SAV.—Wonder, Oh wonder!

VIDU'.—*(Aside)* Ho, Slave's son, magician, what is the use of your showing the gods and the Apsarases? If you want to have him pleased, then show Ságariká.

(*Enter* VASUNDHARA').

VASUNDHARA'—(*Approaching the* KING) Prosperity, prosperity, to the lord!

Minister Yaugandharáyaṇa begs to say—Here has arrived Vasubhûti, the prime minister of Vikramabáhu, along with Bábhravya, our Chamberlain. So Your Majesty should be pleased to see him at this very happy moment. I, too, will just come, having finished what remains of the business to be done.

VA'SAVA.—My dear, let the magic-show stand over. The chief minister, Vasubhúti, has come from my maternal uncle's house. So my husband should see him at once.

KING—As the Queen says. (*To the magician*) Good man, you may stop now.

MAGICIAN—As Your Majesty commands.

(*Waving the bunch of feathers again*; *departing*). But one more performance of mine should be necessarily seen by Your Majesty.

KING—Good man, we shall see.

VA'SAV.—Káñchanamálá, go you and give him a reward.

KA'NCHA.—As Your Majesty orders. (*Exit with the* MAGICIAN).

KING—Vasanṭaka, go forth and conduct Vasubhûti hither.

VASAN.—As Your Majesty commands. (*Exit with* VASUNDHARA').

(*Enter* VASUBHU'TI *and* BA'BHRAVYA *followed by* VASANTAKA).

VASUBHU'TI—(*Looking all round*). Oh, the magnificence of the lord of the Vatsas! For here,

Attracted by the Prosperity-securing elephant while looking attentively at the noble (*lit.* favourite) steeds; captivated by the strain of music, when standing for a moment in the conclaves of (tributary) princes; and with the wealth of the King of Simhala forgotten all at once, I am made as a rustic by the objects of great curiosity met (*lit.*, lying) at the very door. (12)

BA'BHRAVYA—Vasubhûti, at the thought that I shall see my master to-day after a long time, I am experiencing an indescribable change of condition owing to great joy. For,

My great satisfaction lends help to-day to my age: it aggravates yet more the increase of tremor, through nervousness; it obscures the more my dim eye-sight with veils of tears; and it renders more dull my speech in broken words owing to the choking of the throat. (13)

VIDU'.—(*Stepping forward*) Come this way, this way, Your Excellency.

VASUBHU'TI—(*Seeing the jewel-necklace on Vidu'shaka's neck, aside*) Bábhravya, I perceive this is the very jewel-necklace which was given by the King, to the princess at the time of her departure.

BA'BHRAVYA—Minister, there is resemblance. What then, shall I ask Vidúshaka how he got it?

VASU.—Bábhravya, don't you, don't you do so. On account of the abundance of gems in a great royal household, similarity of ornaments is not difficult to be found. (*They walk on*).

VIDU'.—Sir, here is His Majesty; let the Minister approach.

VASU.—(*Advancing*) May Your Majesty prosper!

KING—(*Rising*) Noble one, I bow to you.

VASUBH.—May you be of long life!

KING—A seat, a seat, for the noble one.

VIDU'.—Here is a seat. May the minister sit down.

(VASUBHU'TI *sits down*).

BA'BHRAVYA—Sire, Bábhravya bows down to you.

KING—*(Placing his hand on his back)* Bâbhravya, sit here.

BA'B.—*(Sits down).*

VIDU'.—Minister, here is Queen Vàsavadattâ bowing to you.

VA'SAVA.—Noble sir, I salute you.

VASU.—Long-lived one, may you obtain a son like the king of Vatsa!

(All sit down).

KING—Noble Vasubhùti, is it all well with His Honour, the King of Simhala?

VASUB.—*(Looking up and sighing)* Sire, I do not know what to say.

(Remains with face hung down).

VA'SAV.—*(With dejection; to herself)* Oh, fie, fie! What will Vasubhúti tell now?

KING—Tell us what this is. Noble one, my soul is almost distracted.

BA'BHRAVYA—*(Aside)* Minister, even after a long time this must be told; speak it out then.

VASU.—*(With tears)* Sire, it is not possible to communicate it; yet here I tell it, ill-fated that I am. That Ratnàvalî, of long life, his daughter, who being already sought in marriage was bestowed upon (betrothed to) Your Majesty by the lord of Simhala, on hearing that Vásavadattá had perished in a fire.

KING—*(Aside)* Queen, what falsehood is this that your maternal uncle's minister is uttering?

VA'SAVA.—*(Smiling)* Husband, it cannot be known who utters a falsehood.

VIDU'.—What happened to her then?

VASU.—She, while being brought to Your Majesty's presence was drowned in the sea owing to ship-wreck. *(Remains weeping, with face cast down).*

VA'SAV.—*(With tears)* Ah, I am undone, unlucky that I am. Ah! Cousin Ratnávalì, where are you now? Give me a reply.

KING—Queen, take heart, take heart! Inscrutable is the course of fate. These two themselves, I say, who went down through shipwreck and rose up again (were saved) are instances unto you. *(Points to* VASUBHU'TI *and* BA'BHRAVYA*).*

VA'SAV.—Husband, it is proper; but whence such luck in my case?

(A great uproar behind the scenes).

Here, in the inner apartment, has broken out, all of a sudden, this fire, imparting to the mansions the beauty of golden turrets by its masses of flames, having its intense heat indicated by its scorching the tops of the thick-grown trees of the garden, making the pleasure-mountain dark like a watery cloud by its smoke descending on it and causing distress to the women-folk by its burning heat. (14)

Moreover,

This fire has sprung up, to give veracity as it were, to the rumour about the Queen's being burnt, which was formerly circulated in Lâvâṇaka. (15)

(All look about in alarm).

KING—*(Suddenly rising)* How now! A fire in the harem! Alas! Queen Vâsavadattâ is burnt! Alas! My darling Vásavadattâ!

VA'SAVA.—Husband, save, save!

KING—Ah! How was the Queen not noticed, through extreme flurry, though standing here! Queen, take heart, take heart.

VA'SAV.—Husband, I did not say that for my sake. Here is poor Ságarikâ perishing, restrained with a chain by my cruel self. So let my husband rescue her.

KING—How now, Queen, Ságarikâ perishes! Here I go.

VASU.—Sire, why is the part of a moth played when there is no grave cause for it?

BA'BHRAVYA—Sire, Vasubhûti says the right thing.

VIDU'.—*(Seizing the* KING *by the upper garment)* Friend, do not, indeed, do this rash act.

KING—*(Dropping the upper garment)* Fie, fool Ságariká is being destroyed; why is life still sustained? *(Having acted entering the fire and gesticulating being overpowered by smoke)*

Desist, desist, O fire; give up this continuous column of smoke; why do you display this lofty circle of flames? What (harm) will you do to me who was not consumed by the fire of separation from my beloved, having the burning heat of the fire at the time of universal destruction? (16)

VA'SAVA.—How is it that my husband has resolutely acted thus, following the words of me, a miserable creature! So I too will follow my husband.

VIDU'.—(*Walking forth and standing in the front*) Madam, I too will be your guide on the way.

VASUB —How now! Vatsarâja has already entered the fire. So it behoves me who have witnessed the decease of the princess also to make an offering of myself just here (in this fire).

BA'BHRAVYA—Alas! Sire! Why is this race of Bharata causelessly consigned to (the domain of) uncertainty? Or rather, what is the use of talk? I too will act in a way befitting my devotion.

(*All act entrance into the fire*).

(*Enter* SA'GARIKA' *bound with fetters*).

SA'GAR.—(*Looking into the quarters*) Oh, fie! The fire has burst into flames all round. (*Reflecting with gratification*) Fortunately the fire will, to-day, put an end to my suffering.

KING—Ah! Here is Ságarikâ standing with the fire close upon her. I will then quickly attend to her. (*Hastily approaching*) Ah, darling, why do you still remain calm (unconcerned) when there is cause for haste (or, flurry)?

SA'GAR.—(*Seeing the* KING, *to herself*) How now! My husband! On seeing him I have again got a desire for life. (*Aloud*) Let master save, let master save!

KING—O timid one, dismiss your fear. Let this thick effusion of smoke be borne for a moment. (*Looking forth*) Alas, Oh fie! This garment dropped from your breasts has taken fire. (*Observing*) Why do you stumble again and again! (*Marking closely*) How is it that you are fettered with a chain? (*Girding up his loins*) I will quickly bear you away from here. Take hold of me, dearest. (17)

(*Embracing her by the neck and gesticulating the pleasure of touch, with eyes closed*). Oh, the heat I felt disappeared in a moment. Cheer up, darling, cheer up.

Evidently the fire does not burn you although touching you, since, O darling, this your touch removes heat itself. (18)

(*Opening the eyes, looking in the quarters and letting go the hold of* SA'GARIKA') Oh! A great wonder!

Where is that fire gone? The inner apartment is in the same state (as before)—(*Seeing* VA'SAVADATTA') How now! This is the daughter of the King of Ujjayinî!

VA'SAVA.—(*Feeling the body of the* KING *with joy*). Luckily my husband has his body unharmed.

KING—This is Bábhravya !

BA'BHRAVYA—Sire, now we have been brought back to life.

KING—This Vasubhu'ti !

VASUB.—May the great King prosper !

KING—And this my friend !

VIDU'.—Prosperity, prosperity to Your Honour !

KING—Does my mind rove (as) in a dream; or can this be magic ? (19)

VIDU'.—Oh, entertain no doubt, this is, indeed, magic. It was said by that whore's son, the magician, that Your Highness should perforce see one more feat of his magic. So it is just that.

KING—My Queen, here is Ságariká brought by me at your bidding.

VA'SAVA.—Husband, I know it.

VASUB.—(*Seeing* SA'GARIKA' ; *aside*) Bàbhravya, this girl is like the princess.

BA'BH.—Minister, the same occurs to my mind too.

VASUB.—(*To the* KING) Sire, whence is this girl ?

KING—The Queen knows it.

VASU.—Queen, whence again is this damsel ?

VA'SAV.—Minister, she was delivered over into my hands by minister Yaugandharáyaṇa, saying that she was obtained from the sea. Hence it is that she is called Ságariká.

KING—*(To himself)* Delivered by Yaugandharayana ! How can he do a thing without informing me !

VASUB.—*(Aside)* Bábhravya, since there is a very similar necklace of gems on Vasantaka's neck, and the maiden also is brought from the sea, she is clearly Ratnávalî, the daughter of the king of Simhala.

(Advancing; aloud) Long-lived one, Ratnávalî, are you reduced to this plight ?

SA'GA.—*(Observing* VASUBHU'TI, *with tears)* How now ! Minister Vasubhûti !

VASUB.—*(Weeping)* Ah, I am undone, unfortunate that I am ! *(Falls on the ground)*.

SA'GAR.—Ah father, Ah mother! Where are you? Give me a reply. (*Dropping on* VASUBHU'TI *faints*).

VA'SAV.—(*In confusion*) Noble Chamberlain, is this my cousin, Ratnàvalî?

BA'BHRAVYA—Madam, this is she.

VA'SAV.—(*Clasping* RATNA'VALI') Take heart, sister, take heart.

KING—How now! This is the daughter of Vikramabâhu, the king of Simhala, of high descent.

VIDU'.—(*Touching the jewel-necklace; to himself*) I knew from the very beginning that such an ornament could not belong to an ordinary person.

VASU.—(*Rising*) Long-lived one! Revive, revive. Don't you see, this your elder sister is ill at ease; embrace her, therefore.

SA'GAR.—(*Reviving, and seeing* VA'SAVADATTA'; *to herself*) I have, indeed, given offence to the Queen; so I cannot show my face to her. (*Remains with head downcast*).

VA'SAVA.—(*With tears, stretching forth her hands*) Come, come; O extremely hard-hearted one, now at least show affection. (*Clasps her at the neck*; RATNA'-VALI' *gesticulates stumbling; aside*) Husband, I am ashamed of this my cruelty; so remove her fetters.

KING—(*With satisfaction*) As the Queen says. (*Does accordingly*).

VA'SAV.—Husband, I have, indeed, been made (to act like) a wicked woman by minister Yaugandharayaṇa, by whom, although knowing, nothing was told.

(*Then enter* YAUGANDHARA'YANA).

YAUGAN.—When, at my request, separation from her husband was consented to by the Queen, then it was that she was placed in (subjected to) great distress by arranging for your getting another wife: true that this attainment of the sovereignty of the world by Sire will give joy to her; still, through shame, I am not able to show my face to her. (20)

(*Reflecting for a moment*) Or, what is to be done? Such is the vow of devotion to one's master, that it takes little account, in its execution, even of those worthy of the highest respect. (*Looking on*) Here is His Majesty. Let me then approach. (*Approaching*) Prosperity, prosperity to my lord! Sire, pardon me for what was done by me without informing you.

KING—Yaugandharáyaṇa, tell what you did without informing me.

YAUGAN.—May Sire sit down. I will relate everything.

(All sit down according to their positions).

YAUGAN.—*(With hands folded)* Listen, Sire. Of this daughter of the king of Simhala, it was predicted by a seer (Siddha) that whoever would accept her hand in marriage would be the sovereign of the whole world. Then, when she was not given (to Sire) by the lord of Simhala, avoiding mental affliction to Queen Vásavadattá, although repeatedly sought by us for Sire, through our belief in that (prophecy)—

KING—What then?

YAUGAN.—Then having got a report circulated that the Queen was burnt in the fire at Lâvânaka, Bàbhravya was (again) sent to his presence.

KING—What followed has been heard by me. Now with what object was this girl delivered into the hands of the Queen?

VIDU'.—Oh, it can just be known, though untold. That placed in the inner apartment she might easily cross the range of your eyes.

KING—*(Smiling)* Yaugandharàyaṇa, has your motive been well grasped by Vasantaka?

YANGAN.—As Your Majesty says.

KING—The Magician's affair also, I think, was of your own design.

YAUGAN.—Sire, it was. How else could Sire have seen her, confined in the inner apartment? And when not seen, how could she have been recognized by Vasubhûti? *(Smiling)* Now that her cousin is recognized, the Queen is the chief authority as to how to dispose of her.

VA'SAVA.—*(With a smile)* Noble one, why don't you say clearly—Give Ratnávalî to him (the King)?

VIDU'.—Noble lady, you have well guessed the minister's intention.

VA'SAVA.—*(Extending her hand)* Come, Ratnávalî, come. Let this much at least, worthy of a sister, happen at my hands.

(Decorating RATNA'VALI' *with her own ornaments, taking her by the hand, and approaching the* KING*)* Husband, accept this one.

KING—*(Stretching forth his hands, with satisfaction)* What favour of the Queen is not esteemed by me?

VA'SAVA.—Husband, at a distance are her paternal relations; so act in such a way that she will not remember her kinsmen. *(Gives her to him).*

KING—As the Queen commands.

VIDU'.—*(Dancing about)* Bless me, Oh, Ho! The whole earth has now, indeed, come into the hands of my dear friend.

VASUBH.—Long-lived one, rightly, indeed, do you possess the title of Queen!

YAUGAN.—Now my labours have borne fruit. Sire, say what further good (lit., desirable thing) shall I do unto you?

KING—Is there anything to be desired beyond this? For

Vikramabàhu is made one with me; this my darling Ságarikà, the most precious object on the surface of the earth, the sole cause of the acquisition of the earth bound by the seas, is gained; the Queen has been pleased owing to the recovery of her sister; and the Kosalas are conquered; you, the ablest of ministers being there, what blessing do I not possess for which I can entertain a wish? (21)

Still let there be this—

(The Actors' Benediction).

May Indra, sending down showers as desired, make the earth yield luxuriant crops; may eminent Bràhmaṇas give satisfaction to the celestials with sacrifices duly performed; may there be union of the good, as long as the world exists, conducing to increased happiness; and may the (abusive) utterances of the wicked, difficult to be controverted and indelible like the adamantine glue, be completely laid at rest!! (22)

(Exeunt Omnes).

(End of Act IV. named AINDRAJA'LIKA*).*

(Here ends the NA'TIKA' *called* RATNA'VALI', *the composition of* KING ŚRI'HARSHA*).*

NOTES.

P. 1. Following the time-honoured practice of Sanskrit writers, the poet begins his work with the usual *mañgala* (the benedictory stanza or stanzas) which in the case of dramas, is technically called Nândî. Such *mañgala* is thought to be necessary for the removal of obstacles and the safe completion of a work. This Nândî generally consists of one or two s'lokas, sometimes of three as here, and very rarely of four.

In the case of the present play, however, as in that of the Veṇîsaṃhára, two additional s'lokas are found in some printed editions and MSS., but their authenticity may well be questioned. See remarks under those.

P. 1. S'l. 1. In this Śl. the handful of flowers thrown by Párvatî (comp. in this respect the first Śl. of Veṇî.), instead of Pârvatî herself, is referred to as competent to grant protection. For, Hindu poets often refer to something connected with, or some act (*Cf.* the first s'l. of the Mâl.-Mâdh., Mudrâ. &c.) of their favourite deity instead of to the deity directly, as a mark of great humility The handful of flowers was thrown by Pârvatî when she was sent by her father to propitiate S'iva (तदाराधने) while practising penance on the Himâlayas after he had lost Satî (see Kum. I. 53,54). According to Kum., however, the *Añjali* was offered at the feet of S'iva (व्यकीर्यत त्र्यम्बकपादमूले पुष्पोच्चयः पल्लवभङ्गभिन्नः। III. 61).

The idea is this:-Pârvatî wished to place the offering of flowers on S'iva's head. With this object she raised herself on the tips of her toes. The view of her developed limbs caused S'iva to cast wistful eyes on her. At this Pârvatî felt bashful owing to the feeling of love; her hand shook nervously; and the *Kusumâñjali*, meant to fall on S'iva's head, missed its destination and fell between the two.

पादाग्रस्थितया &c.—Construe—तदाराधने पादाग्रस्थितया मुहुः स्तनभरेण नम्रतामानीतया शम्भोः सस्पृहलोचनत्रयपथं यान्त्या सपुलकस्वेदोद्गमोत्कम्पया ह्रीमत्या गिरिजया शिरसि ईहितः क्षिप्तः [सन्] अन्तरे विश्लिष्यन् कुसुमाञ्जलिः वः पातु।

पादाग्र०—Dissolve पादाग्राभ्यां or-ग्रयोः स्थितया. This she did to reach the lofty head of S'iva. मुहुः—Often, repeatedly; may also be taken with पादाग्र०. स्तनभरेण नम्रतामा०—made to bend down, brought to a stooping posture. नम्रस्य भावः

नम्रता; नम्रस्य being सामान्ये नपुंसकं; otherwise we should expect नम्राता (नम्रायाः भावः) as the Vârtika—स्वतलोर्गुणवचनस्य (इति वक्तव्यं) providing पुंवद्भाव does not apply in the present case. For शुक्लादय एव इह गुणाः remarks the प्रौढमनोरमा. शुक्लाया भावः शुक्लत्वं-ता; गुणवचनस्य किम् । कर्त्र्या भावः कर्त्रीत्वं; Sid.-Kau. For similar instances, *cf.* उपेत्य सा दोहददुःखशीलतां Rag. III.; स्तुतेन पाण्डोः कलमस्य गोपिकां निरीक्ष्य मेने शरदः कृतार्थता । Kir. IV. 9; क्षीबतामुपगतास्त्वनुवेलं &c. S'is'. X. 34. This is a favourite idea with Sanskrit poets; *cf.* Kum. III. 54; Meg. II. 22; अतनुकुचभरानतेन भूयः &c. S'is'. VII. 66. This explains the सस्पृहलोचनत्व of S'iva.

शम्भोः--शं सुखं भावयति उत्पादयति इति; fr शं happiness, welfare and भू which has a causal sense here (अन्तर्भावितण्यर्थोऽत्र भवतिः Sid.-Kau.) with the aff. उ (डुः) by the Vârtika—मितद्र्वादिभ्य उपसंख्यानम् । सस्पृह०—लोचनानां त्रयं लोचनत्रयं; now see com. For the change of पथिन् to पथ see Gr. § 280 Pâṇ V. 4. 14. *Cf.* हरस्तु किंचित्परिलुप्तधैर्यः उमामुखे—व्यापारयामास विलोचनानि । Kum. III. 67 (अनेन भगवतो रतिभावोदय उक्तः । Malli.)

ह्रीमत्या—ह्रीः अस्या विद्यते असौ ह्रीमती तया। This properly means 'bashful' but here it means 'who came to be bashful,' felt ashamed (when S'ambhu looked at her with longing eyes and she was affected with emotion). ईहितः—wished or intended (to fall on the head); ईह् properly means 'to act bodily' (चेष्टायां); but as action depends upon wish (for the order is—जानाति, इच्छति, यतते &c.) it has often the sense of 'to wish;' *cf* माधुर्ये मधुबिन्दुना रचयितुं क्षाराम्बुधेरीहते। Bh. तेने हा तेनेहा (तेन ईहा) मधुकरेण कथम् । Bv.

सपुलक०—Here we have three of the eight सात्त्विक भावs or involuntary manifestations of strong feeling arising from *Satva* (for these, see Intro.), *viz.* horripilation (see note on संरोहत्पुलका next S loka), perspiration and tremor. As S'ambhu looked at Pârvatî with loveful eyes, there was a reciprocation of feeling on her part also. *Cf.* तदनु युगपदीशः पार्वतीवक्त्रपद्मे स्मितविकसितगण्डे प्राहिणोल्लोचनानि । पुलकिततनुरन्तर्भावमावेदयन्ती दरमुदितमुखेन्दुः सा च सव्रीडमस्थात् ॥ Pâr-P. III. 9. See Kum. III. 68. विभ्रश्यन्—The preposition वि reverses the sense of भ्रंश्; so this either means 'getting loose and falling down' (not being properly thrown) or 'not reaching its destination,' falling in the middle (not being thrown with sufficient force). ०अञ्जलिः—properly means 'the cavity formed by joining the hollowed palms;' hence, secondarily (by Lakshaṇâ), the thing contained therein;

here the flowers. अन्तरे—अन्तं राति इति अन्तर that which reaches the end; hence, the interval or space between two things. वः—According to S'âstrî Nigudkar, must be taken in a wider sense, *i. e.* as meaning-you and all of us युष्मानस्मानन्यांश्च। He remarks—व इति 'त्यदादीनि सर्वैर्नित्यम्' इति एकशेषः। एतेन व इत्यस्य युष्मानित्यर्थकरण व्याकरणानाभिज्ञत्वमूलकम्। पान्वित्याशीषि लोड्विधानेन इतराशीःप्रार्थने सूत्रधारस्य नान्दीपठनफलाभावप्रसङ्गात्।

In this s'l. there is S'ṛingâra manifested, its substraum being S'iva and Pârvatî (आलम्बनविभाव). Its permanent sentiment is रति or love, as indicated by Śiva's सस्पृहलोचनत्व, and Pârvatî's स्वेदोद्गम &c. which are its अनुभाव and Pârvatî's ह्रीमत्व which is a व्यभिचारिभाव. For the technicalities, see Introduction.

The figure of speech in this s'l. is *Kâvyaliṅga* as the falling in the middle of the handful of flowers is explained by such epithets as ह्रीमत्या, स्तनभरेण &c.

P. 2. S'l. 2. Herein the poet passes on to another scene, *viz.* that of the first meeting in private of Pârvatî and S'iva after marriage.

Constr. नवे सङ्गमे औत्सुक्येन कृतत्वरा (किं तु) सहभुवा ह्रिया व्यावर्तमाना बन्धुवधूजनस्य तैस्तैः वचनैः पुनः आभिमुख्यं नीता अग्रे वरं दृष्ट्वा संरोहत्पुलका आत्तसाध्वसरसा हसता हरेण श्लिष्टा गौरी वः शिवाय भवतु।

औत्सुक्येन—औत्सुक्य eagerness. The instr. is हेतौ. सहभुवा—सहभूः inborn, natural; fr. सह + भू with the aff. क्विप् added कर्तरि. This may also be taken with औत्सुक्येन. ह्रिया—हेतौ तृतीया. तैस्तैः—Here तद् refers to the speeches of inducement or persuation used on such occasions (is प्रसिद्धार्थत्वपर). The repetition indicates वीप्सा or totality, by the rule नित्यवीप्सयोः। Pâṇ. VIII. 1. 4. (आभीक्ष्ण्ये वीप्सायां च द्योत्ये पदस्य द्विर्वचनं स्यात्। Sid.-Kau.) वीप्सा (वि + ईप्सा) lit. means 'the desire to include every case of every one of a group:' as वृक्षं वृक्षं (*i. e.* all) सिञ्चति. Pârvatî's friends used every word of encouragement to induce her to approach her husband. बन्धुवधू०—may be taken as (1) बन्धुः प्रियः beloved यः वधूरूपो जनः वधूजनः female friends or relatives तस्य; or (2) बन्धुः a kinsman or relative; बन्धूनां वध्वः (the wives of) तासां जनः समूहः. For जन meaning 'a body or collection of' *cf.* सखीजनस्ते किमुतार्द्रसौहृदः। Vik. I. 9.; ज्ञातिजनास्निग्धाभिः वनदेवताभिः। S âk. IV.; नापेक्षितो गुरुजनः *Ibid.* V. 16.

आभिमुख्यं—अभिमुखस्य भावः the state of standing before or in front of; by adding य (ष्यञ्) to अभिमुख.

वरं—वृणोति, वरतीति वा वरः the husband; fr. वृ + अच् (अ) कर्तरि by पचाद्यच्। वरो जामातृवोढारौ इति विश्वः। आत्तसाध्वस०—आत्त p. p.

p. of दा with आ; by the rule अच उपसर्गात्तः । Pâṇ. VII. 4. 47.; the vowel of the root दा preceded by a preposition ending in a vowel is replaced by त् when the root is followed by a termination beginning with त् and having an indicatory क् (किति). ०साध्वसरसा—may mean—(1) आत्तः साध्वसस्य साध्वसरूपो वा रसो यया who experienced the emotion of fright. साध्वस flurry, agitation; रस anything experienced; hence 'feeling'; *cf.* परायत्तः प्रीतेः कथमिव रसं वेत्ति पुरुषः । Mudr. IV. 4. Or (2) आत्तौ साध्वसं fear च रसः love च साध्वसरसौ यया who was inspired with fear and love. The first way is better, as the feeling of love is indicated by the epithet संरोहत्पुलका. संरोहत्पु०—With the hair of her body standing on end. In erotic poetry this रोमाञ्चविक्रिया is considered as the first outward indication of love, and is often referred to by poets; *cf.* Vik. I. 11, Kum. VII. 77, Rag. VII. 22, &c.

हसता—For, the embarrassed condition of his wife amused him a great deal.

S'l. quoted in K.-P. VII, (see under Kârikâ 15) as an illustration of the principle that the actual mention of an Accessory (व्यभिचारिभाव) when it is not suggested by an Ensuant (अनुभाव) peculiar to itself, does not constitute a fault. Here the Accessory औत्सुक्य cannot be represented by the Ensuant त्वरा, as that may be caused by Fear, Anger, and the like. Hence for a clear and unmistakable apprehension of the Accessory its mention by its own term is neccessary.

The figure of speech is *Svabhâvokti*. Some think that there is समासोक्ति, but for that, according to the K.-P., the epithets ought to be S lishṭa or paronomast

S'l. in foot-note—सम्प्राप्तं &c.—In some editions and MSS. this is given as part of the benediction. But it does not seem to be genuine. The quibbling on words in it is too much even for the somewhat artificial style of Harsha. Again it is inconsistent with the reverence the poet is expected to have for S'iva or even for Vishṇu. We cannot expect him to make either Pârvatî or Laksmî call her husband निर्लज्ज even in प्रणयकोप.

This S'l. has a double application: it refers to Pârvatı and S'iva as also to Lakshmî and Krishṇa, each clause having a double meaning. Constr. ll. 1, 2. पुरा मकरध्वजेन मदर्थे स्वत्तः मथनं संप्राप्तम् । तत् हे निर्लज्ज मम पुरो बहुमार्गगां वोढुं तव युक्तम् । ll. 3–4–(1) हे कृष्णकण्ठ ग्रहं मुञ्च स्वभावकुटिलां तामेव अनुनय इति अद्रितनया

रुषा यमाह स वः पायात्। (2) हे कृष्ण कण्ठग्रहं मुञ्च मावकुटिलां सामेव अनुनयस्व इति लक्ष्मीः रुषा यमाह &c.

मकरध्वज—(1) मकरस्य प्रतिकृतिः इति मकरः by adding कन् in this sense, which is then dropped in the case of ध्वज or केतु. The God of Love; lit. the Makara-bannered; so called from the sea-monster subdued by him and represented on his banner. (2) मकर by implication (उपलक्षण) means 'sea animals'; hence, the milky ocean (*cf.* झषकेतन), Lakshmî being one of the 14 jewels churned out of it. *Cf.* the well-known verse—लक्ष्मीः कौस्तुभपारिजातकसुरा धन्वन्तरिश्चन्द्रमा &c. (See A. Dic.).

मथनं—(1) Destruction. For the story see Kum. III. 66 71-72; S'iva—P. Adh. 11. (2) Churning. This is derived from मथ् 1st Conj.; and not from मन्थ् 9th Conj. which will give मन्थन. त्वत्तः—(2) Although Vishṇu did not take part in the churning he was indirectly connected with it. For the churning was conducted under his directions; he also supported the mountain Mandara by assuming the form of a tortoise. मदर्थे—(1) In connexion with me, on my account. (2) For my sake. अर्थे at the end of a comp. also occurs as अर्थं and sometime as अर्थाय, with an adverbial force. *Cf.* तद्दर्शनादभूच्छंभोर्भूयान्दारार्थमादरः। Kum. VI. 13; प्रत्याख्याता मया तत्र नलस्यार्थाय देवताः। Nalop. XIII. 19.

तद्युक्तं—To be read with a *Káku* (*i. e.* a change of voice indicative of fear, grief &c.) and implying that it is not युक्त. बहुमार्गगां—Lit. going by various routes, having many courses; here the Ganges which is त्रिपथगा 'three-coursed' (the first course being through the Heavenly region, the second over the Earth and the third along Pâtâla or the lower regions. Gaṅgâ, being borne on his head by S'iva, is often represented by Sanskrit poets as exciting Párvatí's jealousy on that account. *Cf.* Mudrá I. 1. (2) Kubjâ (whose real name was Sairandhrî) the female servant of Kamsa, seems to be meant here. She was deformed being crooked or bent in three parts of the body. *Cf.* दास्यस्म्यहं सुंदर कंससंमता त्रिवक्रनामा ह्यनुलेपकर्मणि। &c. Bg. X. 1st half, XLII. 3. While Ráma and Krishna were passing through the main road of Mathurá, they saw her carrying unguents to to Kaṃsa, and asked her if she would give those to them. Readily acceeding to their wish, she applied the unguent to their bodies. Pleased by this act Kṛishṇa planted his feet on her feet and holding her by the chin made her straight. Touched by him she became the best of beauties (मुकुन्दस्पर्शनात्सद्यो बभूव

प्रमदोत्तमा ।). She then being enamoured of him requested him to visit her house which he promised to do after killing Kaṃsa. For further particulars see B. P. X. 1st half Ch. 47. 1–10.

Some understand this to refer to Sarasvatî, but that does not seem probable. This and the epithet भावकुटिला cannot be very well taken with सरस्वती. वोढुं·वोढुः—*V. l.* is not good as it implies a habitual act. स्वभावकुटिलां—(1) Naturally crooked (going in a zigzag or meandering way) Even if separated as भाव०, भाव will mean the same as स्वभाव. (2) भावकुटिलां—भावेन भावे वा by intention or thought कुटिला crooked, insincere; not honest in her professions. *Cf.* Mṛich. IV. 16. कृष्णकण्ठ०—S'iva got the epithet नीलकण्ठ (here called कृष्ण० for the S'esha) on his drinking the poison Hálâhala, which turned his neck black. ग्रहं—Your hold *i. e.* embrace. Fig. of speech S'lesha.

P. 3. In this s l. S'iva is represented as describing to his wife Pârvatî (Satî, now restored to him)—the scene at Daksha's sacrifice when destroyed by him.

Allusion:—Daksha, at the instance of the sages, gave his daughter Satî to S iva in marriage; but he was never wholly reconciled to the uncouth figure and the loathsome practices of his son-in-law. He once performed a sacrifice at which all the gods except S'iva were invited. He did not invite his daughter also to be present at the ceremony. Satî, however, persuaded her husband to go. But on finding herself slighted and her husband grossly abused by her father, she was exasperated, threw herself into the flaming sacrificial fire and perished. According to another account, she sat down in contemplation, fixing her mind on her husband, and relinquished her body derived from Daksha, by generating fire into it. For other particulars see B. P. IV. 4, especially 24–27; *Cf.* also Kum. 1. 27. When the terrible news reached S'iva, he got highly incensed and took dire vengeance on Daksha. According to one account he himself went to the sacrifice, completely destroyed it, pursued Daksha who assumed the form of a deer and decapitated him. According to another account he tore off a lock of his matted hair and dashed it on to the ground. From it sprang up the fierce Vîrabhadra with a thousand arms. S'iva asked him to go, accompanied by the Gaṇas, and to destroy Daksha's sacrifice, and also himself went there to assist in the work of demolition referred to in the above s'loka.

Construe:—त्रयोपि अमी बह्वयः क्रोधदग्धैः त्रिभिः दृष्टिपातैः उपशमिताः। त्रासार्ताः चपलगणहृतोष्णीषपट्टाः ऋत्विजः अधः पतन्ति । दक्षः स्तौति अस्य पत्नी करुणं विलपति देवैः अपि विद्रुतं च। इति देव्यै मखमथनविधौ शंसन् आत्तहासः शिवः वः पातु।

क्रोधेद्धैः—Kindled by, *i.e* firey with or glowing with, wrath. **क्रोधोद्धैः**—*V. l.* क्रोध एव उद्धः अग्निः येषु fiery. This is faulty because उद्ध is an obscure word, and it is a bad compound. Perhaps धो is a mislection for धे. **क्रोधान्धैः**—*V. l.* blinded, bedimmed—will not do as the idea of overpowering light is necessary to explain the putting out of the three fires. **त्रिभिः—मुहुः** *v. l.* does not make good sense; for it shows that the glare of the eyes was not so powerful as to put down the fires at once. **अमी**—Here used for ते, 'those well-known' It cannot be taken as 'these' (पुरोवर्तिनः ।) as S'iva cannot be supposed to be describing to his wife the scene at the destruction of the sacrifice at the time it took place; for Satî had burnt herself before that. **अथोपि वह्नयः**—वहति देवेभ्यो हव्यमिति वह्निः fr. वह्+नि Uṇâdi; the principal office of fire being that of conveying the oblations offered to the gods; *cf.* the S'ruti अग्निमुखा वै देवाः. **त्रयः**—These are (1) गार्हपत्य (गृहपतिना नित्यं संयुक्तः by गृहपतिना संयुक्ते ञ्यः। Pâṇ IV. 4. 90) or the sacred fire perpetually kept up by a householder (being transmitted from father to son) and from which fires for sacrificial purposes are lighted. (2) आहवनीय (आहूयते प्रक्षिप्यते हविरत्र) in which the oblations to the gods are offered; and (3) दक्षिणाग्नि or the ceremonial fire. They are collectively called त्रेता. *Cf.* A's'valâyana—पिता वा एषोग्नीनां यद्दक्षिणः पुत्रो गार्हपत्यः पौत्र आहवनीयः। See Ms. II. 231.

त्रासार्ताः—They were frightened at the terrible sight of Vîrabhadra and the havoc wrought by him and the gaṇas; for the easy fright taken at such scenes by the priests *cf.* संभ्रमोऽभवदपोढकर्मणामृत्विजां च्युतविकङ्कतस्रुजाम्। Rag. XI. 25. **ऋत्विजः**—Lit. sacrificing at stated times; see com. Here priests officiating at a sacrifice. *Cf.* अग्न्याधेयं पाकयज्ञानग्निष्टोमादिकान्मखान्। यः करोति वृतो यस्य स तस्यर्त्विगिति स्मृतः॥ Ms. II. 43.

The four chief priests officiating at a sacrifice are होतृ, उद्गातृ, अध्वर्यु and ब्रह्मन्. At grand sacrifices, such as the one referred to here, there are sixteen priests, each one of the four principal ones having three assistants; these are (1) होता, मैत्रावरुण, अच्छावाक् and ग्रावस्तुत्; (2) उद्गाता, प्रस्तोता, प्रतिहर्ता and सुब्रह्मण्य; (3) अध्वर्यु, प्रतिप्रस्थाता, नेष्टा and उन्नेता; and (4) ब्रह्मन्, ब्राह्मणाच्छंसी, आग्नीध्र and पोता.

चपल—mischievous, actively busy. The Gaṇas are so by nature; *cf.* मा चापलायेति गणान्व्यनैषीत् Kum. III 41. **गण**—A troop of demigods called Pramathas, who attend on S'iva and are under the superintendence of Gaṇesha, one of the demigods. They are said to be 63 crores in number. See notes on

Kum. I. 55. उष्णीषपट्टा:—उष्णं ईषते (हिनस्ति removes) इति उष्णीषं (fr. ईष् 1 A.+क: *i. e.* अ) a turban; उष्णीषार्थं पट्टा: cloths worn as turbans. पट (fr. पट् to go, 1st conj.) is the usual word; पट्ट is got by adding त to पट् (बाहुलकात्त:). अध: पतन्ति—As the priests running about in terror were pulled by their turbans they fell down.

दक्ष:—A celebrated *Prajâpati,* one of the ten sons of Brahman, being born from his right thumb, and the chief of the patriarchs. दक्षस्त्वजायताङ्गुष्ठाद्दक्षिणाद्भगवानृषि: । B. P. see A.'s Dic. करुणं—piteously, in a manner to excite compassion. कृपणं *V. l.* meaning 'helplessly, miserably' is better. This may better be taken with विद्रुतम्.

आत्तहास:—Who began to laugh. S'iva laughed heartily as he thought of the miserable plight in which Daksha found himself for his folly in insulting the goddess and of the ease with which he routed the sacrifice. अट्टहास:—*V. l.* Here an adj. meaning 'laughing loudly,' see com. This will also do. अट्टहास, when a noun means 'a loud, boisterous laugh' and is particularly applied to the loud laugh of S'iva. *Cf.* राशीभूत: प्रतिदिनमिव त्र्यम्बकस्याट्टहास: । Meg. I. 60; गिरिशाट्टहासकास. Das.

The *Rasa* or flavour of the S'l. is रौद्र or the terrific. Its permanent mood (स्थायी भाव) is 'anger' Vîrabhadra is its material or essential excitant (आलम्बन विभाव). Figure—*Anuprâsa.*

S'l. 4. जितं—Prosperity to the moon. जि in such cases has the sense of 'to prosper', with the additional sense of 'salutation to' implied. *Cf.* K.-P. जयत्यर्थेन च नमस्कार आक्षिप्यते &c. Com. on I. 1. द्विजवृषभा:—the best of, illustrious, Brâhmaṇas; उपमानोत्तरपदकर्मधारय. वृषभ is one of the words of the व्याघ्रादि class, which coming latter in a Karm. comp. indicate excellence or pre-eminence. See com. निरुपद्रवा:—This implies previous trouble, and its cessation is now wished for. The three statements in these two lines are very significant. They covertly refer to change in the religious belief of S'rî-Harsha himself. Thus the triumph of the moon means Harsha's triumphling over his strong bias towards Buddhism. The homage to the gods implies the King's belief in Brâhmaṇism; while द्विजवृषभा: &c. is meant to show that the Brâhmanas would no longer be persecuted.

सस्यसस्या—सस्य (or शस्य) means the fruit of a tree, and also corn.; 'rich in the yield of fruit and corn of every kind; producing plentiful harvest.' *Cf.* भवतु वसुमती सर्वसम्पन्नसस्या ।

Mṛich. X. 61. The fulfilment of this wish depends upon that of the three previous ones. For when the Brâhmaṇas perform the holy rites properly and the gods are well pleased, there is timely rain; and the moon (the lord of herbs-ओषधीपतिः) shining properly, not being obscured by untimely clouds, the plants thrive. *Cf.* Bg. III. 11, 14. and अग्नौ प्रास्ताहुतिः सम्यगादित्यमुपतिष्ठते । आदित्याज्जायते वृष्टिर्वृष्टेरन्नं ततः प्रजाः । Ms. III. 76.

प्रतपतु—Here तप् is intrans.; *Cf.* तमस्तपति घर्मांशौ &c. S'âk. V. 14; सूर्ये तपत्यावरणाय दृष्टेः &c. Rag. V. 13.

चन्द्रवपुः—'having a body like *i.e.* as gladdening as, that of the moon.' This is generally taken as an adj. to नरेन्द्रचद्र. But there is tautology in this, as comparison with the moon is implied in नरेन्द्रचन्द्रः. It is better, therefore to take चन्द्रवपुः as a part of the wish and construe नरेन्द्रचन्द्रः चन्द्रवपुः सन् (gladdening the people like the moon by his person, and not oppressing them like the previous kings), प्रतपतु (display his power, reign gloriously). *Cf.* the S'loka कर्मणा मनसा वाचा &c. quoted in the Introduction.

Fig.—समासगा उपमा.

These four S'lokas constitute what is called the Nândî. About the genuineness of the first three of these there is no question, as they are found in all the MSS. and printed editions. The fourth also seems to be genuine as it is found in most of the printed edd. Even H. H. Wilson had it in the MS. he used for his translation of the Ratnâvalî. Again it is possible that Harsha might have written it to please the people after his reversion to Brâhmaṇism. But we cannot be very certain on this point.

P. 4. नान्द्यन्ते—नान्दी-For definition see com.; नन्दन्ति देवता अस्यामिति नान्दी; fr. नन्द् with घञ् (अ) and the fem. aff. ई; some derive it as आशीर्योगादिना नन्दतीति नन्दः; नन्द एव नान्दः by adding अ स्वार्थे (प्रज्ञादित्वादण्); ततः स्त्रियां ङीप् ।

This forms an essential part of the theatrical preliminaries and is of four kinds:—नमस्कृतिर्माङ्गलिकी आशीः पत्रावली तथा । नान्दी चतुर्धा निर्दिष्टा नाटकादिषु धीमता ॥ According to Bharata the principal events of the plot should be covertly indicated in the Nândî and this is done here also. Thus the first S'l. refers to Sâgarikâ's कुसुमायुधपूजन by offering flowers to him, and other incidents connected with that. The second s'l. refers to Sâgarikâ's getting nervous in the presence of Vatsarâja and his seizing her by the hand, and some other incidents of the second Act. See com. The third S'l. hints at the incidents of the third and fourth Acts, such as Vâsavadattâ's irritation at her husband's conduct, and the consequent obstruction caused by her, Sâgarikâ's lamentation in the words हा तात &c. p. 79 and the confusion and bustle caused by the fire exhibited by the magician. According to those who include the fourth s'l. in the Nândî the third S'l. refers to the incidents of the third Act alone and the fourth to those of the fourth, *viz.* the victory gained by Rumaṇvân for the King and the King's gaining the hand of Ratnâvalî, now appearing in her true character.

The discussion as to the *Padas* the Nândî should consist of, or the meaning of the term Pada (for these see Râghavabhaṭṭa's com. on नान्दी S'âk. I) is useless to the general reader and has been here dispensed with.

P. 5. (नान्द्यन्ते) सूत्रधारः—To complete the stage-direction here and other similar ones, supply आह, कथयति or some such word. The Sûtra. continues to speak after reciting the Nândî.

As the Sûtradhara is mentioned after the Nândî, the question arises—who recited the Nándí, and if the सूत्र० did it why should his name not precede the benedictory S'lokas. The answer is that the Sûtra. generally recited the Nándî, according to the precept of Bharata—सूत्रधारः पठेत्तत्र &c. (see com.); also because, he, as a Brâhmaṇa, was qualified to give a blessing. But his name is not put first, as nothing but auspicious words can begin a poetic composition. Again, the Sútradhâra, it seems, did not assume his character as such, until after the Nāndî was recited. For a fuller discussion on the subject see our Vik. or S'âk., note on the word; also Jagaddhara's remarks in his com. on the Mâl.-Mâdh.

सूत्रधारः—Lit. the holder or regulater of the thread of dramatic business; he is the chief manager who assigns to the various actors the characters they are to represent, instructs them and takes a leading part in the Prologue.

It is probable the term originally applied to the exhibitors of puppet-shows who sat behind a curtain and made the puppets move as they moved the strings; and that the drama in its present form is a development of such shows. See notes to Vik.

अलमतिविस्तरेण (or ०प्रसक्तेन)—Here अलं has the sense of prohibition (वारण). विस्तर means amplification, prolixity, *fr.* विस्तृ+अप् (भावे); with घञ् (अ) we have विस्तारः (extent); mark the difference between the two; विस्तारो विग्रहो व्यासः स च शब्दस्य विस्तरः ।

Ak. प्रसक्त means the same. The whole means—'enough of:' 'nothing is to be gained by the prolongation of the theartical preliminaries;' see com. Here अतिविस्तर is the करण of the साधन or विधानक्रिया which is understood, and therefore takes तृतीया. For it is remarked in Nyâsodyota—a क्रिया which is understood implies instrumentality just as well as one actually mentioned; so this is equivalent to साध्याभावात् विस्तरो न कर्तव्यः। The constant use of this expression in plays shows that the prolix preliminaries were found to be tiresome by the audience of later times.

वसन्तोत्सवे—It seems it was usual in ancient India to exhibit dramatic performances on the occasion of some fair or festival (as a great conclave of people was likely to be present on such occasions). The spring festival, which may be likened to the carnival or saturnalia of the Romans, was formerly celebrated from about the middle of the bright half of Chaitra to the full moon, to mark the return of spring, when Kámadeva or the God of Love was worshipped as described further on. According to some, the season commenced from the fifth day of Mâgha called Vasantapañchamî and lasted for two months. It is now identified with the Holî festival which is celebrated from the full-moon day of Phálguna to the 5th of the dark half of the same month and in which people of all grades of society mix and take liberties with one another. The Bhavishyottara Purâṇa gives a detailed description of the festival, for which see Wilson's note on this; H. Th. p. 264.

श्रीहर्ष०—For Harsha, see Introd.; देवस्य,–देव fr. दिव् to shine originally meant 'shining, brilliant;' then it came to signify a god (*cf.* Latin *deus*)—is used as a term of respect and greatness after the names of kings; *cf.* Vikramâkadeva, Vikramadeva &c. पादपद्मो०—Gaining their living, subsisting, by the support of the lotus-like feet of; a respectful way of saying 'the humble vassals of'. अपूर्व०—अपूर्व should better be taken with रचना: अपूर्वा such as has not been displayed before, novel, extraordinary (and attractive). If taken with वस्तु the statement is not correct. रचना is the judicious arrangement of the various parts and incidents so as to lead them to a charming end. The poet means that he has borrowed the plot, but presented it in a novel way.

रत्नावली-Properly the name of the princess of सिंहल and the Heroine of the play; the same signifies the play of that name by tranference of an epithet (अभेदोपचार); see Sid.-Kau. on शारीरकं भाष्यं Pâṇ. IV. 3. 88. The poet's other play प्रियदर्शिका is similarly named after the heroine. This is according to the rule—नाटिकासट्टकादीनां नायिकाभिर्विशेषणम्। नाटिका—see Intro. परम्परा—is a word by itself (अव्युत्पन्नं प्रातिपदिकं); a line or series of. The reading कृतेति...श्रुता is bad, as the presence of इति prevents श्रुता being syntactically connected with नाटिका; it must be श्रुतम्. प्रयोगतः—by way of being represented; actually staged. °ह्लादिनः—°जनस्य हृदयमाह्लादयतीति तस्य. अनुग्रहबुद्ध्या—Lit. with the thought of favour, *i. e.* with a wish to favour us. *Cf.* प्रणयिषु वा दाक्षिण्यादथ वा सद्वस्तुपुरुषबहुमानात् &c. Vik. I. 2. यथावत—See com.; 'in due 'form;' with strict attention to rules; *i. e.* in a faultless manner; or fully, everything as written being exhibited.

नेपथ्यरचनां—नेपथ्य is derived by Bhânujî Dîkshita as निनः (fr. नि *n.* the eye) to the eye, or नेः नेतुः (fr. नी a leader) to the leader, पथ्यं good; pleasing; hence (1) dress or (2) decoration; it also means (3) the tiring-room (where the decorations are made or the actors attire themselves); and (4) the drop-curtain जवनिका. °रचना here means—The arrangement of the tiring-room (such as the assignment of parts to the actors, giving them instructions as to costume, acting, and so on). आवर्जितानि—p p.p. of वृज् cau. with आ, to incline &c.; inclined, drawn to or attracted. सामाजिक—those who assemble in an assembly, the audience. ठक् (इक) is added to a word denoting combination in the sense of 'those who assemble there;' or समाजं रक्षन्ति इति those who keep an assembly by their presence. निश्चय:—conviction, firm belief.

S'l. 5. निपुणः—Having the skill attained by the observation of the ways of the world and by the study of the Śâstras and good poems. Here निपुणत्व also includes the idea of शक्ति 'genius or poetic inspiration,' as observed by Mammaṭa: *cf.* शक्तिर्निपुणता लोकशास्त्रकाव्याद्यवेक्षणात्। Kâv. I 2. गुणग्राहिणी—capable of appreciating merits (otherwise our dramatic skill will be useless). *Cf.* "And as you are known. The first and happiest hearers of the town," &c. &c. Shakespeare, Henry VIII. Prologue.

हारि—हर्तुं शीलमस्य naturally attractive or charming. The word is generally used as the latter member of a comp., as मनोहारि, चेतोहारि &c. वत्सराज—वत्सानां राजा वत्सराजः; King of the Vatsa country (for which see Introd., Geography of the play). This was Udayana.

Udayana was a king of the lunar race, the son of Sahasrânika and the hero of a popular story. His geneology is thus given in the Kathâs.—पाण्डु—अर्जुन—अभिमन्यु—परीक्षित्—जनमेजय—शतानीक—सहस्रानीक—उद-यन. In the Vishṇu P., however, he is said to be the son of a second S'atânîka, the 19th in succession from Janamejaya, which seems to be more probable. According to Lalitavistara (a work in Sanskrit on the life and doctrines of Buddha) he was born on the same day as Buddha. Mahâsena, also called Chaṇḍa-Mahâsena—king of Ujjayinî, had a daughter, called Vâsavadattâ, whom he wished to give in marriage to Vatsarâja. (According to another account he wished to give her to a king named Sañjaya. In the meantime Vâsavadattâ saw Udayana in a dream and being enamoured of him contrived to inform him of her love). With this object he enticed Udayana to his city and kept him a captive there. Being engaged to teach music to Vâsa- adattâ, Udayana gained her heart and by the advice of his minister, Yaugandharâyaṇa, managed to carry her off from her father. They were afterwards married in great pomp.

हारि चरितं—This is proved by the many references to his name; *cf.* उत्तेजयामि सुहृदः परिमोक्षणाय यौगन्धरायण इवोदयनस्य राज्ञः । Mṛich. IV. 26; प्राप्यावन्तीनुदयनकथाकोविदग्रामवृद्धान् Meg. I. 30; प्रद्योतस्य प्रियदुहितरं वत्सराजोऽत्र जह्रे । Ibid. I. 33; वासवदत्ता च राज्ञे संजयाय पित्रा दत्तमात्मानमुदयनाय प्रायच्छत् । Mal.-Mâd. II.

नाट्ये—नाट्य is the pantomimic representation of situations; gesticulation, acting. वयं—himself and the band of actors. The plural is not आदरार्थे here, as the Sūtra. refers to himself in the 4th line (मद्भाग्योपचयात्). वस्तु—a thing, a fact or an item. Distinguish this from वस्तु in अपूर्ववस्तुरचना० *supra*. एकैकं—एक repeated is to be taken as a Bah. Comp. by 'एकं बहुव्रीहिवत्' Pâṇ. VIII. 1. 9, and dissolved as एकमेकं एकैकं, the case-termination of the first being dropped by virtue of its being a comp. ०फल—is money and reputation. पदं—object, abode or source. पुनः—implies पक्षान्तर 'what then (when).' उपचय-growth, development, excess. समुदितः—has appeared all together, is combined. गुणानां—favourable circumstances, advantages or excellences; *cf.* एकैकमप्यनर्थाय किमु यत्र चतुष्टयम् । Hit. I.

S'l. quoted in S.-D. and D.-R. as an instance of प्ररोचना (or that which attracts the attention of the audience to the representation by a commendation of the play &c.) one of the *angas* of भारती वृत्ति; it is defined as—निवेदनं प्रयोज्यस्य निर्देशो देशकालयोः । काव्यार्थसूचकैः शब्दैः सभायाश्चित्तरञ्जनम् । कविकाव्यनटादीनां प्रशंसा च प्ररोचना ॥

This introductory passage (from अद्याहं to the end of this S'l.) is found almost the same in the other two plays of the poet, with some slight variations to suit the context; *e. g.* इन्द्रोत्सवे for वसन्तोत्सवे, सिद्धराज or बोधिसत्त्व for वत्सराज &c. in Nâg. See Introd.

P. 6. संगीतकं—means here a song or songs accompanied by instrumental music, and dancing; a concert. अनुतिष्ठामि—the reader will see that this wish of the Sûtra. is not fulfilled, owing to his wife not being in the proper mood for it. Almost the same expression occurs in Mud. I. यावत्—'Just,' indicates immediate action. आर्ये—A wife is to be so addressed in dramas. तावत्—Lit. 'so much' (as to come here), has in such expressions the force of 'please' in English. Or it may mean 'for a while' (अवधि). Supply after this आगम्यतां as the impersonal form is more polite than the active आगच्छ or एहि. आर्यपुत्र—Lit. the son of the venerable one (*i. e.* the father-in-law), is the prescribed mode of addressing a husband in dramas. For the use of the Prâkṛita by women, see Introd. p. 9.

From the use of the Prâkṛita by women and the minor characters in dramas, it appears that, although the Prâkṛita dialects came into general use about the fifth century B. C., they were at first used by women, even of the higher classes, and by the uneducated people generally. The principal branches of the Prâkṛita were Mâgadhî or the Eastern branch, spoken in Magadha (modern Behar) and S'aurasenî or the Western branch, spoken in the Doab or the region between the Ganges and the Jumna.

नियोगः—नियुज्यते अस्मिन्निति, an order to be executed, a task. It also means a duty assigned to a particular individual; *cf.* त्वमपि स्वं नियोगमशून्यं कुरु (constantly occurring in dramas); न खलु तातनियोग एव S'ák. I. &c. रत्नावलीदर्शन—Here रत्ना. by Lakshaṇâ, means, 'the representation on the stage of the play Ratnâvalî.' नेपथ्यं—dress.

त्वं-तुमं *Cf.* Marâthî तुम्ही and Gujarati तमे. दुहिता—Lit. the milker; fr. दुह् + the Uṇâdi aff. तृ. there being no guṇa. The task of milching the cattle was assigned to daughters in the early Aryan society (as they only could be safely entrusted with that work). The fem. affix ई is not added as the word belongs to the स्वस्रादि class. See Sid.-Kau. on Páṇ. IV. 1. 10. Yáska derives it as दुर्हिता (one who is ill-placed) or दूरे हिता (placed at a distance from her father's home after marriage) देशान्तर—properly a region separated by a large river; hence a distant country (महानद्यन्तरं यत्र तद्देशान्तरं). दत्ता—means here वाग्दत्ता promised to be given, betrothed. आत्मापि मे &c.—

Even my own self is not perceptible to me, I am not cognizant of myself even (so much beside myself I am with anxiety).

P. 7. S'l. 6. द्वीपात् &c.—द्वीप fr. द्वि + अप् (the अ of अप् is changed to ई after द्वि. अन्तर् and prepositions; अन्तरीप, प्रतीप &c.); see com.

घटयति-cau. of घट् 1. A. to happen (अभिमतं घटेत Mâl.-Mâdh. I. 9.) and not घट् 10th conj. which has घाटयति; 'brings about' accomplishes;' *cf.* तटस्थः स्वानर्थान्घटयति च मौनं च भजते । Mâl.-M. I. 14. Or it may mean 'brings in close contact with,' 'unites'. अभिमुखी०—Lit. with the face turned towards; hence favourably disposed, propitious. The fig. of speech may be अप्रस्तुतप्रशंसा. This S'l. gives a forecast of the principal events, by referring to the rescue of Ratn. from the waters of the sea, and her being brought from a distant land and attached to the Queen's apartments.

नेपथ्ये—In the post-scenium, or tiring-room. भरतपुत्र—भरतस्य पुत्र इव पुत्रः भरतपुत्रः-A follower of the science propounded by भरत; an actor; by transferrence of epithets भरत also means 'an actor,' as in तत्किमित्युउदासते भरताः। Mâl. M. I. एवमेतत् &c.—This speech of Yaugandharâyaṇa from behind the scenes forms the first *aṅga* or element of the *Mukhasaṃdhi* called उपक्षेप or the hinting of the Bîja or seed, *viz.*, Yauga. s attempt, assisted by favourable fate, to unite Ratn. with his master.

यौगन्धरायण—The faithful minister of Udayana, ever devoted to his master's cause. Wherever King Vatsa is mentioned, his associates, Yaugandharâyaṇa his minister, Vasantaka his companion, and Rumaṇavat his general, are mentioned. भूमिका—the part assigned to an actor in a drama.

नेपथ्यग्रहणाय—*i. e.* the dress suited to the parts they had to assume. The reading वयमपि अनन्तरकरणीय &c. (अनन्तरं यत्करणीयं तस्य वेशस्तद्ग्रहणेन by putting on the dress suited to what we have to do next—see foot-note) found in the Cal. ed. does not seem to be original. It is not in the style of the poet. Again अनन्तरकरणीय and अपरभूमिकया are almost pleonastic; for अनन्तरकरणीयं is अपरभूमिकाग्रहणं. Thirdly, नेपथ्यग्रहणाय accords better with the previous तद् गृह्यतां नेपथ्यम् p. 6.

प्रस्तावना—प्रस्तावयति (that which introduces the subject-matter) इति; fr. प्रस्तु cau. + अन् (युच्) added कर्तरि and fem. आ. प्रस्तावना or the Prelude, also called आमुख (although the former is generally used in plays) is a dialogue, full of interesting speeches between the Sûtradhâra and one of the actors or the actress, bearing on their own business and hinting or leading to the incidents immediately to be introduced. See com. There are five varieties of प्रस्तावना, of which the present is कथोद्घात, as Yaugandharáyaṇa enters, catching up the words of the Sútradhâra. See com.

यौगन्ध०—एवमेतत् &c. Here we have the बीजन्यास or the casting of the seed. See D.-R. p. 5.

P. 8. अन्यथा—otherwise (*i. e.* if the favourableness of Fate be not admitted). Here Yau. finds the statement of the Sûtra. verified in his case. क-क—The repetition of क indicates great incongruity or disparity between two assertions. It is often used by Kâlidása, see Rag. I. 2, Mál. III. 2. Śâk. II. 18, &c. सिद्धादेश०—सिद्ध—a seer, one who has obtained miraculous or superhuman power by the practice of *Yoga*, such as त्रिकालज्ञान, &c.; तस्य आदेश: (authoritative) statement or telling. The आदेश was that whoever married her would become an emperor. See Act. IV. प्रार्थिता—formally asked, solicited.

सिंहलेश्वर०—This was Vikramabáhu; see Act IV. For सिंहल see Introd. यानभङ्ग—यान is any vehicle or conveyance; here used for a ship; प्रवहण *v. l.* means the same thing. ०मग्नोत्थितया:—shows that she was fortunate enough to find a plank at the moment she rose up from water. ०निमग्नाया: *v. l.* who fell into the water. ०निम्नगाया: *v. l.* 'who sank in the water' —is not a good reading and is probably a mislection for निमग्नाया:. फलकं—फलहक *v. l.* a plank. ०कासादनं—This refers to the Sûtradhâra's मध्यादपि जलनिधे: । S'l. 2 *supra.* कौशाम्बीय:- see com.; a resident of Kaus'âmbî, the capital of Udayana; see Introd. संभावनं-may mean—(1) finding her; or (2) सम्यग्भावनं taking care of her and rendering assistance to her. ०चिह्नाया:- She was recognized as a princess from the costly jewel-necklace she wore, and the merchant being a native of Kaus'âmbî, knew that the marriage of the daughter of the King of Siṃhala with his master was being negotiated for by Yaugandharâyaṇa, and so he at once concluded that she was no other than the princess of Siṃhala and brought her to Kaus'âmbî.

सहर्षे—The fore-mentioned happy happenings augured well for the King, and he is delighted to think that his object would be fulfilled now. सर्वथा—In every way; hence, very assuredly. अभ्युदया:—Prosperity of every kind. The pl. shows that the King would not only get the princess but success in his campaigns against his enemies. एनां-should rather be एतां,

as the proper form of एतद् is not used before. The use of एतद् is to be justified by supposing her to be mentally present before him. सगौरवं—This he did to show to the queen that the maiden was not an ordinary girl and was, therefore, to be treated with special consideration. युक्तं—For he knew that thereby the King would get a chance of seeing her and thus be drawn to her. Hereir we have the बीजन्यास the casting or sowing of the seed, (see D.-R. p. 5) which is developed hereafter as the plot progresses. We shall not, hereafter, refer in the Notes to the various technicalities of dramaturgy in connexion with this as they are given in the com.

कञ्चुकी—So called probably from the long loose robe he wore (कञ्चुकः अस्यास्तीति). The Kañch. is a character peculiar to the Sanskrit drama. He was the superintendent of the inner apartments of kings, being a Bráhmaṇa, old, endowed with a number of good qualities, and a clever man of business. See com. Bâbhravya, it seems, was sent by Yaugandharâyaṇa to the King of Siṃhala with a request to give his daughter in marriage to his master. वसुभूतिना—Viu.'s presence at Kaus'âmbî is necessary for the identification of Ratnávali; hence its importance in the development of the plot. कथं कथमपि—अपि added to कथं has the sense of 'indefiniteness or indescribability;' the repetition of कथं serves to intensify the meaning: so the whole means 'with great difficulty.' कोसलो०—For कोसल see Introd. रुमण्वन्—The general of Udayana. ०प्रायं—Here प्राय means बाहुल्य; see com.; so this, at the end of comp.s, means-for the most part; almost; nearly. धृतिं—धृति may mean—(1) संतोष 'satisfaction'; *cf.* चक्षुर्बध्नाति धृतिं Vik. II. 8; किं भुङ्क्ते भुवनत्रये धृतिरसौ Nâg. I. 6; or (2) धैर्य 'fortitude,' stability; he means—I feel nervous about it, as suggested by the last line of the next s'l.

P. 9. S'l. 7. स्वामिनः &c.—Construe—इत्थं देवेन दत्तहस्तावलम्बे स्वामिनः वृद्धिहेतौ अस्मिन्प्रारम्भे; or स्वामिनः वृद्धिहेतौ अस्मिन्प्रारम्भे इत्थं देवेन दत्तहस्तावलम्बे सति (now that the support of the hand is thus given to it). दत्तहस्ता०—दत्तहस्त also means the same thing; *cf.* अवयवैर्दत्तहस्ता Veṇ. II. 21; चित्रलेखादत्तहस्ता Vik. p. 20. सिद्धेः—सिद्धे *v. l.* सिद्धिविषये 'as regards success;' here सिद्ध must be taken in the sense of सिद्धि, त being added भावे. स्वेच्छा०—Acting of my own motion or will (*i. e.* without the King's knowledge and approval). The S'l. is quoted in the D.-R. (with the reading ०कारी for ०चारी) as an instance of Parinyâsa, one of the angas of *Mukhasamdhi*). भीत एवास्मि—His endeavour was to advance his master's cause: hence he should have no fear, and yet he has it. The fig. of speech in this S'l. is अनुगुण; अत्र प्राक्सिद्धप्रारम्भस्य देवानुकूल्यवर्णनादनुगुणालंकारः । Nig. S'.

अभिहन्य०--Some read मधुरं (adv. modifying अभिहन्य०) 'agreeably', 'sweetly', before this; but this is superfluous, as the idea is expressed by मृदु which follows. Again it will have to be construed with अभिहन्यमान which is not separate, but part of a comp. मृदु—mellow, pleasantly sounding (being gently beaten). मृदङ्ग--So called as it was originally made of clay (मृद् अङ्गमस्य). चर्चरी०—चर्चरी has a variety of meanings: it means (1) 'a kind of song,' thus defined-द्रुतमध्यलयं समाश्रिता पठति प्रेमभरान्नटी यदि । प्रतिमण्ठकरासकेन वा द्रुतमध्या प्रथमा हि चर्चरी ॥ (2) 'the clapping of hands' (which is the meaning here, as the word गीत already occurs in the comp.);(3) 'a mode of walking' as in चर्चरिकयोपविश्य Vik. IV. p. 145; (4,5) see com. ०मह--a festival; fr. मह् पूजायां and अ (अज् or घ). This is the same as the Vasantotsava referred to before. महीयांसं—greatly enhanced, excessive (celebrated with great rejoicings). This is fully described in Váts. Kám. (I. Adhi. 5) wherein the Com. remarks—मदनमहोत्सवः वसन्तस्य प्रथमवासरे. देवः—The king is so addressed in dramas.

S'l. 8. The epithets herein are paronomastic and apply to both वत्सेश्वर and कुसुमचाप, there being thus a verbal resemblance between the two; the king is described as coming like मदन himself, eager to see his own festival. विश्रान्त०—(1) विग्रह war; with regard to whom all talk about war is at rest; for Udayana had conquered all his enemies (see S'l. 9 *infra* राज्यं निर्जितशत्रु and his subjects enjoyed the blessings of peace; (2) विग्रह body; for Madana's body was reduced to ashes by S'iva. रतिमान्—(1) रति love, attachment; जनस्य चित्ते वसन् अत एव रतिमान possessed of the love of his subjects; some take it to mean 'full of love,' a gallant (as shown by his private life); but that does not seem to be intended here, as the attribute चित्ते वसन् will have no significance. (2) रति the wife of Káma; रतिमान् being always accompanied by Rati. see Kum. III. 35. रतिमान् in the first case may also mean having a liking for, *i. e.*, interest in, the rejoicings of the people (रतिमान् अभ्युपैति).

जनस्य चित्ते वसन्—(1) By his good government Udayana had secured a place in the hearts of the people; (2) naturally dwelling in the heart; *cf.* the epithets मनसिज, मनोभू &c. प्रियवस॰—(1) वसन्तक name of the Vidûshaka, the King's constant companion; (2) वसन्तक the God of spring, who is described as a constant associate of Kâma; *cf.* मधुश्च ते मन्मथ साहचर्यात् Kum. III. 21; इत्युक्तो वचनं तस्मै तथेत्योमिति तद्वचः । गृहीत्वा शिरसा कामः सदारः सवसन्तकः ॥ Siva P. Adh. X. एव—is to be construed as दर्शनाय एव (पर्युत्सुकः). पर्युत्सुकः—Anxious, eager. निजमहो॰—(1) निज because inaugurated by himself or due to his good rule. (2) Celebrated in his honour. The dat. is used तादर्थ्ये. Although उत्सुक governs the Instr. or the Loc. (by प्रसितोत्सुकाभ्यां तृतीया च) पर्युत्सक does not, as the injunction समासप्रत्ययविधौ तदन्तविधिप्रतिषेधः interferes. अभ्युपैति—The Present tense here does not go against the p. p. p. अधिरूढ in the preceding paragraph; for there Yangandha. saw him on the terrace of the palace, and now approaching the road-side.

For the figures in the s'l. see com.; छेकानुप्रास means the similarity (but in different ways) of a group of letters (as वसन् here) occurring once—छेको व्यञ्जनसंङ्घस्य सकृत्साम्यमनेकधा ।

P. 10. कार्यशेषं—What remains of the business to be accomplished, *viz.* Ratnávalî's union with the King. This refers to the employment of the magician, mentioned in the fourth Act, for obtaining the consent of the Queen to the match. विष्कम्भकः—(विष्कम्नातीति from स्कम्भ् 5, 9 P. with वि to fasten or fix, and aff. अण्) is an interlude, showing concisely the connexion between those subordinate parts of the story; which are not enacted on the stage and those to follow. It may be in the form of a monologue (as here) or a dialogue which may be carried on by low (नीच) characters who speak Prâkrit or by the middle ones (मध्यम) who speak Sanskrit, when it is called शुद्ध or pure; or by the low and middle ones, in which case it is called मिश्र or mixed. See also p. 30, note on प्रवेशक.

विदूषकः—The Vidú., who by the rules ought to be a Brâhmaṇa, is the constant companion and trusted friend of the hero of a play, playing the same part towards him that the female companion and confidante plays towards the heroine. His business is to excite mirth by his ridiculous appearance, age and quaint dress. He assists the hero or king in his love-intrigues and is allowed not only full liberty of speech but free access to the female apartments also. He is thus more than the buffoon of the Western drama. He is variously named, as Vasantaka, Kusuma, Maitreya or so. "His attempts at wit," remarks M. Williams, "which are never very successful, and his allusions to the pleasures of the table, of which he is a confessed votary, are absurdly contrasted with the sententious solemmity of the despairing hero, crossed in the prosecution of his love-suit. The shrewdness of the heroine's confidantes never seems to fail them; but the clumsy interference of the Vidúshaka in the intrigues of his friend only serves to augment his difficulties and occasions many an awkward dilemma'.

Sl. 9. राज्यं—This tecnnically includes the seven elements of a kingdom mentioned by Kâmandaka; *cf.* स्वाम्यमात्यश्च राष्ट्रं च दुर्गकोशौ बलं सुहृत् । परस्परोपकारीदं सप्ताङ्गं राज्यमुच्यते ॥ योग्य—worthy, fit; the fitness lying in his ability and consummate statesmanship. सचिव—सचिं वाति fr. सचि friendship and वा to go + अ (कः). उपसर्ग—calamity, trouble; fr. सृज् with उप+अ (घञ्) added कर्मणि or भावे.

प्रद्योतस्य सुता—Here the poet evidently refers to Vásavadattâ. He also does the same in Priy.; *cf.* सपरिजनं प्रद्योतं विस्मयमुपनीय वादयन् वीणाम् । वासवदत्तामपहरामि &c. III. 6; also I. 7. Kâlidása in his Meg. also calls Vása. the daughter of Pradyota (see Meg. I. 33); and the commentators of Meg. say that प्रद्योत was another name of Chaṇḍamahásena, king of Ujjayinî, whose daughter Vâsa. really was. According to the Kathás. Pradyota was the King of Magadha, quite different from Mahásena; and his daughter's name was Padmâvatî who was given in marriage to Udayana at his own desire. See Kathás. XIII. 19, 20. See Introd. वसन्तसमयः—The spring season, so favourable to enjoyment. The King might well regard the spring as coming to serve him to complete his happiness; *cf.* अथ समाववृते कुसुमैर्नवैस्तमिव सेवितुमेकनराधिपम् । यमकुबेरजलेश्वरवज्रिणां समधुरं मधुरञ्चितविक्रमम् ॥ Rag. IX. 24. Some take this (but this does not seem to be intended) as an adj. qualifying त्वं meaning 'one behaving like the spring' *i. e.* contributing to pleasure; see com. इति—for these six reasons. कामं—as much as he likess. मम पुनः—*cf.* with this Yaugan.'s निजमहोत्सवदर्शनाय. This S'l. establishes the character of the hero as धीरललित. *Cf.* with this Nâg. I. 7, and Târâḍîda's description in Kâd. स राजा बाहुदण्डेन विजित्य सकलद्वीपवलयां वसुन्धरां शुकनासनाम्नि मन्त्रिणि सुहृदीव राज्यभारमारोप्य सुस्थिताः प्रजाः कृत्वा......प्रशमिताशेषविपक्षतया विगलितशङ्कः......यौवनसुखमनुबभूव । p. 98.

P. 11. श्री वयस्य &c.—The king is to be addressed as वयस्य or राजन् by the Vidû.; *cf.* Bharata वयस्य राजन्निति वा भवेद्वाच्यो महीपतिः। विदूषकेण &c.एवं न्विदं-Vid. first endorses the King's view, but then, as suits his character, says that the festival may rather be looked upon as *his,* and furnishes the reason for such a supposition in the words यस्य कृते &c.

ममैवैकस्य ब्राह्मणस्य—*cf.* a similar passage in Nâg. ही ही भोः संपूर्णा मनोरथाः प्रियवयस्यस्य। अथ वा न हि न हि भवत्या मलयवत्याः। अथ वा नेतयोः। ममैवैकस्य ब्राह्मणस्य। p. 47. ब्राह्मणवटुकस्य—*v. l.* of me, a poor Bráhmaṇa. For comp. see com. बटु primarily means a pupil; क added to it implies commiseration; a poor or helpless pupil, and then secondarily (by Lakshaṇá) any poor person. The reading ब्राह्मणस्य is preferred because the Vid. is not likely to speak disparagingly of himself, especially when he was complimented by the King in the way mentioned above. मन्त्रयते—is spoken; although मन्त्र्, according to the Dhátupátha means 'to speak or confer in private (गुप्तपरिभाषणे),' it is often used in plays in the sense of 'to speak.'

प्रेक्षस्व &c.—The three long compounds ending in कौतूहलस्य, शोभिनः and सुखस्य are adjectives qualifying मदनमहोत्सवस्य. मधुमत्त &c. For comp. see com. मधु is wine prepared from the flowers of Madhûka (*Bassia Latifolia*). कामिनीजन—sportive young women. स्वयंग्राहः—voluntary seizing तेन गृहीतः voluntarily seized; qualifies नागर जनः (०गृहीतश्चासौ नृत्यंश्च). The form ग्राह in the sense of ग्रहण, although used by Kálidâsa (*scil.* कण्ठे स्वयंग्राहनिषिक्तबाहुं Kum. III. 7) is anomalous (although Mallinâtha finds a defence for it; see our note *ad. loc.*) as घञ् (अ) is not available. Some say स्वार्थयन्ता वृच् (by adding अच् to ग्रह् cau. used in the primitive sense). It is better to read स्वयंग्रह; we get ग्रहणं ग्रहः by adding अच् (अ) to ग्रह् भावे. स्वयंग्राहगृहीत may also be taken with शृङ्गक-syringes taken in their hands by the ladies of their own accord. शृङ्गक—शृङ्ग a syringe; शृङ्गमेव शृङ्गकं, क being added स्वार्थे. Probably horns perforated at the end were originally used as syringes. ०प्रहारनृत्यन् dancing by reason of being struck. नागर—a citizen (as opposed to ग्राम्य a rustic); hence one well versed in love-matters; a gallant.

उद्दामताड्यमान—स्वच्छन्द *v. l.* means 'beaten ceaselessly' (lit. unchecked). सुवृत्त *V. l.* well-rounded, well- shaped. मर्दल—मर्द (beating or friction) लाति इति; a kind of Mridanga (तबला says Nig. S'., but that does not seem to be intended here, as the Mardalas spoken of here were carried about by men walking through the streets and were sounding loudly). ०मर्दलैः उद्दामा (see com.) greatly deepened or swelled by; the word here may be उद्दामा swelling unrestrained (उद्गतं दाम a fastening; hence restraint or check यस्मात् सः) or उद्दामः (*cf.* उद्दामेन द्विरदपतिना संनिपत्याभियुक्तः । Uttar. III. 6); in this case explain-उद्गतो दामाया: उद्दामः; दामन् is both *n.* and *fem.*, when *fem.* it optionally assumes the form दामा by डाबुभाभ्यामन्यतरस्याम् । Pāṇ. IV. I. 13. Or this may be taken separately ०मर्दलैः उद्दामचर्चर्याश्च शब्देन मुखराणि &c. चर्चरी —here, a kind of song. रथ्यामुखं—The outlets or openings of streets. पटवास—a kind of scented powder (called अबीर or बुक्का.) of a yellowish red colour. पिञ्जरित—From पिञ्जर *m.* a yellowish-red colour; पिञ्जरः सञ्जात एषामिति पिञ्जरितानि. पिञ्जरीकृत *v. l.* is a *Chvi*-formation-अपिञ्जराणि पिञ्जराणि सम्पद्यन्ते तथा कृतानि. सश्रीकता—Charmingness; श्रिया सह वर्तते इति सश्रीकः charming तस्य भावः सश्रीकता. The final क is added by the rule शेषाद्विभाषा (and not by नद्युतश्च), so we have सश्रीः also.

P. 12. कोटि—कोटि may mean—(1) extremity, limit, and परा कोटि the farthest limit; or (2) excess. स्यात्कोटिरश्रो चापाग्रे संख्यभिदप्रकर्षयोः । इति विश्वः.

S'l. 10. पिष्टातकौघैः—पिष्टमतति इति पिष्टातः fr. अत् to go + अ (अण् कर्मणि); पिष्टात एव पिष्टातकः the same as पटवास. ओघ—a collection or heap of; here, handfuls of. कुङ्कुम०—कुङ्कुम saffron; क्षोद powder, dust. गौर—reddish. भरनमितशिखैः—which have caused the crests (or the heads) to bend low on account of their weight (implying that they were worn in a thick mass). कैङ्किरातैः—the wreaths of the As'oka flowers (see com.) which are of a reddish-yellow colour. Some take किंकिरात to mean 'the yellow कुरण्टक flowers'. The idea is that the upper parts of the bodies of the people were yellow with the glitter of the gold-ornaments, while their heads were yellow with the thick mass of the As'oka wreaths. ०शिरःशेखरैः *v. l.*—Nig. Ś. explains—भरेण पुष्पाणां नमितानि शिरांसि तेषां शेखरैः आपीडैः कैंकिरातैः wreaths of the as'oka flowers which served as ornaments to the heads &c. But this is not very satisfactory. It will, perhaps, be better to take शेखर in the sense of 'head dress.' Mr. Godbole takes कैंकिरातैः in the sense of 'gallants, amorous persons' (fr. किंकिरात Cupid)-by gallants wearing garlands, which &c. But this does not directly add to the पीतत्व of the city.

वेषाभिलक्ष्य०—वेष includes the idea of both, the ornaments worn by the people and their dresses. So heavily were the people loaded with gold-ornaments and so rich and magnificent were their costumes that the collective wealth of the city, estimated from these, seemed to exceed that of Kubera. For the somewhat extravagant description here, *cf.* Shakespeare's Henry VIII, Act I, scene I.

> To-day the French,
> All clinquant, all in gold, like Weathen gods,
> Shone down the English; and, to-morrow, they,
> Made Briton India; every man that stood
> Showed like a mine. Their dwarfish pages were,
> As cherubins, all gilt; the madams too,
> Not used to toil, did almost sweat to bear
> The pride upon them, &c. &c.

शातकुम्भ—gold, so called from its being supposed to be found in the mountain शतकुम्भ. एकपीता—Wholly yellow; yellow all over. The atmosphere was yellow with the powder thrown all round, while the streets were yellow being thickly crowded with the people also yellow as described above.

Sl. 11. धारायन्त्र—a fountain. संतत—continuous, uninterrupted. The म् of सम् is optionally dropped before तत and हित (by समो वा ततहितयोः), so we have सतत also. पूर—a mass or quantity of (as the idea of flow is expressed by संतत). प्लुते—read प्लुते—covered over. सर्वतः—goes with प्लुते. सान्द्रविमर्द—heavy or close treadings (by the feet). सर्वं—is better taken with सैन्दूरीक्रियते. प्राङ्गणे—प्रकृष्टमङ्गनं प्राङ्गणं a spacious yard; the न is changed to ण as it is a संज्ञा by the rule पूर्वपदात्संज्ञायाम्.

उद्दाम°—See com., moving unrestraimed, treading at will; or boisterous. प्रमदाः—Young women in high glee; or drunken women. कपोल—The reading कपाल is bad, as it is generally applied to the skull-bone or the portion of the skull of a dead body; and even if it be made somehow to mean 'the forehead' the rhetoricians would find the ग्राम्यतादोष in that. सैन्दूरं—Made of or dyed with vermillion. चरणन्यासैः—Properly the settings of the feet on the ground; hence, secondarily, the foot-prints. पुरः कुट्टिमं—The pavement or paved floor in front of the court-yard. The two words may also be taken as compounded. The pavement was completely reddened by the treadings of the people as they moved about with their wet soles carrying the red paint dropping from the cheeks of the women walking with wanton steps.

P. 13. सुविदग्ध—Very clever, (in amorous sports); skilled in that business, सीत्कार—The hissing sound (lit. the emitting of the sound *sît*) caused by a sensation of pain or so. *Cf.* मया दृष्टाधरं तस्याः ससीत्कारमिवाननम्। Vik. IV. 21. वारविला॰ a courtesan, a harlot; वार 'a multitude' with any word signifying a woman added to it has this sense; *e. g.* वारस्त्री.

Sl. 12. ॰सान्धकारे—The Vidú. directs the attention of the King to another quarter where the courtezans were sporting with amorous persons. The dense cloud of the scattered scented dust, not being mixed with saffron, added to the gloom of the approaching evening and the King, looking from above, could see the people but dimly by the glitter of the gems they wore, and the scene appeared to him like the one presented by Pâtála, which is said to be perpetually shrouded in darkness, with the Nâgas moving about. The Nâgas, according to one account, are semi-divine beings, having a human form with the hood of a serpent rising behind their necks (see our Nâg., note on the word नागकन्यका p. 18). The epithets प्रकीर्ण॰, मणिवि॰, उद्यत॰, and the pun on भुजङ्ग give the points of similarity. मणिविभूषण—(1) ornaments containing jewels; (2) the gems (in their hoods) serving as ornaments. उद्यतफ॰—(1) with the hood-like syringes raised up; (2) with raised hoods looking like syringes.

मां—The use of the accus. here is somewhat questionable. The poet seems to follow the general rule गतिबुद्धिप्रत्यवसानार्थ &c. Pân. I. 4. 52, *i. e.* in the case of verbs implying 'motion, knowledge' &c. (see A. G. § 44) the subject of the primitive verb is put in the acc. case, in the causal. But Bhaṭṭoji Dikshita and others hold that the addition of the Várṭika 'दृशेश्च' implies that the word बुद्धि in the Sûtra refers to verbs implying knowledge of a general kind and not of a particular kind, such as घ्राणजन्यज्ञान, श्रवणजन्यज्ञान &c., and will not apply to verbs like स्मरति; we must say घ्रापयति, स्मारयति, देवदत्तेन. Some defend the acc. by saying that Patañjali allows the प्रयोज्यकर्म to स्मरयति when he says स्मरयत्येनं (कोकिलं) वनगुल्मः स्वयमेव। (see Bhâshya on Pâṇ. I. 3. 67). स्मरयत्येव वनगुल्म इत्यत्र तु णेरणाविति सूत्रे भाष्यप्रयोगादेव कर्मत्वं बोध्यम्। Tatvabodhinî. संस्मरयति—There is some grammatical inaccuracy also here. As the King merely thought of Pâtála at the sight before him, we should expect the form स्मारयति. स्मरयति is the form when the sense is 'makes one yearn after a thing' *i. e.* when स्मृ is used in the sense of आध्यान or उत्कण्ठापूर्वकं स्मरणं (and not चिन्ता merely). The King could not have got a longing for a thing he had not actually seen. Perhaps the poet used it for the sake of the metre. It is a weak defence to say that the King longed to see what appeared like Pâtâla and so had उत्कण्ठा.

मदन०—adv. विसंष्ठुलं unsteadily, unevenly. For विसं० *cf.* मुहूर्तनिर्व्यूढविस्मयविसंष्ठुलोद्वेलद्विस्तीर्यमाण &c. Mâl.-Mâd. VII. p. 152. मदवश०—*V. l.* under the influence of passion. मदनवशावेषं (मदनस्य वशा मदनवशा तस्याः वेषं) वहन्ती—*V. l.* bearing the appearance (वेष) of one under the influence of love. वसन्ताभिनयं—with gesticulations indicative of the spring-festival. अभिनवं *v. l.* -in a novel or strange manner.

P. 14. द्विपदीखण्डं—द्विपदी is a kind of Prâkṛita song adapted to music. It consists of four feet or quarters, with 13 *mâtrâs* in each. It is of four kinds, for which see com.

S'l. 13. The southerly breeze or the wind from the Malaya mountain is invariably described by Sanskrit poets in connexion with the Spring; *cf.* Kum. III. 25; and, as it excites passion, being cool and charged with the fragrance of the sandal trees in which the mountain abounds, it is called the Messenger of Kâma. Comp. with this the description of Spring at the beginning of the 5th Ch. of D.K., Pûrvapiṭhikâ.

दूतकः—The क in this and in the next S'loka is added स्वार्थे, merely for rhythm. मुकुलायित—made to possess blossoms; see com.; it may also be taken as the p. p. p. of the cau. of the denom. from मुकुल (मुकुल इव आचरति मुकुलायते) by adding य (क्यङ्). But then the intended sense is not got directly. मुकुलीकृत० *v. l.* is explained in the com. बहु०—The propriety of बहु is this—as it was the beginning of Spring, the south-wind had caused many of the mango-trees to blossom (and not all yet). घन—*v. l.* for बहु is not good, for that would mean that the breeze caused only the shady mango-trees to blossom. शिथिलित०—This it did by reminding them of the spring season, which was the season for enjoying the company of, and not for getting angry with, their husbands. *Cf.* for a similar thought त्यजतमानमलं बत विग्रहैर्न पुनरेति गतं चतुरं वयः। परभृताभिरितीव निवेदिते स्मरमते रमते स्म वधूजनः॥ Rag. IX. 47; *cf.* also Kum. III. 32.

Sl. 14. विकसित०—Qualifies युवतिसार्थकः; through whom the As'oka and Bakula trees have come into blossom. For women causing the blossom of trees, see further, notes on

S'l. 18. ०मेलकः—may mean 'a crowd, a multitude'; or मेलनं (company, union with). मेलः एव मेलकः; 'मेलके संगसंगमौ' इत्यमरः। The प्रियजन॰ meant are those that are absent. उत्कण्ठितप्रियमेलकः- *v. l.* The compound is clumsy. It must be taken as प्रियमेलके प्रियसंगमे उत्कण्ठितः; the परनिपात of प्रिय॰ being explained by taking the comp. as one of the राजदन्तादि class. प्रतिपालना॰—Being affected by great longing they are unable to wait longer. साम्यति—feels uneasy, pines away. *Cf.* गाढोत्कण्ठाललितलुलितैरङ्ग-कैस्ताम्यतीति। Mâl.-Mâd. I. 15. Some read भ्राम्यति (भम्मइ). wander about (hoping to meet their lovers). Nig. S'. who reads उत्कण्ठितप्रियमेलकः takes this S'l. as a continuation of the preceding one (the two forming a युग्म) and gives a very ingenious explanation of the different epithets. He makes it mean—The south-wind, which has caused the Bak. and As'o. trees to blossom, which brings together lovers pining for each other's company (उत्कण्ठिताश्च ते प्रियजनाश्च तेषां मेलकः संगमयिता। मिल संगमने कर्तरि ण्वुल्। शेषषष्ठ्या समासः), which makes separated beloveds unable to wait (प्रतिपालने असमर्थाः येन) and which makes young women long for the company of their husbands (अर्थेन पतिसमागमरूपेण सहिताः सार्थाः तादृशीः करोतीति सार्थकः। सार्थशब्दात्तत्करोतीति णिजन्ताण्ण्वुल्। युवतीनां सार्थकः युवतिसा॰), causes trouble (तमधातुरन्तर्भावितण्यर्थः). But the S'âstrî himself condemns this interpretation as requiring a great deal of twisting and straining and as containing the fault समाप्तपुनरात्तान and then interprets it in the way we have done. These two s'lokas are in the Dvipadî style. The following is a Gîti.

S'l. 15. मृदुलानि—मृदुर्गुण एषामस्तीति मृदुलानि possessed of softness, soft, *i. e.*, capable of being pierced by the flowery arrows. लब्धप्रसरैः—which have got scope for action or access.

P. 15. क्रीडारसः—interest in, ardour or passion for sport. मधुरोऽयमासां निर्भरः क्रीडा॰ *v. l.*-Here निर्भरः is the predicate, मधुरः क्रीडारसः निर्भरः। We have dropped मधुर as it is the निर्भरत्व that is described in the next S'loka. आसां-as two maids only are introduced here we should expect the dual (instead of आसां) in the King's speech; so the general term परिजनस्य has been preferred here.

S'l. 16. पीडयेव — hould better be taken with every line. आकुलः—disordered, dishevelled. As the braid of hair got loosened the garland tied round it slowly dropped down. The poet fancies that the केश॰ was grieved, as it were, to lose the beauty imparted to it by the flowers. **केशपाश:**--The luxuriant hair; a Nitya-samâsa. पाश when forming the second member of a comp., implies excellence (*e. g.* कर्णपाश:), and as excellence lies, in the case of hair, in its abundance, it means 'a collection or mass of.' पाश: पक्षश्च हस्तश्च कलापार्थाः कचात्परे । Ak. पाश also implies 'censure,' 'depreciation,' as in भिषक्पाश:, छत्रपाश:. **क्षीबायाः**—क्षीब p. p. p. of क्षीब् 1. A'. to be intoxicated or drunk. **द्विगुणतरं**—द्विगुण itself has an intensive force; तर adds to the intensity or greatness. तर and तम are sometimes thus added to imply greater excess, as in युधिष्ठिरः श्रेष्ठतमः कुरूणाम्; says the Kâs'iká—यदा च प्रकर्षवतां पुनः प्रकर्षो विवक्ष्यते तदातिशायिकान्तादपरः प्रत्ययो भवत्येव । **क्रन्दत:**—cry with a very great force, *i.e.*, give rise to an unusually loud jingle. **पाद०**—There is also a pun on this—they fall at her feet to implore her not to dance with such violence. **व्यस्त:**--irregularly tossed or thrown about. **०अनुबन्ध**—continuity, uninterrupted succession of the jerks or quakes. *Cf.* उत्कम्पोऽल्पोऽपि पीनस्तनभरितमुरः क्षिप्तहारं दुनोति । Veṇî. II. 22. **पीडयेव उरो हन्ति**—The necklace being itself thrown about with violence struck against her bosom in order to induce her not to tread so carelessly and violently. But this it did, fancies the poet, painfully. **स्तनभर** &c.—भर implies full development. **०विनमत्**—the idea is a favourite one with Sanskrit poets; *cf.* आवर्जिता किंचिदिव स्तनाभ्यां &c. Kum. III. 24. **०मध्यभङ्ग०**—adv. modifying क्रीडन्त्याः.

एतासां बद्धपरिकराणां *v. l.*—परिक्रियते वस्त्रादिकमस्मिन् इति परिकरः the loins, the waist; बद्धः परिकरो याभिः who have girded up their loins; *i. e.* busily engaged in dancing. **मानयिष्यामि**—do honour to it by taking part in it.

P. 16. **हताश**—Lit. one whose hopes are destroyed (on account of his folly, wickedness &c.), hence a fool, a wicked man. **खण्ड:**—a kind of sugar not perfectly dried and used in lumps. It is finer than मत्स्यण्डिका (granulated sugar) but less refined than शर्करा. **करीअन्ति**—*cf* the Marâthi करितात; mark that the Prâkrit has no Âtmanepada. **मोदकाः क्रियन्ते**—bears testimony to the Vid.'s extreme fondness for edibles. This trait of his character is often referred to in Sanskrit plays; *cf.* एष खण्डमोदकसश्रीक उदितो राजा द्विजातीनां Vik. III. p. 71 (and the King's remark on that, *viz.* सर्वत्रौदरिकस्याभ्यवहार्यमेव विषयः ।); किं मोदकखादिकायाम् । S'âk. I. p. 48.

P. 17. **हञ्जे**—A particle of address used in the case of low female characters, such as दासीs, चेटीs &c. It may be used, as here, also by low characters when addressing each other. भट्टिनी:—भट्टिणी is usually translated into Sanskrit as भर्त्री. It is a respectful form of address adopted by servants towards the Queen. आज्ञापयति—and विज्ञापयति are polite ways of saying 'tells, informs, says,' though sometimes they may have their proper sense also. When a person in a superior position says something to his subordinate the verb आज्ञापय् is used; while when a person of an inferior rank says something to his or her superior विज्ञापय् is the verb used. दास्याःपुत्रि—A comp. with *aluk* of the Gen. termination as censure is meant. The Vid. says this, out of humour, to please the King. उत्सवात्—The abl. is ल्यब्लोपे 'having set aside or surpassed' (अतीत्य), *i. e.*, a festival more welcome than the one there already was.

स्वस्तिवाचनकं—from स्वस्ति (an indec. meaning 'a blessing') and वच् cau. and अन (ल्युट्) करणे; स्वस्ति वाच्यते अनेन that by which one is made to utter the word स्वस्ति, *i. e.*, pronounce a blessing. The usual form of address to the Brâhmaṇas is 'स्वस्ति भवन्तोऽधिब्रुवन्तु;' to which they reply आयुष्मते स्वस्ति. It may also be explained as स्वस्ति इत्यस्य वाचनं स्वस्तिवाचनं (ल्युट् added भावे) the pronouncement of a blessing; तत्प्रयोजनमस्य by adding छ (ईय) which then disappears by the rule पुण्याहवाचनादिभ्यो लुग्वक्तव्यः। Vârtika (not noticed in the Sid.-Kau.) on Pâṇ. V. 1. 110. Such स्वस्तिवाचन is necessary on all auspicious occasions, according to the Smṛiti–सम्पूज्य गन्धपुष्पाद्यैर्ब्राह्मणान् स्वस्ति वाचयेत्। धर्म्ये कर्मणि माङ्गल्ये संग्रामाद्भुतदर्शने ॥ The Prâkrit सोत्थिवाचणं is also translated into Sanskrit as स्वस्तिवायनं (often shortened into वायन, Maráthi वाण), though ०वाचनं is better; *cf.* पुण्याहवाचन, शान्तिवाचन &c. It is a present of a small quantity of rice, a coconut, a piece of cloth &c.; or sometimes of sweetmeats alone, with *Dakshiṇá*, and is given to a Brâhmaṇa (or to a woman whose husband is living) on such occasions as वटसावित्री व्रत, मङ्गलागौरी व्रत, मकरसङ्क्रमण &c.

P. 18. मकरन्दो०—मकरन्द means floral juice or honey; hence the same implies the abundance of flowering plants in it. मलयमारुता०—The mountain Malaya is identified with the southern portion of the Ghats, running from the south of Mysore and forming the eastern boundary of Travancore. It is specially known for its sandal trees, and cardamoms. It is separated from the Sahya mountain on the north by the Canara Hills. It is reckoned as one of the Kulaparvatas. सहकार—a kind of mango tree known for the fragrance of its blossoms which attracts bees (see Rag. VI. 69) and therefore a favourite haunt of lovers. It is probably so called for this reason. ॰सङ्गीत—is vocal music mixed with instrumental music; here the latter was furnished by the hum of the bees. ॰श्रुतिसुखं—This reading is preferable to ॰मुखरं as it better expresses its attractiveness. मुखरं simply means 'resounding with.' ॰दर्शितादरं—It has shown its regard for you, on your coming to visit it, by furnishing a canopy and by providing music for your reception.

P. 19. S'l. 17. Construe इह हि अधुना मधुप्रसङ्गं प्राप्य उद्यद्द्रुमकान्तिभिः किसलयैः ताम्रां त्विषं बिभ्रतः, कलैः भृङ्गालीविरुतैः अविशदव्याहारलीलाभृतः, मुहुः मलयानिलाहतिचलैः शाखासमूहैः घूर्णन्तः अमी द्रुमा मत्ता इव भान्ति । मधुप्रसङ्ग—There is a pun on the word मधु; (1) मधोः प्रसङ्गः the time of the vernal season; (2) मधुनः प्रसङ्गः contact of wine. उद्यत्—shooting or branching out, (when in the process of formation) hence the comparison to tender leaves. *Cf.* तवाधरस्पर्धिषु विद्रुमेषु पर्यस्तमेतत्सहसोर्मिवेगात् । ऊर्ध्वाङ्कुरप्रोतमुखं कथंचिद्दूरादपक्रामति शङ्खयूथम् ॥ Rag. XIII. 13. ताम्रां त्विषं &c. The redness of the tender leaves is compared to the flush of wine. *Cf.* मद्याताम्रे तरुण्या मुखशशिनि next S'l. कल-indistinct but sweet. लीला—the sportive act of. घूर्णन्तः—(1) moving backward and forward; (2) reeling.

भ्रान्ति—*v. l.* construe अमी द्रुमाः मधुप्रसङ्गमधुना भ्रान्तिं प्राप्य मत्ता इव दृश्यन्ते मधुप्रसङ्ग॰—॰प्रसङ्ग एव मधु तेन by the liquor in the shape of (the influence of) spring; or (2) by the wine of the juice of the spring flowers. This reading is bad as it is difficult to assign a meaning to भ्रान्ति; for, if we take it in the sense of भ्रमण (unsteadiness or staggering) that idea is already contained in घूर्णन्तः. If it be taken to mean उन्मत्तता (the whirling of the brain or excitement in which judgment is suspended) or intoxication, then there is tautology with मत्ता (उन्मत्ततां प्राप्य मत्ता इव दृश्यन्ते). To avoid this difficulty इव must be taken as constituting an उपमा; the trees being worked up by the intoxicating influence of the spring appear like drunken people. But this is to destroy the beauty of the S'loka. Again, भ्रान्ति does not account for the red appearance of the trees, although it explains the other two actions.

S'l. 18. गण्डूषसेकासवः—The wine sprinkled over the trees in mouthfuls by women to cause them to blossom. वास्यते—is scented as it were (as the trees had to drink it with their roots). Wine is often described as being flavoured with the perfume of flowers before it was drunk. *Cf.* सुरभिगन्धपराजित केसरम् । पतिषु निर्विविशुर्मधुमङ्गनाः &c. Rag. IX. 36; also Sis'. X. 3 (भग्नबालसहकारसुगन्धो &c.). The reading वाम्यते found in Jîvânada's ed. is vitiated by ग्राम्यतादोष or vulgarism; see Dandin's Kâv. D. I. 95. Or we may separate ०सव इव, as ०सवे इव (see com.) taking ०सवे as an adj. qualifying मूले. As soon as the root has wine supplied to it in mouthfuls, it is covered (वास्यते) with a shower of flowers. तरुण्या मुखशशिनि &c.—The implication is that as soon as the women, exhilarated with wine, treated the Champaka trees with their gentle and dexterous smiles and thus satisfied their cravings, the latter at once put forth flowers. अशोकपादा०—The As'oka requires to be struck with their feet by beautiful women to make it blossom. *Cf.* असूत सद्यः कुसुमान्यशोकः स्कंधात्प्रभृत्येव सपल्लवानि । पादेन नापैक्षत सुन्दरीणां संपर्कमासिञ्जितनूपुरेण ॥ Kum. III. 26.

For the poetic convention (कविसमय) mentioning certain trees as blossoming under certain conditions, see the S'l. स्त्रीणां &c. quoted in the com. निर्भरं—adv. निःशेषेण भरो यथा स्यात्तथा; excessively, greatly.

P. 20. अनुहरन्ति—As the imitation here is casual and not habitual, we have the Par.; otherwise by the rule हरतेर्गतताच्छील्ये we should get the Âtm., as in पैतृकमश्वा अनुहरन्ते. पूजोपकरण—The materials of worship, such as flowers, rubbed sandal, *akshatás,* fragrant powder (*Bukká*), &c. विभवतः—According to their ranks or positions. निरन्तरो०—may mean (1) with flowers thickly grown; or (2) ever blossoming. नवमालिका—a kind of double jasmine, with large and fragrant white flowers. On account of its beauty and fragrance, the Nav. flower is regarded as one of the five flowery arrows of Cupid. अकाल—out of the proper time or season; the sense of the neg. particle is तदन्यत्व here. श्रद्धालुना—श्रद्दधाति इति fr. श्रद्+धा +आलुच् added कर्तरि साधुकारिणि (fully believing).

P. 21. आत्मगतं—See Intro. p. 6. प्रमादः परिजनस्य—By परिजन she refers to the servants that had accompanied her; she means that they should have asked Sâgariká to stay behind. यस्यैव &c.—Ever since Ságariká was committed to her care by the minister, Vása. had taken care to keep her away from the sight of the King; but her presence now alarmed her; for she feared that her superior charms and youth might captivate the King and thus raise a rival to her. She, therefore, asks

Sâgarikâ, under some pretext, to go away. °पराधीने—For comp. see com; 'in the power of another,' *i. e.*, not in a position to look to another's business. मदपराधीनपरि° *v. l.*-may mean (1) when the servants are in the power of intoxication; or (2) मद् अपराधीन not dependent on me, have been given liberty to-day.

दृष्टिगोचरे—गोचर within the reach of or cognizible by the senses; from गो + चर्+अ (घ:); see com.; दृष्टि°—within the reach of vision.

P. 22. परिजने—जातौ एकवचनं; the whole body of servants. पुन:—However, on my part. प्रेक्षिष्ये—This resolve on the part of Sâga. defeats the object of the Queen. She sees the King, is impressed by his beauty, and love for him germinates in her mind. Thus we have here समाधान, one of the *aṅgas* of *Mukhasamdhi*. प्रद्युम्नं—प्रकृष्टं द्युम्नं बलं यस्य; here the image of the god of love. Prad. was the son of Krishṇa by Rukmiṇî. He was Káma re-born by the grace of Śiva moved by the lamentations of Rati, his wife. See Kum. VI. 42. Hence he is spoken of as one with Kâma. He killed the demon S'ambara.

P. 23. S'l. 19. कुसुम°—The bow-staff of Kâma consists of flowers (whence his name कुसुमधन्वन् &c.). नियमेन—(1) by means of a vow, such as the observance of a fast, &c. नियमस्तु स यत्कर्मानित्यमागन्तुसाधनम् । Amarar. (2) by regularity, as required (that it should easily bend). कथं—shows surprise. कुंकुमचर्चिका—Applying saffron with the fingers. स्वहस्तदत्तै: कुसुमकुङ्कुम-चन्दनवासोभि: *V. l.* has been accidentally omitted from the foot-notes. अर्च्यतां—Wilson says—

"According to *Bhavishyottara-Purâṇa*, the worship of Kâmadeva was instituted by *S'iva* in pity of the fate to which he had confined him. On the thirteenth of *Chaitra* the worshipper having bathed was to adore the portrait or the image of Kâmadeva either in person, or as in the present instance, in one of his manifestations, attended by his wives *Rati* and *Prîti*, his friend Vasanta, ...represented in a grove of As'oka trees, or placed in the shade of one of them, with flowers, fruits, and perfumes. It was in a grove of As'oka trees that Kâma incurred S'iva's wrath, whence the selection of that tree. ° ° ° ° A rather longer prayer is addressed to the god in *Tithi-Tattva*—'God, armed with a flowery bow, salutation be to thee! Salutation be to thee, who bearest a fish on thy banner! Salutation to thee who shakest the firmness of divinities and saints! Son of Mâdhava, Kandarpa, the foe of *S'ambara*, lord of Rati, glory to thee, the mind-engendered, the subduer of the whole universe! ...Glory to the destroyer, to Kâma, the embodied form of the god of gods, the agitator of the hearts of Brahma, Vishṇu, S'iva and Indra.' "

P. 24. S'l. 20. प्रत्यग्र—new, fresh. मज्जन—(1) a bath; (2) the act of being sprinkled with. विविक्त—bright, transparent. It is well known how a bath, just after it is performed, imparts a glow of brightness and freshness to a fair complexion. (2) clean. कौसुम्भराग॰—(1) कुसुम्भस्यायं कौसुम्भ: राग: a dye prepared from the Kusumbha flowers (which are of a bright yellowish-red colour) or it may mean 'saffron-colour.' तेन रुचिर: (charming) स्फुरन् (flashing forth, looking bright) अंशुकान्त: (the border of the wearing garment) यस्या: सा; (2) pleasing with its shining red tints (अंशु) like those of the safflower. मकरकेतनम॰—goes only with त्वं. बालप्रवाल॰—see com. The Queen touching the As'oka tree with her hand in the act of worshipping the image of Kâma, appeared like a creeper growing on a tree having tender foliage. The saffron marks made on the tree are the *Bâlapravâlas*.

This S'l. is quoted in the Kâv.—P. X. as an instance of the fault of an *Upamá*, called प्रक्रमभङ्ग (difference) of persons. For here the common verb विभ्राजसे must be changed to विभ्राजते to make it agree with लता. विभ्राजते is, therefore, suggested as a better reading, as it can agree with लता and also with भवती (understood) referring to प्रिया in the Vocative case.

S'l. 21. In this S'l. the advantage to the tree from the touch of the hand is poetically described. उद्भिन्नापर॰—Touched by the Queen's delicate hand the As'oka appeared to have put forth a shoot, more delicate (and lovelier) than those it already had. For the comparison of the hand to a sprout *cf.* किसलयै: सलयैरिव पाणिभि: । Rag. IX. 35, and of the arm of a woman to the twig of a tree, कोमलविटपानुकारिणौ बाहू । S'âk.I. 19.

S'l. 22. अनङ्गोयं &c.—The reference is to Kâma's incineration by S'iva. See note on संप्राप्तं मकरध्वजेन मथनं, additional benedi. S'l., p. 2. अनङ्गत्वं—Although the image had an *aṅga* the deity represented by it had not, and could not experience the pleasure of the touch.

॰सत्कारं—The act of showing respect or rendering honour to; fr. सत् respect आदरानादरयो: सदसती । पूजाया: पूजारूपो वा सत्कार:. This was not only in the fitness of things, but necessary. For the Bhav.-P. directs—"Having offerred adoration to the mind-born divinity, let the wife worship her husband, with ornaments, flowers and raiment, thinking internally with entire complacency 'This is the god of love.'" Wilson.

P. 25. उत्क्षिप्त०—Lit. thrown up and so drawn away from the proper point of attention; hence completely occupied by, overpowered by. विटप—The expanse or cluster of the shoots of a tree (or creeper) growing from the main stock; स्कन्धादूर्ध्वं तरोः शाखा करभो विटपो मतः इति । विटपो न स्त्रियां स्तम्बशाखाविस्तारपल्लवे । Medini. कथं प्रत्यक्षः &c.—कथं expresses susprise. By the time Ságarikâ came back, Madana's worship was over and the King was being worshipped. She saw the King who was extremely handsome, and she mistook him for the god of love; and hence her surprise at seeing the god of love worshipped in person. अमोघदर्शनः—The sight of a deity is supposed to bring on its reward; it cannot go in vain; and so Sága. wishes that she should also be favoured by the deity. दृष्टं यद्र०—She had waited there to see how Kâma was worshipped—whether he was worshipped in the same manner as at her father's house or otherwise. This being done, she now thinks of going away. यावन्न कोपि &c.—She feared because she was told by the Queen to go away at once, and not because she saw the King by not obeying the Queen; for she had no knowledge then that it was the King that was seen by her.

P. 26. विलेपन०—See *supra* note on स्वस्तिवाचन p. 17. वैतालिकः—Lit. one who sings in different *tâlas*; a kind of bard or poetical panegyrist whose duty it was to announce the fixed periods of the day, (see Vik. II. 1,) by singing a song (or two) describing in eulogistic terms the king's grandeur, his valour &c. Sometimes two bards are mentioned.

S'l. 23. आस्थानीं—The audience-hall or chamber where the king received the tributary princes in the morning and evening. संपतन्—congregating from all sides. सरोरुह &c.—has a double sense, as applying to पादान् (1) the feet (the plu. used to indicate respect) and (2) rays:—(1) having the lustre (beauty) of lotuses; (2) depriving the day-lotuses of their beauty, *i. e.*, causing them to fade. प्रीत्युत्कर्ष०—(1) may also mean joy and prosperity. उदयनस्य—may also be taken as an adj. qualifying तव (rising ever more in prosperity).

P. 27. कथमयं &c.—Sâgarikâ is agreeably surprised to learn from the song of the bard that her *Kusumáyudha* is no other than King Udayana himself to whom she was betrothed by her father. यस्याहं &c.—The same occurs in Priy. II. p. 16.

The gen. यस्य is used as there is no dative in Prâkrit. प्रेषण—Lit. sending on an errand, hence, service. सन्ध्यातिक्रमः—the passing away or advance of the evening twilight, dusk. It may also 'mean the passing away of the time for the performance of the evening rites.' The first only is probably intended. उपल०—परिकल्पितः *v. l.* means 'brought into the mind, thought of.'

S'l. 24. उदयतटा०—पटान्त० *v. l.*—hidden by the curtain of. But the comparison of a mountain to a curtain is strange. परिपाण्डुना मुखेन—The part of the eastern sky palely lit up by the beams of the moon about to rise is called the face of the eastern quarter. *Cf.* Kâlidâsa हरति मे हरिवाहनदिङ्मुखं, Vik. III. 6. हृदयस्थितं—For the paleness is brought on by constant thought about the lover. This S'l. is quoted in the Subhâshitâvalî, with the reading उदयनगा० for ०तटा०, which is better.

मन्दभागिनी—मन्दः भागः share or portion (of luck) यस्याः न पारितः—was not possible for me to be seen, *i. e.*, I could not see him. पार् though given as a root of the 10th cl. is more properly a denom. from पार the other bank, or the cau. of पृ, and means 'to carry to the other side, to accomplish fully;' and then to be able to do anything.

P. 28. S'l. 25. तिरस्कारिणा—Throwing into the background, eclipsing or surpassing, being spotless (all bright). *Cf.* हृत्वा पद्मवनद्युतिं प्रियतमेवेयं दिनश्रीर्गता। Priy. II. 10. विनिर्जितानि—Because her face is the subduer of the moon who conquers (causes to fade) the day-lotuses. विच्छायतां— छाया is कान्ति or lustre; विच्छाय० the state of being lustreless or darkened. गच्छन्ति—Because disgrace at the hands of equals is more unbearable and causes greater humiliation.

स्वपरिवार०—परिवार्यते अनेन इति; also परीवारः; retinue, suit. The courtezans had accompanied the Queen that day as it was a festival day. भृङ्गाङ्गनाः—The female bees are mentioned as females have a more melodious voice than males. लीयन्ते मुकु०—The lotuses closed up at the approach of night and assumed the state of buds again and the bees were encased therein. This the poet describes as a voluntary act on the part of the bees owing to their being put to shame by the sweeter songs of the Queen's attendant courtezans. The fact of the bees being shut up in closing lotuses is often referred to by poets. *Cf.* त्वां कारयामि कमलोदरबन्धनस्थं S'âk. VI. 20; बभूव तत्र प्रचलितभ्रमरं च पद्मम्। Rag. V. 68, न पङ्कजं तद्वलीनषट्पदम्। Bhatti. II. 19.

ACT II.

In this Act the love of Ságariká for the King, which has already germinated and struck root in her heart in the Mukhasaṃdhi, is described as growing in intensity; and this is in accordance with the canon पूर्वं रक्ता भवेन्नारी पुमान्पश्चात्तदिङ्गितैः।

P. 29. व्यग्र०—विगतमग्रमस्य व्यग्रः 'one whose point (keeness) is gone;' hence occupied or busy with; व्यग्रेण पञ्जरे वा व्यग्रौ हस्तौ यस्याः. We know from the first Act that Sâgarikâ had entrusted the cage of the Sâriká to the care of Susaṃgatâ; hence the entrance of the latter here with the cage. मम हस्ते &c.—*Cf.* सारिका मया पुनः सुसङ्गताया हस्ते निक्षिप्ता। *supra* p. 22.

अनन्यसदृशः—This refers to the King's trying to make the Navamálikâ blossom out of its season. The maid attributes it to the influence of some deity. वृत्तान्तः—This refers to the way in which the King was to accomplish his object.

अवधीर्य—अवधीर is not expressly mentioned in the 10th class, but is accepted there as a denom. from धीर; if अवधीरय् be regarded as a root by itself the form will be अवधीरयित्वा. श्रीपर्वतात्—Śrîparvata, also called श्रीशैल, is a holy place, still visited by pilgrims, near the Krishṇá river, in the Karnul zilla, about 120 miles from Hyderabad. The temple of Mallikârjuna (one of the twelve Jyotirliṅgas) is on a small hill in its neighbourhood and the two were probably designated, according to Dr. Sir Bhandarkar, by the name S'rîśaila. It is represented as the place for the attainment of miraculous powers, and as such is also referred to in the Mâl.-Mâd. I., (see p. 18). धार्मिकस्य-धर्मं चरतीति अधीते वा; fr. धर्म+इक (ठक्) दोहदं—दोहं ददाति that which brings about the desired object. Properly the hankering or desire felt by a woman *en ceinte*, the satisfaction of which ensures good progeny. Hence such a craving felt by plants; and hence, again, any preparation or medical recipe which enables plants to put forth flowers or fruits even out of their season.

P. 30. वर्तिका—a brush for drawing pictures. समुद्गक a casket; here a small box containing the painting materials प्रवेशक—like विष्कंभक is an interlude meant to acquaint the audience with those events, not represented on the stage, which have already occured or are to occur in the near future. But there is this difference between the two—It is carried on by low characters only, speaking प्राकृत (and is therefore not distinguished into मिश्र and शुद्ध); it comes between any two Acts (and thus cannot come at the beginning of the first Act, as विष्क० does); and in it more than two characters can also take part.

अनुबन्ध—is 'fastening after,' clinging to; hence, persistence in; *cf.* हृदय दुर्लभजनं प्रार्थयमानं त्वं कस्मान्मां दुःखितां करोषि । Priy. III; दुर्लभः प्रियस्तस्मिन्भव हृदय निराशम् । Mâlav. II. 4.

P. 31. नृशंस—The cruelty lies in forsaking one who was friend from birth. स्त्रीजनं प्रहरन् &c.—For there is no chivalry in striking a woman, and especially in the case of one so well known for his bravery. So in Nâg. II. भगवन् कुसुमायुध......मां पुनरनपराद्धामप्यबलेति कृत्वा प्रहरन्कथं न लज्जसे ।. अथ वाऽनङ्गोसि—and therefore without a heart; and so you cannot feel pity for me and are not therefore to blame. सर्वथा &c.—So her ill luck is wholly to blame for bringing about the circumstances leading to her death. *Cf.* सर्वथा मरणं वर्जयित्वा कुतो मे हृदयस्य निर्वृतिः । Priy. III. p. 20.

दुर्निमित्तेन—Ill omen, *viz.* her heart persistently feeling love for the King; or, this may refer to Kâma's shooting his arrows at her. अवश्यं मरणं *v. l.*—अवश्यं is unnecessary after सर्वथा. सावष्टम्भं—अवष्टम्भ is supporting or steadying the heart; hence सा०, 'with firmness.' एकमनाः—एकस्मिन्मनो यस्याः focussing, concentrating her mind on one object. यथासमीहितं—She means that she would then put an end to her life. अग्रहस्तः—is usually solved as a Karm. Now in a Karm. such as नीलोत्पल, there is सामानाधिकरण्य, *i. e.*, उत्पल and its नीलत्व are identical. But in the present case अग्र and हस्त are not identical. But according to Vâmana they may be regarded as such metaphorically, through the relation of अवयव (a part) and अवयविन् (the whole of which it is a part). See com.

P. 32. स्वैरं—ईरणं ईरः fr. ईर् to prompt, to go &c.; स्वः ईरः यस्मिन्कर्मणि तद्यथा तथा; according to one's motion or pleasure; hence, gently, stealthily, walking. अथ वा—This modifies her previous ejaculation. There is nothing to praise you. It is but natural that. न कमलाकरं &c.—राजहंसी—The royal swan or flamingo is described as a white bird of the goose tribe with red legs and a red bill. *Cf.* सागरं वर्जयित्वा कुत्र वा महानद्यवतरति । क इदानीं सहकारमन्तरेणातिमुक्तलतां पल्लवितां सहते । Śâk. III. p. 72. जलनिधिमनुरूपं जह्नुकन्यावतीर्णा । Rag. VI. 85. उत्तानीकृत्य—stretching upwards, *i. e.*, raising up. प्रच्छादयन्ती—Notice the pres.

she was concealing it, had no time to conceal it, and so it was seen by Susaṃgatá. क एष:—Although Sus. knew who was drawn, she purposely asks the question to elicit the truth from her friend.

P. 33. सस्मितं—The smile indicates that she knows the truth. निपुणत्वं—may have a double sense:—(1) Your skill in drawing; (2) Your cleverness in hiding the truth. शून्यं—void of interest, defective (being unaccompanied by that of Rati). सनाथं—नाथ 'a master;' सनाथ 'one having a master to look after;' *cf.* सनाथा इदानीं धर्मचारिण: । S'âk. I.; hence, 'accompanied by, joined to,' in which sense it is commonly used. व्यपदेशेन—व्यपदिश्यते अनेन by which one is led away; fr. दिश् with वि and अप and affix घञ् (अ); hence a pretext.

सासूयम्-With an air of censure or chiding; disapprovingly. असूया तु दोषारोपो गुणेष्वपि । Amara. अन्यथासम्भाविनि—may mean (1) You who pass or represent things otherwise; or (2) you who misread things, or think otherwise of me; *cf.* अलमस्मान्न्यथा सम्भाव्य S'âk. I. She means to say-you think otherwise of me, *i. e.* regard me as having no interest in you. This is preferable, as appears from the reading असद्भाविनी 'thinking improperly of.' भवितव्यं—Pot. p. p. used impersonally, means 'what must or ought to be.' *Cf.* further on-कारणेन भवितव्यम्.

P. 34. पुन:—But again (used भेदे). मेधाविनी—see com.; मेधा is that faculty of the mind by which one grasps ideas and retains them, retentive memory; मेधाविनी having strong memory, talented. Here it is the name of the Sârikâ due to her having a strong memory, as is clear from Susaṃgatá's speech at p. 47 (मेधाविन्या मेधाविलम्). आलापस्य गृहीताक्षरा—is a comp. सापेक्षत्वेऽपि गमकत्वात् being equal to गृहीतालापाक्षरा. गृहीतार्था *v. l.* is not noticed in the foot-notes. It means 'having caught the contents (*i. e.* the words) of'. But here अर्थ has to be taken in a restricted sense. मदनावस्थां नाटयति—The reading सन्तापं नाट० should rather have been adopted, as she was already समदनावस्था. दीर्घिका—is a large oblong well or artificial pond containing lotus-plants. मृणालिका—the same as मृणाली fem. fr. मृणाल (a tender lotus-shoot) which is more common. Lotus leaves and stalks are mentioned as being usually resorted to for allaying the fever of love.

P. 35. S'l. 1. दुर्लभ &c.—These three are adduced as the reasons for her love being विषम uneven, that cannot take a smooth course—which is sure to lead to trouble and misery.

दुर्लभजना०—In the first place her love is for a person difficult to obtain, being far out of her reach. As दुर्लभजन is here emphatic, Prof. Ray proposes to render the Prâkrit as दुर्लभजन अनुराग (being equal to दुर्लभजने अनुरागः) which is certainly better. लज्जा गुर्वी—And to add to her difficulty her sense of shame is very great, so that she cannot directly or indirectly make the disclosure to the King. And to make matters worse she was not her own master and so had no independence of action (being entirely in the power of the Queen). The only course, therefore, left to her, she thinks, is to find solace in death. प्रियसखि &c.—This is elliptical for प्रियसखि यदा प्रेम एवं विषमं तदा &c.; मरणं &c.—may be taken as a question: see com.; or नवरं may be taken as a comp. of न (not नञ्) with वरं, 'that than which none is better, the best'. Some take नवरं in the sense of केवलं; 'णवरः केवले' इति प्राकृतप्रकाशे वररुचिः नेपथ्ये कलकलः—*V. l.* The addition of कलकल which means 'a mixed noise' is unnecessary as the S'lokas that follow show that there was no Kalakala. The breaking loose of the monkey and the confusion caused by that are described by some one behind the curtains.

S'l. 2. कण्ठे कृत्ता०—When the monkey broke off the chain, part of it that was attached to the neck remained hanging down, and this he dragged along as he ran about. दामन्—*n.f.* a rope for fastening, hence, here, a chain. हेला—sport, hence, wanton movement. चक्रवाल—a belt, a circle. दत्तातङ्कोक्र०—may also be taken as a सापेक्षत्वेपि गमकत्वात्समासः being equivalent to दत्ताक्रनातङ्क like आलापस्य गृहीताक्षरा *supra*. D.—R. reads ०क्रो गजानां...मन्दुरातः. अश्वपालैः—the stable-keepers. प्लवंगः—प्लवेन by bounding motion गच्छतीति प्लवङ्गः by affixing अ (खच्) to गम् before which a nasal is added to the first member; by adding डः (अ) we get प्लवगः also. It was customary to keep a monkey, especially a male one, in the horse-stable, as a safeguard against evil-eye-influence and against evil spirits. *Cf.* the Persian proverb, as quoted by Wilson—'The misfortune of the stable be on the monkey's head' (*Bilai Tahila ba ser i maimum*). मन्दुरा—a stable for horses.

S'l. 3. वर्षवरैः—Eunuchs. ये त्वल्पसत्त्वाः प्रथमाः क्लीबाश्च स्त्रीस्वभाविनः। जात्या न दुष्टाः कार्येषु ते वै वर्षवराः स्मृताः॥

P. 36. पर्यन्ता०—परिगतः अन्तः पर्यन्तः 'the border all round;' now see com. नाम्नः सदृशं—*cf.* the derivation of किरात, किरं पर्यन्तभूमिं अततीति one constantly moving, *i. e.,* living on the borders of hills or mountains. Name of a wild tribe of mountaineers, like the Bhils, and classed as Mlechchhas by Aryanwriters. They were forced into service and employed as watchmen by kings. This is also translated as 'the mountaineers, the guardians of the bounds, acted in a style accordant with their name, *i. e.* they did valiantly, not running away from the monkey.' P. Mitra's trans. of S.-D., p. 63. But this is against the general drift of the s'l.

नीचतया—stooping still low; and hence शनकैः; as they had shortened their forms they could not walk quickly. According to Prof. Ray नीचता has a double sense—खर्वता and अनुदारता (*i. e.* they walk like mean, poor-spirited persons). Servants such as those mentioned in the S'l. were employed as assistants in harems. *Cf.* अन्तःपुरे वर्षवराः किराता मूकवामनाः । म्लेच्छाभीरशकाराद्याः स्वस्वकार्योपयोगिनः ॥ D.-R. II. 44, 45.

तमालविटपा०—They thought of the Tamâla grove, as the *tamâlas* being of a dark colour could afford them better shelter. The Tamâla grows on the slopes of the Malabar hills. It has thick leaves of a dark-green colour, which are used in spices.

सुस्थिते—'O you who are quite at ease;' hence one who does not take thought of the future; thoughtless. किमद्यापि चित्र०—She means, the picture-board is not a matter of great concern;-it is the Sârikâ that must be first attended to, as she has escaped from her cage now. दधिभक्त—an Inst. Tat.

P. 37. सुसंगते ज्ञायते &c.—The Vidû. is described as monkey-like in appearance; *cf.* एष खलु आलिखितवानर इव...आर्यमाणवकस्तिष्ठति Vik. II. p. 28; अये कपिलमर्कट.&c. Nâg. III. p. 54.

प्रहृष्टः—पटाक्षेपेण *v. l.* with a toss of the curtain. This stage-direction (like अपटीक्षेपेण) is used when a character enters suddenly, either owing to haste or under the influence of some emotion, such as fear, joy or sorrow, and without the usual introduction ततः प्रविशति. This is out of place here as the entrance of Vidú. is previously intimated. For दोहद see p. 29. निरन्तर—so as to leave no space between. वर्धयिष्यामि—is short for दिष्ट्या वर्ध०, *i. e.* say दिष्ट्या भवान्वर्धते.

P. 38. परोक्षाम्—परोक्षा may be explained as अक्षेभ्यः परा: (beyond senses) पर being changed to परो when अक्ष follows; or as अक्ष्णः परं परोक्षं Avya.; by the rule प्रतिपरसमनुभ्योऽक्ष्णः and then adding अ मत्वर्थे; in either case the comp. is irregular. Explain similarly प्रत्यक्षा. यथानिर्दिष्टः—यथा निर्दिष्टः यथा० a comp. सुप्सुपा.

S'l. 4. **उद्दामो०**—The adjectives apply to the creeper, Nava., and a woman in love. Thus उद्दामो० means (1) having a luxuriant (उद्दाम) growth of buds (कलिका); (2) whose love-longing is excessive. **विपाण्डुररुचं**—(1) having a brilliant appearance (being covered with blossoms); (2) with a very pale complexion (owing to pining). **प्रारब्धजृम्भां**—जृम्भा the opening of buds; yawning. **आयासं**—(1) its being tossed ; (2) pain experienced by her. **श्वसनोद्गमैः**—(1) The upheavels of the wind ; (2) the heavings of sighs. **समदनां**——(1) With the Madana tree; (2) full of passion or love.

This s'l. is quoted in the D.—R. as an instance of पताकास्थान by तुल्यविशेषणता (*i. e.* having paronomastic adjectives), which is defined as प्रस्तुतागन्तुभावस्य वस्तुनोऽन्योक्तिसूचकम् । पताकास्थानकं तुल्यसंविधानविशेषणम् ॥ "That which by the mention of something foreign to the matter in hand indicates the present business going forward or some future incident either by a similarity of situation or the use of paronomastic attributes, is called Patâkâsthâna." See D.–R. p. 5.

तद्वृत्तान्त—The news about the blossoming of Navamâliká.

P. 39. S'l. 5. The genuineness of this s'l. is questionable. It is omitted in some editions.

पुरुषोत्तमः—*Cf.* उत्तमः पुरुषस्त्वन्यः परमात्मेत्युदाहृतः । यस्मात्क्षरमतीतोऽहमक्षरादपि चोत्तमः । अतोऽस्मि लोके वेदे च प्रथितः पुरुषोत्तमः॥ Bg. XV. 17,18. **मणि**—The celebrated gem called कौस्तुभ, obtained at the churning of the ocean. The reference to the flight of the enemies at the sight of the gem is not clear. **हताः**—struck down, *i. e.* overpowered by. **मन्त्रबलात्**—*Cf.* तवाभिधानाद् व्यथते नताननः सुदुःसहान्मन्त्रपदादिवोरगः। Kir. I. 24.

लक्ष्मणवीर०—वीर properly ought to go with लक्ष्मण; but then the comp. will be वीरलक्ष्मणः; लक्ष्मणवीर may be defended on the principle of बहुलग्रहण; *cf.* जेत्रः स चित्रं रतिजानिवीरः। Nai. VII. 85. But if this cannot be allowed, वीर must be taken with वानरभटाः. **मेघनाद**—He was the bravest and most distinguished of the sons of Râvaṇa. By his power of becoming invisible, which he had obtained from S'iva, he captured Indra and bore him off to Laṅká. Brahmâ with the other gods hurried thither and procured his release, giving the victor the title of Indrajit. In the great war he seriously wounded not only the chief monkey warriors, Sugrîva, Aṅgada, Nala, Susheṇa and others, but Râma and Lakshmaṇa also, and went away leaving them unconscious on the battle-field. They were, however, brought back to consciousness and had their wounds healed by inhaling the smell of the healing herbs brought by Hanumân from Káilâsa. साटोपम्—आटोप pride, self-importance. The Vidú. feels proud as his party has won, the King's favourite creeper Navamálikâ having flowered before Mâdhavî, the Queen's favourite one.

P. 40. संभवः—may mean-existence or possibility. प्रभावः- *v. l.* power; how can such prevail here.

S'l. 6. स्पष्टाक्षरं—A starling speaks more clearly than a parrot. अनिर्हारि—Not resounding or spreading out so as to be heard at a distance; and hence it cannot be human voice.

भयालुकः—(Additional readings) timid by nature; but the affix आलु added to भी is against Pâṇini; the allowed forms are भीरु, भीरुक or भीलुक. पिशुन—wicked; here Vidú., as suits his character, wittily compares his stick, which was crooked, to a wicked man's heart. कपित्थफल—a wood-apple (कवठ in Marâthi). *Cf.* दास्याःपुत्र दुष्टपारावत तिष्ठ तिष्ठ । यावदनेन दण्डकाष्ठेन सुपकमिव चूतफलमस्मात्प्रासादाद्भूमौ पातयिष्यामि । Mṛich. V.

P. 41. एषा भणति &c.—From here the Sárikâ is represented as reproducing, *verbatim,* the conversation between Sâgarikâ and Susaṃgatá. This habit of these birds is often referred to by Sans. poets; *cf.* अयमपि च गिरं नस्त्वत्प्रबोधप्रयुक्तामनुवदति शुकस्ते मञ्जुवाक्पञ्जरस्थः । Rag. V. 74; दम्पत्योर्निशि जल्पतोर्गृहशुकेनाकर्णितं यद्वचः प्रातस्तद्गुरुसन्निधौ निगदतस्तस्योपहारं वधूः । &c. Amarus'a. It is difficult, however, to imagine how the bird could do it with such preciseness. But that is not the poet's concern. He wants to acquaint the King with Sâgarikâ's love for him, which is necessary for the future development of the plot, and uses this device.

कामदेव &c.—Under the pretext of; *i. e.,* she passed the picture off as Kâmadeva's. तत्—See com. छोटिका—The sharp sound produced by the snapping of the thumb and the middle finger.

P. 42. यद्येवं--If so, *i. e.,* if she is दर्शनीया as you say. कुरकुरायते—see com.; कुर is an imitation of an indistinct sound; the affix डाच् (आ) is added to such a word, before which it is doubled, when it consists of at least two syllables (and when it is not followed by इति). It then takes the affix क्यष् and we get कुरकुरायति-ते. चतुर्वेदी—Explain—चतुरवयवा वेदाः चतुर्वेदाः; चतुर्वेदाः सन्त्यस्य चतुर्वेदी, इन् being added मत्वर्थे. ऋचः पठितुं—The Vidû. mistakes the *gâthâ* sung by the Sârikâ for a verse of the Ṛig-Veda.

P. 43. महाब्राह्मण--This is ironical. The word महत् when prefixed to certain words (see com.) expresses reproach. श्लाघ्ययौवना—Lit. one whose youth is praiseworthy, hence endowed with all the charms of youth जीवितनिरपेक्षया—by one grown regardless of life. वक्र०—Crooked, round-about speeches. मामनासा०—The Vidú. has always a high regard for his master; to him none is more handsome or accomplished than he, and hence he thinks that the picture drawn by the maiden must have been the King's, as, in his opinion, none could be passed off as the god of love. *Cf.* in this respect—राजा—माढव्य अनवाप्तचक्षुःफलोसि येन त्वया दर्शनीयं न दृष्टम्। विदू०—ननु भवानग्रतो मे वर्तते। S'ák. II.

S'l. 8. दुर्वारां—irresistible, that cannot be got rid of. कामिनां—one affected by love, love-stricken.

P. 50. शिशुशुक०—शिशु (young children) also unknowingly repeat what they hear. Some read शुकशिशु०; but there is no propriety in saying 'repeated by *young* parrots,' as grown-up parrots are equally ignorant of the sense of what they repeat. धन्यानां—That is, those that hear it are blessed, as then they can seek out such girls and try to secure them. श्रवणपथा०—'Becomes the guest of' *i. e.* is casually heard by.

गता दास्याःपुत्री। अत्र तावद् &c.—The Sârikâ is no more useful for the furtherance of the plot The poet's purpose was to take the King and his friend to the plantain-bower, where the picture-board was left. The Sârikâ's flight to the bower was the device used to serve this purpose. The Vidú. therefore says, never mind the Sárikâ; let us sit here; &c. उद्वेल्लत्—fluttering, shaken up; qualifies दलानि. बालकदली &c.—The stone-slab was fenced round by young plantain-trees in order that it should be kept cool.

उद्घाटित०—Some read ऊनोद्घाटित (partially opened) द्वारेण. The whole passage is also read as—भो वयस्य एतेन उद्घाटितद्वारेण दृष्टवानस्मि तस्याः सारि० पञ्ज० भवि०। राजा—वयस्य निरूप्यताम्। विदू०—यद्भवानाज्ञापयति। (परिक्रम्यावलोक्य च) एषोपि...गृह्णामि। (गृहीत्वा &c.) भो वयस्य &c.

P. 45. पारितोषिकं—Lit. that which is meant to give satisfaction; परितोष+इक; a reward.

S'l. 9. Here also the attributes are paronomastic. The maiden is compared to a female swan. लीलावधूतपद्मा—(1) Who surpasses Lakshmí by her grace; (2) who has shaken or agitated the lotuses by her sport. कथयन्ती &c.—Indicating

special leaning towards (love for) us (नः gen.); (2) displaying to us (नः dat.) the great movement (flapping) of her wings. मानसं—(1) the heart; (2) the lake of that name. चित्रगता—(1) delineated in the picture; (2) with a graceful (चित्र) gait or varied motion.

S'l. 10. विधाय &c.—अपूर्व—extraordinary, because always full and always present. ०दुःस्थितः—In the presence of this moon, the lotus that formed his seat closed up and consequently Brahmá could not sit comfortably on it (being pressed from all sides by the closing petals). For figures see com. According to some there is also the fig. अतिशयोक्ति in this. This S'l. is quoted in the Subhâshitâvalî as of S'rî-Harshadeva.

P. 46. गुल्म—a cluster or clump of. निर्वर्णयन्—Eying closely, gazing intently. वर्णयन्—*v. l.* Describing. निर्वर्ण० is better, as the King had his eyes fixed on the picture when Sus. saw him. The stage-direction 'राजानं चालयित्वा' also shows that the King was lost in his admiration of the picture. But if we read शृणुवस्तावत् in Sus.'s previous speech and the following stage-direction as उभे आकर्णयतः, then the reading वर्णयन् must be preferred.

अवनतमुखी—We should have preferred the reading रुदितमुखी, for when Susamgatâ saw her friend, tears were trickling down from her eyes (as shown by the stage-direction सास्रं or सास्रा p. 31) and so she was painted, as is clear from the King's words जललवप्रस्यन्दिनी लोचने। s'l. 11.

इमं जनं लघुं करोषि-इमं refers to the King and not to herself, as some take it. She means—In your fondness for jokes, you are lowering the King by representing him as loving *me*, who am only a servant of the Queen.

P. 47. सुखयति—brings delight to; denom. from सुख *n.* (सुखं गमयति) or adj. (सुखमस्यास्तीति सुखं by adding the possessive aff. अ) सुखं करोति. जीवितमरणयोरन्तरे—she was sure of death; *cf. supra* मरणं शरणं S'l. 1; but now, as her picture was already before the King, her life hung on his reply; if he would say—'Yes,' she had reason to live. In case he would say 'no', death was certain. Thus she stood on the boundary-line between life and death. So says the similarly placed Dushyana—अत्रान्तरे श्रवणकातरतां गतोस्मि ॥ S'âk. III. 9.

S'l. 11. कृच्छ्रात्—When the eyes were cast on her thighs, they could not leave them easily (owing to their beauty). ०स्थले-स्थल here implies excellence which consists in the expanse of the नितम्ब (प्रशस्तो नितम्बः नितम्बस्थलम्). त्रिवली—तिस्रो वल्यस्त्रिवल्यः; the comp. is allowed as it is a संज्ञा. If it be not regarded as a संज्ञा then the comp. will have to be taken as one of the शाकपार्थिवादि class: त्रिविभक्ता वली त्रिवली. The त्रिवली (three folds of skin near the waist) forms an almost invariable part of the description of a beautiful woman by Sanskrit poets; *cf.* मध्येन सा वेदिविलग्नमध्या वलित्रयं चारु बभार बाला। Kum. I. 39; सौधारोहणपरिपाटया वलित्रयं, D.—K.; दधन्ति मध्येषु वलीविभङ्गिषु। Kir. VIII. 24. ०विषमे—rugged, difficult to be crossed. Hence निस्पन्दतामा० 'motionless through exhaustion owing to the difficulty of crossing.' तृषितेव—As if thirsty (as one would be after ascending a mountain). साकांक्षं—The sight was eagerly looking at the eyes as they were shedding the water of tears. A thirsty person also eagerly looks at the source of water. ईक्षते—looks at (and does not leave them, as it did the other parts).

सखि श्रुतं त्वया—The King's reply was as Sâgarikâ had wished it. So Susaṃgatá asks her this question. But modesty does not allow her to say 'yes'. Again it was the picture that the King admired; there was nothing in the S'l. to show that the King loved her. So she asks her friend to hear the King who was praising rather the skill of the painter than her own self. विज्ञान—special skill.

P. 48. यस्य ईदृश्योपि &c.—The Vidû. means-when maidens whom you admire admire you, you ought to think highly of yourself, but you do not d it, your attention being solely absorbed by the beauties of maidens. पराभवः—means here slight, disregard. बहुमानः—The King means-I do not think lightly of myself (पराभव), but I regard it as a great honour done to me that she has painted me.

S'l. 12. बाष्पाम्बु &c.—It should be remembered that tears were falling from Sâgarikâ's eyes while she was engaged in drawing the King's picture. Some of these drops fell on the picture itself, and these are referred to here by the King. ०शीकरकण—शीकर drops कण small particles into which the drops were broken as they fell on the hard board. The appearance of perspiration is one of the eight सात्त्विक भावs due to the sensation produced by ardent love. It thus indicates the King's love.

मनोरथोपि ते &c.—The King's words अनया लिखितोहमिति &c. and the indication of love for her fill Sâga. with great joy.

It was more than what she had expected from the King. She had regarded him as a दुर्लभजन. Her most fervent expectation was that he might treat her with some consideration—perhaps respond to her love out of pity. Hence she says मनोरथोपि ते &c.

S'l. 13. परिम्लानं—Greatly or entirely (परि) faded. This implies great heat. पीन—p. p. of प्याय्, 1. Â. to grow or swell. पीन is the form when it refers to a limb of the body (स्वाङ्ग); otherwise प्यान or पीन. परिमिलन—close contact with; the proper form is परिमेलन. So this is a poetic license. Such forms when used by great writers are justified by the maxim संज्ञापूर्वको विधिरनित्यः. To avoid the grammatical anomaly some propose the reading परिमिलितम०.

P. 49. न्यास—placing or arrangement of. श्लथ—languid, drooping, owing to the torment. आक्षेप—throwing out, exuding कृशाङ्गी—thin-bodied (naturally, and not emaciated).

S'l. 14. मन्मथोत्थां—मन्मथ is derived as मननं मत् consciousness; मथाति इति मथः the destroyer of (fr. मथ्+अच्); मतो मथः मन्मथः. मान्मर्थायां—*V. l.* मन्मथस्य इयं-of, caused by, Madana. ०परिणाह—extent, large expanse; so in S'ák.—स्तनयुगपरिणाहाच्छादिना वल्कलेन S'l. read before S'l. 18; p. 20. म्लापिताभ्यां—The reading ग्लापि० is not good, as ग्लानि refers more to the mental than to the physical condition.

पीनस्तनो०—क्लिश्यमान suffering from, being withered. The heat was great owing to the पीनत्व of the breasts. ०स्तनस्खलनक्लि०—*V. l.* pining because dropped from. But we cannot expect such an observation from the Vid.; it will suit in the mouth of a gallant only.

जडप्रकृते—जडा dull, incapable of discrimination प्रकृतिः यस्य. Also जलं (डलयोरभेदात्) प्रकृतिः source यस्य, sprung from water.

P. 50. S'l. 15. किं शोषमा०—With the instinct of a true gallant the King thinks that the garland was withering (pining) for being displaced from Sága.'s breasts; and calls it foolish (जडप्र०) for doing so. The reason is stated in the next two lines न सूक्ष्मतंतोरपि &c.—*cf.* for a similar description, मध्ये यथा श्याममुखस्य तस्य मृणालसूत्रान्तरमप्यलभ्यम् । Kum. I. 40. This sl. is also found in the Subháshitâvali, as Harsha's.

असम्बद्धं—inconsistently, inappropriately. For in the preceding verse he addressed the inanimate garland as though it were a sentient being. यस्य कृते &c.—The sentence is so worded that Sâgar. should understand by it the King, and when she suspects that and asks a question, Susaṃgatâ passes off the matter by saying 'I mean the picture-board, though you suspect something else (the King)'. For a parallel *cf.*—बकुलावलिका—एष उपारूढराग उपभोगक्षमः पुरतस्ते वर्तते । मालविका—(सहर्षम्) किं भर्ता । बकुला०—न तावद्भर्ता एषोऽशोकशाखावलम्बी पल्लवगुच्छकः । Mâ'. III. p. 55. This illustrates one of the *aṅgas* of Pratimukhasaṃdhi, called नर्म (परिहासवचः).

P. 51. सरोषम्—Sâgarikâ is angry that her friend should thus make fun of her and says that she would go away, not being able to understand her enigmatical speeches.

असहना—One who cannot brook delay or bear a joke. सुसं० दृष्ट्वा ससंभ्रमं—Vidú. was in a hurry to warn the King as he did not know that Susaṃgatâ, though the Queen's maidservant, was interested in Sâgarikâ's well-being.

विज्ञातः—fully known; this speech of Susaṃgatâ is quoted in the S.—D. as an instance of वज्र or a speech in harsh words which comes as a thunderbolt (gives a shock). It is quoted in D.-R. as an instance of भयनर्म or jest meant to frighten. Here Sus. pretends to be a partisan of the Queen and seeks to frighten the King as a matter of joke.

अपवार्य—This stage-direction is used when a character says something to another by turning towards him or her, preventing others from hearing it by screening them with the palm of the hand with three fingers raised, so as to look like three banners; तद्भवेदपवारितम् । रहस्यं तु यदन्यस्य परावृत्य प्रकाश्यते । त्रिपताककरेणान्यानपवार्यान्तराकथाम् ॥ S.—D. मुखरा—निन्दितं मुखं (वचनं) अस्याः, fr. मुख + र a possessive (मतुप्) affix. It means-garrulous, speaking disagreeably. गर्भदासी—Lit. one who is a slave from conception; a born slave; used as a term of contempt.

P. 52. ०प्रसादेन—The inst. is हेतौ by reason of, on the strength of, my lord's favour. एष एव मे &c.—Here we have उपन्यास (one of the *aṅgas* of प्रतिमुखसन्धि) which consists in the use of conciliatory words meant to remove the unpleasantness caused by a joke.

एतेन कार्यं भविष्यति—Vidû. means that in case Sâgar. should, by some chance, slip from the hands of the King, the board might be a source of comfort to him; but we shall find further on, that like other devices of the Vid. this also proves to be a source of embarrassment to him.

P. 53. पद्मास्यपदमपि—This is स्तम्भ, one of the eight *Sáttvika bhâvas.*

S'l. 16. दृशः—The plural is used as Brahmâ has eight eyes. पृथुतरीकृताः—extended wider (in order to have a full view of). जितनि॰—This epithet has no special propriety. चलितानि—चल् (कम्पने) to shake, does not lengthen its अ in the causal; *cf.* क्षितिं सशैलां चलयन्निषुभिः। Kir. XIV. 50; चलयन्भ्रूकुटीचस्तथालकान्। Rag. VIII. 53. ॰ललाम॰—ललामं-म वा भूता ललामभूता a comp. of the सुप्सुपा class. Some take this as a Tat. Or if भूत be taken in the sense of सम 'like', dissolve ललामेन तुल्या ललामभूता, a Nitya-samâsa. So in S'âk. अहं तु तामाश्रमललामभूतां शकुन्तलां &c. II. p. 51. ललामभूतः स पौरवाणां, III. p. 72. The metre of this s'l. is faulty since the pause which ought to be at the 8th syll. is misplaced in the 2nd and 4th lines, not being at the end of a *pada*. Willson quotes—

Ventidius to Antony.
"You :—
Were—sure the chief, and best of human race.
So perfect that the gods who formed you wondered
At their own skill, and cried, a lucky hit
Has mended our design." All for Love.

सासूयं—Sus. had gone expressly for bringing the picture-board, while she brought the King; hence the reproach. Of course the *asúyâ* was only outward.

S'l. 17. भामिनि—From भामः anger+इन् having to an excess; or अवश्यं भामते fr. भाम् 1 A. to be angry, with इन् (णिनिः), irascible, passionate. The King was told that Sâga. was angry with her friend and he still found her in that mood. Hence he addresses her as भामिनि. इयं—may refer to दृष्टि or to Susamgatâ (although you look angrily at her she loves you and will not resent it). खेदं करिष्यति—will cause trouble (exhaustion) to you. *Cf.* ताम्यत्यूरुयुगं नितम्बभरतः। Nâg. II. 6. खेदं गमिष्यति *V. l.*-will feel oppressed.

S'l. 18. पाणिरस्यस्याः &c.—She thus combines in herself the properties of both; here is her अपूर्वत्व. पारिजात—The tree produced at the churning of the ocean. As it was produced along with nectar, it is spoken of here as shedding nectar. स्वेदच्छद्मा—The appearance of perspiration produced by the touch of her lover is one of the Sáttvikabhávas; *cf.* Vâtsyáyana—कन्या तु प्रथमसमागमे स्विन्नाङ्गुलिः स्विन्नमुखी च भवति। &c. *Cf.* ज्ञाते स्वेदापदेशादविरतममृतं स्यन्दते व्यक्तमेतत्। Priy. III. 11.

अतिनिष्ठुरा—अदक्षिणा *v. l.* not polite, ungenerous. युक्तः कोपा०—युक्तं कोपानुबन्धं कर्तुं *v. l.* which is equivalent to युक्तं कोपानुबन्धस्य) करणं, the तुम् in कर्तुं being added भावे.

P. 55. एषा खलु &c.—The words here are so arranged as to have two different meanings. While the Vidû. meant to say—This is another (second) Queen Vâsa. (on account of her stubbornness of anger), the King and others took him to mean—Here comes another, Queen Vâsavadattá; and hence their confusion. अत्र–In this unexpected situation. अन्तरयित्वा—keeping between as a screen, hence, hidden by.

S'l. 19. In this s'l. Sâg. and रत्नावली (a necklace of gems) are compared. The various epithets apply to both. कण्ठमनीत्वा–(1) not embraced; (2) not taken to (placed round) the neck. प्रकटरागा—(1) whose attachment was manifest; (2) whose lustre or radiance is clear (bright).

P. 56. अथ (कुसुमिता)—is प्रश्नार्थे (indicates a question). त्वं चिरयसि—This is of course false. He says so in order that the Queen should not get the least inkling of what happened between him and Sâgarikâ. मुखरागारेव &c.—This brings out the wounded pride of the Queen. The glow on the King's face was, of course, due to his meeting with Sâgarikâ. But the Queen mistook it for the glow of triumph over her on account of the flowering of the Navamâlikâ. Hence her refusal to go to see the creeper. फलकः पतति—The Vidû. in his wild joy dances with out-stretched arms forgetting all about the picture-board, which falls down and only serves to expose the King's secret. This inadvertence of the Vidû. is well known and often leads his friend into a situation of embarrassment *Cf.* the dropping down of the birch-leaf from the hands of the Vidú., with a similar result, in Vik. II, and of the ornaments leading to Chârudatta's conviction in Mṛich. Some read after फलकः पतति, तद् दृष्ट्वा विषादं नाटयति. But the subsequent speech of the Vidû. shows that he does not at all feel sorry for it, but is on the contrary self-confident. It is, therefore, rejected.

P. 57. इयं पुनः—This again, *i. e.*, who ought not to be here. वैलक्ष्य—fr. विलक्ष one that has lost the point of attention or aim (लक्ष्यते इति लक्षं); bewilderment, confusion, embarrassment. आत्मा—one's own form. यदि ईदृशी दृष्टपूर्वा— This apparently means—If such a one was ever seen by us, *i. e.*, the form painted is pure invention. The Vidû. also says the truth-for he really means such a one was only seen by us for the first time.

P. 58. घुणाक्षरं—घुण is a kind of insect that bores holes into wood. In the course of its incisions in the wood it happens to trace out a figure which resembles a letter of the alphabet. Hence घुणाक्षरं means 'any accidental resemblance.' Kâñch. says that it may be quite by accident that the figure drawn by the King resembles S'agariká. ऋजुके-Here क is कुत्सायां (implies reproach) 'you silly one'. वक्रभणितानि—equivocal speeches, speeches which have another than the plain meaning. प्रेक्षमाणाया:--The apparent meaning is-My looking at the picture with a steadfast gaze has produced headache. The real meaning is—The sight of the woman by your side has produced headache.

S'l. 20. न घटते—does not fit in, is not proper. ज्ञास्यसि--According to the rule 'अनुपसर्गाज्ज्ञः,' ज्ञा when used by itself ought to take the Âtm., but the Sútra refers to cases where the क्रियाफल refers to the agent, as धर्मं जानीते. Here the knowledge that the statement is false (मृषा) does not benefit the Queen and so the Paras. is used. This Śl. illustrates पर्युपासनं (the reconciling of one who is offended), one of the *angas* of प्र० संधि. This is quoted in the Subháshitâvalí under the heading अनुनय. अन्यथा—*i. e.* I am offended.

P. 59. अकाल--Because she came at an improper time (अप्रशस्तः कालः), *i. e.* at the time of Sâgariká's meeting. आभिजात्यात्—Through nobility of birth. Being noble-born and well-bred, she suppressed her anger; that is all.

S'l. 21. भेदकारि--penetrating the heart, because it was a smile of anger. प्रभुतया--must be taken with every line; she did all that as she had perfect self-control. च-च-The two चs indicate simultaneity of action. भ्रूभङ्ग, भेदकारि हसित and ०जडीकृतं चक्षुः indicated her anger; वदनं नीतं परां नम्रतां &c.—indicated her प्रश्रय or modesty of demeanour, decorum. *Cf.* with this Priya. III. 13. After S'l. 21, some read विदू०-गता देवी वा० तत्कस्मात्त्वं &c. see foot-notes. राजा—मूढ न लक्षितस्त्वया देव्याः कोपः। तत्सर्वथा देवीप्रसादनं मुक्त्वा नान्यमत्रोपायं पश्यामि। These two speeches are evidently an interpolation. There is no अरण्यरुदित in what the King says. Again, they repeat what is already said in the previous speeches of the Vid. and the King.

देवीमेव प्रसा --The reading देवीसकाशं गच्छाव: is better and should have been preferred. For as the Queen did not show her anger openely, her प्रसादन was out of question, as remarked by the King himself in S'l. 20. The King now simply wishes to go to ascertain the real state of the Queen's mind. Besides we do not find any attempt at pacification on the part of the King early in the next Act. The true occasion for that arises in that Act. कदलीगृहो नाम—The Act is named after the Plantain.—bower, that being the main scene of action.

ACT III.

P. 60. आकाशे—This stage-direction is used when a character addresses a speech to a person not present on the stage, shows that he hears replies and repeats them for the information of the audience, with the words किं ब्रवीषि &c.; see com. कौशाम्बिका—from her name she appears to be a native of Kaus'âmbí and in service of the King. कर्णं दत्वा--In order to hear a supposed reply. कोऽपि काल:--is idiomatic for 'a long time has elapsed' and constantly occurs in literature. सोत्प्रासम्--उत्प्रास from अस् to throw with उद् and प्र; a taunt, sarcasm; उत्प्रासनं तूपहासो योऽसाधौ साधुमानिति। S-D. सन्धिविग्रह—Properly, peace and war. These are the chief of the six expedients to be used by a king in foreign politics. [The remaining four are:—यान or leading an expedition against an enemy, all things being favourable; आसन or blockading, or, sitting quiet, waiting for a favourable opportunity; द्वैधं or duplicity; and आश्रय or resorting to a fort, seeking the help of a powerful king, &c.]. Kâñch. humourously uses these terms, with reference to the Vidû. in the sense of his planning (or busying himself with) a union between the King and Sâgarikâ, and bringing about thereby a quarrel between the King and Vâsavadattâ. रहस्यं--रहो भवं a secret, fr. रहस्+यत्

P. 61. चित्रशालिका—चित्राणां शाला चित्रशाला सैव चित्रशालिका a picture-hall. It was probably a small building where painting was taught and pictures kept. वर्जयित्वा--Having omitted, excepting. It is properly an absolutive but it has lost its character as such and is used like a preposition. *Cf.* मुक्त्वा, विहाय &c. used similarly. प्रतीकारं--This means of course that she should try to bring about Ságarikâ's union with the King.

अद्य—goes with प्रदोषे. वृत्तान्त—an incident, affair. प्रसादीकृतं—The reward was given that Susangatâ should keep good watch over Sâgarikâ. तया सह भर्तुः समागमो भविष्यति—*Cf.* a similar plan formed for the union of the King with A'raṇyakâ in Priy. III. It was this—For the amusement of the Queen the adventures of Vatsarâja, while a prisoner at Ujjayinî, *viz.*, how Vâsavadattâ was placed under his tuition in music, how he won her love and managed to steal away with her, &c., should be represented on the stage; there Âraṇyakâ was to play the part of Vâsava. and Manoramâ, her friend, was to represent the King. It was arranged that Manoramá, dressed as the King, when about to appear on the stage, should contrive to remain back, while the King himself should enter the stage and act his own part.

P. 62. हतासि—हताशा *v. l.*—One whose hopes ought to be destroyed on account of one's wickedness; hence wicked, cursed. ॰वत्सलां—वत्सोऽस्या अस्तीति वत्सला affectionate; fr. वत्स affection and ल added मत्वर्थे (in the sense of possession). The reward given and the confidence put in Susa. bear out the Queen's वात्सल्य. उत्ताम्यन्त्या—This shows how loving the Queen was. The news of her husband's indisposition not only made her forget her anger but buried her in deep anxiety.

मिष—is छल or pretext, meant to deceive or mislead. दन्त॰—दन्त ivory; तोरण the outer gate; see com. वलभी—The top-most room of a mansion (सौधोर्ध्ववेश्म). So in Priya. IV.—एषा खलु देवी तयैव सह दन्तवलभ्यां तिष्ठति । प्रविशति उपविष्टः—is a dramatical technicality; it means—is discovered seated, the curtain being lifted up.

P. 63. S'l. 1. उपशमः—allaying, mitigation. तां प्रति—is better than सम्प्रति, as we have it already in the first line. तदा प्राप्तः—see p. 54. सान्द्र—thick; this is necessary to make the sandal-juice compare with the touch of her hand.

S'l. 2. चल—Unsteady, in motion; hence, difficult to hit. दुर्लक्ष्यं च—and it is difficut to be seen, being atomic accord- to the Naiyâyikas. This adds to the difficulty. *Cf.* तत् (मनः) च प्रतिजीवं भिन्नमणु नित्यं च । Tark.-Kau. समं—Simultaneously. In the first place, it was difficult to hit the mind; Kâma being the greatest marksman, could have, at the most, hit it with one arrow. But here the wonder was that it was hit with all the arrows and at one and the same time. This is meant to indicate that his affliction was very great.

कुसुमधन्वन्--विषमायुध *v. l.* one having an odd number of (*i. e.* five) weapons (arrows); the God of love. It also means 'one whose weapons are hard'.

S'l. 3. मनोभवस्य--मनसि भवतीति (पचाद्यच्) मनसि भवो यस्य इति वा. अस्मद्विधः--*i. e.*, suffering from love-torment, being separated from their beloveds.

P. 64. विप्रतीपं--विशेषेण प्रतीपं विप्र० quite reversed. प्रतिगता आपो अत्र इति प्रतीपं from प्रति + अप् water + अ, अप् being changed to ईप् after द्वि, अन्तः, or a preposition. विप्र० दृष्टं--The relation is now seen to be reversed. For the पञ्चत्व (the state of being five) which belonged to your arrows has now been transferred to कामिजन३ they being reduced to the state of five (led to death), while असंख्यत्व which formerly belonged to the Kâmijanas has now been transferred to your arrows. अधुना--*Now* that I am hit and so know it by personal experience. अन्तर्निगूढ--and hence more to be feared. ०संरम्भ--the vehemence or impetuosity of. कोपसंभारायाः--*v. l.* her accumulated (*i. e.* excessive) anger. लोचनगोचर--गावश्चरन्त्यत्र इति गोचरः, 'that to which the senses move,' range of. The Queen has looked angrily at Sâga.; this does not augur well for her. तपस्विनी--Lit. one practising penance and thus without the means of self-protection; hence one deserving protection or pity; helpless.

S'l. 4. ह्रिया--She felt ashamed because she loved one who was (according to her present position at least) beyond her reach. वैलक्ष्यं--shame with confusion. अधिकं--because *friends* smile. प्रायेण--Both प्राय and प्रायस् are used. आतङ्कः--uneasiness or disquietude of the mind; *cf.* अस्यास्तान्निमित्तोऽयमातङ्को भवेत्. S'âk. III. p. 68; or deep pain, anguish. विधुरा--विगता धूः कार्यभारोऽस्याः; *lit.* one unable to undertake any responsibility; hence helpless, disconsolate; *cf.* मदनदहनोद्दाहविधुराम्, Mâl.-Mâd. II. 3.

कौशाम्बीराज्य--The kingdom of Vatsa, Kaus'âmbi being the capital. प्रियवचनं--By प्रिय he means the meeting with Sâgarikâ arranged by him.

P. 65. समीहिताभ्यधि०--The King wanted to know only about the well-being of Sâgarikâ; but now he was to have an interview with her. This reading is, therefore, preferable to समीहितकार्यसिद्ध्या. सगर्वम्--Vidû. is proud of the success achieved by him in his mission.

बृहस्पति--बृहतां पतिः; स् is inserted and त् dropped when the comp. refers to the deity of that name; otherwise बृहत्पति

न खलु चित्रं—The king pays a compliment to the Vidt. by this. He means—There is nothing to be wondered at in this. This is nothing compared to what your wit can achieve. हस्तं—The comp is faulty. हस्त should not have been compounded. The readings here are not very satisfactory.

P. 66. गुर्वनुरागी॰—The Sun is here represented as a lover going to meet his bride, the evening सन्ध्या, according to his engagement with her. This is quite in keeping with the matter in hand. The King also will shortly do the same.

वारुणीवधू *v. l.*—वारुणी the western quarter, presided over by Varuṇa. The west is also represented as the bride of the sun; *cf.* मानमानपरविग्नमितायाश्चुम्बति स्म मुखमुद्गतरागः । पद्मिनी किमु करोतु वराकी मीलिताम्बुरुहनेत्रपुटाऽभूत् ॥ Vik.-Ch. XI. 9. अनुसरति—अनु goes with काननं, and is a कर्मप्रवचनीय; काननमनु लक्ष्यीकृत्य सरति moves towards.

S'l. 5. The idea worked out herein is this—The chariot of the Sun has but one wheel; so he is anxious as to how it will be able to travel round the world the next day, being weakened by its journey round the world that day. He therefore, rests on the peak of the setting-mountain, pulls off the wheel of the directions and carries it off with him, as it were, that it should serve as the second wheel for his chariot. एकचक्रः—*cf.* रथस्यैकं चक्रं भुजगयमिताः सप्ततुरगा निरालम्बो मार्गश्चरणरहितः सारथिरपि । रविर्यात्येवान्तं प्रतिदिनमपारस्य नभसः क्रियासिद्धिः सत्त्वे भवति महतां नोपकरणे ॥; also एकचक्रो रथो यन्ता विकलो विषमा हयाः । आक्रामत्येव तेजस्वी तथाप्यर्को नभस्तलम् ॥ Daṇḍin. प्राप्तुं—to come to the point of starting (the rising mountain).

सन्ध्यामृष्टा॰—आमृष्ट wiped off, snatched away; *cf.* for this sense आमृष्टं नः परैः पदम् । Kum. II. 31. ॰कृष्ट *v. l.* pulled or drawn away, *i. e.*, contracted—means nearly the same thing. परिकर—a collection. हेमार॰—see com.; the rays of the sun shooting upwards in all directions and of a golden hue at dusk are here spoken of as the spokes of the *dikchakra*. The sun's chariot is golden (*cf.* हिरण्मयेन सविता रथेन &c. Ṛigveda I. 35. 2); so it is but proper that the spokes of its wheels also should be golden. परिकरैः स्पष्ट॰ *v. l.* where the instr. is हेतौ (on account of). ॰हेमारपंक्तिः—*v. l.* qualifies अर्कः; this means-who has the circle of spokes in the form of his rays ready. This is not so satisfactory as the reading in the text. स्पृष्टहेमार॰—*v. l.* means —the line of spokes of which is touched (seized) by the sun with his करs (rays-hands) for drawing it towards himself.

This yields a good sense, but then it is not clear what the हेमारपंक्ति is made of.

P. 67. S'l. 6. In this S'l. the day-lotus-plant (पद्मिनी), which closes its flowers at sunset and opens them at sunrise, is described as the sun's spouse, consoled by him at the time of his departure to the nether world. The sense of a lover consoling his beloved at the time of separation is also hinted at It is fully explained in the com. पद्मनयने—This reading is preferable to ०वदने. For the सरोरुहिणी is spoken of here as सुप्ता on account of the closing up of the lotuses; and as it is the eye that is closed in sleep, it follows that the पद्म is regarded as the eye of the पद्मिनी. *Cf.* in this respect the latter half of the S'l. from the Vikram.-Ch. quoted above; also तदेतदु न्मीलय चक्षुरायतं महोत्पलं प्रत्युषसीव पद्मिनी । Vik. I. 5. पद्मनयने in the second case means 'having lotus-like eyes.' समयः—(1) time; (2) may also mean condition, agreement, *viz.* सुप्ता &c. प्रत्यायनं—conviction, assurance (that she should feel cheerful). सरोरुहिणी—(2) having a lotus in her hand (for sport). Poets represent young girls as carrying a lotus in their hands for sport; *cf.* लीलाकमलपत्राणि गणयामास पार्वती । Kum. VI. 84; हस्ते लीलाकमलं &c. Meg. II. 2. सर्वः—(2) a clever lover. अस्तमस्तक०—(1) with his rays resting on the setting-mountain; (2) with his hand placed on her drooping head.

This s'l. is quoted in the Das'-R. as an instance of पताका-स्थानक (that which indicates by the mention of something extraneous, the matter in hand that is begun or is about to happen, being characterized by parity of situation or attributes) by similar situation.

बहलीकृत—rendered dense and magnified. Darkness covering the intervals between the lines of forests made them appear like a compact mass and also extended their limits. संनिवेश—situation, arrangement. गृहीतघन०—This added to their darkness. पीवर—Stout, fat (being well-developed and advanced in age). Such only are quite dark.

P. 68. समन्तात् &c.—Some read सहर्षं before this, but there is no special reason for the King to feel joy here.

S'l. 7. स्थगयति—The root स्थग् though not mentioned by Pāṇini is recognized by later writers being included in the चुरादि list (चुरादीनामाकृतिगणत्वात्) and is often used by poets; *cf.* विश्वङ्मोहः स्थगयति Uttar. III. 38; निमित्तशून्यैः स्थगिता रजोभिः । Bhaṭṭi. XII. 69; स्थगयासि पुनरोष्ठं पाणिना दन्तदष्टम् । Śis'. XI. 34.

अन्यामपि दिशं—अन्या अपि दिशः *v. l.* noticed by Mr. Joglekar, is better, as the darkness would envelop all space at once. ॰पुरविभागान्—The comp. may also be taken as अद्रींश्च द्रुमांश्च पुरविभागान् (the different parts of the city) च. It is natural that the King should speak of the mountains and trees in the distance in general and the different parts of the city in particular. तिरयति—Denom. fr. तिरस् (तिरः करोति). भुवनस्यै॰—*Cf.* असत्पुरुषसेवेव दृष्टिर्निष्फलतां गता। Mṛich. I. 34. हरकण्ठ—The neck of Hara is taken as a standard of blackness, owing to its being turned black as the effect of the Hâlahala poison drunk by him.

संसक्त—intermixed, in close contact with each other. पिण्डीकृत—massed together, solidified.

S'l. 8. पाली—a row; also पालि. According to Prof. Chakravartî this line is quoted in a comm. as पालीयं चम्पकानां परिमलविलसत्षट्पदश्रेणिभाजाम्. पाटला—The trumpet flower-tree (Maráthi पाडळी). Its flowers have a good smell; *cf.* Śák. पाटलसंसर्गिसुरभिवनवाताः I. 3.

P. 69. आघ्राया॰—The repetition indicates frequency, having inhaled the smell every time. विविधं—various; each tree was known by the peculiar smell of its flowers. द्विगुणतर-अतिशयेन द्विगुणं simply means 'excessively dense'. The comp. should properly be ॰तमसानिह्नुतः according to the rule ओजः-सहोऽम्भस्तमसस्तृतीयायाः (अलुक्) Páṇ. VI. 3. 3. The present instance may be treated as a case of poetic license. *Cf.* for a similar use सततनैशतमोवृतमन्यतः। Kir. V. 2; वञ्चयिष्यसि कुतस्तमोवृतः कामुकेति चकुषुस्तमङ्गनाः। Rag. XIX. 33. Prof. Ray defends the लुक् here by referring to the dictum समासप्रत्ययविधौ तदन्तग्रहणं नास्ति. निपतन्म॰—Some read ॰करकुसुमा॰ as one comp.; but it was not possible for the Vidū. to see the bees settling on flowers; he could only see them coming to the garden. आमोद—is fragrance exceedingly gratifying.

मसृण—smooth. सुखायमानः—feeling or experiencing ease or pleasure; pre. p. of the denom. of सुख (सुखं वेदयते, सुख+क्यङ्) It is properly the person walking that feels the pleasure, but it is transferred (उपचरित) to चरणसंचार. देवीवेष॰—This is to remind the King of the plan settled, that he should not take Sága. for the real Queen. कोपि—strange, which cannot be explained. परिभाविन्—disregarding, slighting, not caring for.

P. 70. Śl. 9. विशद—bright, cheerful. रसात्—through pleasure. रमयतितरां—such acts on her part please the lover all the more. संकेतस्था—waiting in the place appointed or keeping the engagement.

मम वेषं कृत्वा—मम वेषधारिणी v. l. is faulty; as we have to take recourse to सापेक्षसमास, मम being connected with वेष. अभिसारि॰—अभिसृ to go to meet a lover with carnal desire.

P. 71. कृतावगुण्ठनः—This in order that he should not be recognized. एषा स्फुटमेव &c. Vidú. wanted to compliment S'aga. by saying that she looked exactly like Vásav.; so perfect was the disguise. Vâsav., however, understood him to mean—This is clearly Queen Vásav. (and not Sâgarikâ) and hence her confusion. हताश—You, whose object is foiled; unfortunate one. उद्गच्छति मृगलाञ्छनः—After this some editions have—वासव॰—(ससंभ्रममपवार्य ।) भगवन्मृगलाञ्छन मुहूर्तं तावदपवारितशरीरः (with your body hidden) भव (i. e. do not rise) येन प्रेक्षिष्येऽस्य भावानुबन्धं (the continuous flow or depth of love). We should have inserted this in the text. It is natural for Vâsa. to wish that the moon should rise a little later; so that she might hear the King actually professing his love for Sâgariká, without the fear of her identity being discovered.

P. 72. अये—expresses surprise. Some read for this—(सोत्कण्ठमात्मगतम्). But this speech of the King cannot be आत्मगत as it is heard by the Vidúshaka.

S'l. 10. आदौ—At its beginning. आसन्ने—supply प्रियासमागमे. अभ्यर्ण--p. p. p. of अर्द् with अभि; close at hand, imminent. *Cf.* for the idea स्मर एव तापहेतु...दिवस इवाभ्रश्यामस्तपात्यये जीवलोकस्य । S'âk. III. 10.

उत्कण्ठा॰—उत्कण्ठा is चिन्तन with a great longing. Some define it as—रागे त्वलब्धविषये वेदना महती तु या । संशोषणी च गात्राणां तामुत्कण्ठां विदुर्बुधाः ॥ ॰या निर्भरं greatly, excessively यथा तथा. प्रिये सागरिके—This is necessary; otherwise he might escape when the mistake is discovered, by saying—'I did not address Sâga., but you'.

S'l. 11. रम्भागर्भ—The interior of a plantain tree, (i. e., the stump deprived of its outer skin) which only resembles the thighs in colour and plumpness; तेन निभं Inst. Tat.; according to some निभ when used as an उत्तरपद has the sense of तुल्य 'equal'; in this case it is a नित्यसमास (॰गर्भेण तुल्यं). *Cf.* स्युरुत्तरपदे त्वमी । निभसंकाशनीकाशप्रतीकाशोपमादयः । Amara. The रम्भागर्भ is cold, and the comparison to that is appropriate here (though otherwise found fault with by Kâlidâsa—एकान्तशैत्या-

कदलीविरोषाः । जातास्तदूर्वोरुपमानबाह्याः । Kum. I. 36) as the King was suffering from a feverish heat. मृणालोपमौ—This also may be a Bah. or निरयसमास like the above. निःसंक—*Cf.* ll. 1,2 of S'l. 9 *supra*. विसुरानि—nerveless, languid. दर्शयति—shows his impatience. निर्वापय—cau. of वा with निर्, to soothe, to gladden.

P. 73. साहसिक:—From सहस rashness, precipitancy and aff. ठक् (इक); see com.; विश्रब्धा—*i. e.*, dismissing all fear (at the thought that he is the King) and reserve. नित्य—always, without cessation. रुष्टा—in ill-humour. कटुकिते—fr. कटुक bitter, see com. मधुरवच°—He means to say—The harsh words constantly grating against the ears have made them harsh; so something soothing must be put in. Let your sweet words do that. आर्यवस°—She means that Vasan. also has uttered equally bitter words.

P. 74. स्मरिष्यसि—She means—you will have to repent afterwards for having uttered these words when your plan is brought to light and you pay the penalty for that.

°कपोलसंनिभ:—*i. e.* reddish (as the moon is at the time of rising). The cheek of a delicate and fair-skinned woman is tinged red with the flush of anger.

S'l. 12. स्वहस्ता°—When the moon appeared on the top of the rising-mountain he was of a pale-white colour, while the face of Ságariká had all the splendour of the full moon. Now the poet, by means of an *Utpreksha* (read in the com. श्लेषाश्रयोत्प्रेक्षा instead of °योपमा) makes the King say—Look, there is the moon, with uplifted *Karas* (rays-hands) ready to retaliate as it were, on finding his splendour totally robbed.

प्रकृतिजडत्वं-natural dullness of intellect, want of discretion; also °जलत्वं (डलयोरभेदात्) wateriness, the moon being supposed to be formed of water; *cf.* सलिलमये शशिनि रवेर्दीधितयो मूर्छितास्तमो नैशम् । क्षपयन्ति &c. Varâhamihira; and अस्त्वेवं जडधामता तु भवतो यद्व्योम्नि विस्फूर्जसे । quoted in K.-P. X.

S'l. 15. The moon's जडत्व (want of discretion) is explained in this S'l. The various purposes served by the moon are also served by the face. Again, the moon of the face is always present and full, while the real moon is not so; the latter should have had the discretion not to rise; but he has risen; hence his जडत्व.

हन्ति—(1) overshadows, eclipses; (2) destroys, causes to disappear; because day-lotuses fade at moon-rise. नयनानन्दं—*cf.*

कलाशेषा मूर्तिः शशिन इव नेत्रोत्सवकरी। Mál.-Mád. II. 3; न हन्ति किं— *i. e.* it does (see com.). झषकेतनस्य—(1, 2) of love or passion. So Bhavabhûti ज्वलयति मनोभवाग्निं (मालती) Mál.-Mád. III. 6. The moon also is an inflamer of passion; *cf.* Śák. III. 3; अदिदीपदिन्दुरपरो दहनः कुसुमेषुमत्रिनयनप्रभवः। Śiś. IX. 42; Nigudkar Śâstrî quotes—प्रभावस्यास्तु तं दृष्ट्वा ववृधे कामसागरः। चन्द्रस्येवोदये प्राप्ते पर्वण्यां सरितां पतिः॥ Harivaṃśa. In the second case झष॰ may also mean 'the Ocean' whose waters begin to swell at moon-rise (a reference to the flow-tide). वक्त्रेन्दौ—वक्त्रमेव इन्दुः is a Rûpaka. अभ्युद्गतः—Some read उज्जृम्भते; but अभ्युद्गतः better accords with the preceding उदितः and स्थितः. वक्त्रे चन्द्रमसि स्थिते किमपरः शीतांशुरुज्जृम्भते is the reading found in the Rasagaṅgádhara. This line with the reading अभ्युद्यतः is quoted in the K.-P. with the remark अत्र अपरत्वमिन्दोरनुगुणं न तु वक्त्रस्य प्रतिकूलमिति रूपकस्य साधकतां प्रतिपद्यते।

अमृतेन—The Inst. is हेतौ, 'owing to the possession of'. बिम्बाधरे—बिम्बसदृशः अधरः बिम्बाधरः a comp. of the शाकपार्थिवादि (मध्यमपदलोपि) class; बिम्बाधर इति वृत्तौ मध्यमपदलोपिन्याम् Vâmana (in his अलंकारवृत्ति). बिम्बमिवाधर इति वा where इव has the sense of तुल्य and is dropped. The lower lip of a beautiful woman is often likened to the Bimba fruit (which when ripe is bright red); *cf.* बिम्बाधरं स्पृशसि चेद्भ्रमर प्रियायाः। Śák. VI. 20; दष्टवत्यधरबिम्बमभीष्टे Śiś. X. 53; यत्र बिम्बाधराणां Meg. II. 7; इमां दधाराधरबिम्बलीलाम् Nai. VII. 52. The figures of speech in this S'l. are रूपक and प्रतीपध्वनि; and according to some आक्षेप.

P. 75. जीवितसंशयः &c.—As the King was caught red-handed, Vidū. thinks that the punishment to be meted out would be severe. अन्यगतानि—to another, *viz.* to Sâgarikâ. अन्यां गतानि अन्य॰; अन्यां takes पुंवद्भाव by the rule सर्वनाम्नो वृत्तिमात्रे पुंवद्भावः। The pronouns become *mas.* when parts of a comp. or a Taddhita formation.

P. 76. व्यलीक—an offence, an unworthy or reprehensible act, a transgression.

S'l. 14. आताम्रतां—ताम्रयोः भावस्ताम्रता। आ ईषत् ताम्रता आता॰। a Prádi Tat. विलक्षः—embarrassed or full of shame. विवर्णः—*v. l.* विगतः वर्णः यस्य one who has lost his colour, on account of the consciousness of having done something wrong; hence wicked; or वर्ण may mean praise स्तुतिः; one who is not to be praised—deserves to be condemned—means the same.

लाक्षाकृतां—लाक्षा a kind of red dye largely used by women in ancient times for dyeing the soles of their feet and sometimes the lips. *Cf.* निष्ठ्यूतश्चरणोपभोगसुलभो लाक्षारसः केनचित् S'âak. IV. 5.

Sir M. Williams says—"Lâkshâ-alakta or alaktaka, 'lac,' a red dye prepared from an insect analogous to the cochineal insect. This minute red insect is found in great numbers in the Pâlâs'a, (Indian fig tree), and some other trees. It punctures its bark whence exudes a resinous milky juice with which it surrounds itself in a kind of nest, and which, when dry, may be broken off and used for various purposes.

मूर्ध्ना—*i. e.* by rubbing the head against the feet. कोपोपरागः—उपराग is an eclipse (राहुग्रास); the moon when eclipsed appears reddish; anger is here compared to Râhu, eclipsing the moon of the Queen's face. *Cf.* रमणकेलीकलहकोपोपरागपल्लवितकेरलीकपोल &c. Mâl.-Mâdh. III. p. 76. The removal of the flush of anger from the Queen's face depended on her being appeased, and that was possible only if she relented. परं—used as an adv.; पर means great or only (केवल); so परं means 'to a great degree (if you will be exceedingly kind to me)', 'or, only'.

ईदृशं—*i. e.* treacherous, which can easily transfer its love to another. Although there is an air of despair and resignation in this speech of the Queen, yet the use of the third person and its very tone express her great resentment. अपण्डिते—fr. पण्डा sharp, penetrating intellect; see com., 'You who cannot read the King's mind correctly'. अत्र—in this case *i. e.*, when the king's heart is quite alienated from me, and attached to another.

P. 77. अरण्यरुदितं—which cannot be heard by another and hence is useless; hence, any useless or futile attempt. कथं न कृतः &c.—He means—The Queen did not inflict corporeal punishment upon us; is not that a favour? उपहससि—Because the Vidú. spoke in a jesting tone including him also in his remark अक्षतशरीरौ. *Cf.* मूर्ख नायं परिहासकालः। Vik. II. p. 60. अनर्थः—*viz.* the knowledge of the love-intrigue by the Queen and the possibility of her committing suicide on that account. This is explained in the next S'loka. ०नर्थक्रमः—*v. l.* (a series of misfortunes) is bad, as only one अनर्थ is referred to in the next S'l.; ०कन्द—*v. l.* a source of calamity; is good in itself, but it does not harmonize with आपतितः.

S'l. 15. समारूढा—grew in intensity, developed; or rose to the highest pitch. ०बहुमानात्—On account of our affection being mutually esteemed. Some read समारूढप्रीतिः as one word, making it an attribute of प्रिया. This makes the construction smooth, no doubt. But the first better explains why the King also should not have been guilty of such conduct and why the Queen should resent it so much. प्रतिदिनं—दिने दिने इति अनु०, day by day. प्रिया मु०—This is the calamity feared by the King. प्रकृष्टस्य &c. प्रेम्णः सम्बन्धे स्खलितं any blundering with regard to &c.; or better, प्रेम्णः may be taken with अविषह्यं, to far-gone love any failing on one's part &c.; *cf.* in this case दूरारूढः प्रणयोऽसहनः Vik. IV. p. 93.

ततः प्रविशति &c.—As Sága. enters alone the plan settled seems to be that Sâgariká, to avoid suspicion, should go alone, dressed as Vâsava. and that Susaṃgatà should meet her at the rendezvous. सोद्वेगं—Although she started to go, the thought troubled her that she might have been watched (as appears from her words केनापि न लक्षितास्मि) and hence her उद्वेग. Notice the reading इदा नाहमनेन विरचितभट्टिनीवेषेणाविनीता (ill-trained, imprudent) केनापि &c.; see foot-note.

P. 78. मूढः—dazed, out of one's wits. अत्र—*i. e.* to ensure the safety of Ságariká. ज्ञातसंकेतवृत्तान्तया—After reflection Sága. comes to the conclusion that the Queen was sure to get knowledge of the meeting arranged between her and the King and that she, hunting her out there, would subject her and her friend to the severest rebuke and ill-treatment. Hence her resolve to put an end to her life. वरं—means मनाक् (a little) प्रियं (something to be preferred out of two alternatives although itself not much desirable). परिभूता—insultingly treated.

P. 79. अनाथा—Having no one to look after, forlorn. अशरणा—having no one to protect, helpless. Or as नाथ means a master and hence a protector, शरण may be taken in its second sense of गृह or shelter, shelterless.

साहस०—सहसि भवं साहसं; तत्र भवः इत्यण्; fr. सहस+अ. अकार्य—a reprehensible deed; अ has the sense of अप्राशस्त्य.

S'l. 16. स्वार्थः प्रयत्नोऽयं &c.—The Queen might say-Now that you do not care for me, why do you seek to save my life ? Expecting such a question the King says—It is not so much to save your life that I am trying, but to save mine; for मम कण्ठ० &c. प्रिये—By addressing her thus, he reassures her of his love-You are still my darling.

अथ वा एनं प्रेक्ष &c.—The sight of her lover inspired love of life in her; but that was only for a moment; the next moment she thinks of carrying out her first resolve.

P. 80. S'l. 17. अतिमात्रं—Adv. modifies कृतेन understood; *cf.* न खलु न खलु मुग्धे साहसं कार्यमेतद्व्यपनय करमेतं पल्लवाभं लतायाः। Nág. II. 11. चलितमपि—For it was already कण्ठगत. जीवितेशे—and so she could prevent his life from going out. बाहुपाशं—The noose formed by the arms, which is necessary to chain life to his body. This may also mean 'your excellent arm,' प्रशस्तः बाहुः बाहुपाशः as पाश is one of the words expressing excellence, the comp. being of the *Nitya* class. कण्ठे कृत्वा स्पर्शं नाटयन्—Here we are to suppose that the King not only fastened her arm round his neck but also embraced her (the reading कण्ठे गृहीत्वा makes it clear) as appears from IV. 2 and 3. अनभ्रा वृष्टिः—A shower without the appearance of clouds and which, therefore, is not expected; hence, the sudden occurrence of anything that is welcome; *cf.* अपमेघोदयं वर्षं Kum. IV. 54;—किमयमनभ्रः सुधावर्षः। Mál. Mâd. X. 10.

अकालवाता॰—which will blow off the shower.

P. 81. वरं स एव जनो &c.—Kâñch. means—Both of you are, in a way, guilty now—he of infidelity to you, you of want of courtesy or breach of decorum. So if you go and forgive him now, he only will remain a दुर्जन, as he has no excuse for his conduct.

मुग्धे—*i. e.* one who does not know how to respond to acts of love. अद्यापि—although I have actually placed your arm round my shoulder.

P. 82. After तथा करोति some read राजा—आकर्णायतलोचने &c.; see foot-note. But the verse does not seem to be genuine. It is not in Harsha's style; it is out of place after विफलमनोरथाः क्रियामहे; it repeats ideas that have already occurred. The expression अम्बुधरैरिवोन्नतकुचैः is unpoetic.

अलीकदाक्षिण्येन—False courtesy or display of unreal love. By this she refers to the King's words जीवितेशे &c. (s'l. 17), इयमनभ्रा वृष्टिः, and मध्यस्थतया विफलमनोरथाः क्रियामहे.

Sl. 18. सहजाभिजात्य॰—The King means to say—my behaviour towards the Queen was simply a matter of formality, due to the Queen's high birth and lofty character. It was a dry thing (wanting in रस) after all; while my real love *you* only possess.

युक्तमेतत् &c.—This is ironical and is meant to express her great resentment. सदृशं—in keeping with a husband's behaviour towards his loving wife.

P. 83. मोहित—Deluded wrongly made to believe. दुर्नय—ill-conceived policy; refers to the meeting planned by him.

P. 84. अकृतपुण्यया—Had she a good stock of religious merit she could have died as desired and her misery would have ended. The reading कथमकृतपुण्यैर्मर्तुमप्यात्मन इच्छया न प्राप्यते is a general statement, intended to support a particular case. अवापितं *v. l.* is bad as it has to be taken in the sense of पारितं according to the principle धातूनामनेकार्थत्वात्. विपद्यमानं-being subjected to misery.

कृतदीर्घरोष०-For usually whenever the Queen saw the King a loving smile bloomed on her face. सुसंभृत—well stored-up, gone to its climax. क्रमोद्गत—*v. l.* which gradually (as each incident happened) rose up (swelled). क्रमोद्धतं *v. l.* also means the same (क्रमेणोद्धता रुट् यस्याः). सर्वाकार—सर्वेणाकारेण *i. e.*, in the three ways mentioned before. सर्वारम्भ—*v. l.* is bad for आरम्भ means 'what one undertakes;' or an undertaking; or an act on one's part; so this will mean 'pained or made uneasy by every act or effort of mine;' but this has no connexion with what precedes.

ACT IV.

P. 85. लज्जावति—लज्जालुके *v. l.* लज्जते इति तच्छीला लज्जालुः सैव लज्जालुका; here आलु (आलुच्) which is added कर्तरि and ताच्छील्ये is irregular, as लज्ज् is not included in the list of the roots that take it. Nigudkar S'ástri derives it in another way for which see com. अयि—is used here in the sense of अनुनय or entreaty. She addresses Fate entreatingly that it should relent and favour Sâgarikâ. असामान्य—समानमेव सामान्यं, य (ष्यञ्) being added स्वार्थे; स्त्रियां सामान्या; now see com. प्रतिपादय—give: for this sense *cf.* अर्थिभ्यः प्रतिपाद्यमानं &c. Bh. Nîti.; गुणवते कन्या प्रतिपादनीया S'ák. IV. p. 87.

P. 86. पट्टांशुक—पट्ट means here 'Silk'; पट्टनिर्मिते अंशुके पट्टांशुके. न खलु—asks a question with a hope to the contrary; has a mishap &c., I hope not; *cf.* न खलु तामभिक्रुद्धो गुरुः । Vik. III. p. 66; Kum. IV. 24. अत्याहितं—a great mishap or calamity (अतीव आधीयते स्म मनसि); or an act involving risk to life;

अस्याहितं महाभीतिः कर्म जीवानपेक्षि च। Amara. *Cf.* न खलु किमप्यत्याहितं S'âk. I. p. 27; मया अस्याहितमुपलब्धम्। Vik. IV. p. 92; for the second sense, *cf.* पाण्डुपुत्रैर्न किमप्यत्याहितमाचेष्टितं भवेत्। Veṇ. II

सोद्वेगम्—Some read after this हा भवति साग० &c. (see footnote); but this is quite out of place in Vidû.'s mouth. आर्यवसन्तकस्य हस्ते—Although such was not the injunction of Sága., Susaṅgatá says it purposely to induce Vasan. to take it, that it might be seen by the King and enlist his sympathy thereby.

P. 87. ईदृशे प्रस्तावे—When such is the drift of circumstances, at such a juncture; *i. e.,* when Sâg.'s life is in peril; तस्याः अलं० समागमः—Here समागम means 'acquisition' (प्राप्ति). so तया समागमः also.

P. 88. परिच्छदः— परिच्छाद्यते अनेनेति; fr. छद् cau. with aff. अ (घ) करणे; that by which one is surrounded or covered any attendant thing; *cf.* सेना परिच्छदस्तस्य Rag. I. 19; a garment' dress; here an ornament. महाकुल०—see com. Here प्रसूता is used in the sense of जाता; *cf.* तदन्वये शुद्धिमति प्रसूतः &c. Rag. I. 18. महाभिजनया—*v. l.* महान् अभिजनो (कुलं) यस्याः 'of noble birth,' is better.

सव्याजैः—व्याज is deceit, a feint (intended to mislead); see see com. The King had to take oaths to assure the Queen of his future fidelity to her; but he took care to use words conveying one meaning to the Queen while, at the same time, they had another which would leave him free to pursue his love-intrigue. वैलक्ष्येण परेण—Whenever the King met the Queen, he showed that he was greatly ashamed of his past conduct. प्रत्यापत्ति &c.—The cons. is न हि तथा प्रत्या० उपागता यथा रुदत्या ......स्वयं कोपः अपनीतः तदा उपागता। प्रत्यापत्ति—return (to her usual disposition). प्रत्यासत्ति—*V. l.* is not so good, as it requires a great deal of twisting to take it in the sense of 'reconciliation'; it properly means 'close contiguity or connexion;' hence close adherence to reconciliation. प्रत्यासत्तिमु० मम तथा *v. l.*—makes the construction smooth (देवी तथा मम प्रत्यासत्तिमुपागता &c.) but then एव and स्वयं lose their force; see com.

P. 89. सागरिकाचिन्तैव—Although we are told in III. 19, that three things troubled him, the first two were of vital importance to him, *viz.* the reconciliation of the Queen (who else, he feared, would put an end to her life; see III. 15) and the plight of Ságarikâ. He was free from anxiety about the first now; but Sâga. still continued to be in the same miserable state and the thought about that troubled him. Why should it do so? Why not forget her? He assigns the reason in the next S'l. Sâga. was in his heart; if she was uneasy, he was also uneasy.

S'l. 2. ०तापने विलीव—This may be questioned; for although the King embraced her, Sâga. remained apathetic, see p. 81 (किमपापि मध्यस्थतया &c.). The पनत्व not being on Sâga.'s part the विलय is inconceivable. Again the idea of विलय does not well harmonize with the comparison to the interior of a lotus, which is easily crushed, but does not melt. It must be remembered, however, that the King is speaking under distraction. ०मार्गैः—The pl. is used because five holes were made by the five arrows. Sâga. being liquified entered his heart through these five channels. This S'l. is given in the Subhâshitâvalî as S'rîharsha's, under the heading 'विरहिणां प्रलापाः,' with the second line read thus-कण्ठग्रहप्रसमरापघने निलीय.

०परिक्षामामपि &c.—*cf.* एवमुत्सुकोपि प्रियदर्शनो देवः। S'âk. VI. p. 149. भावनीयला०-*cf.* श्लाघ्ययौवनां p. 49. द्वितीयाचन्द्रः—The moon appearing on the 2nd night of the bright half of a lunar month which is crescent-shaped (क्षीण) appears especially beautiful. Its appearance is hailed with great delight and reverence by the people.

P. 90. S'l. 3. कामं—Very much, greatly. अदक्षिणं—दक्षिण is one who is generous-minded, noble. He means—Sâga. died for me; but I did not follow her, being अदक्षिण. दक्षिणा भवत—This may mean—you should be kind to me and grant my request; or rather, I was अदक्षिण towards her; you at least be दक्षिण and follow her. गजगामिनी—He means-although stepping like an elephant she walks fast. (An elephant, although apparently walking slowly, is a swift walker).

P. 91. निरनुरोधा-See com.; अनुरोध fr. अनुरुध् + अ (घञ् भावे) means 'regard or consideration for' (which makes one look to the interest of another). निरनुरोधिता *v. l.* the state of being regardless, want of consideration for; साधु निरनुरुणद्धीति निरनुरोधिनी तस्या भावः. निरनुक्रोशा *v. l.* pitiless. अन्यथ...प्रेषिना—Mark the nobility of Vidú.'s mind. Although the necklace was given to him, he says that it was sent for the king.

S'l. 4. तुल्यावस्था—for his body also had obtained Sâga.'s कण्ठाश्लेष and then lost it.

P. 92. धृति—contentment, keeping the mind at ease. It is one of the 33 Vyabhichâribhâvas, see D.-R. IV. 12. धृति—

v. l. (keep up) life;—has no propriety. वेत्रहस्ता—वेत्र a cane-staff, usually worn by door keepers; *cf.* Kum. III. 45, Rag. VI. 26. खड्गहस्ता—*v. l.* there is no special reason why Vasu. should have worn a sword as the times were not turbulent and the people enjoyed the blessings of peace; see I. 9 *supra.* भागिनेय:—For deriv. see com. (भगिनी+एय). ०तुकाम:—The nasal of the infinitive is dropped before काम and मनस्.

P. 93. करितुरग०—The three of the four constituents of an ancient Indian army, the chariots being dropped by this time, as too cumbrous for advanced warfare. Comp. the description here with that of the expedition against Vindhya-ketu, at p. 6, Priy. दुर्निवार—difficult to be kept back, irresistible. समावेशयितुं—to arrange in battle-order. परिभव—This insult, *scil.* the blocking up of the passage. हास्तिकं—a multitude of elephants. वेपते इव—The Vid., of course, says this for fun.

S'l. 5. तत्क्षणं—स एव क्षणो यस्मिन्कर्मणि तद्यथा तथा. विग्विदन्धम्—shows the vastness of his army. ०पृतनापीडबन्धेन—पृतना an army, hence a multitude, आपीड a close and compact array, बन्ध formation. वेगात्—may go with विमुञ्चन् or better with निपत्य. ०पत्ति:—As Rumanvat's infantry advanced to meet the opposing force, it was crushed by the elephants of the Kosala king. ०पत्ति—*v. l.*—०घटाभि: उत्पिष्टा: पत्तयो येन तं कोसलाधिपतिं; in this case the पत्तय: are to be taken as belonging to Rumanvat. प्रत्यैच्छत्—opposed. वाञ्छितास्रि—The object desired was a duel with the Kosala-King. रभस-may mean joy, or beter still his ordour or chivalrous spirit. वाञ्छिताधि०—*v. l.* is bad, as it makes no sense; for आधि means मानसी व्यथा; so the meaning will be whose vigour was doubled by the anxiety wished for by him; but this is absurd. So to give it some meaning, the आधि must be taken to refer to the enemy (शत्रो: आधि: येन) which is not directly got from the compound.

P. 94. Sl. 6. अस्त्रव्यस्त०—The readings here are uncertain. As it is, the comp. must be taken as अस्त्रै: व्यस्तानि शिरस्त्राणि येषां तानि । शस्त्रकषणोत्कृत्तानि च उत्तमाङ्गानि यस्मिन्. But this gives rise to an awkward comp. The reading अस्तव्यस्त० is also not satisfactory. It means 'thrown off disorderly' (अस्तानि च व्यस्तानि च) scattered pell-mell. Prof. Ray takes व्यस्त in the sense of 'upturned.' Dissolve in this case अस्तानि च तानि व्यस्तानि च शिरस्त्राणि येषु तादृशै: शस्त्रकषणै: कृत्तानि &c. व्यूढा—there flew (विन्यस्ता);

व्यूढो विन्यस्तसंहतौ इत्यमरः । वर्मोद्गमद *v. l.* is grammatically wrong. आहूय—ह्वे with आ in the sense of 'to challenge' is Âtm. (स्पर्धायामाङः । अन्यत्र पुत्रमाह्वयति). भङ्गप्रतीपा°—becoming opposed to भङ्ग or defeat; encouraging his soldiers to fight and not allowing them to give way. भग्ने प्रधाने बले—*v. l.* when the main body of the army was broken (had given way). This reading is better as it praises the valour of the Kosala-king and thereby brings into greater relief the prowess of Rumaṇvat. The epithet एकेनैव also becomes more appropriate in this case. Some read after this—राजा—कथमस्मदीयान्यपि बलानि भग्नानि । But as observed by Prof. Ray, it is not clear that the main force that was broken belonged to Rumaṇvat, till the addition of the fourth line. In the absence of the fourth line the प्रधानबल would appear to be of कोसलपति; so the interruption is premature and absurd.

समरव्रणित—व्रणा अस्य सञ्जाता इति व्रणितं; प्रहारव्र°—*v. l.* (see ft.-note) is rejected as प्रहार is unnecessary, व्रण being due to प्रहार; again we are not told that Rumaṇvat's army consisted of elephants for the most part; and even supposing he took with him the elephants from the enemy's army, he could not have taken all. दीयतां मत्प्रसादः—प्रदर्श्यतां मत्प्रसादः *v. l.* in this case प्रसाद would mean the result of *i. e.* a reward worthy of.

P. 95. ऐन्द्रजालिकः—इन्द्रजाल magic (इन्द्रस्य जालं माया deceit illusion; Indra is the presiding god of magic. Some take इन्द्र to mean परमात्मा). इन्द्रजालेन दीव्यति; or see com.; पिच्छिका—a bunch of peacock's feathers carried by jugglers and magicians, which they wave about to produce a sort of hypnotic influence on the eyes of the spectators before whom they perform.

S'l. 7. The reading पणमह चलणे violates the metre. °पिनद्ध—tied up, inseparably connected with. इन्द्रजाले लब्धसाक्षस्य *v. l.*—'who derived knowledge of magic by direct intuition'-*i. e.* "magic appeared, of itself, to Indra, who had not to resort to any other indirect means". Ghâte.

शम्बरस्य—Name of a demon, regarded as the patron of magic, as also the composer of several incantations. Magic is called शाम्बरी माया after him. He carried off Pradyumna and threw him into the sea, but was slain by him afterwards. मायासुप्र°—*i. e.* renowned for his magical skill. सुपरीक्षितसर्वजगतः *v. l.*—who could take a good view of the whole world (by his magical power).

P. 96. S'l. 8. किं धर०—Some read किं with देव and the line as धरणीए मिअअङ्को &c. "We see from this" remarks Wilson, "that the pretensions of the necromancers of India were not inferior to those of their brethren of the west, nor of dissimilar purport." किं बहुना &c.—This is read as the first line of the next S'l. instead of मङ्ग &c., as किं जल्पितेन बहुणा. हृदयेनेहसे—By this he means that he would also show Sâgarikâ, whom the King longed so much to see.

भो वयस्य अ० भव—In some Editions these words are omitted; and the speech is given as ईदृशस्तेऽव० *i. e.* as addressed to the magician. अवष्टम्भ—self-confidence (with which he has spoken); or this may mean आरम्भ: the beginning, the preliminary part.

युष्मदीय:–See com.; Vâsa.'s father was the ruler of Ujjayinî, to which the magician belonged.

P. 97. ज्ञातिकुल—Properly the paternal relations; here all those connected with her father's house. नाभिकुल—*v. l.* means the same thing–those conncected by the navel or womb, descendants of the same parents. सपिंडास्तु सनाभय: Amara. बहुमान:—Kâñch. gives a different colouring to the Queen's remarks. उज्जयिनीत:......पक्षपात: She means—It is not undue partiality that you have for the magician; it is the high regard that you have for those connected with your parental house that makes you take interest in him. The reading माईकुल (मातृकुल) is bad as Vâsa.'s mother did not belong to Ujjayinî.

गर्जितम्—*i. e.* he has talked boastingly of his own skill in magic.

S'l. 10. सिद्ध &c.—A class of semi-divine beings characterized by great holiness and purity and having the eight superhuman faculties or *Siddhis*, *viz.* अणिमा महिमा चैव लघिमा गरिमा तथा । । प्राप्तिः प्राकाम्यमीशित्वं वशित्वं चाष्ट सिद्धयः ॥ चारण—Heavenly choristers or bards, whose duty it is to move about (as they have access to any place in the universe: *cf.* लोकालोकविचारिचारणगणै: Nâg. V. p. 108) and sing songs in praise of the glorious deeds of gods or god-like heroes; *cf.* चारणेभ्यस्त्वदीयं जयोदारणं श्रुत्वा &c. Vik. I. p. 21. सुरवधू०—The heavenly nymphs or *Apsarases*; here वधू means स्त्री; *cf.* ऊरूद्भवा नरसखस्य मुने: सुरस्त्री Vik. I. 3.

P. 98. S'l. 11. दोर्भि:—उपलक्षित: marked or characterized by. The Inst. is उपलक्षणे. सधनु &c.—For dissolution and the special names of the weapons, see com.

ऐरावत:—इरा उदकानि सन्त्यस्मिन् इरावान् the sea, इरावति भव: ऐरावत: sprung from the sea. The celebrated elephant produced at the churning of the ocean and appropriated by Indra. त्रिदश०—The word त्रिदश is variously derived, as तिस्र: दशा: stages of life येषां, they not having the fourth (that of old age); or तृतीया दशा येषां always in youth; the word त्रि standing for तृतीय as in त्रिभाग; or त्रिरावृत्ता दश परिमाणमेषां; Bah. दिव्य०—दिवि भवा दिव्या: fr. दिव्+यत्, Pán. IV. 2. 101. "This is something like the masque in the Tempest (of Shakespeare)" Wilson.

P. 99. मातुलगृ०—shows that विक्रमबाहु was the maternal uncle of Vâsavadattá. प्रत्युद्गम्य—प्रत्युद्गम् means 'to go forward to receive a person'. अनुभाव:—here means 'what impresses a man with one's dignity, power or greatness' (अनुभावयतीति । पचाद्यच्); hence magnificence, grandeur.

S'l. 12. जयकुञ्जर—कुञ्ज: (हस्तिहनु: दन्तौ वा an elephant's chin or tusk) अस्यास्तीति कुञ्जर: an elephant; जयस्य जयावहो वा कुञ्जर: जय[कु]ञ्जर:—also called गन्धहस्तिन्—an elephant of extraordinary strength and size and endowed with all the auspicious signs, whose possession ensured prosperity to a king. *Cf.* यस्य गन्धं समाघ्राय न तिष्ठन्ति प्रतिद्विपा: । तं गन्धहस्तिनं प्राहुर्नृपतेर्विजयावहम् ॥ Ancient imperial kings had such an elephant in their possession. *Cf.* गन्धमादननाम्ना गन्धहस्तिना सनाथीकृतैकदेशं (राजकुलं विवेश) Kád. p. 142; यात्रासु दिक्पालपुरीं विलुण्ठ्य न दिग्गजान् केवलमग्रहीय: । पलायितास्ते जयसिन्धुराणां गन्धेन सप्तच्छदबान्धवेन ॥ Vikra.-Ch. I. 84.

तुरगाणि०—Perhaps Harsha had the scene at his own royal gate in view when he wrote this S'loka. *Cf.* Báṇa's description of the noble steeds and the mountainous elephant Darpasâra he met at the royal gate. H.-Ch. II. It seems the king's choice horses and elephants were kept in the spacious courtyards of palaces; *cf* Kir. I. 16.

P. 100. सद्यो विस्मृत &c.—Vasu. was the minister of a petty king. He had never witnessed such grand scenes as were presented to his sight at the gate of Vatsarája. The fine horses, the wonderful elephant, the conclave of kings and the melody of music so filled him with surprise that he looked quite bewildered like a rustic going to a big city where everything is a wonder to him. द्वा:स्थेनैव कुतूहलेन-the wonderful objects just at the door (what will be my state when I shall see the inside then). ग्राम्य:—ग्रामे भव: (aff. य); also ग्रामीण.

अद्य खलु चिरात् &c.—*cf.* विजयसेनः-अद्य स्वामिपादा द्रष्टव्या इति यत्सत्यमनुपमं कमपि सुखातिशयमनुभवामि। Priy. p. 6.

S'l. 13. **कम्पस्य**–The Kañchukin is an old man; and generally he refers to his condition as an old man on his entrance. Here the effects of old age are described as intensified by the ecstatic joy he felt at his being able to see his master after a long time. **जडयति**–A denom. from जड; तर, changed तरां, added, intensifies the meaning.

P. 101. **संवादः**—Agreement; hence, similarity. **आयुष्मान्-अतिश्रेयान्** *v. l.* अतिशयितं श्रेयः यस्य one blessed with great fortune, exceedingly prosperous. **पृष्ठे हस्तं दत्वा**—as a mark of great familiarity and royal favour.

P. 102. **आकुल इव**—इव almost. **पर्याकुलयसि** *v. l.* पर्याकुलं करोषि throw into agitation, perplex. **चिरमपि स्थित्वा कथ०**—He means to say—Even if you hesitate for a long time, you will have to tell it as it will not be possible for you to keep back the fact from the King; so it will be better to tell it at once. **अलीकं**—The King was right in thinking so, as the demand was made by Yauga. without his knowledge. **वास०—(स्मित्वा)**. The Queen smiled because she knew the truth, being a party to the plan formed by Yaugan.; but she gives an evasive reply, not wishing to disclose the plan at this stage. She could not say that Vasu. was right, as in that case she would have been forced to explain the matter; only she did not know that Sâga. was the maiden sought by the minister.

अस्माभिरानीय०—Some Edd. omit अस्माभिः; but it is necessary, as the King knows then at once that the two, Vasubh. and Bâbhravya were with her on board the same ship when she was wrecked. And hence his remark further on ननु एतावेव ते निदर्शनम्.

This speech of Vasubhûti is differently read (see foot-notes) being amplified in a way in which the entire plan of Yaugandharâyaṇa is revealed. But the additions are evidently interpolations. In the first place a politician like Yaugandharâyaṇa was not likely to communicate his plot, which was kept a profound secret, to the minister of the very king whom he was going to dupe. Even supposing Vasu knew it, he could not have given such a detailed account of it in the presence of Vâsavadattâ, nor could he have said to the King's face–लावाणकेन वह्निना देवी दग्धेति वार्तामुत्पाद्य देवेन तदन्तिकं बाभ्रव्य.

प्रहित:. Again Yaugand. himself gives out his plot further on, so its premature disclosure here destroys the poetic effect. And further, when Yaugand. comes to the point इति प्रसिद्धिमुत्पाद्य तदन्तिकं बाभ्रव्यः प्रहितः, the King interrupts him, saying ततः परं श्रुतं मया. This shows that what preceded was not heard by him and so was not told by Vasubhúti.

मन्दभागिनी—मन्दः small भागः share of luck अस्ति अस्याः; unfortunate.

P. 103. दुरवगाहा गतिः &c.—दुःखेनावगाह्यते इति; गाह् + अ (घञ्) कर्मणि. Nobody can scrutinize the ways of Fate; no one knows what Fate may bring to pass-who knows Ratnâvalî, too, might have been saved, as these two were saved by Fate.

निदर्शनं—निदर्श्यते is illustrated अनेन; an instance proving a statement; *cf.* हिमसेकविपत्तिरत्र मे नलिनी पूर्वनिदर्शनं मता । Rag. VIII. 45. भागधेयं—भाग एव भागधेयं, धेय being added स्वार्थे; *cf.* रूपधेय and नामधेय. It is masc. when meaning कर or tribute (अन्यं भागधेयं S'âk. p. 56).

S'l. 14. हेमशृङ्गाश्रयमिव—The quadrangular houses set apart for ladies had plain tops; as the yellowish red flames tapering at the top rose above them from all sides they seemed to furnish them (the houses) with turrets of gold, as it were. सान्द्रोद्यान°—The heat was so great that it affected the trees of the garden also, causing their tops to wither. पिशुनित—*p. p. p.* of पिशुनय् a denom. from पिशुन 'one who indicates' (सूचक). सजलजलधर—धरतीति धरः, जलस्य धरः जलधरः the holder of water, a cloud; so there is an apparent tautology here; but जलधर is a word रूढ in the sense of any cloud, full-of-water or empty (according to poetic ideas). क्रीडामहीध्रं—महीं धरतीति महीध्रः; धृ + अ (कः) कर्तरि; क्रीडाया महीध्रः an artificial hillock in a garden for sport. प्लोषार्त—प्लोषेण प्लोषाद्वा आर्तः distressed.

S'l. 15. लावाणके—लावाणक was a village in the country of Vatsa, near Magadha. Some read लावणक but लावाणक is the correct name of the city as will appear from—युक्त्या लावाणकं यामः सह देव्या नृपेण च । पर्यन्ते मगधासन्नवर्ती हि विषयोऽस्ति सः ॥ Kathâsar. XV. 119. Prof. Ray quotes the following from Bhása, to verify this—लावाणके हुतवहेन हताङ्गयष्टिं तां पद्मिनीं हिमहतामिव चिन्तयामि । where the metre will not admit the form लावणक. For the allusion see *infra* note on ला° वह्निना...प्रवादमुत्पाद्य p. 111

कथं देवी वासवदत्ता दग्धा—The sudden announcement of the fire called up to the King's mind the past occurrence at

Lâvâṇaka, and in the heat of the agitation he thought that Vâsavadattâ was actually burnt though she was then by his side. The student will see further on that the fire was but the magician's trick, employed by Yauga. as the best means to procure the release of Sâga. and to get her identity disclosed in the presence of the King and the Queen.

P. 104. संयमिता—संदानिता *v. l.* p. p. of दान् 1 conj. with सम्; it has the same meaning as बद्धा. अकारणं—Here अ has the sense of अप्राशस्त्य; when there is no grave cause for it; for such a slight reason; does not mean 'without cause'. पतङ्गवृत्तिः—वृत्ति behaviour, mode of action. The moth throws itself headlong into a flame and perishes.

उत्तरीये गृहीत्वा—The Vidû. being on perfectly familiar terms with the King takes hold of his upper garment; Vasubh. and Bâbhravya could only respectfully remonstrate. किमद्यापि प्राणा: &c.—This speech ought to be अपवार्य.

S'l. 16. धूमानुबन्ध—a continuous flow of smoke. चक्रवालं—a circling mass of; चक्राकारेण वलते इति fr. चक्र + वल + अच् (अ); or चक्रमिव वाल: a circular mass यस्य.

P. 105. अध्यवसितं—done with a firm or resolute mind. पथ्युपदेशकः-पथ उपदेशकः Gen. Tat. *i. e.* I will also enter fire and die before you Some think that the objection to compounds in अक is not universal, as Pâṇ. himself says जनिकर्तुः प्रकृतिः and तत्प्रयोजको हेतुश्च. ०पुत्रीविपत्तेः—For, it was his belief that the princess had perished. इहैव—इह is emphatic; he had already made up his mind to die and not to show his face again to the king of Simhala, without Sâgariká. So he thinks that this was the best occasion to carry out his resolve. अकारणं—अवस्तुनि *v. l.* for such a trifling matter. भरतकुलं—For Udayana belonged to the race. संशयतुलां—in the balance of doubt (about its existence) *i. e.* doubt in one scale, weighed against the continuity of the race in the other, it being not known which would outweigh the other.

आसन्नहु०—*i. e.* within the reach of fire. संभावयामि—Lit. honour (by helping), hence help, attend to. एष...त्वरयतीव मां केसरवृक्षकः । यावदेनं संभावयामि । S'ák. I. p. 21. संभ्रमे—Supply कर्तव्ये, when you ought to be hurrying about to get out of the reach of fire. मध्यस्थतया—indifferent to your safety.

P. 106. आर्यपुत्र—The King had addressed her as प्रिया; he had also reciprocated her love; so she has the satisfaction of calling him आर्यपुत्र when speaking to herself. पुनरपि—For she had no desire to live, as is clear from her previous speech. भर्ता—Speaking aloud, she addresses him in the usual style.

S'l. 18. यत: संतापं—For her touch deprives the fire of its burning power.

S'l. 19. हुतवह:—हुतस्य वह: the carrier of oblations to the gods, fire; *cf.* वह्नि. अवन्ति°—For Vâsav. had entered the apartment and gone to the place where the King was.

P. 107. स्वप्ने मति: &c.—For but a moment ago the whole apartment was a scene of destruction; suddenly the fire vanished and everything appeared in its original state; was that a dream?

इयं त्वद्वचनात् &c.—The King now found himself in an awkward position; he was rather in a hurry to go to the rescue of Ságarikâ, when there were others at hand to go. So he tries to pass off the matter by saying this. The Queen smiles at his defence and says ironically "yes, I know it." राजपुत्र्या:—सदृशी having the sense of तुल्य is construed with the Inst. or Gen. by तुल्यार्थैरतुलोपमाभ्यां तृतीयाऽन्यतरस्याम् । तुल्य: सदृश: समो वा कृष्णस्य कृष्णेन वा । Sid.-Kau.

P. 108. सागरिका—See com. for derivation. मामनिवेद्य—The reader knows that Yau. had done all that on his own responsibility; see *supra* I. 8 (स्वेच्छाचारी भीत एवास्मि भर्तु:).

ईदृशीमवस्थां—For she was in chains at that time. The sight was too much for the faithful and tender-hearted minister to bear and he falls down overpowered by emotion. वत्तुभूतेरुपरि &c.—For he was like a father to her.

कथमुदात्तवंशस्य &c.—The King is agreeably surprised to find that she who was so long considered as of a humble origin was a princess.

P. 109. परिच्छदो भवतीति—After this Prof. Ray adds the stage-direction—इति रत्नमालां रत्नावलीकण्ठे समर्पयति, with the remark—'The jester here does what is most natural.' If this be genuine, it only brings into greater relief the nobility of the Vid.'s mind already displayed by him when offering the same to the King although he was expressly told that it was presented to him by Ságarikâ. See our remark on अन्यच्च मन हस्ते तया &c. p. 91.

कृतापराधा—Her fault lay in impersonating Vásavadattâ and going to meet the King. अतिनिष्ठुरे—Because as she thought she had the hardness of heart not to tell her (the Queen) that she was related to her. Ratnâvalî, however, did not know anything herself about the relationship, until it was announced by a bard in Act I, that she was in the household of King Udayana; and even after that she could not tell it out of modesty; *cf.* लज्जा गुर्वी II. 1. इदानीमपि तावत्—So in Priya. एहि अलीकशीले। इदानीमपि ते भगिनीस्नेहं दर्शय. स्खलितं नाटयति—This draws the Queen's attention to Sâg.'s being in chains. नृशंसतया—*Scil.* her putting Sâg. into fetters. नृन् शंसति destroys इति नृशंसः, hence, cruel; नृशंसस्य भावः नृशंसता. अमात्ययौ० दुर्जनीकृतास्मि—She knew that in her jealous pride she did not treat Sága. in a manner worthy of a Queen. She now tries to find a defence for her ill-treatment of Sâga. by saying that Yaugand. was responsible for that.

S'l. 20. देव्या मद्वचनात् &c.—This refers to Yaugandharâyaṇa's attempt to bring about a family alliance between Vatsarâja and the powerful King of Magadha, who had a beautiful daughter, named Padmávatí. But this was not possible so long as Vâsavadattâ lived, as Padmâvatî's father did not like that his daughter should hold a secondary position in the King's household Yaugand., therefore, persuaded Vâsavadattâ to suffer, for state purposes, a temporary separation from her husband, and while the royal household was at Lávâṇaka, set fire to the royal camp, while the King was out a-hunting. The poet, however makes mention of this incident in connexion with Ratnâvalî.

कलत्रसंघटनया—Some read कलत्रानाघटनया; देव्यन्यकलत्र० परं नापिता. The कलत्र meant here is, of course, Ratnâvalî, although the original reference is to Padmávatî. According to the plot of the play Ratnâvalî was to be the second wife of the King, but the Queen did not yet know that Sága. was that Ratnâvalî, and that her union with the King was imminent.

P. 110. अयं स्वामित्वलाभः—Yaugan. speaks of Udayana's acquisition of universal sovereignty after his marriage with Ratnávalî, as almost an accomplished fact, so firm was his belief in the prophecy.

अत्यन्त०—For comp. see com. निरनुरोध०—He means—In the loyal discharge of one's duty towards the master one cannot allow considerations of the feelings of others, however respectable, to come in one's way.

देव क्षम्यताम्—Some add before this the stage-direction पादयोर्निपत्य; but that is derogatory to the dignity of the prime minister; again, if genuine, we expect something like मा मैवम् or उत्तिष्ठ in the following speech of the King. सार्वभौमः—सर्वभूमेः ईश्वरः । तस्येश्वर इत्यण् ।

P. 111. अथेयं देवीहस्ते &c.—A similar question is asked in the Svap.-Va's.—अथ पद्मावत्या हस्ते किं न्यासकारणम् । (विहस्य) परिज्ञातायाश्च &c.—This is a hint to the Queen that she should give her sister in marriage to the King. In Jîvânanda's Ed. this part of the speech is assigned to the King, with a corresponding change in the following speeches of Vâsava. and the Vidû., *viz.*—अज्जउत्त...फुडं देहि मए...। विदू०—पिअवअस्सस्स अभि०. But the speech is appropriate in Yauga.'s lips alone, as it is natural that the suggestion should come from him. To put it in the mouth of the King is to go against propriety and make him forget his dignity.

P. 112. भगिनिका०—In the absence of her (Ratnâvalî's) parents she was entitled to give her away like that. को देव्याः प्रसादः &c.—*i. e.* सर्वोपि बहु मन्यते मया तथायमपि (so this one also is received with respect). तत्तथा कुरु &c.—*cf.* for similar requests यथा नौ प्रियसखी बन्धुजनशोचनीया न भवति तथा निर्वाहय । S'âk. III. p. 79; तद्यथेयं मे प्रियसखी स्वर्गस्य नोत्कण्ठते तथा वयस्येन कर्तव्यम् Vik. II. p. 87. पृथ्वी खलु &c.—Because the gaining of the hand of Ratnâvalî meant the gaining of supremacy over the whole world. स्थाने देवीशब्दं &c.—Vasu. was struck with the magnanimity of the Queen who gave Ratnâvalî to the King without betraying the least sign of jealousy. In some editions this speech is given as Bâbhravya's; but it suits Vasubhûti better. Some read after this—वासवदत्ता रत्नावलीमालिङ्ग्य देवीशब्देन प्रसादं करोति ।. इदानीं सफल०—Some attribute the speech to बाभ्रव्य; see foot-note; some read देव इदानीं सफलः परिश्रमः संवृत्तः. प्रियमुपकरोमि—This use of उपकृ is somewhat strange; but it has become technical as it is found in almost all the plays. Perhaps it means उप समीपे करोमि bring near to, confer; *cf.* उपहरामि the variant in S'âk.

S'l. 21. आत्मसमतां—Lit. made like my own self. He means—by the marriage-tie a firm ally is secured in Vikra., who would henceforth regard my interest as identical with his. This may also mean 'raised to our rank;' but it will not do here; for that is an advantage to Vikra. and not to the speaker.

प्रासेयं—Sâgar. is not dismissed so summarily; three epithets are used to point out her importance, *viz.* उर्वीतले सारं, •प्राप्त्यैकहेतुः and प्रिया (loved by me).

P. 113. **किं नास्ति त्वयि** &c.—किं नामास्ति विधेयं *v. l.* where विधेयं means 'what is to be accomplished, an object to be gained. **अमात्यवृषभे**—See द्विजवृषभाः p. 3.

भरतवाक्यं—This is a stage-direction. It refers to the concluding s'loka (or s'lokas) of a play, so called because, like the Nândî, it is repeated by भरत or the chief actor, divested of his dramatic character, as all acting is over. भरतप्रस्तावनानन्तर नटवाक्याभावादत्र भरतवाक्यमित्युक्तिः। Râghavabhaṭṭa on S'âk. It contains an expression of wish for general prosperity, &c.

S'l. 22. **उद्दाम**—Of luxuriant growth, abundant. **वासवः**—This is variously explained as वसोः अपत्यं पुमान्; or वसवो देवाः वसूनि रत्नानि वा अस्य सन्ति इति; ज्योत्स्नादित्वादण्. Indra, the god of the firmament and the dispenser of rain; *cf.* तव भवतु बिडौजाः प्राज्यवृष्टिः प्रजासु। S'âk. VII. 34. **इष्टां**—as desired; *i. e.* timely, and as much as is necessary. **इष्टैः**—Here इष्ट means an इष्टि or यजन, the aff. क्त being added to यज्, भावे (to form an abstract noun); distinguish this from the preceding इष्टां where क्त is added कर्मणि (to form p. p. p.). **त्रैविष्टपाः**—The gods; see com **प्रीणनं**—This is done by offering oblations to them; *cf* इष्टान्भोगान्हि वो देवा दास्यन्तो यज्ञभाविताः। Bg. III. 12. This is the service the gods expect from mortals in return for the favour from heaven; *cf.* त्वमपि विततयज्ञो वज्रिणं (स्वर्गिणः v. l.) प्रीणयस्व। S'âk. VII. 34. **राजमुख्याः**—*V. l.* will do equally well; it will be clear from the quotation above and Raghu. I. 26 &c., that it was the duty of kings also to offer sacrifice to gods through Brâhmaṇa priests.

आकल्पान्तं—कल्प is the period of the world's duration It extends over one thousand cycles of the four yugas. **समुपचितसुखः**—It is better to take the सुख as referring to the people at large, and not to good men alone. This same s'l. occurs as the concluding stanza of the Priya. with the readings स्थिरसमुपचिता (स्थिरा steady चासौ समुपचिता grown, developed) संगतिः for समुपचितसुखः संगमः, and दुःसहाः for दुर्जयाः in the third and fourth lines. **दुर्जयाः**—difficult to be put down by argument. **वज्रलेपाः**—वज्रवद् like a diamond or the thunderbolt, कठिनः hard लेपः यासां leaving a permanent (pain ful) impression on the mind. वज्रलेप also means a kind of cement, so called because things joined with it adhere permanently; for its preparation see Bṛihatsaṃ. Ch. 57; this meaning also will do; वज्रलेप इव स्थिताः वज्रलेपाः.

The third and fourth lines are also differently read as— आकल्पं सूक्तिकीर्तिः विलसतु सुकवेर्हृद्यसद्वृत्तरत्ना नाम्ना रत्नावलीयं सकलजनमनोनाटिका नाटिकास्तु । Construe-सुकवेः of the great poet सूक्तिकीर्तिः (the fame arising from the good composition, the play) आकल्पं विलसतु (shine forth, endure); इयं हृद्यसद्वृत्तरत्ना हृद्यानि charming सतां वत्सराजयौगन्धरायणादीनां वृत्तानि deeds रत्नानि यस्याः तादृशी इयं नाम्ना रत्नावली नाटिका सकलजनस्य मनसः नाटिका (that which causes to dance-bound with joy, hence, the delighter of) अस्तु. Also as—आकल्पान्तं क्रियासु-सुः क्रममुपरचितं—क्रतुषु समुचितं—संगतं सज्जनाश्च निर्विश्लेषावकाशं पिशुनजनवचोवर्जनाद्वज्रलेपम् ॥ But the meaning of this is not clear.

The subha shitas occurring in the play.

(The figures refer to the pages of this edition)

I. SENTENCES.

	Page
अचिन्त्यो हि मणिमन्त्रौषधीनां प्रभावः ।	39
इयमनभ्रा वृष्टिः ।	80
कष्टोऽयं खलु भृत्यभावः ।	8
किं पुनः साहसिकानां पुरुषाणां न संभाव्यते ।	73
घुणाक्षरमपि कदापि संभवत्येव ।	58
न कमलाकरं वर्जयित्वा राजहंस्यन्यत्राभिरमते ।	32
प्रकृष्टस्य प्रेम्णः स्खलितमविषह्यं हि भवति ।	77
मनश्चलं प्रकृत्यैव ।	63

II. ŚLOKAS.

तीव्रः स्मरसंतापो
  न तथादौ बाधते यथासन्ने ।
तपति प्रावृषि नितरा-
  मभ्यर्णजलागमो दिवसः ॥ p. 72

दुर्वारां कुसुमशरव्यथां वहन्त्या
  कामिन्या यदभिहितं पुरः सखीनाम् ।
तद्भूयः शिशुशुकसारिकाभिरुक्तं
  धन्यानां श्रवणपथातिथित्वमेति ॥ pp. 43–44

द्वीपादन्यस्मादपि
  मध्यादपि जलनिधेर्दिशोऽप्यन्तात् ।
आनीय झटिति घटयति
  विधिरभिमतमभिमुखीभूतः ॥ p. 7

INDEX OF IMPORTANT WORDS.

(The figures refer to the pages of this Edition).